BARRON'S POCKET GUIDE TO
CORRECT SPELLING

Fourth Edition

Francis Griffith

Former Professor of Education
Hofstra University

Revised edition by
Mary Elizabeth, M.Ed

P9-DDD-770

Acknowledgments
The following material is copyright by the author and used by permission of the author.

Tables on pages 27–30 copyright © 2003 by Mary Elizabeth, expanded from pages 153–156 in her book *Painless Spelling,* published by Barron's Educational Series, Inc. and copyright by the author.

Table on pages 31–32 copyright © 2003 by Mary Elizabeth, expanded from pages 243–248 in her book *Painless Spelling,* published by Barron's Educational Series, Inc. and copyright by the author.

Chart on pages 36–37 copyright © 2004 by Mary Elizabeth. All rights reserved.

Chart on pages 51–59 copyright © 2004 by Mary Elizabeth, expanded from pages 15–19 in her book *Painless Spelling,* published by Barron's Educational Series, Inc. and copyright by the author.

The Homophone List on pages 262–327 copyright © 2004 by Mary Elizabeth. All rights reserved.

All inquiries should be addressed to:
Barron's Educational Series, Inc.
250 Wireless Boulevard
Hauppauge, New York 11788
http://www.barronseduc.com

Library of Congress Catalog Card Number 2004041131
International Standard Book Number 0-7641-2691-1

Library of Congress Cataloging-in-Publication Data
Griffith, Francis J.
    Barron's pocket guide to correct spelling / Francis Griffith.—
4th ed. / rev. ed. by Mary Elizabeth.
      p.   cm.
    Rev. ed. of: A pocket guide to correct spelling.
    ISBN (invalid) 0-7641-2691-1
    1. Spellers. 2. English language—Orthography and spelling—
Handbooks, manuals, etc. I. Title: Pocket guide to correct spelling.
II. Title: Correct spelling. III. Mary Elizabeth, M. Ed. IV. Griffith,
Francis J. Pocket guide to correct spelling. V. Title.

PE1145.2.G7   2004
428.1′3—dc22   2004041131

PRINTED IN CHINA
9 8 7 6 5 4 3 2

Contents

Introduction

This 4th edition of *Pocket Guide to Correct Spelling* is intended for use by office professionals, business executives, authors, proofreaders, students, and other writers who either need ONLY to quickly verify spelling and hyphenation or need spelling tools BEYOND what they find in the standard dictionary.

This book has six elements to help you both verify your spelling in a particular instance AND improve it for the long term. First, it contains a guide to becoming a better speller that explains some of the difficulties of spelling in English. Second, it features a comprehensive list of spelling rules, both for ready reference and for study, should you wish to further your understanding. Third, it presents a thorough analysis of the kinds of situations in which spelling errors arise and how to get around them when looking up words in the pocket guide (or any dictionary). Fourth, to help you look up words that you do not already know how to spell, it includes an extensive chart of the ways sounds are spelled in English—this, also, is useful for ANY look-up situation. Fifth, the list of over 24,000 commonly misspelled words, alphabetized and divided so that you can see the points at which you can hyphenate them, has been brought up-to-date using *Merriam-Webster's Collegiate Dictionary, Eleventh Edition* (referred to hereafter as Merriam-Webster's). The list was revised in two ways after little-used words were removed. Initially, other lists of important, high-frequency words were consulted, and those words likely to be misspelled but not appearing in the 3rd edition of this book were added. Special emphasis was given to words that are considered important for preparing for standardized college or graduate-study entrance exams, such as the SAT I, ACT, GMAT, and GRE. Also, many words that have been added to the new edition of Merriam-Webster's and that have entered the English language since 1970 were added. Some of these new words are compound words or words that originated in other languages, and many of them present spelling issues simply because they are new. So words that describe our culture and society such as might be used in a broad range of journalism venues and personal and business correspondence are included, along with current legal, business, scientific, technical, computer, and medical terms, useful to specialists and consumers. Sixth, with what is perhaps the largest list of homophones assembled in a book of this kind—more than 2,100—you can go well beyond the common knowledge of *there/their/they're* and *your/you're* as sets of words that are confused because they have identical sound but different spellings and meanings.

The guide's handy size is an important advantage. Focusing on spelling and syllabication while skirting all the other information that makes a dictionary so valuable—and so bulky—it provides the important hyphenation information that your spell-checker doesn't give you, without forcing you to search through pronunciation, etymologies, definitions, synonyms, antonyms, and the other elements of a dictionary entry. Not intended as a substitute for a dictionary, the guide has a wealth of information found in no dictionary, and you will find it a valuable supplement.

Spelling deserves emphasis because all written, typed, and e-text messages require that we spell words in order to set them down. Whether what you have to say is formal or off-the-cuff, the spelling of any message can either promote communication by transmitting the message clearly while remaining invisible (if it is entirely correct) or interrupt communication when it draws a reader's attention away from the content of what is being said to the format (if it contains errors). Worse than merely interrupting the reader, misspelling may distort communication (if one word is substituted for another) or give a negative impression of the writer's competence. With the wide variety of spelling aids (not aides;-) offered here, you are likely to find assistance for spelling issues in many different situations, and in ways that will help you to actually improve as a speller, rather than just become dependent on a source.

How to Become a Better Speller

The first step in improving your spelling is to realize that learning to spell is a lifelong process! Well, that's natural, since new words are continually entering the language, and since new work and life experience both bring about the need for new vocabulary.

The second step is to realize that there are multiple acceptable spellings and pronunciations for many words in English. A single dictionary demonstrates this. Start looking at more than one, and the variety is even more impressive. Sometimes there's only one correct answer. But you can write *good-by, goodby, good-bye,* or *goodbye* and be correct.

Third, words are sounds written down. If you think about them this way—as the letters being a code to convey what we hear—then the different possibilities for spelling various sounds may make more sense to you.

Fourth, US English vocabulary derives from many languages. Therefore many rules have exceptions. Don't expect to have consistent one-to-one correspondence between sounds and spellings, as in a language like Spanish. Instead, learn to rely on patterns within, among, and between words.

Once you have safely tucked away those concepts, a few basic strategies will stand you in good stead.

A. Learning a New Word.
1. Write the word several times, spell it aloud, or both, to reinforce the spelling pattern. Make your choice depending on your favored learning style(s).

2. Say the word aloud to help imprint it in your mind. Associate a mental image with it as you speak.
3. Make up a memorable sentence with the word in it.
4. If there are any spelling difficulties in the word, make up a mnemonic, or memory aid, to help you remember the correct spelling.

B. Using the Sound/Sight Strategy for Dealing with Groups of Words That Have Any Kind of Pattern That You Wish to Understand.

1. Look for visual patterns.
2. Listen for sound patterns.
3. Notice how the sound patterns correspond to the visual patterns.
4. Consult the spelling rules for an explanation of the relationship. If no existing rule covers the case, consider modifying one or making one up.
5. Look for more words that fit your rule.
6. Check your rule for exceptions.

C. Making a Ready-Reference for Yourself of the Spelling Facts You Most Need.

Include, as appropriate:

1. words that you often have to look up (so you don't have to look them up anymore!).
2. spelling rules that you find most helpful.
3. any sets of homophones that you find confusing, with definitions that will help you distinguish them.

D. Experimenting Until You Discover an Approach to Learning More About Spelling That Works for You.

1. Some people use a word-a-day approach and continually increase their vocabulary by learning to spell new words of interest.

2. Others prefer to learn the spelling rules in an order that appeals to them.

3. Some find the homophone list to be of interest and expand their knowledge using that tool.

E. Using Tools Such as This Book, as Needed, for Assistance.

1. Assemble the references and resources that meet your needs so that you have them to call upon.

2. Take the time to look through the various offerings in this guide, using sticky notes to mark pages you want to return to, as desired.

3. Use underlining or a highlighter to mark sections of particular interest so that you can spot them easily.

4. Identify which spelling issues (see page 43) affect you the most and adopt strategies to help you over-come them as well as to deal with any resulting confusion.

Spelling Rules

Spelling rules are descriptions that cover as much as possible of the English language in an attempt to give us a guide for making correct decisions about our language use. Because the English language is made up of words from so many different languages, it is almost inevitable that there will be exceptions to the rules. Still, learning the rules that cover the predominance of cases can help you assemble words that you previously had to remember individually into useful groups, making the task of recalling proper spelling much easier.

PLURALS

In most cases, we judge how to form a word's plural by examining the word in question, particularly its ending. Sometimes, groups of words require special treatment, in which case memorizing the group characteristics can be helpful.

General Rule for Forming Plurals

➤ a. Add *s* to the singular form of most common and proper nouns to form the plural.

> hyenas, cheesesteaks, kazillions, bungees, clarinets, Nguyens, Smiths

➤ b. If the noun ends in a sound that will not unite with *s* alone—soft *ch, j, s, sh, ss, x, z,* or *zz,*—add *es*.

> churches, hajjes, Woodses, Nashes, mosses, crucifixes, waltzes, buzzes

Nouns Ending in *i*

➤ Add *s* to the singular form of most nouns ending in *i* to form the plural, with the following exceptions:

alkalies (or alkali), taxis (or taxies), chilies

Nouns Ending in *o*

➤ a. Add *s* to the singular form of nouns with a final *o* that is preceded by a vowel to form the plural.

zoos, duos, studios, cameos, taboos, ratios, bamboos, cuckoos, stereos

➤ b. Add *s* to the singular form of most nouns with a final *o* that is preceded by a consonant to form the plural in most cases, if the word is from a Romance language and for *photos*.

Italian words, including musical terms:

violoncellos, pianos, altos, octavos, casinos

Spanish words:

aficionados, amigos, amontillados, Latinos

Portuguese words:

albinos

Latin words:

egos, infernos

French words:

do-si-dos

➤ c. Add *es* to the singular form of a few nouns with a final *o* that is preceded by a consonant to form the plural.

> heroes (except for the meaning submarine sandwich, where the plural is heros), potatoes, tomatoes, dingoes, lingoes

➤ d. Add either *es* OR *s* to the singular form of many nouns with a final *o* that is preceded by a consonant to form the plural. Here are some examples.

S Is First Spelling Listed	*ES* Is First Spelling Listed
avocados or avocadoes	desperadoes or desperados
banjos or banjoes	echoes or echos
cargos or cargoes	grottoes or grottos
commandos or commandoes	hoboes or hobos
halos or haloes	mosquitoes or mosquitos
zeros or zeroes	mottoes or mottos
	noes or nos
	tornadoes or tornados
	volcanoes or volcanos

Nouns Ending in *y*

➤ a. Add *s* to the singular form of common and proper nouns with a final *y* that is preceded by a vowel to form the plural, except if the vowel spells a consonant sound (see b).

> bays, monkeys, Sundays, Mays, decoys, turkeys, guys

➤ b. For common nouns, change the *y* to *i* and add *es* to the singular form with a final *y* that is preceded by a consonant to form the plural. This is also true of common nouns in which there is a consonant **sound** spelled by a vowel just before the *y* (like the \w\ spelled by *qu* in *colloquy*).

> bunnies, cities, soliloquies, funnies, flies

➤ c. For proper nouns, add *s* to the singular form with a final *y* that is preceded by a consonant to form the plural (with some exceptions, including those noted).

> Peggys and Sallys, the O'Malleys, two different Garden Citys

Exceptions:

> the Alleghenies, the Rockies, the Smokies

Nouns with an Internal Vowel Change

➤ a. Some nouns require an internal vowel change to form their plural (and some change more than the vowel, actually).

Singular	Plural
foot	feet
goose	geese
tooth	teeth
louse	lice (animals); louses (contemptible people)
mouse	mice
man	men
woman	women
person	people

➤ b. Compounds that end with these words form their plurals in identical fashion.

> forefoot/forefeet, dormouse/dormice, gentleman/gentlemen, craftsperson/craftspeople

➤ c. Words ending in *–man* that are not compounds are made plural by adding *s*. This is also true of *mongoose*, which is not a compound.

> humans, Normans, Burmans, caimans, Oklahomans, Romans, shamans, Walkmans™

Nouns Ending in *f, ff,* or *fe*

➤ a. Add *s* to the singular form of most nouns ending in *f, ff,* or *fe* to form the plural.

> belief/beliefs, bailiff/bailiffs, fife/fifes

➤ b. Some nouns change *f* or *fe* to *ves.*

> elf/elves, leaf/leaves, wife/wives, life/lives

➤ c. Some nouns ending in *f* have more than one plural form and *staff* does as well. This is further complicated by differing British and US usage, so check a dictionary.

> beefs/beeves, wharfs/wharves, scarfs/scarves, hoofs/hooves, staffs/staves, dwarfs/dwarves

For two of these words, the two plurals actually have distinct meanings: *Beefs* can be the plural of the *beef* that means "complaint" as well as the *beef* that refers to the animal, but *beeves* refers exclusively to the animal. The plural of *staff* meaning "officers of a business" or a "group of assistants" must be *staffs*, but the clef on which music is written can be pluralized *staffs* or *staves* (and this also is sometimes called a *stave* in the singular).

Plural Forms from Other Languages

➤ a. Form the plural of some nouns from foreign languages
   by using the pattern from the language of origin.

Latin Origins

Singular	Plural
alumnus	alumni (us ➜ i)
bacillus	bacilli
cactus	cacti
fungus	fungi
nucleus	nuclei
radius	radii
analysis	analyses (is ➜ es)
basis	bases
crisis	crises
diagnosis	diagnoses
hypothesis	hypotheses
parenthesis	parentheses
bacterium	bacteria (um ➜ a)
datum	data
medium	media
ovum	ova
alumna	alumnae (a ➜ ae)
antenna (insect feelers)	antennae
formula	formulae
larva	larvae
vertebra	vertebrae
criterion	criteria (on ➜ a)

French origins

> madame/mesdames, monsieur/messieurs

Hebrew origins

> cherub/cherubim, kibbutz/kibbutzim,
> seraph/seraphim

Italian origins

> solo/soli, virtuoso/virtuosi

➤ b. Some words that follow this pattern have an additional plural formed by adding *s* or *es* to the singular form. (See the next category.) When there are two plurals, neither is wrong, except by context—for example, in a publication that has style guidelines that require the preferred plural from a particular source or that sets a standard of Anglicized spellings (altered to English form).

NOTE: This next chart does not attempt to cover all words from the previous chart.

Singular Form	Plural Following Language of Origin	Plural by Adding *s*
solo	soli	solos
virtuoso	virtuosi	virtuosos
medium	media	mediums
curriculum	curricula	curriculums
memorandum	memoranda	memorandums
matrix	matrices	matrixes
vortex	vortices	vortexes
fungus	fungi	funguses
gladiolus	gladioli	gladioluses

(continued)

(continued)

Singular Form	Plural Following Language of Origin	Plural by Adding *s*
cherub	cherubim	cherubs
seraph	seraphim	seraphs
automaton	automata	automatons
criterion	criteria	criterions
phenomenon	phenomena	phenomenons
antenna	antennae	antennas
formula	formulae	formulas
vertebra	vertebrae	vertebras
adieu	adieux	adieus
beau	beaux	beaus

➤ c. Several words have two plurals, one of which is identical to the singular:

> apparatus or apparatuses, nexus or nexuses

➤ d. Some Latin words have simply a plural formed with *es*.

> censuses, consensuses, hiatuses, impetuses, prospectuses, sinuses

Nouns with Two Different Plural Forms Indicating Different Meanings

➤ Some nouns have two different plural forms each having a distinct meaning. Here are some examples.

Singular	Plural #1 and Meaning	Plural #2 and Meaning
brother	brothers (two boys born to the same parents)	*brethren (members of the same society; e.g., the Quakers)
die	dies (tools used to stamp; dadoes)	dice (numbered cubes used for games)
genius	geniuses (brilliant people; marked abilities)	genii (imaginary spirits, like the one in *Aladdin*)
index	indexes (tables of contents)	indices (algebraic signs)

* Old English plurals: Besides brother ➔ brethren, two other English nouns form their plural with an *en* ending: ox ➔ oxen and child ➔ children.

Identical Singular and Plural Form

Words from the Biological Sciences

One Plural Form
➤ a. Some nouns have the same singular and plural form. One subsection of this group is fish, game, and livestock names.

   bison, moose, sheep, swine

Two Plural Forms
➤ b. Some nouns may either use an identical form as the plural or use a regular plural formed with *s* or *es* (preferred form first). The distinction is used to separate discussion of the animal collectively (the singular form used as the plural) from a reference to different varieties or species referred to collectively (the regularly constructed plural form).

Preferred Plural	Second Plural
antelope	antelopes
cod	cods
crabs	crab
deer	deers
elk (for animals)	Elks (for members of fraternal organization)
fish	fishes
flounder	flounders
grouse	grouses
herring	herrings
quail	quails
reindeer	reindeers
salmon	salmons
shrimps	shrimp
trout	trouts

➤ c. Two plurals are also available for *offspring* and *sperm* with the form identical to the singular being preferred and the other being formed regularly with *s*.

Nationalities and Countries of Origin
➤ d. Form the plurals of many words indicating nationality or place of origin identically to the singular form. In some cases, a form with *s* is an alternate.

Chinese, Norse, Swiss

American Indians/Native Americans
The *Chicago Manual of Style* (7.10) says that current usage for American Indian/Native American tribes should use *s* to form the plural universally. This contradicts Merriam-Webster's, which gives several different standards (details follow). The names of American

Indian/Native American peoples should be checked
individually—AND ALWAYS, IF POSSIBLE, WITH
THE PEOPLES THEMSELVES—because they follow
several different patterns and preference has changed
over time. The usage most prevalent in Merriam-
Webster's is listed first.

Two Plural Forms
➤ e. Form the plural of most American Indian/Native
American tribes in two ways, the preferred one being
identical to the singular, the second being formed
with *s*. Singular forms, including variant spellings,
are listed in the chart.

Abenaki/Abnaki	Apache	Cherokee
Chippewa	Comanche	Cree
Creek	Delaware	Eskimo
Hopi	Lakota	Mahican/Mohican*
Maya	Mohawk	Mohegan/Mohican*
Navajo/Navaho	Ojibwa/Ojibway/Ojibwe	Omaha
Pawnee	Penobscot	Pueblo
Shawnee	Tlingit	Ute
Zuni		

* The Mahicans and the Mohegans are separate tribes, both of which
have *Mohican* as an alternate spelling.

➤ f. For other tribes, there are two plurals, the preferred
one being formed regularly with *s* and the second
being identical to the singular form.

Hurons/Huron   Seminoles/Seminole
Shoshones/Shoshone   Dakotas/Dakota,
Blackfeet/Blackfoot   Ottawas/Ottawa

➤ g. For yet other tribes, there are two plurals, the preferred
   one being identical to the singular and the second being
   spelled with *es*.

   Huichol/Huicholes

One Plural Form

➤ h. In some cases there is one plural form, which is identical to the singular.

   Anasazi, Illinois, Iroquois, Sioux

   NOTE: There are a few tribes for which the plural is
   formed regularly by adding *s*.

   Inca/Incas, Aztec/Aztecs

*Words That Can Be Understood as Either
Singular or Plural*

➤ i. Some nouns have only one form that can be understood as singular OR plural (depending on context)
   or have a plural form that is identical to the singular
   form. This group of words is a diverse set that is not
   easy to characterize overall.

aircraft	alms	amends
bellows	bourgeoisie	chassis
corps	counsel (a person)	congeries
economics	forceps	headquarters
humankind	means	politics
précis	rendezvous	samurai
scissors	series	shambles
species	sweepstakes	two bits
United States		

Compound Nouns

➤ a. Form the plural of compounds that are spelled
   closed-up (as single words) just as you would the
   final element. If the word is a measurement ending in
   –ful, add *–s* at the end. Rarely, both elements of the
   word are pluralized.

> pigsties *or* pigstyes, pillowcases, hairbrushes,
> jackknives, stepchildren, microfungi *or*
> microfunguses, tablespoonfuls, menservants

➤ b. To form the plural of hyphenated compounds, locate
   the main noun and form its plural in the usual way.

> attorney-at-law ➜ attorneys-at-law
> man-of-war ➜ men-of-war
> mother-in-law ➜ mothers-in-law
> passer-by ➜ passers-by
> runner-up ➜ runners-up

   CAUTION: Watch out for ODDBALLS like these:

> twelve-year-old ➜ twelve-year-olds
> drive-in ➜ drive-ins
> court-martial ➜ courts-martial OR court-martials

➤ c. For the plural of open compounds (compounds written as two separate words), if one of the words is an
   adjective, make the noun element plural.

> musk oxen, postmasters general, art schools,
> flower children, bay leaves

Plurals of Letters, Figures, Characters, Symbols, Signs, and Digits

➤ a. Form the plural of capital letters used as words or acronyms, abbreviations without inner punctuation, and numerals used as nouns (such as dates) by adding *s* to the singular form. (Words as words are set in italic type, but the *s* is roman.)

> ABCs, 1930s, URLs, vol./vols., Boeing 737s, IOUs
> The acronym *SADD* has two *D*s.

➤ b. Form the plural of lowercase letters and abbreviations with two or more interior periods or with a combination of capital and lowercase letters by adding an apostrophe and *s*. (Words as words are set in italic type, but the *s* is roman.)

> *p*'s and *q*'s, PhD's

➤ c. Where confusion might arise without an apostrophe (as with symbols), use an apostrophe.

> +'s, −'s, #'s, B♭'s, ñ's

POSSESSIVES

➤ a. Form the possessive of most singular nouns, as well as most plural nouns that are irregular (i.e., do not end in *s*), by adding an apostrophe and *s*.

> child's, pork pie's, country's, mouse's, ox's, alumni's, Jeannette's
> children's, mice's, oxen's, alumnae's

➤ b. Form the possessive of most plural nouns that end in
    s by adding an apostrophe only.

> pigs', editors', medical centers', rocking horses',
> jubilees', the Lewises'

➤ c. Form possessives in the expression "For __ sake"
    with only an apostrophe when the noun ends with an
    s or *s* sound.

> for old times' sake   for goodness' sake
> for appearance' sake   for Jesus' sake
> for convenience' sake   for pity's sake

➤ d. If a proper noun has two or more syllables and ends
    in the sound /ēz/ or has an unpronounced *s* in the sin-
    gular, an awkward appearance may be avoided by
    adding an apostrophe only.

> Sophocles' plays, the Euphrates' banks, Xerxes'
> strategy, Descartes' reasoning, Albert Camus' essay

➤ e. Possessive pronouns are formed from determiners
    (sometimes mistakenly called possessive adjectives)
    and are mostly formed by adding *s* with no apostro-
    phe, first person singular being an exception.

Subject Pronoun	Determiner	Possessive Pronoun
I	my	mine
you	your	yours
he	his	his
she	her	hers
it	its	its
we	our	ours
they	their	theirs

Joint and Separate Ownership

➤ a. Show possession of multiple owners listed in
   sequence by adding a possessive ending to the final
   name only.

> Marjorie and Mary's song; Senators Mulholland,
> Vadehra, and Wong's bill; Drs. Santana, Rochefort,
> Lipsky, and Santopietro's practice

➤ b. Show individual possession of similar (or identical)
   articles by changing each name to reflect possession.

> Marjorie's and Mary's poems; Senators
> Mulholland's, Vadehra's, and Wong's reelection
> campaigns; Drs. Santana's, Rochefort's, Lipsky's,
> and Santopietro's volunteer work

CONTRACTIONS

➤ Form most contractions by replacing one or more letters (or numbers) with an apostrophe.

Pronoun + verb:

> 'tis, it's, they're, we've, I'd, it'd (it had/it would),
> let's (let us)

Verb + negative adverb:

> wouldn't, isn't, aren't (also used for am + not in
> interrogative), needn't

First two digits of year:

> class of '91

Shortened word form:

> e'er (ever), 'tude (attitude), rock 'n' roll (rock and
> roll), o'er (over)

Exceptions: Sometimes there are letter changes as well as omissions.

am/is/are not → ain't   will not → won't

Sometimes there are letters omitted from more than one spot, but only one apostrophe is used.

shall not → shan't

SUFFIXES

Syllable Juncture Rules

Syllable junctures are the points at which syllables meet. When we join suffixes to words, we create syllable junctures, and there are four important patterns. The patterns that occur at syllable junctures can help us remember how to spell a word.

Doubling Final Consonant

➤ a. Double the final consonant before adding a suffix that begins with a vowel for monosyllabic words that end in a single consonant preceded by a single vowel.

hop/hopped, big/bigger, flat/flattest, hot/hotter, rat/ratted, stem/stemmed, whip/whipping

Exceptions:

bus/buses, words formed from *gas* (except *gassing* and *gassy*)

➤ b. Double the final consonant before adding a suffix that begins with a vowel for multisyllabic words that end in a single consonant preceded by a single vowel and have the accent on the last syllable. If the accent shifts to an earlier syllable when you add the suffix, do not double the consonant.

prefer/preferred/preference, occur/occurrence, acquit/acquittal, forget/forgettable

Exceptions:

chagrin/chagrined, transfer/transferable/transference

Words Ending in *C*
The letter *c* can make two different sounds: \k\, and \s\ when followed by *i, e,* or *y*. To prevent a change in pronunciation, a spelling change is introduced when a suffix is added to some words ending in *c*.

➤ To maintain the pronunciation of *c* as \k\, add a *k* in most cases to words ending in *c* before adding a suffix beginning with *e, i,* or *y*.

bivouac/bivouacking, colic/colicky, frolic/frolicker, picnic/picnicked

Words Ending in *E*
➤ a. In most cases, drop a silent *e* before a suffix beginning with a vowel and retain it before a consonant. For words that end in *ce* or *ge*, keep the *e* before suffixes beginning with *a, o,* or *u* so that the pronunciation will not change from soft (\s\ or \j\) to hard (\k\ or \g\).

hope/hoping, rate/rating, wipe/wipers, sale/salable, blue/bluish, advantage/advantageous, trace/traceable

Exceptions: Keep the *e* in *dye, singe,* and *tinge* to distinguish results from *die, sing,* and *ting.*

➤ b. Drop the *e* in many words that end in a silent *e* that is immediately preceded by another vowel (not *e*):

due/duly, argue/argument, true/truly

Exceptions: These individual words do NOT drop the *e*, as one would expect:

> mile/mileage, acre/acreage, hoe/hoeing, line/lineage

These individual words do NOT maintain the *e,* as one would expect before a consonant.

> abridge/abridgment, acknowledge/acknowledgment, awe/awful, judge/judgment, nine/ninth, whole/wholly, wise/wisdom, nurse/nursling

➤ c. Words ending in *ie* usually drop the *e* and change *i* to *y.*

> vie/vying, die/dying

Words Ending in *Y*

➤ For most words ending in *y* following a consonant, change *y* to *i* for any suffix except one beginning with an *i*. In other cases, retain the *y.*

> happy/happiness, tidy/tidier, pity/pitiful, ruby/rubies, icy/iciest, accompany/accompaniment, beauty/beautiful

Exceptions: Y is retained in forms of *baby* and *city:*

> baby/babyish, city/citywide

Y is retained before the suffixes -*ship* and -*like*:

> lady/ladyship/ladylike

Y is retained in most one-syllable adjectives when the suffix begins with a consonant. Sometimes there are alternate forms, so checking a dictionary is wise.

> fry/fryer, fly/flyer *or* flier, shy/shyness/shier *or* shyer, sly/slyly, dry/drier *or* dryer, wry/wryness

Particular Endings

A number of homophonous (sound-alike) endings cause trouble for spellers. Here is some brief advice to help you sort your way through a few of the most troublesome.

-able/-ible

A few rules can help you begin to distinguish between *-able* and *-ible*.

➤ a. Most times when the ending is added to a whole word, you use *-able,* and when it is added to a base that cannot stand alone as a word, you add *-ible.*

Whole Word	Nonword
depend ➜ dependable	aud ➜ audible
break ➜ breakable	ed ➜ edible

➤ b. If the base word ends in silent *e*

1. preceded by a soft *c* \s\ or *g* \j\, keep the *e* and add *-able.*

   manage   manageable
   notice   noticeable

2. without a soft *c* or *g,* drop the *e* and add *-able.*

   love ➜ lovable
   use ➜ usable

➤ c. If the *-ion* form of the word is

1. spelled *-ation,* add *-able.*

admire	admiration	admirable
tolerate	toleration	tolerable
transport	transportation	transportable

2. spelled without an *a*, add *-ible*, even though it IS a whole word.

contract	contraction	contractible
produce	production	producible

3. spelled with *ss* or *ns*, add *-ible* after the *ss* or *ns*.

permit	permission	permissible
comprehend	comprehension	comprehensible

Exceptions: collapse, which ends in silent *e,* becomes *collapsible.* Also, *potable, insuperable,* and *ineffable,* the base words of which are not words in their own right, are formed with *-able.*

-cede/-ceed/-sede

This confusion is most easily dealt with by memorizing the one word that ends in *-sede* and the five that end in *-ceed*. The other ten end in *-cede*.

> *-sede:* supersede
> *-ceed:* exceed, glacéed, proceed, succeed
> *-cede:* accede, antecede, cede, concede, intercede, precede, recede, retrocede, secede, supercede

-ance/-ence

In general, words with *-ance* and *-ence* must simply be learned. But here are a few clues to help guide you to choose the correct ending for some words:

- If the suffix is preceded by soft *c* \s\ or soft *g* \j\, then you can tell that *-ence, -ent,* and *-ency* are used because *e* following *c* and *g* causes soft pronunciation, while *a* causes hard \k\ and \g\.
- In parallel fashion, if the suffix is preceded by hard *c* \k\ or hard *g* \g\, then you can tell that *-ance, -ant,* and *-ancy* are used because *a* following *c* and *g* causes hard pronunciation, while *e* causes soft \s\ and \j\.

- If a verb ends in *r* preceded by a vowel and the accent is on the last syllable, it uses the suffix form *-ence*.

  occur/occurrence, prefer/preference, refer/reference

-ise, -ize, -yze

At one time, the spelling *-ise* distinguished a word with origins in French and *-ize* pointed to origins in Greek and Latin, but this usage is not followed in the United States. Here are some clues to help you.

- All the fourteen words that end in *-yze* are spelled *alyze* or *olyze*. The most often used are *analyze, psychoanalyze, overanalyze, paralyze, electrolyze,* and *catalyze*.
- The spelling *-ise* often given as the second spelling of an *-ize* spelling, as in *centralize, carmelize,* and *capitalize*. In some cases, this is a British variant.
- Some examples of *-ise* as a first spelling include:

  advertise, compromise, disguise, exercise,
  merchandise, otherwise, reprise, sunrise, surprise

- Some examples of *-ize* include:

  apologize, baptize, criticize, jeopardize, realize,
  recognize, subsidize, symbolize, vocalize

PREFIXES AND ASSIMILATION

A prefix is one or more syllables attached to the beginning of a word or root to change its meaning. When a prefix is added, the spelling of the original word or root is not changed, but the spelling of the prefix may accommodate to the beginning of the word or root for easy pronunciation. This adaptation is called *assimilation*. See the following tables.

Following tables © 2003 by Mary Elizabeth. All Rights Reserved.

Old English

Prefix	Meaning	Examples
a-	on, in	abed, aboard, afoot, asleep
a-	up, out, away	arise, awake
be-	around, about, away, thoroughly	behead, beloved, beset
mis-	wrongly, badly, not correct	misapply, misinterpret, mismanage, misspell, mistake
out-	to a greater degree, located externally or outside	outboard, outdo, outhouse, outlive, outshine, outshoot
over-	over, excessively	overcompensate, overdrive, overdue, overrun, oversee
un-	not, opposing	unaccompanied, undo, unhappy, unlock, untrue

Greek

Prefix	Meaning	Examples
a-	without, not	amoral, apolitical
amphi-	around, both	amphibious, amphitheater
anti-	against, opposite	antibody, antipathy, antiseptic
auto-	self	autobiography, automobile
bi-	two, twice	bicycle, bimonthly
cata-	down, away, against	cataclysm, catastrophe
dia-	through, together	dialogue, diameter
eu-	good, pleasant	eulogy, euphemism
hemi-	half	hemiplegic, hemisphere
hyper-	extra, over, excessive, beyond	hypercritical, hypertension, hyperthermia

(continued)

Greek (continued)

Prefix	Meaning	Examples
hypo-	under, beneath, below	hypocritical, hypodermic, hypothesis
macro-	large	macrobiotic, macrocosm
micro-	very small	microcosm, micromanage, microscope
neo-	new	neolithic, neologism, neonatal, neo-Nazi
para-	beside, similar to, beyond	paragraph, paranormal, paraphrase, paraprofessional
peri-	about, around	perimeter, periscope
pseudo-	false, pretended, not real	pseudonym, pseudopod, pseudoscience

Latin

Prefix	Meaning	Examples
ab-	away, from	abduct, abject
ante-	before, prior to	antebellum, antediluvian
circum-	around, on all sides	circumference, circumnavigate
contra-	against	contradict, contraindicated
counter-	opposite	counteract, counterrevolution
de-	reversal, removal, away, from, off, down	deactivate, decapitate, decode, decrease, delouse, demean, destroy
dis-	do the opposite of, not, absence of	disagreeable, disaccord, disband
equi-	equal	equidistant, equilateral, equivalent

Latin (continued)

Prefix	Meaning	Examples
extra-	beyond, outside	extracurricular, extraordinary, extraterrestrial
inter-	among, between	intermurals, international, interplanetary, interstate
intra-	within	intramurals, intramuscular, intravenous
mal-	bad, wrongful	malignant, malodorous, maltreatment
multi-	many	multicolored, multiform, multimillionaire, multinational
non-	against, not, without	nonentity, nonessential, nonexistent, nonsense, nonstop, nonviolence
per-	throughout, thoroughly	perambulate, perennial
post-	after, following	postdate, postgraduate, postpone, postscript
pre-	before	preclude, prefix, preheat, prejudge
pro-	forward, in place of, favoring	proclaim, prolong, pronoun, prorate
re-	again, back, backward	reappear, relinquish, repair, repay, replace
retro-	back, backward	retroactive, retrorocket, retrospect
semi-	half, twice	semiannual, semicircular, semidetached, semiformal
super-	above, extra, over	supernatural, supersaturated, superscript, superstar

(continued)

Latin (continued)

Prefix	Meaning	Examples
trans-	across, beyond	transcontinental, transpolar, transport
tri-	three, every third	triangle, tricycle, trimonthly
ultra-	beyond, excessively	ultraconservative, ultramodern, ultrasonic, ultraviolet
under-	below, beneath	underground, underhanded, underwater, underwear
uni-	one	unicycle, unison

Assimilating Prefixes

Some prefixes change (or assimilate) their final consonant to the first letter of the word part they join to make pronunciation easier. The different forms that a prefix takes are called *allomorphs*. To tell, for example, if the *a* you see is the prefix *a-* or an allomorph of *ad-*, look at the etymology in the dictionary entry. The earliest origins of the word—or the first-listed etymologically related word—will likely break down the word into its components, and you'll be able to see which prefix is being referenced, by spelling and meaning. One thing to look for is doubled consonants at the syllable juncture—often a sign of an assimilated prefix.

Following table © 2003 by Mary Elizabeth. All Rights Reserved.

Prefix	Meaning	Assimilated Form	Examples
ad-	to, toward	*a* before *gn, sc, sp, st*	ascribe, aspire, agnomen, astringent
		ac before *c*	accompany
		ac before *q*	acquaintance
		ad before *j*	adjoin
		af before *f*	affirm
		ag before *g*	aggrieve
		al before *l*	allot
		an before *n*	annotate
		ar before *r*	arrest
		as before *s*	assort
		at before *t*	attune
in-	not, into	*i* before *g*	ignominy
		il before *l*	illegal
		im before *b, m, p*	imbibe, immortal, impurity
		ir before *r*	irrational
		in the rest of the time	incapable, infertile, interminable, etc.
com-	with	*co* before *g, h,* and most vowels	cogent, cohere, coalesce, coefficient, coincide, cooperate
		col before *l*	collaborate
		com before *b, m, p*	combative, commensurate, complain
		cor before *r*	corroborate
		con before other consonants	conjecture, confide, concede, etc.
ob-	against, toward	*o* before *m*	omit
		oc before *c*	occur
		of before *f*	offend
		op before *p*	oppose
		ob the rest of the time	observe, obtuse, obvious, etc.

(continued)

(continued)

Prefix	Meaning	Assimilated Form	Examples
sub-	under, near	*suc* before *c*	succeed, succinct
		suf before *f*	suffix
		sug before *g*	suggest
		sum before *m*	summon
		sup before *p*	suppose
		sur before *r*	surreptitious
		sus sometimes before *c, p, t*	susceptible, suspect, sustain
		sub the rest of the time	subaudition, submarine, subnormal, etc.
syn-	together, with	*sym* before *b, m, p*	symbiotic, symmetry, sympathy
		syl before *l*	syllable
		sy before *s* and *z*	system, syzygy
		syn the rest of the time	syncretic, syndrome, synergy

COMPOUND NOUNS AND ADJECTIVES

There are three kinds of compound words.

1. Open compounds are spelled as two or more words.

   Saint Francis Hospital, acid snow, baby back ribs, crop circle

2. Hyphenated compounds are spelled with one or more hyphens connecting the words.

   eco-conscious, drag-and-drop, hip-hop, op-ed, nurse-practitioner

3. Closed compounds are spelled as single words.

   biofeedback, benchmark, downsize, grandfather, socioeconomic

- Some compounds are *nonce constructions,* created for one-time use. An example is *look-up,* as used on page iv.
- *Permanent compounds* have established a place in the language and are found in the dictionary. There is a tendency for open and hyphenated compounds to become closed as they gain in use. (This tendency is offset by the length in some cases.) Because this is a continually changing area, it is good to check a dictionary.
- Some open compounds used as phrasal adjectives appear before a word or words that they modify: A hyphen may make the meaning clearer.

Rules for groups of compounds and nonce compounds (compounds invented for a particular writing situation) are so complex that it is well to refer to the *Chicago Manual of Style, Words Into Type, New York Times Manual of Style and Usage, Associated Press Stylebook, A Guide to MLA Documentation, APA Publication Manual,* or whichever style guide is the authority in your field or place of work for detailed information, rather than working from an oversimplified list, so only two rules are given here.

Numbers

- Hyphenate the spelled-out numbers twenty-one through ninety-nine, as well as simple fractions used as nouns, adjectives, and adverbs.

  three-eighths, seventy-two, thirty-five, one-half

Modifier Placement and Hyphenation

• Compounds used as modifiers before a noun MAY take a hyphen but be spelled open after the noun.

> a well-prepared performance, the performance was well prepared

WORDS WITH *IE/EI*

➤ a. When a word has the sound of long *e* \ē\, it is most likely spelled with *i* before *e*. Exceptions—that is, cases in which the sound is long *e* and the *e* comes first in the spelling—include words in which the vowel combination follows *c* AND the following words:

caffeine	codeine	deil
disseise	either	Keith (proper name)
leisure	Neil (proper name)	neither
obeisance	plebeian	protein
Reid (proper name)	reive	seisin
seize	seizing	seizure
sheik	weir	weird

➤ b. After *c*, put *i* before *e* in *ancient, financier, specie,* and *species.*
➤ c. In cases in which the sound of the vowel combination is long *a* \ā\ or long *i* \ī\, or short *e* \e\ or short *i* \i\, spell the sound as *ei*, except in the words *friend, sieve, mischief,* and *handkerchief.*
➤ d. If the two vowels spell separate sounds, there should be no problem.

SILENT LETTERS

Spelling can be made confusing by letters that provide visual information but are not heard to make a distinct sound. This can occur when letters are present to create a sound in combination with other letters, as in *air* or *chap*—but these letters are auxiliary and are different than other silent letters in the way that they contribute to the sound of a word. They are also covered in the chart on pages 36–37 and are not considered further here.

The following are instances of some of the reasons that we end up with unvoiced letters that we refer to as silent:

- Letters that represent a meaning segment but are not pronounced in a specific word form as in *resign/ resignation* or that appear in words that reflect the spelling of the country of origin, as in *khaki*.
- Letters added into a Middle English word to reflect its etymology by scholars who thought this was important (*dette* ➔ *debt, receit* ➔ *receipt*).
- Letters that signal something about the pronunciation of other letters in the word, as with the silent final *e* that distinguishes *fate* from *fat*.
- Letters remaining in the word, though the pronunciation has changed over time, as in *light*.
- Letters that fall before other letters that make the sequence of sounds difficult to pronounce distinctly, as in *handkerchief*.

While one may say the following:

- *b* is often silent before *m* and *t*
- *c* can be silent before *t* and *s*
- *g* may be silent before *m, n*, and sometimes *l*
- *k* is silent before *n*
- final *e* is often silent

a list of examples is likely to be more useful. Remember: Some of these instances may not be silent in your particular dialect.

SILENT A	scent	gnat	SILENT H	SILENT K
accidentally	scepter	gnaw	ah	knack
aesthetic	science	gnome	annihilate	knave
bread	scissors	gnu	cheetah	knead
cocoa	Tucson	imbroglio	exhaust	knee
logically	victual	intaglio	exhibition	kneel
musically		malign	exhort	knell
realistically	**SILENT CK**	phlegm	Gandhi	knew
romantically	blackguard	reign	gherkin	knickers
stoically		resign	ghost	knife
	SILENT D	seraglio	hallelujah	knight
SILENT B	handkerchief	sign	heir	knit
bomb	handsome		herb	knob
climb	Wednesday	**SILENT GH**	honest	knock
comb	Windsor	bough	honor	knot
crumb		bought	hour	know
debt	**SILENT E**	caught	hurrah	Knox
doubt	bridge	daughter	khaki	knuckle
dumb	clue	eight	Messiah	
indebted	fixed	height	oh	**SILENT L**
lamb	serve	high	Pooh	calf
limb		hight	rheum	caulk
numb	**SILENT LF**	might	rhubarb	chalk
plumber	halfpenny	neighbor	rhyme	colonel
subtle		night	rhythm	could
thumb	**SILENT G**	ought	Sarah	folk
tomb	align	right	vehement	half
womb	champagne	straight		Norfolk
	consign	taught		salmon
SILENT C	design	though	**SILENT I**	should
Connecticut	diaphragm	thought	business	talk
czar	feign	through		walk
indict	foreign	tight		would
muscle	gnarl	weigh		
scene	gnash			

SILENT M	prompt	**SILENT S**	**SILENT TH**	whole
mnemonic	psalm	aisle	asthma	whose
	pseudonym	apropos		wrap
SILENT N	psychiatrist	bourgeois	**SILENT U**	wreak
autumn	psychiatry	debris	biscuit	wreck
column	psychology	island	building	wren
condemn	psychother-	isle	guard	wrestling
damn	apy	viscount	guess	wretch
hymn	pterodactyl		guest	wriggle
monsieur	ptomaine	**SILENT T**	guide	wrinkle
solemn	raspberry	ballet	guilty	wrist
	receipt	castle	guitar	write
SILENT O		Christmas		wrong
jeopardy	**SILENT RCE**	fasten	**SILENT UE**	
leopard	Worcester-	gourmet	plague	**SILENT Z**
people	shire	listen	rogue	chez
		mortgage	tongue	laissez faire
SILENT P	**SILENT RH**	often	vogue	rendezvous
Campbell	amenorrhea	rapport		
clapboard	catarrh	ricochet	**SILENT W**	
corps	hemorrhage	soften	answer	
coup	myrrh	thistle	Greenwich	
cupboard	Tyrrhenian	whistle	sword	
pneumatic	Sea		two	
pneumonia			who	

Chart ©2004 by Mary Elizabeth. All Rights Reserved.

24,000-Word
Ready-Reference

HOW TO USE THE READY-REFERENCE WORD LIST

Introduction

The following list consists of words commonly used in formal and informal writing: correspondence, news publications, magazines and journals, and books. Included are words from current events, business, computer technology, health, and other disciplines, as well as a select group of proper nouns.

The list gives the most frequently used forms of the words (the root word is not always included if its form can be inferred and/or it is rarely used), forms that are troublesome to spell, and forms that differ significantly in hyphenation from other derivatives. It excludes many one-syllable words; however, all words of whatever description that most frequently appear on the SAT I, ACT, and other standardized tests are included.

Centered dots show word divisions for hyphenating at the end of a line of print or type. Words that are not broken into syllables should not be hyphenated (see page 41 if you wish to further develop your understanding of hyphenation rules). Hyphens that are part of the word are shown as hyphens.

Occasionally in the list, due to space considerations, a lengthy word such *underrepresentation* (page 242) has been divided at a hyphenation point. In cases such as these, the center dot has been retained at the end of the line, rather than replacing it with a hyphen. This has been done to avoid confusion, and to avoid giving the impression that this particular syllabication point is any different than any other.

Because there are no definitions, there is no difference in the information for a word standing alone and a word standing as the first word in a compound word. For example, since *chan·nel surf·ing* is included, it includes all the information about the hyphenation of *chan·nel* that you would find were it listed separately. Therefore, there is often no separate listing unless it is expected that the word might get lost in the compound.

Some words have multiple spellings, also known as *variant spellings*. The preferred spelling may vary by region or dialect. Because Merriam-Webster's is the source for this book, the preferred spelling from that source is preferred here, and other spellings are labeled with an asterisk (*). This does not mean that other spellings are incorrect, but if you have chosen a spelling labeled with an asterisk, you may wish to check a dictionary to find out more information.

Words that may appear to be variant spellings but are actually completely separate (*envoi* and *envoy*) are marked with a plus sign (+). Sometimes, one of the words can be both a word in its own right AND a variant of another word. In such a case, it is marked with both an asterisk and a plus sign (for example, *smoothy*+ and *smoothie**+). If you are not certain that you've got the word you want, check in a dictionary. Words that are variants but are in the dictionary with no reference to each other are not marked. When you see * or +, you may wish to first check the homophone list beginning on page 262—often you may find the information you need there.

NOTE: The choice of words in some cases is a matter of cultural/social importance. *Bipolar disorder*, for example, is currently preferred to *manic-depressive illness.* Some tribes prefer to be called American Indians, while others wish to be referred to as Native Americans. This guide does not offer assistance in this area in the list, but it alerts you here to the importance of sensitive word choice.

Organization of the List

This list of words is organized just as the dictionary is: Alphabetical order is used, and open compounds (a single concept consisting of two or more words with a space between, like *a priori*) are alphabetized as if there were no space (so you will find *a priori* after *apricot*, not at the very beginning of the list).

Hyphenation

Words that have hyphens in them retain their hyphens in the list. Occasionally in the list, due to space considerations, a hypenated compound word such as *under-the-counter* (page 242) has been divided at a hyphen. In these cases, a **double hyphen** (=) has been used to show that the hyphen is not just for the end of the line and should be retained when the word is written as a unit on one line. *Hyphenation points*—points where you can break the word at the end of a line of text — are shown by small dots. Note that this kind of break has a different purpose from the kind of break that shows separate syllables for pronunciation; quite often it divides a word very differently. The two types of syllable division are not interchangeable. But in both cases, one-syllable words are not divided.

NOTE: When a word is divided in text, the hyphen belongs at the end of the first line, not at the beginning of the second.

The rules for end-of-line division are listed below. The first five rules are universal and are reflected in the word divisions shown in the list. Others are context dependent, and so must be left to the discretion of the writer. *The Chicago Manual of Style, Fifteenth Edition,* was consulted in preparing this section.

1. A word may not be divided after an initial single-letter syllable. In such cases, this syllable is joined to the second syllable in a multisyllable word.

    abate   abol·ish

2. A word may not be divided before a final single-letter syllable. In such cases, this syllable is joined to the preceding syllable in a multisyllable word.

    mouthy   idea   piz·ze·ria

3. Division is made after a vowel unless this contradicts one of the preceding rules or is contrary to pronunciation. Diphthongs are treated as single vowels.
4. Two consonants that separate vowels are generally divided.
5. A final syllable with no vowel except a "silent" *e* is not divided from the rest of the word.

    quelled   nixed

The following rules are for you to use as guidelines in making decisions about hyphenation. The first three rules are based on the principle of respecting word parts.

1. In a hyphenated word, the best point of division is the point at which the hyphen occurs.

2. In a closed compound word (a compound word with neither a hyphen nor a space), the best point of division is a point between words.
3. Breaks after prefixes and before suffixes are preferable to other breaks in words in which those parts occur. If there is a double consonant before *-ing,* the second consonant is included with the suffix.

   The next four rules deal with words that are not usually hypenated.

4. If a word part would be misleading when a word is hyphenated, don't hyphenate.

   wo-men   pray-er

5. Avoid dividing proper names if possible.
6. Also try to avoid dividing numbers expressed as figures.
7. Try not to break URLs or e-mail addresses across lines, as errors are likely to occur. (For the same reason, do not follow them with punctuation: Try to word sentences so that they are not the final element, or set them off on their own line.)

Finding Words on the List

Spelling Issues and How to Get Around Them When You're Looking Up Words

This section does two things: It enumerates as thoroughly as possible the main issues that lead to misspelling and identifies how these issues may lead to problems using the word list (some of them don't affect looking up words, but are problematic only when you're trying to spell a word without a reference source to guide you) and what strategies to follow if you find this to be the case. In general, if the word isn't where you thought it would be, the first strategy to follow is always to scan the page a bit to see if the word is nearby. (Note that the list in this book is NOT a full unabridged dictionary list; it is not even the size of a collegiate dictionary: The nonappearance of a word does not mean that you've spelled it incorrectly—it may simply not be listed, although I've tried to include what's most useful and important.)

All examples in this book are listed in Merriam-Webster's—that is, they are part of what is now considered the English language.

Some of the typical problems include the following:

• There is a pattern, but you don't know what it is.
• There is a pattern, but it's deceptive.
• There is no pattern.
• It seemed to you that there was a pattern that in reality doesn't exist.

Issues Due to Similarity
• *Same spelling, multiple pronunciations*—The words *coyote, rodeo,* and *tomato* all have multiple pronunciations that change (depending on the word) the vowel sound, number of syllables, and/or stressed syllable. Obviously the letters may reflect some pronunciations better than others. If you can't find your word in the list, use the chart on page 52 to check other possible spellings of the sound(s) in your word that can be said more than one way.
• *Same pronunciation, multiple spellings* (or same pronunciation, multiple spellings AND multiple meanings for one or more of the spellings)—The words *principal/principle* and *fat/phat* are pronounced identically but spelled differently. If you do not know the difference already, you will not be able to distinguish

them in the word list, but a flip to the homophone list
on page 262 will help you identify which is which. If
you can't locate the word in the homophone list, the
sound chart can help you locate alternate spelling
possibilities.

• *Similar spellings*—When completely unrelated words
  have similar spellings, like *diary/dairy*, your mind
  becomes accustomed to seeing (in this case) the vowels in both orders, so neither one catches your attention nor registers as "wrong." If you look up a word in
  the list on page 60, there will be nothing to indicate
  that you may have found the incorrect word, whereas
  if you look up the word in a dictionary, and the meaning you thought it had just isn't there, it might jog you
  to realize what's happened.

Issues Due to Unfamiliar Spelling

• Words of non-English origin, as one might expect,
  may follow orthographic patterns of which we know
  nothing. Thus, neither *qiviut* (Inuit for the undercoat
  of a musk-ox) nor *qintar* (an Albanian monetary unit)
  has a *u* after the *q*. An awareness of a word's origins
  might alert you to not expect English spelling patterns
  and to use the sound chart to find alternate spellings if
  your first instincts don't lead you to the word.

• *Neologisms,* or new words, may always cause spelling
  difficulties simply because they're new to us, if for no
  other reasons. A word like *hoodie* (1992) new to
  eleventh edition of the dictionary, has the ending
  sound \ē\, which has several different spellings. In
  this case, knowledge of word suffixes might preclude
  your needing to consult the sound chart—but you
  could always look there, if necessary.

- A unique spelling for a sound will, obviously, not form a pattern and may thus present a memory problem; *eo* for the sound of long *e* in *people* is an example. The center and far right-hand columns of the sound chart will help you locate less usual or singleton spellings.
- Exceptions to a well-known rule may also cause spelling problems. Many kindergartners learn that "When two vowels go walking, the first one does the talking," but words like *thief* defy this logic. Again, the sound chart will help you. But for some other rules, for example, "If the singular form of a noun ends in a sound that will not unite with *s* alone—soft *ch, j, s, sh, ss, x, z,* or *zz*—add *es*," the sound chart would NOT help you discover that the preferred plural of *matrix* is *matrices.* (Fortunately, you can find the plural form of a word listed in a dictionary in the entry for the singular form. But this example is included to indicate that there may be times that only a dictionary—neither reasoning from rules nor using the resources included in this volume—can provide the information you need.)
- Accent marks—while they do not change alphabetical order, and therefore do not affect looking up words— do affect spelling correctness. The word *übercool* is given in the entry for the prefix *über-* (*uber-* is actually acceptable as well).
- Words with contrasting spellings to indicate gender, as in *fiancé/fiancée* and *protégé/protégée,* don't create alphabetizing problems with their accents, but they are problematic because, if you do not already know, you cannot tell by looking which is which. Again, consult the homophones list.
- Words with more than one acceptable spelling may be as difficult to find as a word that you've misspelled

for any other reason. Sometimes you may find British and American English differences (as in *cosy/cozy*) or simply variant American English spellings (as in *yogurt/yoghurt*). In either case, scanning the page, and if that doesn't yield results, referring to the sound chart are good ideas.

Pronunciation
- In words with silent letters, the spelling will not match the sound, so these words are often problematic to spell. *Wednesday* is a perennial problem. The sound chart includes spellings with silent letters, so it can help you out in such situations. You also may wish to refer to the silent letter lists on pages 36–37.
- The pervasive unaccented vowel sound (schwa), which can be made by any single vowel and a number of combinations in English, is so frequently necessary to look up that it's the first item on the sound chart. *Arithmetic* is one example of a word with the schwa sound spelled with an *e*.
- When our pronunciation of a word omits a syllable, as in *mathematics* (the *e* is not pronounced, and the word has three syllables, not four as it might appear), it is often hard to figure out what goes on in the syllable that isn't heard. You might start by guessing some letter that could spell a schwa sound, but this is not a guarantee. If scanning doesn't help you locate the word, you may need to end up with a dictionary.

Mispronunciation
Since mispronunciations aren't conscious or intended, you probably won't know you're making this kind of mistake when it occurs. But if you can't find a word, it's a possibility to consider, and you might try the strategies listed here, just in case.

- Skipping over a consonant in pronunciation, as you may imagine, may make spelling the word a bit problematic. Many people omit the first *r* when they say the word *February*. Fortunately, the spelling is distinct enough, that scanning a bit will probably bring it into view. If that should fail, a calendar would help in this case. In general, mispronunciation is one of the tougher issues to cope with because often one is not aware that one has missed something. If you simply cannot find a word, asking a friend/colleague or using a misspeller's dictionary can be a next step.

- Adding a vowel in pronunciation is another possible source of errors. If one says "disasterous," one is likely to look for a vowel rather than the *r* following the *t*.

- Transpositions are sometimes made in pronunciation, the most famous probably being the child's version of *spaghetti* (*pasghetti*), and possibly the most common among adults being *jewelry* pronounced as *jewlery*. Because the letters are similar, scanning may help discover the true spelling. If scanning doesn't uncover the word, a misspeller's dictionary may do the trick.

- Sometimes an incorrect model of a word's pronunciation can lead to vowel substitution, so that words that aren't homophones seem to be. *Defused/diffused* is an example. If you don't realize that there are actually two separate words, with separate spellings and pronunciations, you may end up incorrectly using one word in place of the other until someone draws attention to it and explains the situation.

- Omitting or adding a syllable can result from various regional dialectical differences. For example, speakers of certain US dialects referred to as "*r*-dropping dialects" (spoken in the southeastern United States, New York City, and eastern New England) may also add \r\ when a schwa precedes another vowel. The

best thing here is to be aware of your own dialectical
idiosyncracies and to turn to a misspeller's dictionary
if all else fails.

Compound Words
There are three types of compounds: open, with a space
between the words as in *chaos theory* or *channel
surfing;* closed, with the words run together, as in
thirtysomething or *webcam;* and hyphenated, with the
words separated by a hyphen, as in *channel-hopping*
or *open-heart.* Since the type does not affect the alphabetical order, it will not be an issue for looking the
words up, though usually only one rendering is the
correct spelling of the word.

Abbreviation Beginning with Apostrophe
There are not too many examples of this: *'tain't, 'tis,*
and *'tude* (short for *attitude*) are three. In any case, they
do not affect alphabetization—only correct spelling.

Initial Capital
The word *Frankenfood,* the tongue-in-cheek name for
genetically engineered food, after Dr. Viktor Frankenstein
(from Mary Wollstonecraft Shelley's novel of the same
name), takes a capital letter, but this does not affect its
alphabetization—only the correct rendering on paper.

Misapprehension About Meaning Causes Confusion with Another Word
Though *somersault* has nothing to do with *summer* and
kindergarten is from the German, not English *garden*,
misconceptions may lead to mistakes in spelling. The
sound chart on page 51 can be of help here.

Single/Double Consonant Confusion

The words *embarrassment, harassment, occasion, occurred, Massachusetts,* and *Mississippi* are perennially misspelled owing to confusion over which consonants are single and which are doubled. If the correct spelling is not close enough to find by scanning, the sound chart can be of use.

A nonnative speaker may also have difficulty distinguishing the sounds of a language that is not familiar—sounds that are easily separated by a native speaker may seem identical to someone learning a language after their primary language. If English is not your first language, make sure that you know the sounds represented by the symbols in the sound chart.

SOUNDS AND THEIR SPELLINGS

Suppose you cannot find a word in the list (or in any dictionary, for that matter). Here is a chart that details the sounds of the English language and the wide variety of ways they may be spelled. Think about the sounds in the word you are looking for and use the chart to help you consider alternate ways to spell it.

In the chart,

Common means that these are the most frequently occurring spellings of this sound.

Unusual means that these spellings are less frequent.

Oddball means that these spellings are very rare and may even be unique, or singleton, instances.

Following chart © 2004 by Mary Elizabeth, adapted and expanded from pages 15–19 in her book, *Painless Spelling,* copyright by the author. All Rights Reserved.

US English Sounds and Their Spellings

SOUND	SPELLINGS		
	Common	**Unusual**	**Oddball**
schwa \ə\ in an unaccented syllable	*a* as in *balloon* *e* as in *concentration* *o* as in *prison* *u* as in *circus*	*ai* as in *captain* *eo* as in *dungeon* *i* as in *pencil* *ia* as in *special* *iou* as in *anxious* *ou* as in *generous*	*é* as in *protégé* (1st *é*) *eu* as in *chauffeur*
schwa \'ə\ in an accented syllable	*o* as in *oven* *u* as in *button*	*a* as in *attention* *e* as in *them* *i* as in *stirrup* *o_e* as in *come* *oo* as in *flood* *ou* as in *trouble*	*au_e* as in *because* (2nd pronunciation) *e_ _e* as in *terce* *ea* as in *earl* *eu* as in *arbitrageur* *oe* as in *doesn't*
short *a* \a\	*a* as in *bat*	*a_ _e* as in *trance* *au* as in *laugh* *i* as in *meringue*	*a_e* as in *comrade* *ai* as in *plaid*
long *a* \ā\	*a* as in *favor* *a_e* as in *male* *a_ _e* as in *paste* *ai* as in *mail* *ai_e* as in *praise* *ay* as in *may*	*ae* as in *Gaelic* *é* as in *soufflé* *ée* as in *née* *ê* as in *crêpe* *e* as in *rodeo* (2nd pronunciation) *e_e* as in *crepe* *ea* as in *great* *ee* as in *matinee* *ei* as in *veil* *eig* as in *deign* *eigh* as in *neighbor* *et* as in *bouquet* *ey* as in *prey*	*ag_e* as in *champagne* *ai_ _e* as in *taille* *aig* as in *champaign* *aigh* as in *straight* *ao* as in *gaol* *au* as in *gauge* *aye* as in *aye* meaning always *ee_e* as in *feeze* (2nd pronunciation) *eh* as in *eh* *oeh* as in *foehn* (3rd pronunciation) *öh* as in *fohn* *(u)ai* as in *quai* *(u)ay* as in *quay* (2nd pronunciation)

(continued)

US English Sounds and Their Spellings (continued)

SOUND	SPELLINGS		
	Common	**Unusual**	**Oddball**
\ä\ see \o\			

\är\	*ar* as in *car*	*arre* as in *bizarre*
		oire as in *repertoire*
			aar as in *bazaar*
			arr as in *gnarr*
			  (2nd spelling of
			  gnar)
			arrh as in *catarrh*
			ear as in *heart*
			oir as in *au revoir*
			uar as in *guarantee*
			  (2nd pronunciation)

\aů\	*ou* as in *cloud* *ow* as in *frown*	*au* as in *sauerbraten* *hou* as in *hour* *ough* as in *bough*	*ao* as in *Tao* *iao* as in *ciao*
\b\	*b* as in *beefalo* *bb* as in *hobbit*		*bh* as in *bhang* *pb* as in *cupboard*
\ch\	*ch* as in *chimp* *tch* as in *watch*	*c(e)* as in *cello* *t(e)* as in *righteous* *t(i)* as in *question* *t(ure)* as in *creature* *cz* as in *Czech*	
\d\	*d* as in *drum machine* *dd* as in *fiddle* *ed* as in *raddled* *t* as in *kindergarten* (2nd pronunciation)	*ld* as in *should*	*dh* as in *dhow*

US English Sounds and Their Spellings (continued)

SOUND	SPELLINGS		
	Common	**Unusual**	**Oddball**

short e \e\	*e* as in *bet*
	ea as in *bread*
		a as in *any*
		ae as in *aerobic*
		ai as in *said*
		ei as in *leisure*
		  (2nd pronunciation)
		eo as in *leopard*
		ue as in *guess*
			ay as in *says*
			è as in *crème*
			ee as in *been*
			  (2nd pronunciation)
			ie as in *friend*
			oe as in *roentgen*

long e \ē\	*e* as in *me*
	e_e as in *genes*
	ea as in *peal*
	ee as in *peek*
	y as in *happy*
		ae as in *archaeology*
		ay as in *quay*
		ea_e as in *peace*
		ei as in *receive*
		ie as in *thief*
		ey as in *key*
		i as in *curious*
		i_e as in *machine*
		is as in *chassis*
		oe as in *phoenix*
		uy as in *soliloquy*
			a as in *bologna*
			è as in *crème*
			  (2nd pronunciation)
			eo as in *people*
			iere as in *premiere*
			  (3rd pronunciation)
			ière as in *première*
			  (3rd pronunciation)
			ighi as in *Brighid*
			(u)ay as in *quay*

\er\	*air* as in *lair* *ar* as in *parent* *are* as in *snare* *ear* as in *pear*	*aer* as in *aerobic* *aire* as in *millionaire* *eer* as in *eerie* *er* as in *scherzo* *err* as in *error* *eyr* as in *eyrie* *irr* as in *whirr*	*ayer* as in *prayer* *ayr* as in *Ayr* *e'er* as in *e'er* *eir* as in *heir* *ere* as in *ere* *ère* as in *père* *eyre* as in *eyre* *heir* as in *heir* *uar* as in *guarantee* *ur* as in *burial*

(continued)

US English Sounds and Their Spellings (continued)

SOUND	SPELLINGS		
	Common	**Unusual**	**Oddball**
\f\	*f* as in *leaf* *ph* as in *photo*	*ff* as in *difficult* *gh* as in *tough* *lf* as in *calf*	
\g\	*g* as in *gag* *gg* as in *egg*	*gh* as in *yoghurt* *g(u)* as in *guard* *g(ue)* as in *dialogue*	
\h\	*h* as in *human*	*g* as in *Gila monster* *j* as in *junta* *wh* as in *who*	
\hw\	*wh* as in *whale*		*hu* as in *Huai* (2nd pronunciation)
short i \i\	*e* as in *English* *i* as in *bit*	*a_e* as in *advantage* *ia* as in *carriage* *u* as in *busy* *y* as in *abyss*	*ee* as in *been* *i_e* as in *exquisite* *i_ _e* as in *grippe* *ie_e* as in *sieve* *o* as in *women* *ui* as in *build*
long i \ī\	*i* as in *mild* *i_e* as in *mile* *ie* as in *lie* *igh* as in *might* *y* as in *my*	*ai* as in *Thailand* *ay* as in *papaya* *ei* as in *stein* *eigh* as in *heigh-ho* *ey* as in *Rheydt* *eye* as in *eye* *ia* as in *phial* *i(g)* as in *cosign* *uy* as in *buy* *ye* as in *bye* *y_e* as in *rhyme*	*ai_ _e* as in *faille* *aye* as in *aye*[2] *ayyi* as in *sayyid* (3rd pronunciation) *io* as in *viol* (alternate pronunciation) *oy* as in *coyote* *ui_e* as in *guide* *uye* as in *guyed*

---

[2]*aye* meaning *yes*

US English Sounds and Their Spellings (continued)

SOUND	SPELLINGS		
	Common	**Unusual**	**Oddball**
\ir\	*ear* as in *dear* *eer* as in *deer* *er* as in *zero* (2nd pronunciation) *ere* as in *here*	*eir* as in *weird* *ier* as in *tier*	*aer* as in *aerie* (2nd pronunciation) *eor* as in *theory* *eyr* as in *eyrie* (2nd pronunciation) *ier_e* as in *tierce* *iere* as in *premiere* (2nd pronunciation) *ière* as in *première* (2nd pronunciation) *irr* as in *birr* *yr* as in *Tyr*
\j\	*dg(e)* as in *judge* *g(e)* as in *gentle* *j* as in *jump*	*dg(i)* as in *lodging* *d(u)* as in *graduate* *dzh* as in *Adzharia* *gg* as in *exaggerate* *g(i)* as in *giraffe*	*d(i)* as in *soldier* *dj* as in *adjective* *g(a)* as in *gaol*
\k\	*c* as in *camel* *ck* as in *back* *k* as in *kangaroo* *q(u)* as in *conquer*	*cc* as in *accurate* *ch* as in *conch* *cq(u)* as in *lacquer* *c(u)* as in *biscuit* *gh* as in *skeigh* *kh* as in *khaki* *lk* as in *caulk* *q(i)* as in *Iraqi* *que* as in *oblique* *x* as in *phlox* (spells \ks\)	*cch* as in *saccharine* *kk* as in *trekked* *q* as in *FAQs* (spells \ks\)
\l\	*l* as in *latte* *ll* as in *troll*	*sl* as in *isle*	*ld* as in *yauld* *lh* as in *Lhasa apso* *ln* as in *kiln* (2nd pronunciation)

(continued)

US English Sounds and Their Spellings (continued)

SOUND	Common	Unusual	Oddball
		SPELLINGS	
\m\	*m* as in *marginalize* *mm* as in *mommy*	*gm* as in *diaphragm* *lm* as in *balm* *mb* as in *lamb* *mn* as in *limn*	*chm* as in *drachm* *n* as in *tefillin* (alternate pronunciation)
\n\	*n* as in *pin* *nn* as in *inn*	*gn* as in *gnat* *kn* as in *knee* *pn* as in *pneumonia*	*dn* as in *Wednesday* *mn* as in *mnemonic* *nd* as in *handsome* (alternate pronunciation)
\ŋ\	*ng* as in *strong* *n(k)* as in *think*	*ngue* as in *tongue*	*ngg* as in *mah-jongg* *n(x)* as in *anxious*
short o \ȯ\ or \ä\ (Some speakers distinguish these sounds; others don't.)	*a* as in *all* *o* as in *cot*	*au* as in *autumn* *augh* as in *caught* *aw* as in *trawl* *ho* as in *honesty* *oa* as in *broad* *ou* as in *trough* *ough* as in *bought*	*aa* as in *laager* *ah* as in *Utah* *au_e* as in *because*
long o \ō\	*o* as in *no* *o_e* as in *mole* *oa* as in *moat* *oe* as in *doe* *ow* as in *mow*	*au* as in *chauvinist* *eau* as in *plateau* *oh* as in *oh* *ou* as in *soul* *ough* as in *though* *owe* as in *owes*	*aoh* as in *pharaoh* *aux* as in *faux* *eaux* as in *Meaux* *eo* as in *yeoman* *eou* as in *Seoul* *ew* as in *sew* *ho* as in *mho* *ô* as in *Côte* *oo* as in *brooch* *ot* as in *tarot*

US English Sounds and Their Spellings (continued)

SOUND	SPELLINGS		
	Common	**Unusual**	**Oddball**
\ȯi\	*oi* as in *boil* *oy* as in *boy*		*uoi* as in *quoin* *uoy* as in *buoy*
\ȯr\	*ar* as in *quarrel* *or* as in *condor* *ore* as in *galore*	*aur* as in *centaur* *awr* as in *Lawrence* *oar* as in *roar* *oor* as in *door* *our* as in *four*	*awer* as in *sawer* *oer* as in *Boer* *orr* as in *torr*
\p\	*p* as in *potbellied pig* *pp* as in *guppy*	*ph* as in *shepherd*	*gh* as in *hiccough*
\r\	*r* as in *rare*	*rh* as in *rhythm* *rr* as in *terror* *rrh* as in *cirrhosis* *wr* as in *wring*	*l(o)* as in *colonel* *oeh* as in *foehn* *öh* as in *föhn* *rt* as in *mortgage*
\s\	*c(e)* as in *celery* *c(i)* as in *cilia* *c(y)* as in *cyst* *s* as in *slime* *ss* as in *brass*	*ps* as in *pseudonym* *sc* as in *science* *st* as in *listen* *sw* as in *sword* *z* as in *quartz*	*sch* as in *schism* *sth* as in *isthmus* *th* as in *beth* (3rd pronunciation)

\sh\	*c(i)* as in *suspicion*
	sh as in *shoe*
	s(i) as in *scansion*
	ss(i) as in *mission*
	t(i) as in *gumption*
		c(e) as in *oceanic*
		ch as in *chandelier*
		s(u) as in *sugar*
		sch as in *schism*
		  (3rd pronunciation)
		sc(i) as in
		  conscience
		s(e) as in *nauseous*
		ss(u) as in *tissue*
			che as in *cache*
			chs as in *fuchsia*
			psh as in *pshaw*
			zh as in *pirozhki*

(continued)

US English Sounds and Their Spellings (continued)

SOUND	Common	Unusual	Oddball
		SPELLINGS	
\t\	*t* as in *tiger* *tt* as in *cattle*	*bt* as in *debt* *ed* as in *vanished* *nc* as in *chance* (alternate pronunciation) *pt* as in *pterodactyl* *th* as in *thyme*	*cht* as in *yacht* *ct* as in *indict* *dt* as in *Rheydt*
short u \u̇\ in an accented syllable	*o* as in *woman* *u* as in *bull*	*oo* as in *wood* *ou* as in *could*	*oui* as in *bouillion* (2nd pronunciation)
long u \ü\	*ew* as in *stew* *o* as in *to* *oo* as in *soon* *o_e* as in *whose* *u* as in *Ruth* *u_e* as in *June*	*eu* as in *sleuth* *oe* as in *canoe* *ou* as in *you* *ue* as in *blue* *ui* as in *suit*	*ieu* as in *adieu* *ou* as in *coup* (n) *ou_e* as in *coupe* *ou_ _e* as in *mousse* *ough* as in *through* *ougha* as in *brougham* (2nd pronunciation) *oux* as in *doux* *wo* as in *two*
long u with y in front \yü\	*ewe* as in *ewe* *u* as in *human* *u_e* as in *mule*	*eu* as in *feud* *ew* as in *pew* *iew* as in *view* *ue* as in *barbecue*	*eau* as in *beauty* *ieu* as in *adieu* (2nd pronunciation) *u_ _e* as in *butte* *ueue* as in *queue*
\u̇r\	*ear* as in *learn* *er* as in *kernel* *ir* as in *bird* *or* as in *work* *ur* as in *burn*	*ere* as in *were* *eur* as in *entrepreneur* *irr* as in *whirr* *our* as in *courtesy* *urr* as in *burr* *yr* as in *myrtle*	*oor* as in *spoor* *yrrh* as in *myrrh*

US English Sounds and Their Spellings (continued)

SOUND	SPELLINGS		
	Common	**Unusual**	**Oddball**
\v\	*v* as in *love*	*f* as in *of* *lv* as in *calve*	
\w\	*u* as in *suite* *w* as in *wet* *wh* as in *where* (2nd pronunciation)	*(g)u* as in *language* *o* as in *once* *(q)u* as in *conquest*	*hu* as in *Huy*
\y\	*y* as in *yummy*	*i* as in *alleluia*	*j* as in *hallelujah*
\z\	*z* as in *zebra*	*cz* as in *czar* *s* as in *his* *se* as in *turquoise* *ss* as in *possess* (first set of esses) *ts* as in *tsar* *x* as in *xylophone* *zz* as in *buzz*	*thes* as in *clothes*
\zh\	*s(i)* as in *decision* *s(u)* as in *unusual*	*g(e)* as in *garage* *z(u)* as in *azure*	*g(i)* as in *regime* *t(i)* as in *equation*

THE WORD LIST

18-wheel·er
800 num·ber
9/11
9-11

A
aback
aba·cus
aban·don·ment
abase
abase·ment
abas·ing
abash
abate
abate·ment
ab·bé
ab·bess
ab·bey
ab·bot
ab·bre·vi·ate
ab·bre·vi·a·tion
ab·di·cate
ab·di·ca·tion
ab·do·men
ab·duct
ab·duc·tion
abeam
ab·er·rant
ab·er·ra·tion
abet
abet·ted
abet·tor
abey·ance
ab·hor
ab·hor·rence
ab·hor·rent
abide
abil·i·ty

ab·ject
ab·jure
ab·la·tive
ablaze
able-bod·ied
abloom
ab·lu·tion
ab·ne·ga·tion
ab·nor·mal
ab·nor·mal·i·ty
aboard
abode
aboil
abol·ish
ab·o·li·tion
A-bomb
abom·i·na·ble
abom·i·nate
abom·i·na·tion
ab·orig·i·nal
ab·orig·i·ne
abort
abor·ti·fa·cient
abor·tion
abor·tion·ist
abor·tive
abound
about
about-face
above·board
above·ground
ab·ra·ca·dab·ra
abrade
abra·sion
abra·sive
abreast
abridge
abridg·ment

abroad
ab·ro·gate
abrupt
ab·scess
ab·scis·sa
ab·scis·sion
ab·scond
ab·scond·er
ab·sence
ab·sen·tee
ab·sen·tee·ism
ab·sent·mind·ed
ab·sinthe
ab·so·lute
ab·so·lute·ly
ab·so·lu·tion
ab·solve
ab·sorb
ab·sor·bance
ab·sor·ben·cy
ab·sor·bent
ab·sorp·tion
ab·stain
ab·ste·mi·ous
ab·sten·tion
ab·sti·nence
ab·strac·tion
ab·stract·ly
ab·struse
ab·surd
ab·sur·di·ty
abun·dance
abun·dant
abuse
abus·er
abu·sive
abut
abut·ment

abut·ting
abys·mal
abyss
ac·a·deme
ac·a·dem·ic
ac·a·dem·i·cal·ly
ac·a·de·mi·cian
acad·e·my
a cap·pel·la
ac·cede
ac·ced·ed
ac·cel·er·ate
ac·cel·er·a·tion
ac·cel·er·a·tor
ac·cent
ac·cen·tu·ate
ac·cept+
ac·cept·able
ac·cept·ably
ac·cep·tance
ac·cept·ed
ac·cess
ac·ces·si·ble
ac·ces·sion
ac·ces·so·ry
ac·ci·dent
ac·ci·den·tal
ac·ci·den·tal·ly
ac·ci·dent-prone
ac·claim
ac·cla·ma·tion
ac·cli·mate
ac·cli·ma·ti·za·tion
ac·cli·ma·tize
ac·cliv·i·ty
ac·co·lade
ac·com·mo·date
ac·com·mo·da·ting
ac·com·mo·da·tion
ac·com·pa·ni·ment
ac·com·pa·nist
ac·com·pa·ny

ac·com·plice
ac·com·plish
ac·com·plish·ment
ac·cord
ac·cor·dance
ac·cor·di·on
ac·cost
ac·count·able
ac·coun·tan·cy
ac·coun·tant
ac·count·ing
ac·cou·tre
ac·cred·it
ac·cre·tion
ac·cru·al
ac·crue
ac·cul·tur·a·tion
ac·cu·mu·late
ac·cu·mu·la·tion
ac·cu·ra·cy
ac·cu·rate
ac·cursed
ac·cu·sa·tion
ac·cu·sa·tive
ac·cu·sa·to·ry
ac·cused
ac·cus·tomed
acer·bi·ty
acet·amin·o·phen
ac·e·tate
ace·tic
ace·tyl·sal·i·cyl·ic
  acid
ache
achiev·able
achieve
achieve·ment
achon·dro·pla·sia
achy
acid
acid·i·fy
acid·i·ty

ac·i·doph·i·lus
acid·u·lous
ac·id-washed
ac·knowl·edge
ac·knowl·edg·
  ment
ac·me
ac·ne
ac·o·lyte
acorn
acous·tic
ac·ous·ti·cian
acous·tics
ac·quain·tance
  rape
ac·qui·esce
ac·qui·es·cence
ac·quire
ac·quired im·mu·
  no·de·fi·cien·cy
  dis·ease
ac·qui·si·tion
ac·quis·i·tive
ac·quit
ac·quit·tal
acre
acre·age
ac·rid
ac·ri·mo·ni·ous
ac·ri·mo·ny
ac·ro·bat
ac·ro·bat·ics
ac·ro·nym
acrop·o·lis
across
acros·tic
acryl·ic
act
ac·tion·able
ac·ti·vate
ac·tive·wear
ac·tiv·ism

ac·tiv·i·ty
ac·tor
ac·tu·al·i·ty
ac·tu·al·ize
ac·tu·al·iza·tion
ac·tu·al·ly
ac·tu·ar·i·al
ac·tu·ary
ac·tu·ate
acu·ity
acu·men
acu·pres·sure
acu·punc·ture
acute
ad·age
ada·gio
ad·a·mant
ad·a·man·tine
adapt
adapt·able
ad·ap·ta·tion
adapt·er
adap·tive
ad·den·dum
ad·der
ad·dict
ad·dic·tion
ad·di·tion
ad·di·tion·al
ad·di·tion·al·ly
ad·di·tive
ad·dle
ad·dle·pat·ed
ad·dress
ad·dress·able
ad·dress·ee
ad·duce
ad·e·noid
ad·e·noi·dal
ad·ept
ad·e·qua·cy
ad·e·quate

ad·here
ad·her·ence
ad·her·ent
ad·he·sion
ad·he·sive
ad hoc
ad ho·mi·nem
adieu+
ad in·fi·ni·tum
adi·os
ad·i·pose
Ad·i·ron·dacks
ad·ja·cent
ad·jec·ti·val
ad·jec·tive
ad·join
ad·join·ing
ad·journ
ad·journ·ment
ad·ju·di·cate
ad·junct
ad·junc·tion
ad·jure
ad·just
ad·just·able rate
    mort·gage
ad·just·ment
ad·ju·tant
Ad·le·ri·an
ad-lib
ad·min·is·ter
ad·min·is·trate
ad·min·is·tra·tion
ad·min·is·tra·tive
ad·min·is·tra·tor
ad·mi·ra·ble
ad·mi·ral
ad·mi·ral·ty
ad·mi·ra·tion
ad·mire
ad·mir·ing
ad·mis·si·ble

ad·mis·sion
ad·mit
ad·mit·tance
ad·mon·ish
ad·mo·ni·tion
ad nau·se·am
ado+
ado·be
ad·o·les·cence
adopt
adopt·ee
adop·tion
adop·tive
ador·able
ad·o·ra·tion
adorn
adorn·ment
ad rem
ad·re·nal
ad·re·nal·ine
adrift
adroit
ad·sor·bent
ad·sorp·tion
ad·u·late
ad·u·la·tion
adult
adul·ter·ate
adul·ter·a·tion
adul·ter·er
adul·ter·ess
ad·um·brate
ad·um·bra·tion
ad va·lo·rem
ad·vance
    di·rec·tive
ad·vance·ment
ad·van·tage
ad·van·ta·geous
ad·vent
ad·ven·ti·tious
ad·ven·ture

ad·ven·tur·er
ad·ven·ture·some
ad·ven·tur·ous
ad·ver·bi·al
ad·ver·sar·i·al
ad·ver·sary
ad·verse
ad·verse·ly
ad·ver·si·ty
ad·ver·tise
ad·ver·tise·ment
ad·ver·tis·ing
ad·vice
ad·vis·abil·i·ty
ad·vis·able
ad·vise
ad·vis·ed·ly
ad·vis·er
ad·vis·ing
ad·vi·so·ry
ad·vo·ca·cy
ad·vo·cate
ad·vo·ca·tor
adze
ae·gis
ae·on
aer·ate
aer·a·tor
ae·ri·al
ae·ri·al·ist
aer·o·bic
aero·dy·nam·ics
aero·naut
aero·nau·tics
aero·sol
aes·thete
aes·thet·ic
aes·thet·i·cal·ly
aes·thet·i·cism
aes·thet·ics
af·fa·ble
af·fair

af·fect[+]
af·fec·ta·tion
af·fect·ed
af·fec·tion
af·fec·tion·ate
af·fec·tive
af·fer·ent
af·fi·ance
af·fi·cio·na·do[*]
af·fi·da·vit
af·fil·i·ate
af·fil·i·a·tion
af·fin·i·ty
af·firm
af·fir·ma·tion
af·fir·ma·tive
af·fix
af·flict
af·flic·tion
af·flu·ence
af·flu·ent
af·ford
Af·ri·can·ized
     bee
af·fright
af·front
afi·cio·na·do
afield
afire
aflame
afloat
afoot
afore·men·tioned
afore·said
afore·thought
afraid
afresh
Af·ro
af·ter all
af·ter·care
af·ter·glow
af·ter·hours

af·ter·life
af·ter·math
af·ter·noon
af·ter·shave
af·ter·taste
af·ter·thought
af·ter·ward
against
agape
ag·ate
aged
age·less
agen·cy
agen·da
Agent Or·ange
ag·gran·dize
ag·gran·dize·ment
ag·gra·vate
ag·gra·va·tion
ag·gre·gate
ag·gre·ga·tion
ag·gres·sion
ag·gres·sor
ag·grieved
aghast
ag·ile
ag·ile·ly
agil·i·ty
ag·i·tate
ag·i·ta·tor
aglit·ter
aglow
ag·nos·tic
agog
ag·o·nize
ag·o·ny
ag·o·ra·pho·bia
agrar·i·an
agree·able
agree·ably
agree·ment
ag·ri·cul·ture

agron·o·mist
agron·o·my
aground
ague
ahead
ahoy
aid[+]
aide[+]
aide-de-camp
aide-mé·moire
AIDS
ai·ki·do
ai·le·ron
air base
air-con·di·tion·er
air·craft
air·field
air force
air·freight
air·ing
air·lift
air·line
air·lin·er
air·mail
air·man
air·plane
air·port
air rage
air raid
air·ship
air·space
air·speed
air·strip
air·tight
air-to-air mis·sile
air·way
airy
aisle[+]
ajar
akim·bo
akin
al·a·bas·ter

à la carte
alac·ri·ty
à la mode
alarm
alas
al·ba·tross
al·be·it
al·bi·no
al·bum
al·bu·men
al·che·my
al·co·hol
al·co·hol·ic
al·co·hol·ism
al·cove
al den·te
al·der·man
al·der·man·ic
alem·bic
alert
al·fal·fa
al·fres·co
al·ga
al·gae
al·ge·bra
al·ge·bra·ic
al·go·rithm
alias
al·i·bi
alien
alien·ate
alien·ation
alight
align
align·ment
alike
al·i·men·ta·ry
al·i·mo·ny
A-line
A-list
alive
al·ka·li

al·ka·line
al·ka·loid
Al·lah
all-around
al·lay
al·le·ga·tion
al·lege
al·leg·ed·ly
Al·le·ghe·nies
al·le·giance
al·le·gor·i·cal
al·le·go·ry
al·le·lu·ia
all-em·brac·ing
Allen wrench
al·ler·gic
al·ler·gy
al·le·vi·ate
al·ley
al·ley·way
al·li·ance
al·lied
al·lies
al·li·ga·tor
al·lit·er·a·tion
al·lit·er·a·tive
all-night (adj)
al·lo·cate
al·lo·ca·tion
al·lo·path·ic
al·lop·a·thy
al·lot
al·lot·ted
al·lot·ment
all-out (adj)
al·low·able
al·low·ance
al·loy
all-pow·er·ful
all-pur·pose
all right

all-star
all-time (adj)
al·lude
al·lure
al·lure·ment
al·lur·ing
al·lu·sion
al·lu·sive
al·lu·sive·ly
al·lu·vi·al
al·ly
al·ma ma·ter
al·ma·nac
al·mighty
al·mond
al·most
alms
aloe vera
aloft
alo·ha
alone
along·side
aloof
aloud
al·paca
al·pha
al·pha·bet
al·pha·bet·ic
al·pha·bet·i·cal·ly
al·pha·bet·ize
al·pha·nu·mer·ic
al·pine
al·ready
al·so·ran
al·tar⁺
al·ter⁺
al·ter·ation
al·ter·ca·tion
al·ter ego
al·ter·nate
al·ter·nate·ly
al·ter·na·tor

al·though
al·tim·e·ter
al·ti·tude
al·to
al·to·geth·er
alt-rock
al·tru·ism
al·tru·is·tic
alu·mi·num
alum·na
alum·nae
alum·ni
alum·nus
al·ways
Alz·hei·mer's
    dis·ease
amal·gam
amal·gam·ate
amal·gam·ation
am·a·ranth
am·a·ret·to
amass
am·a·teur
am·a·to·ry
amaze
amaze·ment
am·a·zon
am·bas·sa·dor
am·ber
Am·ber Alert
am·ber·gris
am·bi·dex·ter·i·ty
am·bi·dex·trous
am·bi·ence
am·bi·ent
am·bi·gu·i·ty
am·big·u·ous
am·bi·tion
am·bi·tious
am·biv·a·lence
am·biv·a·lent
am·ble

am·bro·sia
am·bro·sial
am·bu·lance
am·bu·lant
am·bu·la·to·ry
am·bush
ame·lio·rate
ame·na·ble
amend
amend·ment
amends
ame·ni·ties
ame·ni·ty
amen·or·rhea
Amer·i·ca·na
Amer·i·can·i·za·
    tion
Amer·i·can·ize
am·e·thyst
ami·a·ble
ami·a·bly
am·i·ca·ble
ami·cus cu·ri·ae
amid
amid·ships
ami·go
amiss
am·i·ty
am·me·ter
am·mo·nia
am·mu·ni·tion
am·ne·sia
am·nes·ty
am·ni·o·cen·te·sis
amoe·ba
amok
among
amor·al
amo·ral·i·ty
am·o·rous
am·o·rous·ness
amor·phous

am·or·ti·za·tion
am·or·tize
amount
amour
am·per·age
am·pere
am·per·sand
am·phet·amine
am·phib·i·an
am·phib·i·ous
am·phi·the·ater
am·pho·ra
am·ple
am·pli·fi·ca·tion
am·pli·fi·er
am·pli·fy
am·pli·tude
am·pu·tate
am·pu·ta·tion
am·pu·tee
Am·trak™
amuck*
am·u·let
amuse
amuse·ment
amus·ing
anach·ro·nism
anach·ro·nis·tic
an·a·gram
anal
an·al·ge·sic
an·a·log+
anal·o·gous
an·a·logue+
anal·o·gy
anal·y·sis
an·a·lyst
an·a·lyt·ic
an·a·lyt·i·cal
an·a·lyze
an·a·pest
ana·phy·lac·tic

ana·phy·lax·is
an·ar·chic
an·ar·chism
an·ar·chist
an·ar·chis·tic
an·ar·chy
anath·e·ma
anath·e·ma·tize
an·a·tom·i·cal
anat·o·my
an·ces·tor
an·ces·tral
an·ces·try
an·chor
an·chor·age
an·cho·rite
an·chor·man
an·chor·wom·an
an·cho·vy
an·cient
an·cil·lary
an·dan·te
and·iron
an·ec·dot·al
an·ec·dote
ane·mia
anem·o·ne
an·es·the·sia
an·es·the·si·ol·o·
     gist
an·es·the·si·ol·o·gy
an·es·thet·ic
anes·the·tist
anes·the·tize
an·eu·rysm
anew
an·gel
an·gel·ic
an·ger
an·gi·na pec·to·ris
an·gio·plas·ty
an·gle

an·gled
an·gler
An·gli·can
an·gli·cism
an·gli·cize
an·gling
An·glo·phile
An·glo·phobe
An·glo-Sax·on
an·go·ra
an·gri·ly
an·gry
angst
ang·strom
an·guish
an·gu·lar
an·gu·lar·i·ty
an·hy·drous
an·i·ma
an·i·mal
an·i·mate
an·i·mat·ed
an·i·ma·tion
an·i·mos·i·ty
an·i·mus
an·ise
an·is·ette
ankh
an·kle
an·klet
an·ky·lo·sis
an·nals
an·neal
an·nex
an·ni·hi·late
an·ni·ver·sa·ry
An·no Do·mi·ni
an·no·tate
an·no·ta·tion
an·nounce·ment
an·nounc·er
an·noy

an·noy·ance
an·nu·al
an·nu·ity
an·nul
an·nul·ment
an·nun·ci·a·tion
an·od·ize
an·o·dyne
anoint
anom·a·lous
anom·a·ly
an·o·mie
an·o·nym·i·ty
anon·y·mous
anoph·e·les
an·o·rak
an·orex·i·a
   ner·vo·sa
an·oth·er
an·swer
an·swer·able
ant·ac·id
an·tag·o·nism
an·tag·o·nist
an·tag·o·nis·tic
an·tag·o·nize
ant·arc·tic
an·te·bel·lum
an·te·cede
an·te·ced·ent
an·te·cham·ber
an·te·date
an·te·di·lu·vi·an
an·te·lope
an·te me·ri·di·em
an·ten·na
an·te·pe·nult
an·te·pen·ul·ti·
   mate
an·te·ri·or
an·te·room
an·them

an·thol·o·gy
an·thra·cite
an·thrax
an·thro·po·cen·tric
an·thro·poid
an·thro·pol·o·gist
an·thro·pol·o·gy
an·thro·po·mor·
   phic
an·ti·bi·ot·ic
an·ti·body
an·tic·i·pate
an·tic·i·pa·tion
an·tic·i·pa·ting
an·tic·i·pa·to·ry
an·ti·cler·i·cal
an·ti·cli·mac·tic
an·ti·cli·max
an·ti·de·pres·sant
an·ti·dote
an·ti·es·tab·lish·
   ment
an·ti·freeze
an·ti·gen
an·ti·his·ta·mine
an·ti·hy·per·ten·
   sive
an·ti·in·flam·ma·
   to·ry
an·ti·lock
an·ti·ma·cas·sar
an·ti·mo·ny
an·tin·o·my
an·ti·ox·i·dants
an·ti·pas·to
an·tip·a·thy
an·ti·phon
an·tiph·o·nal
an·tiph·o·ny
an·tip·odes
an·ti·pov·er·ty
an·ti·quar·i·an

an·ti·quary
an·ti·quat·ed
an·tique
an·tiq·ui·ty
an·ti·Se·mit·ic
an·ti·Sem·i·tism
an·ti·sep·tic
an·ti·so·cial
an·tith·e·sis
an·ti·thet·i·cal
an·ti·tox·in
an·ti·tu·mor
an·ti·vi·rus
ant·ler
ant·lered
an·to·nym
anus
an·vil
anx·i·ety
anx·ious
anx·ious·ly
any·body
any·how
any·more
any·one
any·place
any·thing
any·time
any·way
any·where
aor·ta
apace
apart
apart·heid
apart·ment
ap·a·thet·ic
ap·a·thy
aper·i·tif
ap·er·ture
apex
Ap·gar score
apha·sia

aphid
aph·o·rism
aph·ro·di·si·ac
api·a·rist
api·ary
apiece
ap·ish
aplomb
ap·nea
apoc·a·lypse
apoc·a·lyp·tic
apoc·ry·pha
apoc·ry·phal
apo·gee
apol·o·get·ic
apol·o·get·ics
ap·o·lo·gia
apol·o·gist
apol·o·gize
apol·o·gy
ap·o·plec·tic
ap·o·plexy
apos·ta·sy
apos·tate
a pos·te·ri·o·ri
apos·tle
ap·os·tol·ic
apos·tro·phe
apoth·e·cary
apo·the·o·sis
Ap·pa·la·chians
ap·pall
ap·pall·ing
ap·pa·ra·tus
ap·par·el
ap·par·ent
ap·pa·ri·tion
ap·peal
ap·peal·ing
ap·pear·ance
ap·pease
ap·pel·lant

ap·pel·late
ap·pel·la·tion
ap·pend
ap·pend·age
ap·pen·dec·to·my
ap·pen·di·ci·tis
ap·pen·dix
ap·per·cep·tion
ap·pe·tite
ap·pe·tiz·er
ap·pe·tiz·ing
ap·plaud
ap·plause
ap·plet
ap·pli·ance
ap·pli·ca·ble
ap·pli·cant
ap·pli·ca·tion
ap·pli·qué
ap·ply
ap·point
ap·poin·tee
ap·point·ment
ap·por·tion
ap·por·tion·ment
ap·po·site
ap·po·si·tion
ap·prais·al
ap·praise
ap·pre·cia·ble
ap·pre·ci·ate
ap·pre·ci·a·tion
ap·pre·cia·tive
ap·pre·hend
ap·pre·hen·sion
ap·pre·hen·sive
ap·pren·tice
ap·prise
ap·proach
ap·proach·able
ap·pro·ba·tion
ap·pro·pri·ate

ap·pro·pri·a·tion
ap·prov·able
ap·prov·al
ap·prove
ap·prox·i·mate
ap·prox·i·ma·tion
ap·pur·te·nance
apri·cot
a pri·o·ri
apron
ap·ro·pos
ap·ti·tude
aqua·ma·rine
aqua·plane
aquar·i·um
aquat·ic
aq·ue·duct
aque·ous
aqui·fer
aq·ui·line
ar·a·besque
ar·a·ble
ar·bi·ter
ar·bi·trage
ar·bi·trary
ar·bi·trate
ar·bi·tra·tor
ar·bor
ar·bo·re·al
ar·bo·re·tum
ar·cade
ar·ca·dia
ar·cane
arch
ar·chae·ol·o·gy
ar·cha·ic
arch·an·gel
arch·bish·op
arch·dea·con
arch·di·o·cese
ar·cher
ar·chery

ar·che·type
ar·chi·pel·a·go
ar·chi·tect
ar·chi·tec·ton·ic
ar·chi·tec·tur·al
ar·chi·tec·ture
ar·chives
ar·chi·vist
arch·way
arc·tic
ar·dent
ar·dor
ar·du·ous
ar·ea
are·na
aren't
ar·go·sy
ar·got
ar·gu·able
ar·gue
ar·gu·ment
ar·gu·men·ta·tive
aria
ar·id
ar·is·toc·ra·cy
aris·to·crat
arith·me·tic
ar·ma·da
ar·ma·ment
ar·ma·ture
ar·mi·stice
ar·mor
ar·mory
arm-twist·ing
aro·ma
ar·o·mat·ic
around
arouse
ar·peg·gio
ar·raign
ar·raign·ment
ar·range

ar·range·ment
ar·rang·er
ar·ray
ar·rears
ar·rest
ar·rest·ing
ar·rhyth·mia
ar·riv·al
ar·rive
ar·riv·ing
ar·ro·gance
ar·ro·gant
ar·ro·gate
ar·row
ar·royo
ar·se·nal
ar·se·nic
ar·son
art de·co
ar·te·ri·al
ar·te·rio·scle·ro·sis
ar·tery
ar·te·sian well
art·ful
ar·thrit·ic
ar·thri·tis
ar·ti·choke
ar·ti·cle
ar·tic·u·late
ar·tic·u·la·tion
ar·ti·fact
ar·ti·fice
ar·ti·fi·cial
ar·ti·fi·ci·al·i·ty
ar·til·lery
ar·ti·san
art·ist
ar·tiste
ar·tis·tic
art·ist·ry
art·less
art·work

arty
as·bes·tos
as·bes·to·sis
as·cend
as·cen·dan·cy
as·cend·ing
as·cen·sion
as·cent[+]
as·cer·tain
as·cet·ic
as·cet·i·cism
ASCII
as·cribe
asep·tic
ashamed
ash can
ash·en
ashore
aside
as·i·nine
askance
askew
asleep
aso·cial
as·par·a·gus
as·pect
As·per·ger's
  syn·drome
as·per·i·ty
as·per·sions
as·phalt
as·phyx·i·ate
as·phyx·i·a·tion
as·pic
as·pi·rate
as·pi·ra·tion
as·pire
as·pir·er
as·pi·rin
as·sail
as·sas·sin
as·sas·si·nate

as·sault
as·say
as·sem·blage
as·sem·ble
as·sem·bly
as·sem·bly·man
as·sem·bly·
   wom·an
as·sent[+]
as·sent·er
as·sert
as·ser·tion
as·ser·tive
as·sess
as·sess·able
as·sess·ment
as·ses·sor
as·set
as·sid·u·ous
as·sign
as·sig·na·tion
as·sign·ee
as·sign·ment
as·sim·i·late
as·sim·i·la·tion
as·sis·tance
as·sis·tant
as·sis·ted liv·ing
as·sizes
as·so·ci·ate
as·so·ci·a·tion
as·so·cia·tive
as·sort·ed
as·sort·ment
as·suage
as·suag·ing
as·sume
as·sumed
as·sum·ing
as·sump·tion
as·sur·ance
as·sure

as·sured·ly
as·sur·er
as·ter·isk
astern
as·ter·oid
asth·ma
asth·mat·ic
as·tig·mat·ic
astig·ma·tism
as·ton·ish
as·ton·ish·ment
as·tound
as·tound·ing
as·tral
astray
astride
as·trin·gent
as·trol·o·ger
as·trol·o·gy
as·tro·naut
as·tron·o·mer
as·tro·nom·i·cal
as·tute
asun·der
asy·lum
asym·met·ric
at·a·vism
ate·lier
athe·ism
athe·ist
ath·lete
ath·let·ic
ath·let·ics
at large
at·las
at·mo·sphere
at·mo·spher·ic
atom·ic
at·om·ize
at·om·iz·er
aton·al
atone

atone·ment
atrio·ven·tric·u·lar
atro·cious
atroc·i·ty
at·ro·phy
at·tach
at·ta·ché
at·tach·ment
at·tack
at·tain
at·tain·able
at·tain·ment
at·tar
at·tempt
at·tend
at·ten·dance
at·ten·dant
at·ten·tion def·i·cit
   dis·or·der
at·ten·tive
at·ten·u·ate
at·ten·u·a·tion
at·test
at·tic
at·tire
at·ti·tude
at·tor·ney
at·tor·ney-at-law
at·tor·ney gen·er·al
at·trac·tion
at·trac·tive
at·trac·tive·ness
at·trib·ut·able
at·tri·bute
at·tri·bu·tion
at·tri·tion
at·tune
atyp·i·cal
au·burn
auc·tion
auc·tion·eer
au·da·cious

au·dac·i·ty
au·di·bil·i·ty
au·di·ble
au·di·bly
au·di·ence
au·dio·cas·sette
au·dio·lin·gual
au·di·ol·o·gy
au·di·om·e·ter
au·dio·vi·su·al
au·dit
au·di·tion
au·di·tor
au·di·to·ri·um
au·ger+
aug·ment
aug·men·ta·tion
au gra·tin
au·gur+
au·gu·ry
au·gust
au jus
auld lang syne
au na·tu·rel
aunt
au·ra
au·ral+
au·re·ole
au re·voir
au·ri·cle
au·ric·u·lar
au·ro·ra bo·re·al·is
aus·pic·es
aus·pi·cious
aus·tere
aus·tere·ly
aus·ter·i·ty
au·then·tic
au·then·ti·cate
au·thor
au·thor·i·tar·i·an
au·thor·i·ta·tive

au·thor·i·ty
au·tho·ri·za·tion
au·tho·rize
au·tism
au·tis·tic
au·to·bahn
au·to·bi·og·ra·phy
au·to·bus
au·toc·ra·cy
au·to·crat
au·to·crat·ic
au·to·graph
au·to·im·mune
au·to·mak·er
au·to·mate
au·to·mated
  tell·er
  ma·chine
au·to·mat·ic
au·to·ma·tion
au·tom·a·ton
au·to·mo·bile
au·to·mo·tive
au·ton·o·mous
au·ton·o·my
au·top·sy
au·to·sug·ges·tion
au·to·wor·ker
au·tumn
aux·il·ia·ry
avail·abil·i·ty
avail·able
av·a·lanche
avant-garde
av·a·rice
av·a·ri·cious
av·a·tar
avenge
av·e·nue
aver
av·er·age
averred

aver·ring
averse
aver·sion
avert
avi·ary
avi·a·tion
avi·a·tor
av·id
avid·ity
avi·on·ics
av·o·ca·do
av·o·ca·tion
avoid
avoid·ance
av·oir·du·pois
avow
avow·al
avun·cu·lar
await
awak·en
award
aweigh
awe·some
aw·ful+
awk·ward
aw·ning
AWOL
awry
ax·el+
ax·i·al
ax·i·om
ax·i·om·at·ic
ax·is
ax·le+
aza·lea
az·i·muth
Az·tec
azure

B
bab·ble
bab·bler

ba·boon
ba·bush·ka
ba·by boom·er
ba·by·ing
ba·by·ish
ba·by·sit
ba·by·sit·ter
bac·ca·lau·re·ate
bac·ca·rat
bac·cha·nal
bac·cha·na·lia
bach·e·lor
ba·cil·li
ba·cil·lus
back·ache
back·bite
back·bone
back·drop
back·er
back·fire
back·gam·mon
back·ground
back·hand
back·hoe
back·ing
back·lash
back·log
back·slide
back·stage
back·stop
back·sto·ry
back·swing
back·track
back·up (n)
back·ward
back·yard
ba·con
bac·te·ri·a
bac·te·ri·ol·o·gist
bac·te·ri·ol·o·gy
bac·te·ri·um
badge

bad·ger
bad·min·ton
bad-mouth
baf·fle
baf·fle·ment
bag·a·telle
ba·gel
bag·gage
bag·gy
bag la·dy
bag·man
bag·pipe
ba·guette
Ba·ha'i
Ba·ha·ism
Ba·ha·mas
bail
bai·liff
bai·li·wick
bait
baize
bak·ery
bak·ing pow·der
bak·ing so·da
bal·a·lai·ka
bal·ance
bal·co·ny
bald
bald·ly
bal·der·dash
bale·ful
balk
bal·lad
bal·lade
bal·last
ball bear·ing
bal·le·ri·na
bal·let
bal·lis·tic mis·sile
bal·lis·tics
bal·loon
bal·loon·ist

bal·lot
ball·park
ball·play·er
ball·room
bal·ly·hoo
balm
balmy
ba·lo·ney*+
bal·sam
bal·us·trade
bam·boo
bam·boo·zle
ba·nal
ba·nal·i·ty
ba·nana
ban·dage
ban·dag·ing
Band-Aid™
ban·dan·na
band·box
ban·deau
ban·dit
ban·dit·ry
band·mas·ter
band·stand
band·wag·on
ban·dy
ban·dy-legged
bane
bane·ful
ban·gle
ban·ish
ban·ish·ment
ban·is·ter
ban·jo
bank card
bank·rupt
bank·rupt·cy
ban·ner
banns
ban·quet
ban·shee

ban·tam
ban·ter
ban·yan
bap·tism
bap·tis·mal
bap·tis·tery
bap·tize
barb
bar·bar·i·an
bar·bar·ic
bar·ba·rism
bar·bar·i·ty
bar·ba·rous
bar·be·cue
barbed
bar·bell
bar·ber
bar·ber·ry
bar·ber·shop
bar·bi·tu·rate
bar code
bard
bare·back
bare·faced
bare·foot
bare·hand·ed
bar·fly
bar·gain
barge
bar·hop
bar·i·at·rics
bari·tone
bar·i·um
bark
bar·keep·er
bar·ley
bar·maid
bar·man
bar mitz·vah
bar·na·cle
barn·storm
barn·yard

ba·rom·e·ter
bar·on[+]
bar·on·ess
bar·on·et
bar·on·et·cy
ba·ro·ni·al
bar·ony
ba·roque
bar·racks
bar·racks bag
bar·ra·cu·da
bar·rage
barred
bar·rel
bar·reled
bar·rel·ful
bar·rel·ing
bar·ren[+]
bar·rette
bar·ri·cade
bar·ri·er
bar·ring
bar·rio
bar·ris·ter
bar·room
bar·row
bar·tend·er
bar·ter·er
bar·ware
bas·al[+]
ba·salt
base
based[+]
base·ball
base·board
base·line
base·ment
bash·ful
bash·ful·ly
bash·ful·ness
BASIC
ba·sic

ba·si·cal·ly
ba·sil[+]
ba·sil·i·ca
bas·i·lisk
ba·sin
bas·ing
ba·sis
ba·ses
bask
bas·ket
bas·ket·ball
bas·ket·ful
bas·ket·ry
bas·ma·ti
bas mitz·vah
bas-re·lief
bass
bas·set hound
bas·si·net
bas·so
bas·soon
bass viol
bas·tard
bas·tard·ize
baste[+]
bast·ed
bas·tille
bast·ing
bas·tion
batch
bath
bathe
bath·er
ba·thet·ic
ba·thos
bath·robe
bath·room
bath·tub
bathy·sphere
ba·tik
bat mitz·vah
ba·ton

bat·tal·ion
bat·ted
bat·ten
bat·ter
bat·tered child
  syn·drome
bat·tered spouse
bat·tered wom·an
  syn·drome
bat·tery
bat·tle
bat·tle·field
bat·tle·ment
bat·tle·ship
bau·ble
baud[+]
Bau·haus
baux·ite
bawd[+]
bawdy
bawl
bay·ber·ry
bay·o·net
bay·ou
bay rum
ba·zaar
ba·zoo·ka
beach[+]
beach·comb·er
beach·head
bea·con
bead·ing
bea·dle
beady
bea·gle
bea·ker
be-all and end-all
beam
bean
bean·ie
bear·able
beard

beard·less
bear·er
bear·ing
bear·ish
bé·ar·naise
bear·skin
beast
beast·li·ness
beast·ly
beat·en
beat·er
be·atif·ic
be·at·i·fi·ca·tion
be·at·i·fy
beat·ing
be·at·i·tude
beat·nik
beau
beau geste
beau·te·ous
beau·ti·cian
beau·ti·fi·ca·tion
beau·ti·ful
beau·ti·ful·ly
beau·ti·fy
beau·ty
beaux arts
bea·ver
be·calm
be·cause
bé·cha·mel
beck·on
be·come
be·com·ing
bed-and-breakfast
bed·bug
bed·ded
bed·ding
be·di·zen
bed·fel·low
bed·lam
bed·ou·in

be·drag·gled
bed·rid·den
bed·rock
bed·side
bed·spread
bed·time
bed-wet·ting
beech[+]
beech·nut
beef·eat·er
beef·steak
beefy
bee·hive
bee·keep·er
bee·line
beep·er
bees·wax
bee·tle
be·fall
be·fit·ting
be·fore
be·fore·hand
be·friend
be·fud·dled
be·get
beg·gar
beg·ging
be·gin·ner
be·gin·ning
be·gone
be·gor·ra
be·grime
be·grudge
be·guile
be·guine
be·half
be·have
be·hav·ior mod·i·
  fi·ca·tion
be·hav·ior·al·ly
be·hav·ior·ism
be·head

be·he·moth
be·hest
be·hind
be·hold·en
be·hoove
beige
be·la·bor
Be·la·rus·ian
be·lat·ed
be·lay
belch
be·lea·guered
bel·fry
be·lie
be·lief
be·liev·able
be·lieve
be·lit·tle
bel·la·don·na
belle
belles let·tres
bell·hop
bel·li·cose
bel·lig·er·ence
bel·lig·er·en·cy
bel·lig·er·ent
bel·low
bel·lows
bell·weth·er
bel·ly·ache
be·long·ing
be·loved
be·moan
bench
bench·mark
be·neath
ben·e·dic·tion
ben·e·fac·tor
be·nef·i·cence
be·nef·i·cent
ben·e·fi·cial
ben·e·fi·cia·ry

ben·e·fit
ben·e·fit·ed
ben·e·fit·ing
be·nev·o·lence
be·nev·o·lent
be·night·ed
be·nign neg·lect
be·nig·nan·cy
be·nig·nant
be·nig·ni·ty
ben·zene
ben·zine
be·queath
be·queath·al
be·quest
be·rate
be·reave
be·reave·ment
be·reft
be·ret
be·rib·boned
beri·beri
ber·ry[+]
ber·serk
berth
be·seech
be·set
be·set·ting
be·side
be·sides
be·siege
be·smirch
be·speak
be·spec·ta·cled
bes·tial
bes·ti·al·i·ty
bes·ti·ary
be·stir
be·stow
be·stow·al
best-sell·er
be·ta-blocker

be·ta-car·o·tene
bête noire
be·tray
be·tray·al
be·troth
be·troth·al
bet·ter·ment
bet·tor
be·tween·times
be·twixt and
   be·tween
bev·el
bev·er·age
bevy
be·wail
be·ware
be·wil·der·ment
be·witch
be·yond
bi·an·nu·al
bi·as
bi·ased
bi·ath·lon
Bi·ble
bib·li·cal
bib·li·og·ra·pher
bib·li·og·ra·phy
bib·lio·phile
bi·cam·er·al
bi·car·bon·ate
bi·cen·te·na·ry
bi·cen·ten·ni·al
bi·ceps
bick·er
bi·cul·tur·al
bi·cus·pid
bi·cy·cle
bid·da·ble
bid·der
bid·dy
bi·det
bi·en·ni·al

bier
bi·fo·cal
bi·fur·cate
bi·fur·ca·tion
big·a·mous
big·a·my
big·ot
big·ot·ed
big·ot·ry
big·wig
bike
bi·ki·ni
bi·la·bi·al
bi·lat·er·al
bile
bilge
bi·lin·gual
bil·ious
bilk
bill·board
bil·let
bil·let·doux
bil·liards
bill·ing
bil·lion·aire
bil·low
bil·lowy
bil·ly goat
bi·mod·al
bi·month·ly
bi·na·ry
bin·au·ral
bind·er
bind·ery
bind·ing
binge
bin·go
bin·na·cle
bi·nocs
bin·oc·u·lar
bi·no·mi·al
bio·chem·is·try

bio·de·grad·able
bio·di·ver·si·ty
bio·eth·ics
bio·feed·back
bio·fu·el
bi·og·ra·pher
bio·graph·i·cal
bi·og·ra·phy
bi·o·log·i·cal
bi·ol·o·gy
bi·on·ic
bi·op·sy
bio·rhythm
bio·sphere
bio·ter·ror·ism
bi·par·ti·san
bi·ped
bi·plane
bi·po·lar dis·or·der
birch
bird·er
bird·watch·er
birth·day
birth de·fect
birth·ing room
birth·mark
birth·place
birth·rate
birth·right
birth·stone
bis·cuit
bi·sect
bi·sec·tor
bi·sex·u·al
bish·op
bish·op·ric
bi·son
bisque
bi·state
bis·tro
bitch
bit·ing

bit-mapped
bit·ter·ly
bit·ter·sweet
bi·tu·mi·nous
bi·valve
biv·ouac
biv·ouacked
biv·ouack·ing
bi·week·ly
bi·year·ly
bi·zarre
blab·ber
blab·ber·mouth
black·ball
black belt
black·ber·ry
black·bird
black box the·atre
black·en
black·guard
black·ing
black·jack
black·list
black·mail
black·mar·ket
black·out (n)
black·smith
black-tie (adj)
black·top
blad·der
blade
blah
blame
blame·wor·thy
blanch
blanc·mange
bland
blan·dish·ment
blan·ket
blare
blar·ney
bla·sé

blas·pheme
blas·phe·mous
blas·phe·my
blast
blast·off (n)
bla·tant
blath·er
blaze
blaz·er
blaz·ing
bla·zon
bleach
bleak
bleary
bleat
bleed
bleep
blem·ish
blench
blend·ed fam·i·ly
bless·ed
bless·ing
blight·ed
blind
blind·fold
blind·ly
blind·man's buff
blind·ness
blink
blin·tze
blip
bliss·ful
bliss·ful·ly
blis·ter
blithe
blitz
blitz·krieg
bliz·zard
bloat·ed
blob
bloc+
block+

block·ade
block·age
block·bust·er
block·head
blog
blond+
blonde+
blood
blood bank
blood·cur·dling
blood·hound
blood·less
blood·mo·bile
blood·shed
blood·shot
blood·stock
blood·suck·er
bloody
bloom·ing
bloop·er
blos·som
blotch
blot·ter
blouse
blow-by-blow
blow·hard
blown
blow·out (n)
blow·sy
blow·torch
blowy
blub·ber
blud·geon
blue·beard
blue·bell
blue·ber·ry
blue·bird
blue chip
blue-col·lar
blue·fish
blue·grass
blue-pen·cil

blue·print
blue-rib·bon
blues
blue·stock·ing
bluff
blu·ing
blu·ish
blun·der
blun·der·buss
blunt
blur
blurb
blur·ring
blur·ry
blurt
blush
blus·ter
blus·tery
boa
boar
board·er+
board·ing·house
board·room
board·walk
boast
boast·ful
boast·ful·ly
boat·er
boat peo·ple
boat·swain
bobbed
bob·bin
bob·ble
bob·by
bob·cat
bob·sled
bode+
bo·de·ga
bodh·ran
bod·ice
bodi·less
bodi·ly

bod·ing
body·guard
body mass in·dex
body pierc·ing
bo·gey·man
bog·gle
bo·gus
bo·he·mi·an
boil·er
bois·ter·ous
bold·face
Bol·ly·wood
bo·lo·gna[+]
bo·lo·ney[*]
bol·she·vism
bol·ster
bo·lus
bom·bard
bom·bar·dier
bom·bas·tic
bombed
bo·na fide
bo·na fi·des
bo·nan·za
bon·bon
bond·age
bond·ed
bonds·man
bone·less
bone-dry
bone·head
bon·fire
bon·ho·mie
bon mot
bon·net
bon·sai
bo·nus
bon vi·vant
bon voy·age
bony
boo·by prize
boo·gie-woo·gie

book·bind·ing
book·ie
book·ish
book·keep·er
book·keep·ing
book·let
book·mak·er
book·sell·er
book·store
Bool·e·an
boo·mer·ang
boon·docks
boon·dog·gle
boor·ish
boost·er
boo·tee[+]
booth
boo·tie[*]
boot·leg
boot·lick
boo·ty[+]
booze
bo·rax
bor·de·laise sauce
bor·del·lo
bor·der[+]
bor·der·line
bore·dom
bo·ric ac·id
bor·ing
borne
bor·ough[+]
bor·row
bor·row·er
borscht
bos·om
bossy
bo·tan·i·cal
bot·a·nist
bot·a·ny
botch
both·er

both·er·some
bot·tle
bot·tle·neck
bot·tling
bot·tom·less
bot·tom line (n)
bot·u·lism
bou·doir
bough
bouil·la·baisse
bouil·lon[+]
boul·der
bou·le·vard
bounc·er
bounc·ing
bouncy
bound·ary
bound·er
bound·less
boun·te·ous
boun·ti·ful
boun·ty
bou·quet
bour·bon
bour·geois
bour·geoi·sie
bour·geon[*]
bout
bou·tique
bou·ton·niere
bo·vine
bowd·ler·ize
bowed
bow·el
bow·er
bow·ie knife
bow·knot
bow·legged
bow·ler
bowl·ing
bow·sprit
bow tie

box·car
box·ing
boxy
boy·cott
boy·friend
boy·ish·ly
brace
brace·let
bra·cer
brac·ing
brack·et
brack·ish
brad
brag·ga·do·cio
brag·gart
brag·ger
brag·ging
braid
braid·ing
braille
brain-dead
brain·storm·ing
brainy
braise
brake
brake·man
brak·ing
bram·ble
brand·ing
bran·dish
brand-new
bran·dy
brash
bras·siere
brassy
brat·ty
brat·wurst
bra·va·do
brave·ly
brav·ery
bra·vo
bra·vu·ra

brawl
brawn
brawn·i·er
brawny
bray
bra·zen
bra·zier
breach+
bread-and=
   but·ter (adj)
breadth
break·able
break·age
break·down (n)
break·fast
break-in (n)
break·neck
break·through (n)
break·up (n)
break·wa·ter
breast feed·ing
breast·stroke
breath
breathe
breath·er
breath·ing
breath·less
breath·less·ly
breath·tak·ing
breathy
breech+
breed·ing
breezy
breth·ren
bre·via·ry
brev·i·ty
brew·er
brew·ery
bri·ar
bribe
brib·ery
bric-a-brac

brick·bat
brick·lay·er
brick·work
brid·al+
bride·groom
brides·maid
bridge·work
bri·dle+
bri·dling
brief
brief·case
brief·ing
bri·er*
bri·gade
brig·a·dier
brig·and
bright·en
bril·liance
bril·lian·cy
bril·liant
Brill's dis·ease
brim·ful
brim·stone
brin·dled
brink·man·ship
briny
bri·oche
bri·quette
bris·ket
brisk·ly
bris·tle
bris·tling
Brit·ain
britch·es
brit·tle
broach+
broad·cast
broad·en
broad·loom
broad·mind·ed
broad·side
bro·cade

broc·co·li
bro·chure
bro·gan
brogue
broil·er
bro·ken
bro·ken·heart·ed
bro·ker
bro·ker·age
bro·mide
bron·chi·al
bron·chi·tis
bron·co
bronze
brooch[+]
brood
brood·er
broom·stick
broth
broth·el
broth·er·hood
broth·er-in-law
broth·er·li·ness
brou·ha·ha
brow·beat
brown·ie
brown·ish
brows·er
bruise
brunch
bru·nette
brunt
brushed
brush·fire
brush-off (n)
brusque
brus·sels sprout
bru·tal
bru·tal·i·ty
bru·tal·ize
brute
brut·ish

bub·ble
bub·bly
bu·bon·ic plague
buc·ca·neer
buck·et
buck·et·fuls
buck·le up
buck·skin
buck·wheat
bu·col·ic
Bud·dhism
Bud·dhist
bud·dy
bud·get
bud·gie
budg·ing
buf·fa·lo
buff·er
buf·fet
buf·foon
buf·foon·ery
bug·a·boo
bug-eyed
bugged
bug·gy
bu·gle
bu·gler
build·er
build-up (n)
built
built-in
bul·bous
bulge
bulg·ing
bul·gur
bu·lim·ia
bulk·head
bulk·i·ness
bulky
bull·dog
bull·doz·er
bul·let

bul·le·tin
bull·fight·er
bul·lion[+]
bull·ish
bull·ock
bull·pen
bull's-eye
bul·ly
bul·wark
bum·ble
bum·ble·bee
bum·per
bump·kin
bumpy
bun·dle
bun·ga·low
bun·gee jump
bung·hole
bun·gle
bun·gler
bun·gling
bun·ion
bun·ker
bun·kum
Bun·sen
    burn·er
bun·ting
buoy
buoy·an·cy
bur·den
bur·den·some
bu·reau
bu·reau·cra·cy
bu·reau·crat
bur·geon
bur·gher
bur·glar
bur·glar·ize
bur·glary
buri·al
bur·ied
bur·lap

bur·lesque
bur·ly
bur·nish
bur·noose
burp
bur·ro[+]
bur·row[+]
bur·sar
bur·si·tis
burst
bury[+]
bus·boy
bush·el
bush·ing
bush league
bushy
busi·ly
busi·ness
busi·ness·like
busi·ness·man
busi·ness·per·son
busi·ness·wom·an
bus·ing
bus·tle
busy·body
busy·work
bu·tane
butch·er
butch·ery
but·ler
butt
butte
but·ter·cup
but·ter·fly ef·fect
but·ter·scotch
but·tocks
but·ton
but·tress
bux·om
buy·out
buy·ing
buz·zard

buzz·er
buzz·word
by-and-by (n)
by and large
bye
bye-bye
by-elec·tion
by·gone
by·law
by·line
by·pass
by·path
by-prod·uct
by·stand·er
byte
by·way
by·word

C

ca·bal
ca·bana
cab·a·ret
cab·bage
cab·bie
cab·by*
cab·driv·er
cab·er·net
   sau·vi·gnon
cab·in
cab·i·net
ca·ble mo·dem
ca·boo·dle
ca·boose
cac·cia·to·re
cache
ca·chet
ca·cique
cack·le
ca·coph·o·nous
ca·coph·o·ny
cac·tus
ca·dav·er

ca·dav·er·ous
cad·die[+]
cad·dy*[+]
ca·dence
ca·den·za
ca·det
cadge
cad·re
ca·du·ceus
ca·fé
caf·e·te·ria
caf·fein·at·ed
caf·feine
caf·tan
ca·gey
ca·gi·ness
cairn
cais·son
ca·jole
cal·a·mine
ca·lam·i·tous
ca·lam·i·ty
cal·ci·fi·ca·tion
cal·ci·fy
cal·ci·mine
cal·ci·um
cal·cu·late
cal·cu·lat·ing
cal·cu·la·tion
cal·cu·la·tor
cal·cu·lus
cal·dron*
cal·en·dar
calf
cal·i·ber
cal·i·brate
cal·i·bra·tion
cal·i·co
cal·i·per
cal·is·then·ics
cal·la lily
call·er ID

call for·ward·ing
cal·lig·ra·pher
cal·lig·ra·phy
call·ing
cal·li·ope
cal·lous[+]
cal·low
call-up (n)
cal·lus[+]
calm
ca·lo·ric
cal·o·rie
cal·um·ny
cal·va·ry
calve
calves
ca·lyp·so
ca·lyx
ca·ma·ra·de·rie
cam·ber
cam·bric
cam·cord·er
cam·el
ca·mel·lia
cam·eo
cam·era
cam·i·sole
cam·ou·flage
cam·paign
cam·paign·er
camp·er
cam·phor
camp·site
cam·pus
cam·shaft
can
Ca·na·di·an
can·a·pé
ca·nard
ca·nary
ca·nas·ta
can·can

can·cel
can·celed
can·cel·la·tion
can·cer
can·cer·ous
can·croid
can·de·la·bra
can·did
can·di·da·cy
can·di·date
can·died
can·dle
can·dle·wick
can·dor
can·dy strip·er
ca·nine
can·is·ter
can·ker
can·ker·ous
canned
can·nery
can·ni·bal
can·ni·bal·ize
can·ni·ness
can·ning
can·non[+]
can·non·ade
can·not
can·ny
ca·noe
ca·noed
ca·noe·ing
ca·no·la
can·on*[+]
ca·non·i·cal
ca·non·i·cals
can·on·ize
can·o·py
cant[+]
can't[+]
can·ta·loupe
can·tan·ker·ous

can·tan·ker·ous·ness
can·ta·ta
can·teen
can·ter
can·ti·cle
can·ti·le·ver
can·to
can·ton
can·tor
can·vas*[+]
can·vass*[+]
can·yon
ca·pa·bil·i·ty
ca·pa·ble
ca·pa·cious
ca·pac·i·ta·tion
ca·pac·i·tor
ca·pac·i·ty
ca·par·i·son
ca·per
cap·ful
cap·il·lary
cap·i·tal[+]
cap·i·tal·ism
cap·i·tal·ist
cap·i·tal·i·za·tion
cap·i·tal·ize
cap·i·tol[+]
ca·pit·u·late
ca·pit·u·la·tion
ca·po
ca·pon
ca·price
ca·pri·cious
cap·size
cap·stan
cap·stone
cap·sule
cap·sul·ize
cap·tain
cap·tion
cap·tious

cap·ti·vate
cap·tive
cap·tiv·i·ty
cap·tor
cap·ture
ca·pu·chin
car·a·bi·ner
ca·rafe
car·a·mel
car·at*+
car·a·van
car·a·way seeds
car·bine
car·bo·hy·drate
car·bol·ic acid
car bomb
car·bon
car·bon·ate
car·bon di·ox·ide
car·bon·ic
car·bon·ize
car·bon pa·per
car·bun·cle
car·bu·re·tor
car·cass
car·cin·o·gen·ic
car·ci·no·ma
car·da·mom
car·di·ac
car·di·gan
car·di·nal
car·dio·gram
car·dio·graph
car·di·ol·o·gist
car·di·ol·o·gy
car·dio·pul·mo·nary
 re·sus·ci·ta·tion
car·dio·vas·cu·lar
ca·reen
ca·reer
care·free
care·ful

care·less
ca·ress
car·et+
care·tak·er
care·worn
car·fare
car·ful
car·go
Ca·rib·be·an
car·i·bou
car·i·ca·ture
car·ies
car·il·lon
car·jack·ing
car·load
car·mine
car·nage
car·nal
car·na·tion
car·ni·val
car·ni·vore
car·niv·o·rous
car·ol+
car·om
ca·rouse
car·ou·sel
carp
car·pal tun·nel
 syn·drome
car·pe di·em
car·pen·ter
car·pen·try
car·pet
car·pet·bag·ger
car·pet·ing
carp·ing
car·port
car·rel+
car·riage
car·ri·er
car·ri·on
car·rot+

car·ry·all
car·ry·ing
car·ry·ing-on
car·ry-on (n, adj)
car·ry-out (n, adj)
car·sick
cart·age
carte blanche
car·tel
car·ti·lage
car·ti·lag·i·nous
car·tog·ra·pher
car·ton
car·toon
car·tridge
cart·wheel
carve
ca·sa·ba
cas·cade
cas·cad·ing
ca·sein
case·ment
ca·shew
cash·ier (n)
cash·mere
cash out
cash-strapped
cas·ing
ca·si·no
cas·ket
cas·se·role
cas·sette
cas·sock
cas·ta·net
cast·away (n)
caste
cast·er+
cas·ti·gate
cas·tile soap
cas·tle
cast-off (adj)
cas·tor+

cas·trate
ca·su·al
ca·su·al·ty
ca·su·ist·ry
cat·a·clysm
cat·a·comb
cat·a·falque
cat·a·lep·sy
cat·a·log
cat·a·logue*
cat·a·lyst
cat·a·lyt·ic
cat·a·ma·ran
cat·a·pult
cat·a·ract
ca·tarrh
ca·tas·tro·phe
cat·a·stroph·ic
cat·a·ton·ic
cat·call
catch-22
catch·all
catch·word
catchy
cat·e·chism
cat·e·chize
cat·e·gor·i·cal
cat·e·go·rize
cat·e·go·ry
ca·ter
cat·er·cor·ner*
cat·er·pil·lar
cat·er·waul
cat·fish
ca·thar·sis
ca·thar·tic
ca·the·dral
cath·e·ter
cath·ode
cath·o·lic
Cath·o·lic
cath·o·lic·i·ty

cat·nap
cat·nip
CAT scan
cat·sup*
cat·tail
cat·tle
cat·ty
cat·ty-cor·ner*
Cau·ca·sian
cau·cus
cau·dal
caught
caul
caul·dron
cau·li·flow·er
caulk
caus·al
cau·sal·i·ty
cau·sa·tion
caus·ative
cause cé·lè·bre
cause·way
caus·tic
cau·ter·iza·tion
cau·ter·ize
cau·tion
cau·tious
cav·al·cade
cav·a·lier
cav·al·ry
ca·ve·at
cave-in (n)
cav·ern
cav·ern·ous
cav·i·ar
cav·il
cav·i·ty
ca·vort
cay·enne pep·per
CCD
CD-ROM
cease

cease-fire (n)
cease·less
ce·dar
cede+
ce·dil·la
ceil·ing
cel·e·brant
cel·e·brate
ce·leb·ri·ty
ce·ler·i·ty
cel·ery
ce·les·tial
ce·li·ac
cel·i·ba·cy
cel·i·bate
cel·lar+
cel·lo
cel·lo·phane
cell phone
cel·lu·lar
cel·lu·loid
cel·lu·lose
Cel·si·us
Celt·ic
ce·ment
cem·e·tery
Ce·no·zo·ic
cen·ser+
cen·sor+
cen·so·ri·ous
cen·sor·ship
cen·sure
cen·sus
cen·taur
cen·te·nar·i·an
cen·te·na·ry
cen·ten·ni·al
cen·ter
cen·ter·piece
cen·ti·grade
cen·ti·me·ter
cen·ti·pede

cen·tral
cen·trif·u·gal
cen·trip·e·tal
cen·tu·ri·on
cen·tu·ry
CEO
ce·phal·ic
ce·ram·ic
ce·re·al
cer·e·bel·lum
ce·re·bral
cer·e·bra·tion
ce·re·bro·
    vas·cu·lar
ce·re·brum
cer·e·mo·ni·al
cer·e·mo·ni·ous
cer·e·mo·ny
ce·rise
cer·tain
cer·tain·ty
cer·tif·i·cate
cer·ti·fy
cer·tio·ra·ri
cer·ti·tude
cer·vi·cal
ce·sar·e·an
ces·sa·tion
cess·pool
ce·ta·cean
chafe
chaff·ing
chaf·ing dish
cha·grin
cha·grined
chain
chair·man
chair·per·son
chair·wom·an
chaise longue
cha·let
chal·ice

chalk
chalky
chal·lenge
chal·leng·er
cham·ber
cham·ber·lain
cham·ber·maid
cha·me·leon
cham·ois
cham·o·mile
cham·pagne
cham·pi·on
cham·pi·on·ship
chance
chan·cel·lor
chan·cery
chan·cre
chancy
chan·de·lier
change
change·able
change·less
chang·er
chan·nel-hop·ping
chan·nel surf·ing
chant
chant·er
chan·teuse
chan·ti·cleer
Cha·nu·kah*
cha·os the·o·ry
cha·ot·ic
chap·ar·ral
cha·peau
cha·pel
chap·er·one
chap·lain
chapped
Chap·ter 11
char·ac·ter
char·ac·ter·is·tic
char·ac·ter·i·za·tion

char·ac·ter·ize
cha·rade
char·coal
chard
charge·able
charge-coupled
    device
char·gé d'af·faires
char·i·ot
cha·ris·ma
char·is·mat·ic
char·i·ta·ble
char·i·ty
char·la·tan
char·ley horse
charm·ing
char·ter
char·treuse
chary
chase
chaser
chasm
chas·sis
chaste
chas·ten
chas·tise
chas·ti·ty
cha·su·ble
châ·teau
chat·tel
chat·ter
chat·ter·box
chat·ty
chauf·feur[+]
chau·vin·ism
chau·vin·ist
cheap·en
cheap·skate
cheat
check
check·book
check·er

check·mate
ched·dar
cheeky
cheer·ful
cheer·io
cheer·lead·er
cheer·less
cheery
cheese
cheese·burg·er
cheese·cake
cheesy
chef
chem·i·cal
che·mise
chem·ist
chem·is·try
che·mo·ther·a·py
cher·ish
cher·ry
cher·ry·stone
cher·ub
che·ru·bic
cher·u·bim
cher·vil
chess
chest·nut
che·va·lier
chev·ron
chewy
chiar·oscu·ro
chic+
Chi·ca·na
chi·ca·nery
Chi·ca·no
chick·a·dee
chick·en·heart·ed
chi·cle
chic·o·ry
chide
chief
chief·tain

chif·fon
chif·fo·nier
chig·ger
chi·gnon
Chi·hua·hua
chil·blain
child·bear·ing
child·ish
chil·dren
chili
chili con car·ne
chill·er
chilly
chime
chi·me·ra
chi·me·ri·cal
chim·ney
chim·pan·zee
chi·na
chin·chil·la
Chi·nese
chintz
chintzy
chip·munk
chip·per
chi·rop·o·dist
chi·ro·prac·tic
chi·ro·prac·tor
chirp
chis·el
chi·square
chit
chit·chat
chi·val·ric
chiv·al·rous
chiv·al·ry
chive
chla·myd·ia
chlo·rine
chlo·ro·form
chlo·ro·phyll
chlo·ro·sis

chock
chock-full
choc·o·late
choc·o·laty
choice
choir
choir·boy
choir·mas·ter
choke
chok·ing
chol·era
cho·ler+
cho·les·ter·ol
chomp
choose
choosy
chop·per
chop·py
chop·stick
chop su·ey
cho·ral
cho·rale
chord
chore
cho·reo·graph
cho·re·og·ra·phy
cho·ris·ter
chor·tle
cho·rus
cho·sen
chow
chow·der
chow mein
chrism
chris·ten
chris·ten·ing
Chris·tian
Chris·tian·i·ty
Christ·mas
chro·mat·ic
chro·ma·tog·ra·
  phy

chrome
chro·mi·um
chro·mo·some
chron·ic
chron·i·cle
chro·no·log·i·cal
chro·nol·o·gy
chro·nom·e·ter
chrys·a·lis
chry·san·the·mum
chub·by
chuck·le
chum·my
chump
chunky
church
church·go·er
church·yard
churl
churn
chute[+]
chut·ney
chutz·pah
ci·bo·ri·um
ci·ca·trix
ci·der
ci·gar
cig·a·rette
cig·a·ril·lo
cinch
cinc·ture
cin·ders
cin·e·ma
cin·e·mat·ic
cin·e·ma·tog·ra·
    pher
cin·e·ma·tog·ra·
    phy
cin·na·mon
ci·pher
cir·ca
cir·cle

cir·clet
cir·cu·itous
cir·cu·lar
cir·cu·late
cir·cu·la·tion
cir·cum·cise
cir·cum·ci·sion
cir·cum·fer·ence
cir·cum·flex
cir·cum·lo·cu·tion
cir·cum·nav·i·gate
cir·cum·scribe
cir·cum·spect
cir·cum·stance
cir·cum·stan·tial
cir·cum·vent
cir·cus
cir·rho·sis
cir·ro·cu·mu·lus
cir·ro·stra·tus
cir·rus
cis·tern
cit·a·del
ci·ta·tion
cite[+]
cit·i·fy
cit·i·zen
cit·i·zen·ship
cit·ric acid
cit·ron
cit·ro·nel·la
cit·rus
civ·ic
civ·ic-mind·ed
civ·ics
civ·il
ci·vil·ian
ci·vil·i·ty
civ·i·li·za·tion
civ·i·lize
civ·il·ly
civ·vies

claim
claim·ant
clair·voy·ance
clair·voy·ant
clam·ber
clam·mi·ness
clam·my
clam·or
clam·or·ous
clamp
clan·des·tine
clank
clan·nish
clans·man
clap·board
clap·per
clap·trap
clar·et
clar·i·fi·ca·tion
clar·i·fy
clar·i·net
clar·i·on
clar·i·ty
clash
clasp
clas·sic
clas·si·cal
clas·si·cist
clas·si·fi·ca·tion
clas·si·fied
clas·si·fy
class·less
class·mate
classy
clat·ter
clause
claus·tro·pho·bia
clav·i·chord
clav·i·cle
cla·vier
clean·ness
cleanse

clear·ance
clear-cut
clear-eyed
clear·head·ed
clear·ing·house
cleat
cleav·age
cleave
cleav·er
clef
cleft pal·ate
clem·en·cy
clem·ent
clench
cler·gy
cler·ic
cler·i·cal
cler·i·cal·ism
cli·ché
cli·chéd
click+
cli·ent
cli·en·tele
cliff
cliff·hang·er
cli·mac·ter·ic
cli·mac·tic
cli·mate
cli·mat·ic
cli·max
climb·er
climb·ing wall
clime
clinch·er
cling
clin·ic
clin·i·cal
cli·ni·cian
clink
clin·ker
clip·board
clip·per

clip·ping
clique+
clit·o·ris
cloak
clob·ber
clock·wise
clock·work
clog
cloi·son·né
clois·ter
clone
close
closed-cap·tioned
close·ly
clos·et
clos·ing
clo·sure
cloth
clothe
clothes
clothes·line
cloth·ier
clot·ted
clot·ting
clo·ture
cloud·burst
cloud·less
cloudy
clout
clove
clo·ven
clo·ver
clo·ver·leaf
clown·ish
cloy
cloy·ing·ly
club·by
club·foot
cluck
clue
clump
clum·sy

clung
clunk
clus·ter
clutch
clut·ter
coach
co·ag·u·lant
co·ag·u·late
co·alesce
co·a·li·tion
coarse+
coarse-grained
coarse·ness
coast
coast·line
coat·tail
co·au·thor
coax
co·ax·i·al
co·balt
cob·ble
cob·bler
cob·ble·stone
COBOL
co·bra
cob·web
co·caine
coc·cyx
co·chair
co·chle·ar im·plant
cock·ade
cock-a-leek·ie
cock·a·too
cock·eyed
cock·le·shell
cock·ney
cock·pit
cock·sure
cock·tail
cocky
co·coa
co·co·nut

co·coon
co·cur·ric·u·lar
co·da
cod·dle
code
co·de·fen·dant
co·deine
co·de·pen·den·cy
co·de·pen·dent
co·dex
cod·ger
cod·i·cil
cod·i·fy
co·ed
co·ed·i·tor
co·ed·u·ca·tion
co·ef·fi·cient
co·equal
co·erce
co·er·cion
co·er·cive
co·eter·nal
co·eval
co·ex·ist
co·ex·ten·sive
cof·fee
cof·fer
cof·fin
cog
co·gen·cy
co·gent
cog·i·tate
cog·i·ta·tion
co·gnac
cog·nate
cog·ni·tion
cog·ni·tive
cog·ni·zance
cog·ni·zant
cog·no·men
co·gno·scen·te
cog·wheel

co·hab·it
co·here
co·her·ent
co·he·sion
co·he·sive
co·hort
co·host
coif
coif·fure
coin·age
co·in·cide
co·in·ci·dence
co·in·ci·dent
co·in·ci·den·tal
co·in·sure
co·i·tion
co·i·tus
col·an·der
cold·ly
cole·slaw
col·ic
col·icky
col·i·se·um
co·li·tis
col·lab·o·rate
col·lab·o·ra·tor
col·lage
col·lapse
col·laps·ible
col·lar[+]
col·late
col·lat·er·al
   dam·age
col·la·tion
col·league
col·lect
col·lect·ible
col·lec·tion
col·lec·tive
col·lec·tive·ly
col·lec·tiv·ism
col·lec·tor

col·lege
col·le·gial
col·le·gi·al·i·ty
col·le·giate
col·lide
col·lie
col·lier
col·li·sion
col·lo·ca·tion
col·lo·qui·al
col·lo·qui·al·ism
col·lo·qui·um
col·lo·quy
col·lu·sion
co·logne
co·lon
col·o·nel[+]
co·lo·nial
co·lo·nial·ism
col·o·nist
col·o·ni·za·tion
col·o·nize
col·on·nade
co·lo·nos·co·py
col·o·ny
col·o·phon
col·or
col·or·a·tion
col·or·a·tu·ra
col·ored
col·or·ful
col·or·ing
co·los·sal
col·os·se·um
co·los·sus
co·los·to·my
colt·ish
col·umn
co·lum·nar
col·um·nist
co·ma
co·ma·tose

comb
com·bat
com·bat·ant
com·bat·ive
com·bi·na·tion
com·bine
com·bin·ing
com·bus·ti·ble
com·bus·tion
co·me·di·an
co·me·di·enne
com·e·dy
come·ly
com·er
co·mes·ti·ble
com·et
come·up·pance
com·fort food
com·fort·able
com·fort·er
com·fy
com·ic
com·i·cal
co·mi·ty
com·ma
com·mand
com·man·dant
com·man·deer
com·mand·er
com·mand·ing
com·mand·ment
com·mem·o·rate
com·mem·o·ra·tion
com·mem·o·ra·tive
com·mence
com·mence·ment
com·mend
com·men·da·tion
com·men·da·to·ry
com·men·su·rate
com·ment

com·men·tary
com·men·tate
com·men·ta·tor
com·merce
com·mer·cial
com·min·gle
com·mis·er·ate
com·mis·er·a·tion
com·mis·sar
com·mis·sar·i·at
com·mis·sary
com·mis·sion
com·mis·sion·er
com·mit
com·mit·ment
com·mit·tal
com·mit·tee
com·mode
com·mo·di·ous
com·mod·i·ty
com·mo·dore
com·mon
com·mon·al·i·ty
com·mon-law (adj)
com·mon·place
com·mon·weal
com·mon·wealth
com·mo·tion
com·mu·nal
com·mune
com·mu·ni·ca·ble
com·mu·ni·cant
com·mu·ni·cate
com·mu·ni·ca·tion
com·mu·ni·ca·tive
com·mu·ni·ca·tor
com·mu·nion
com·mu·ni·qué
com·mu·nism
com·mu·nist
com·mu·ni·ty
com·mu·tate

com·mu·ta·tion
com·mu·ta·tor
com·mute
com·pact
com·pac·tion
com·pan·ion
com·pan·ion·able
com·pan·ion·ship
com·pa·ny
com·pa·ra·bil·i·ty
com·pa·ra·ble
com·par·a·tive
com·pare
com·par·i·son
com·part·ment
com·part·men·tal·
    ize
com·pass
com·pas·sion
com·pas·sion
    fa·tigue
com·pas·sion·ate
com·pat·i·ble
com·pat·i·bil·i·ty
com·pa·tri·ot
com·pel
com·pelled
com·pen·di·um
com·pen·sate
com·pen·sa·tion
com·pen·sa·to·ry
com·pete
com·pe·tence
com·pe·ten·cy
com·pe·tent
com·pe·ti·tion
com·pet·i·tive
com·pet·i·tor
com·pi·la·tion
com·pile
com·pla·cence[+]
com·pla·cen·cy

com·pla·cent[+]
com·plain
com·plain·ant
com·plaint
com·plai·sance[+]
com·plai·sant[+]
com·ple·ment[+]
com·ple·men·ta·ry[+]
com·plete
com·plete·ly
com·ple·tion
com·plex
com·plex·ion
com·plex·i·ty
com·pli·ance
com·pli·ant
com·pli·cate
com·pli·ca·tion
com·plic·i·ty
com·pli·ment[+]
com·pli·men·ta·ry[+]
com·po·nent
com·port
com·pose
com·pos·er
com·pos·ite
com·po·si·tion
com·pos men·tis
com·post
com·po·sure
com·pote
com·pound
com·pre·hend
com·pre·hen·si·ble
com·pre·hen·sion
com·pre·hen·sive
com·press
com·press·ible
com·pres·sion
com·prise
com·pro·mise
comp·trol·ler

com·pul·sion
com·pul·sive
com·pul·so·ry
com·punc·tion
com·pu·ta·tion
com·pute
com·put·er
com·put·er·ize
com·rade
com·rad·ery
con·cat·e·na·tion
con·cave
con·ceal
con·cede
con·ceit
con·ceiv·able
con·ceive
con·cel·e·brate
con·cen·trate
con·cen·tra·tion
con·cen·tric
con·cept
con·cep·tion
con·cep·tu·al
con·cern
con·cert
con·cert·ed
con·cer·ti·na
con·cer·to
con·ces·sion
con·ces·sion·aire
con·cierge
con·cil·i·ate
con·cil·ia·to·ry
con·cise
con·clave
con·clude
con·clu·sion
con·clu·sive
con·coct
con·coc·tion
con·com·i·tant

con·cord
con·cor·dance
con·cor·dat
con·course
con·crete
con·cu·bine
con·cu·pis·cence
con·cur
con·cur·rence
con·cur·rent
con·cus·sion
con·demn
con·dem·na·tion
con·dem·na·tory
con·den·sa·tion
con·dense
con·dens·er
con·de·scend
con·de·scen·sion
con·di·ment
con·di·tion
con·do·lence
con·dom
con·do·min·i·um
con·done
con·du·cive
con·duct
con·duc·tion
con·duc·tiv·i·ty
con·duc·tor
con·duit
con·fab
con·fab·u·late
con·fec·tion
con·fec·tion·ary[+]
con·fec·tion·ery[+]
con·fed·er·a·cy
con·fed·er·ate
con·fer
con·fer·ence
con·fer·ring
con·fess

con·fes·sion
con·fes·sor
con·fet·ti
con·fi·dant[+]
con·fi·dante[+]
con·fide
con·fi·dence
con·fi·den·tial
con·fid·ing
con·fig·u·ra·tion
con·fine
con·fine·ment
con·firm
con·fir·ma·tion
con·fis·cate
con·fla·gra·tion
con·flict
con·flu·ence
con·form
con·form·able
con·for·mi·ty
con·found
con·frere
con·front
con·fron·ta·tion
Con·fu·cian·ism
Con·fu·cian·ist
con·fuse
con·fu·sion
con·fute
con·ga
con·geal
con·ge·nial
con·gen·i·tal
con·ges·tion
con·glom·er·ate
con·glom·er·a·tion
con·grat·u·late
con·gre·gate
con·gre·ga·tion
con·gress
con·gress·man

con·gress·per·son
con·gress·wom·an
con·gru·ence
con·gru·en·cy
con·gru·ent
con·gru·ity
con·gru·ous
co·ni·fer
con·jec·tur·al
con·jec·ture
con·join
con·ju·gal
con·ju·gate
con·junc·tion
con·junc·ti·va
con·junc·ti·vi·tis
con·jure
con·jur·er
con·nect
con·nec·tion
con·nec·tive
con·nect-the-dots
con·nip·tion
con·niv·ance
con·nive
con·nois·seur
con·no·ta·tion
con·no·ta·tive
con·note
con·nu·bi·al
con·quer
con·quer·or
con·quest
con·san·guin·e·ous
con·san·guin·i·ty
con·science
con·sci·en·tious
con·scious
con·scious·ness
con·script
con·scrip·tion
con·se·crate

con·se·cra·tion
con·sec·u·tive
con·sen·su·al
con·sen·sus
con·sent
con·se·quence
con·se·quent
con·se·quen·tial·ism
con·se·quent·ly
con·ser·van·cy
con·ser·va·tion
con·ser·va·tion·ist
con·ser·va·tive
con·ser·va·to·ry
con·serve
con·sid·er
con·sid·er·able
con·sid·er·ate
con·sid·er·ation
con·sid·er·ing
con·sign
con·sign·ee
con·sign·ment
con·sist
con·sis·ten·cy
con·sis·tent
con·sis·to·ry
con·so·la·tion
con·sole
con·sol·i·date
con·sol·i·da·tion
con·som·mé
con·so·nance
con·so·nant
con·sort
con·sor·tium
con·spic·u·ous
con·spir·a·cy
con·spir·a·tor
con·spir·a·to·ri·al

con·spire
con·sta·ble
con·stab·u·lary
con·stan·cy
con·stant
con·stel·la·tion
con·ster·na·tion
con·sti·pate
con·sti·pa·tion
con·stit·u·en·cy
con·stit·u·ent
con·sti·tute
con·sti·tu·tion
con·sti·tu·tion·al·
  i·ty
con·sti·tu·tive
con·strain
con·straint
con·strict
con·stric·tion
con·struct
con·struc·tion
con·struc·tive
con·strue
con·sul
con·sul·ate
con·sult
con·sul·tant
con·sul·ta·tion
con·sul·ta·tive
con·sum·able
con·sume
con·sum·er
con·sum·mate
con·sum·ma·tion
con·sump·tion
con·tact
con·ta·gion
con·ta·gious
con·tain
con·tain·er
con·tain·ment

con·tam·i·nant
con·tam·i·nate
con·tam·i·na·tion
con·tem·plate
con·tem·plat·ing
con·tem·pla·tion
con·tem·pla·tive
con·tem·po·ra·ne·
  ous
con·tem·po·rary
con·tempt
con·tempt·ible
con·temp·tu·ous
con·tend
con·ten·tious
con·test
con·text
con·tex·tu·al
con·tig·u·ous
con·ti·nence
con·ti·nent
con·tin·gen·cy
con·tin·gent
con·tin·u·al
con·tin·u·ance
con·tin·u·a·tion
con·tin·ue
con·tinu·ing
con·ti·nu·i·ty
con·tin·u·ous
con·tin·u·um
con·tort
con·tor·tion·ist
con·tor·tions
con·tour
con·tra·band
con·tra·cep·tion
con·tract
con·tract·ible
con·trac·tion
con·trac·tor
con·trac·tu·al

con·tra·dict
con·tra·dic·to·ry
con·tra·dis·tinc·
  tion
con·tra·in·di·ca·tions
con·tral·to
con·trap·tion
con·trari·wise
con·trary
con·trast
con·tra·vene
con·tre·temps
con·trib·ute
con·tri·bu·tion
con·trite
con·tri·tion
con·triv·ance
con·trive
con·trived
con·trol freak
con·trol·ler
con·trol·ling
con·tro·ver·sial
con·tro·ver·sy
con·tu·ma·cious
con·tu·ma·cy
con·tume·ly
con·tu·sion
co·nun·drum
con·va·lesce
con·va·les·cence
con·va·les·cent
con·vec·tion
con·vene
con·ve·nience
con·ve·nient
con·ven·tion
con·ven·tion·al
con·verge
con·ver·gence
con·ver·gent
con·ver·sant

con·ver·sa·tion
con·ver·sa·tion·al·ist
con·verse
con·ver·sion
con·vert
con·vert·ible
con·vex
con·vey
con·vey·ance
con·vey·er*
con·vey·or
con·vict
con·vic·tion
con·vince
con·viv·ial
con·vo·ca·tion
con·voke
con·vo·lut·ed
con·vo·lu·tion
con·voy
con·vulse
con·vul·sion
cook·ie
cooky*
cool·ant
cool·ly
co-op
co·op·er·ate
co·op·er·a·tion
co·op·er·a·tive
co·or·di·nate
co·or·di·na·tion
coo·tie
co-own·er
co·pa·ce·tic
co·pay·ment
cope
copi·er
co·pi·lot
co·pi·ous
cop-out (n)

cop·per
cop·per·head
co·pro·ces·sor
cop·ter
cop·u·late
cop·u·la·tive
copy·right
co·quette
co·quett·ish
cor·al
cor·dial
cor·dial·i·ty
cor·dial·ly
cor·don
cor·do·van
cor·du·roy
co·re·spon·dent
cork·screw
cor·mo·rant
corn·cob
cor·nea
cor·ner
cor·ner·back
cor·net
corn·flakes
cor·nice
cor·nu·co·pia
corny
cor·ol·lary
cor·o·nary
cor·o·na·tion
cor·o·ner
cor·o·net
cor·po·ral
cor·po·rate
cor·po·ra·tion
cor·po·re·al
corps
corpse
corps·man
cor·pu·lence
cor·pu·lent

cor·pus·cle
cor·pus de·lic·ti
cor·ral
cor·rect
cor·rec·tive
cor·re·late
cor·re·la·tion
cor·rel·a·tive
cor·re·spond
cor·re·spon·dence
cor·re·spon·dent
cor·ri·dor
cor·rob·o·rate
cor·rob·o·ra·tion
cor·rode
cor·ro·sion
cor·ro·sive
cor·ru·ga·ted
cor·rupt
cor·rup·tion
cor·sage
cor·tege
cor·tex
cor·ti·co·ste·roids
cor·ti·sone
cor·us·cate
co·sign·er
co·sine
cos·met·ic
cos·me·ti·cian
cos·mic
cos·mo·naut
cos·mo·pol·i·tan
cos·mos
co·spon·sor
cos·sack
co·star
cost-ef·fi·cient
cost·ly
cos·tume
cos·tum·er
co·sy

co·te·rie
co·ter·mi·nous
co·til·lion
cot·tage
cot·ton
cot·ton·seed
couch
cou·gar
cough
couldn't
cou·lomb
coun·cil[+]
coun·cil·lor[+]
coun·sel[+]
coun·sel·or[+]
coun·sel·or-at-law
count·able
count·down
coun·te·nance
coun·ter·act
coun·ter·claim
coun·ter·clock·wise
coun·ter·cul·ture
coun·ter·dem·on·
  stra·tion
coun·ter·es·pi·o·
  nage
coun·ter·feit
coun·ter·foil
coun·ter·mand
coun·ter·pane
coun·ter·part
coun·ter·point
coun·ter·pose
coun·ter·pro·duc·
  tive
coun·ter·sign
count·ess
count·less
coun·tri·fied
coun·try
coun·try·side

coup de grace
coup d'etat
cou·pé
cou·ple
cou·plet
cou·pon
cour·age
cou·ra·geous
cou·ri·er
course[+]
court
cour·te·ous
cour·te·san
cour·te·sy
cour·tier
cous·in[+]
cou·ture
cov·e·nant
cov·er·age
cov·er·all (n)
cov·er·let
co·vert
cov·et
cov·et·ous
cov·ey
cow·ard·ice
cow·ard·li·ness
cow·er
cowl·ing
co·work·er
cow·shed
cox·comb
cox·swain
coy
coy·ote
coz·en[+]
co·zy
crabbed
crab·by
crack ba·by
cracked
crack·er

crack·er·jack
crack·ling
crack·pot
cra·dle
crafts·man
crafts·per·son
crafty
crag·gy
cramp
cran·ber·ry
crane
cra·ni·al
cra·ni·um
crank
cranky
cran·ny
crash·ing
crass
crate
cra·ter
cra·vat
crave
cra·ven
crawl·er
cray·fish
cray·on
crazy
creaky
cream
crease
cre·ate
cre·a·tion
cre·a·tive
cre·a·tiv·i·ty
cre·a·tor
crea·ture
crèche
cre·dence
cre·den·tial
cre·den·za
cred·i·bil·i·ty
cred·i·ble

cred·i·tor
cre·do
cre·du·li·ty
cred·u·lous
creed
creek
creel
creep
creepy
cre·mate
cre·ma·to·ri·um
cre·ma·to·ry
crème de menthe
Cre·ole
cre·o·sote
crêpe su·zette
cre·pus·cu·lar
cre·scen·do
cres·cent
cress
crest·fall·en
Cre·ta·ceous
cre·tin
cre·tin·ism
cre·vasse
crev·ice
crew·el
crib·bing
crick·et
crim·i·nal
crim·i·nol·o·gy
crimp
crim·son
cringe
crin·kle
crip·ple
cri·sis
crisp
criss·cross
cri·te·ri·on
crit·ic
crit·i·cal

crit·i·cism
crit·i·cize
cri·tique
cro·chet
crock·ery
croc·o·dile
cro·cus
Crohn's
   dis·ease
crois·sant
crone
crook·ed
croon·er
crop cir·cle
crop·per
cro·quet
cro·quette
cro·sier
cross-coun·try
cross-eyed
cross-file
cross-in·dex
cross·ing
cross-legged
cross-pur·pose
cross·road
cross sec·tion (n)
cross-stitch
cross·walk
cross·wise
crotch
crotch·ety
crouch
croup
crou·pi·er
crou·ton
crowd
crow's nest
cru·cial
cru·ci·ble
cru·ci·fix
cru·ci·fix·ion

cru·ci·fy
crud
cru·di·ty
cru·el·ty
cru·et
cruise
cruis·er
crul·ler
crum·ble
crum·my
crum·ple
crunch
cru·sade
crus·ta·cean
crusty
crux
crypt
cryp·tic
cryp·to·gram
cryp·tog·ra·pher
crys·tal
crys·tal·line
crys·tal·lize
C-sec·tion
CT scan
C-Span
cub·by·hole
cu·bi·cle
cub·ism
cuck·oo
cu·cum·ber
cud·dle
cud·gel
cui·sine
cul-de-sac
cu·li·nary
cull
cul·mi·nate
cul·mi·na·tion
cu·lottes
cul·pa·bil·i·ty
cul·pa·ble

cul·prit
cul·ti·vate
cul·ti·va·tor
cul·tur·al
cul·ture
cul·vert
cum·ber·some
cum lau·de
cu·mu·la·tive
cu·ne·i·form
cun·ning
cup·ful
cu·pid·i·ty
cu·po·la
cur·able
cu·rate
cu·ra·tive
cu·ra·tor
cur·dle
cure-all (n)
cur·few
cu·rio
cu·ri·os·i·ty
cu·ri·ous
cur·li·cue
curly
cur·mud·geon
cur·rant⁺
cur·ren·cy
cur·rent⁺
cur·ric·u·lar
cur·ric·u·lum vi·tae
cur·ry
cur·sive
cur·sor
cur·so·ry
curt
cur·tail
cur·tain
curt·sy
cur·va·ceous
cur·va·ture

curve
cur·vi·lin·ear
cush·ion
cus·tard
cus·to·di·al
cus·to·di·an
cus·to·dy
cus·tom·ary
cus·tom-built
cus·tom·er
cus·tom·ize
cut-and-dried
cu·ta·ne·ous
cut·away (n)
cu·ti·cle
cut·ie
cut·lass
cut·lery
cut·let
cut·throat
cut·ting
cy·ber·ca·fe
cy·ber·na·tion
cy·ber·net·ics
cy·ber·punk
cy·ber·space
cy·ber·surf·er
cy·cle
cy·clist
cy·clone
cy·clo·ra·ma
cyg·net⁺
cyl·in·der
cy·lin·dri·cal
cym·bal⁺
cyn·ic
cyn·i·cal
cyn·i·cism
cy·no·sure
cy·press
cyst
cys·ti·tis

czar
cza·ri·na
Czech

D

dab·ber
dab·bing
dab·ble
dab·bler
dab·bling
dachs·hund
dac·tyl
da·da·ism
dad·dy
daf·fo·dil
daf·fy
daft
dag·ger
da·guerre·o·type
dahl·ia
dai·ly
dain·ti·er
dain·ty
dai·qui·ri
dairy
dairy·maid
dairy·man
da·is
dai·sy
Da·lai La·ma
dal·li·ance
dal·ly
dal·ma·tian
dam·age
dam·ag·ing
damn
dam·na·ble
dam·na·tion
damned
damp·en
dam·sel
dam·son

dance
dan·de·li·on
dan·der
dan·dle
dan·druff
dan·dy
dan·ger·ous
dan·gle
dank
dap·per
dap·pled
dare·dev·il
dare·say
dark·en
dar·ling
darned
dash·board
da·shi·ki
das·tard·ly
da·ta
da·ta·base
da·ta pro·ces·sor
date·line
date rape
da·tive
da·tum
daub
daugh·ter
daugh·ter-in-law
daunt·less
dau·phin
dav·en·port
da·vit
daw·dle
day·bed
day care
day·dream
day·light
day·time
daze
daz·zle
dea·con

dea·con·ess
de·ac·ti·vate
dead-air space
dead·beat
dead·en
dead-end (adj,v)
dead·ened
dead·en·ing
dead·head
dead·li·er
dead·line
dead·lock
dead·pan
dead·weight
dead·wood
Deaf/deaf
deaf·en
deal·er·ship
deal·ing
dean·ery
dean's list
dearth
death
death·less
death·ly
de·ba·cle
de·bar
de·bark
de·base
de·bat·able
de·bate
de·bauch
de·bauch·ery
de·ben·ture
de·bil·i·tate
de·bil·i·ty
deb·it card
deb·o·nair
de·brief
de·bris
debt
debt·or

de·bug
de·bug·ging
de·bunk
de·but
deb·u·tante
de·cade
dec·a·dence
dec·a·dent
de·caf·fein·ate
deca·gon
de·cal
de·cal·ci·fi·ca·
    tion
de·cal·ci·fy
deca·logue
de·camp
de·cant
de·cant·er
de·cap·i·tate
de·cath·lon
de·cay
de·cease
de·ce·dent
de·ceit
de·ceit·ful
de·ceiv·able
de·ceive
de·cel·er·ate
de·cen·cy
de·cent
de·cen·tral·i·za·
    tion
de·cen·tral·ize
de·cep·tion
de·cep·tive
de·cer·ti·fy
deci·bel
de·cide
de·cid·ing
de·cid·u·ous
dec·ile
dec·i·mal

dec·i·mate
de·ci·pher
de·ci·sion
de·ci·sive
deck·hand
de·claim
de·clam·a·to·ry
dec·la·ra·tion
de·clar·a·tive
de·clar·a·to·ry
de·clare
dé·clas·sé
de·clas·si·fy
de·clen·sion
dec·li·na·tion
de·cline
de·cliv·i·ty
de·coct
de·coc·tion
de·code
dé·col·le·tage
de·com·mis·sion
de·com·pose
de·com·po·si·tion
de·com·press
de·con·ges·tant
de·con·ges·tion
de·con·se·crate
de·con·tam·i·nate
de·con·tex·tu·al·ize
de·con·trol
de·cor
dec·o·rate
dec·o·ra·tion
dec·o·ra·tive
dec·o·ra·tor
dec·o·rous
de·co·rum
de·cou·page
de·coy
de·crease
de·cree

de·crep·it
de·crep·i·tude
de·cry
ded·i·cate
ded·i·ca·tion
de·duce
de·duc·ible
de·duct·ible
de·duc·tion
de·duc·tive
dee·jay
de·em·pha·size
deep·en
deep-root·ed
deep-seat·ed
de·es·ca·late
de·face
de fac·to
def·a·ma·tion
de·fame
de·fault
de·feat·ist
def·e·cate
de·fect
de·fec·tion
de·fec·tive
de·fend
de·fen·dant
de·fend·er
de·fen·es·tra·tion
de·fense
de·fen·si·ble
de·fen·sive
de·fer
def·er·ence
def·er·en·tial
de·fer·ral
de·ferred
de·fi·ance
de·fi·ant
de·fi·bril·la·tor
de·fi·cien·cy

de·fi·cient
def·i·cit
de·file
de·fin·able
de·fine
def·i·nite
def·i·ni·tion
de·fin·i·tive
de·flate
de·fla·tion
de·flect
de·flec·tion
de·flow·er
de·fog
de·fo·li·ant
de·fo·li·ate
de·formed
de·for·mi·ty
de·fraud
de·fray
de·frock
de·frost
deft
de·funct
de·fuse⁺
defy
de·gen·er·a·cy
de·gen·er·ate
de·grad·able
deg·ra·da·tion
de·grade
de·grad·ed
de·grad·ing
de·gree
de·hu·man·ize
de·hu·mid·i·fy
de·hy·drate
de·hy·dra·tion
de·hyp·no·tize
de·ice
de·i·fy
deign

de·ism
de·ist
de·i·ty
dé·jà vu
de·ject
de·ject·ed
de·jec·tion
de ju·re
de·lay
de·lec·ta·ble
de·lec·ta·tion
del·e·gate
del·e·ga·tion
de·lete
del·e·te·ri·ous
de·le·tion
delft
de·lib·er·ate
de·lib·er·a·tion
del·i·ca·cy
del·i·cate
del·i·ca·tes·sen
de·li·cious
de·light
de·light·ful
de·light·ful·ness
de·lim·it
de·lin·eate
de·lin·ea·tion
de·lin·quen·cy
de·lin·quent
del·i·quesce
de·lir·i·ous
de·lir·i·um
   tre·mens
de·liv·er
de·liv·er·ance
de·liv·ery
de·louse
del·ta
del·toid
de·lude

del·uge
de·lu·sion
de·luxe
delve
dem·a·gogue
dem·a·gogu·ery
de·mand
de·mand·ing
de·mar·cate
de·mean
de·mean·or
de·ment·ed
de·men·tia
de·mer·it
demi·god
demi·god·dess
de·mil·i·ta·rize
demi·monde
de·mise
demi·tasse
de·mo·bi·lize
de·moc·ra·cy
dem·o·crat
dem·o·crat·ic
de·moc·ra·tize
de·mo·graph·ic
de·mog·ra·phy
dem·oi·selle
de·mol·ish
de·mo·li·tion
de·mon
de·mo·ni·ac
de·mo·ni·a·cal
de·mon·stra·ble
dem·on·strate
dem·on·stra·tion
dem·on·stra·tive
dem·on·stra·tor
de·mor·al·ize
de·mote
de·mot·ic
de·mur

de·mure
de·mys·ti·fy
de·my·thol·o·gize
de·na·tured
den·dro·chro·nol·
   o·gy
den·drol·o·gy
den·gue fe·ver
de·ni·al
den·i·grate
den·im
den·i·zen
de·nom·i·nate
de·nom·i·na·tion
de·nom·i·na·tor
de·no·ta·tion
de·no·ta·tive
de·note
de·noue·ment
de·nounce
de no·vo
dense
den·si·ty
den·tal
den·ti·frice
den·tist
den·tist·ry
den·ture
de·nu·cle·ar·ize
de·nude
de·nun·ci·a·tion
de·ny
de·odor·ant
de·odor·ize
de·ox·y·gen·ate
de·part
de·part·ment
de·part·men·tal·ize
de·par·ture
de·pend
de·pend·abil·i·ty
de·pend·able

de·pen·dence
de·pen·den·cy
de·pen·dent
de·per·son·al·ize
de·pict
de·pil·a·to·ry
de·plane
de·plete
de·plor·able
de·plore
de·ploy
de·po·lar·ize
de·po·lit·i·cize
de·po·nent
de·pop·u·late
de·port
de·port·able
de·por·ta·tion
de·por·tee
de·port·ment
de·pose
de·pos·it
de·pos·i·tary[+]
de·po·si·tion
de·pos·i·to·ry[+]
de·pot
de·praved
de·prav·i·ty
dep·re·cate
dep·re·ca·to·ry
de·pre·ci·ate
de·pre·ci·a·tion
de·pre·da·tion
de·press
de·pres·sant
de·pres·sion
de·pres·sor
dep·ri·va·tion
de·prive
depth
dep·u·ta·tion
dep·u·tize

dep·u·ty
de·rail
de·rail·leur
de·range
der·by
de·reg·u·la·tion
der·e·lict
der·e·lic·tion
de·ride
de ri·gueur
de·ri·sion
de·ri·sive
der·i·va·tion
de·riv·a·tive
de·rive
der·ma·tol·o·gist
der·ma·tol·o·gy
de·rog·a·to·ry
der·rick
der·ri·ere
der·ring-do
der·rin·ger
der·vish
de·sa·li·nate
des·cant
de·scend
de·scen·dant
de·scent[+]
de·scribe
de·scrip·tion
de·scrip·tive
de·scry
des·e·crate
des·e·cra·tion
de·seg·re·gate
de·seg·re·ga·tion
des·ert storm
  syn·drome
de·sert·i·fi·ca·tion
de·ser·tion
de·serve
des·ha·bille*

des·ic·cant
des·ic·cate
de·sid·er·a·tum
de·sign
des·ig·nate
des·ig·nat·ed
  driv·er
des·ig·nat·ed hit·ter
des·ig·na·tion
de·sign·er drug
de·sir·abil·i·ty
de·sir·able
de·sire
de·sir·ous
de·sist
desk jock·ey
des·o·late
des·o·la·tion
de·oxy·ri·bo·nu·
  cle·ic acid
de·spair
des·per·a·do
des·per·ate
des·per·a·tion
de·spi·ca·ble
de·spise
de·spite
de·spoil
de·spon·dence
de·spon·den·cy
de·spon·dent
des·pot
des·pot·ic
des·po·tism
des·sert
de·sta·bi·lize
des·ti·na·tion
des·ti·ny
des·ti·tute
des·ti·tu·tion
de·stroy
de·stroy·er

de·struc·ti·ble
de·struc·tion
de·struc·tive
des·ul·to·ry
de·tached
de·tach·ment
de·tail·ing
de·tain
de·tain·er
de·tect
de·tec·tion
de·tec·tive
de·tec·tor
dé·tente
de·ten·tion
de·ter
de·ter·gent
de·te·ri·o·rate
de·te·ri·o·ra·tion
de·ter·mi·nant
de·ter·mi·nate
de·ter·mi·na·tion
de·ter·mine
de·ter·rence
de·ter·rent
de·test
de·test·able
det·o·nate
det·o·na·tor
de·tour
de·tox
de·tox·i·fi·ca·tion
de·tox·i·fy
de·tract
de·trac·tion
det·ri·ment
det·ri·men·tal
de·tri·tion
de·tri·tus
deuce
de·us ex ma·chi·na
de·val·u·ate

de·val·u·a·tion
dev·as·tate
dev·as·ta·tion
de·vel·op
de·vel·op·er
de·vel·op·ment
de·vel·op·men·tal·ly
    dis·abled
de·vi·ant
de·vi·ate
de·vi·a·tion
de·vice
dev·il
dev·il·ish
dev·il·ment
de·vi·ous
de·vise
de·void
de·volve
de·vote
dev·o·tee
de·vo·tion
de·vour
de·vout
dewy
dex·ter·i·ty
dex·ter·ous
di·a·be·tes
di·a·bet·ic
di·a·bol·i·cal
di·ac·o·nate
di·a·crit·i·cal
di·a·dem
di·aer·e·sis
di·ag·nose
di·ag·no·sis
di·ag·nos·tic
di·ag·o·nal
di·a·gram
di·al
di·a·lect
di·a·lec·tic

di·a·lec·ti·cian
di·aled
di·a·log*
di·a·logue
di·am·e·ter
di·a·met·ric
di·a·mond
di·a·pa·son
di·a·per
di·aph·a·nous
di·a·pho·ret·ic
di·a·phragm
di·ar·rhea
di·a·ry
di·as·po·ra
di·a·stol·ic
dia·ther·my
dia·ton·ic
di·a·tribe
dice
dic·ey
di·chot·o·my
dic·tate
dic·ta·tion
dic·ta·tor
dic·ta·to·ri·al
dic·ta·tor·ship
dic·tion
dic·tio·nary
dic·tum
di·dac·tic
die·sel
di·et
di·e·tary
di·e·tet·ic
di·e·ti·tian
dif·fer
dif·fer·ence
dif·fer·ent
dif·fer·en·tial
dif·fer·en·ti·ate
dif·fer·en·ti·a·tion

dif·fer·ent·ly
dif·fi·cult
dif·fi·cul·ty
dif·fi·dence
dif·fi·dent
dif·frac·tion
dif·fuse+
dif·fu·sion
dif·fu·sive·ness
di·ges·tion
di·ges·tive
dig·gings
dig·it
dig·i·tal
dig·i·tal·is
dig·ni·fied
dig·ni·fy
dig·ni·tary
di·gress
di·gres·sion
di·gres·sive
di·lap·i·dat·ed
di·lap·i·da·tion
di·late
di·la·tion
dil·a·to·ry
di·lem·ma
dil·et·tante
dil·et·tan·tism
dil·i·gence
dil·i·gent
di·lute
di·lu·tion
di·men·sion
di·min·ish
dim·i·nu·tion
di·min·u·tive
dim·mer
dim·ple
dim sum
dim-wit·ted
di·nette

din·ghy
din·ky
din·ner·ware
di·no·saur
dint
di·oc·e·san
di·o·cese
Di·o·ny·sian
di·ora·ma
diph·the·ria
diph·thong
di·plo·ma
di·plo·ma·cy
dip·lo·mat
dip·lo·mate
dip·lo·mat·ic
dip·per
dip·so·ma·ni·ac
dire
di·rect
di·rec·tion
di·rec·tive
di·rect·ly
di·rec·tor·ate
di·rec·tor's cut
di·rec·to·ry
dirge
di·ri·gi·ble
dirt bike
dirt·i·er
dirt·i·ness
dirty
dis·abil·i·ty
dis·able
dis·abuse
dis·ad·van·tage
dis·ad·van·taged
dis·ad·van·ta·
　geous
dis·af·fect
dis·agree·able
dis·ap·pear

dis·ap·point
dis·ap·point·ment
dis·ap·pro·ba·tion
dis·ap·prov·al
dis·ap·prove
dis·arm·ing
dis·ar·range
dis·ar·ray
dis·as·sem·ble
dis·as·so·ci·ate
di·sas·ter
dis·as·trous
dis·avow
dis·avow·al
dis·band
dis·bar
dis·be·lief
dis·be·lieve
dis·burse
dis·burse·ment
disc
dis·card
dis·cern
dis·cern·ible
dis·cern·ing
dis·charge
dis·ci·ple
dis·ci·pli·nar·i·an
dis·ci·plin·ary
dis·ci·pline
dis·claim
dis·claim·er
dis·close
dis·clo·sure
dis·col·or·a·tion
dis·com·bob·u·late
dis·com·fit
dis·com·fi·ture
dis·com·pose
dis·con·cert
dis·con·nect
dis·con·so·late

dis·con·tent
dis·con·tinu·ance
dis·con·tin·ue
dis·con·ti·nu·ity
dis·con·tin·u·ous
dis·cord
dis·cor·dance
dis·cor·dant
dis·co·theque
dis·count
dis·count·able
dis·cour·age
dis·cour·age·ment
dis·course
dis·cour·te·ous
dis·cov·er
dis·cred·it
dis·cred·it·able
dis·creet+
dis·crep·an·cy
dis·crep·ant
dis·crete+
dis·cre·tion
dis·cre·tion·ary
dis·crim·i·nate
dis·crim·i·nat·ing
dis·crim·i·na·tion
dis·crim·i·na·to·ry
dis·cur·sive
dis·cus
dis·cuss
dis·cus·sion
dis·dain
dis·dain·ful
dis·ease
dis·em·bark
dis·em·body
dis·em·bow·el
dis·en·chant
dis·en·cum·ber
dis·en·fran·chise
dis·en·gage

dis·en·tan·gle
dis·fa·vor
dis·fig·ure
dis·func·tion
dis·gorge
dis·grace
dis·grun·tle
dis·guise
dis·gust
dis·gust·ing
dis·ha·bille
dis·heart·ened
di·shev·el
di·shev·eled
dis·hon·est
dis·hon·or
dis·hon·or·able
dis·il·lu·sion
dis·in·cli·na·tion
dis·in·cline
dis·in·fect
dis·in·fec·tant
dis·in·gen·u·ous
dis·in·her·it
dis·in·te·grate
dis·in·te·gra·tion
dis·in·ter
dis·in·ter·est
dis·in·ter·est·ed
dis·joint·ed
dis·junc·tive
disk
dis·kette
dis·like
dis·lo·cate
dis·lo·ca·tion
dis·lodge
dis·loy·al
dis·mal
dis·man·tle
dis·may
dis·mem·bered

dis·miss
dis·miss·al
dis·mount
Dis·ney·fi·ca·tion
dis·obe·di·ence
dis·obe·di·ent
dis·obey
dis·or·der
dis·or·ga·nized
dis·own
dis·par·age
dis·pa·rate
dis·par·i·ty
dis·pas·sion·ate
dis·patch
dis·pel
dis·pens·able
dis·pen·sa·ry
dis·pen·sa·tion
dis·pense
dis·perse
dis·per·sion
dis·pir·it·ed
dis·place
dis·place·ment
dis·play
dis·please
dis·plea·sure
dis·pos·able
dis·pos·al
dis·po·si·tion
dis·pos·sess
dis·pro·por·tion
dis·pro·por·tion·
ate
dis·prove
dis·pu·ted
dis·pu·ta·tious
dis·qual·i·fi·ca·tion
dis·qual·i·fy
dis·qui·et
dis·re·gard

dis·re·pair
dis·rep·u·ta·ble
dis·re·pute
dis·re·spect
dis·robe
dis·rupt
dis·sat·is·fac·tion
dis·sat·is·fac·to·ry
dis·sat·is·fy
dis·sect
dis·sect·ed
dis·sec·tion
dis·sem·ble
dis·sem·i·nate
dis·sen·sion
dis·sent[+]
dis·sent·er
dis·ser·ta·tion
dis·ser·vice
dis·si·dent
dis·sim·i·lar
dis·sim·u·late
dis·si·pate
dis·si·pa·tion
dis·so·ci·ate
dis·so·ci·a·tion
dis·so·lute
dis·so·lu·tion
dis·solve
dis·so·nance
dis·so·nant
dis·suade
dis·sua·sion
dis·taff
dis·tance
dis·tant
dis·taste
dis·taste·ful
dis·tem·per
dis·tend
dis·ten·sion
dis·till

dis·til·late
dis·til·la·tion
dis·till·er
dis·till·ery
dis·tinct
dis·tinc·tion
dis·tinc·tive
dis·tin·guish
dis·tort
dis·tor·tion
dis·tract
dis·trac·tion
dis·trait
dis·traught
dis·tress
dis·trib·ute
dis·tri·bu·tion
dis·trib·u·tive
dis·trib·u·tor
dis·trict
dis·trust
dis·trust·ful
dis·turb
dis·tur·bance
dis·uni·ty
dis·use
dith·er
dith·y·ramb
dit·to
dit·ty
di·uret·ic
di·ur·nal
di·va
di·van
di·var·i·cate
di·verge
di·ver·gence
di·ver·gen·cy
di·ver·gent
di·verse
di·ver·si·fy
di·ver·sion

di·ver·si·ty
di·vert
di·ver·tic·u·li·tis
di·ver·tic·u·lo·sis
di·vest
di·ves·ti·ture
di·vide
div·i·dend
div·i·na·tion
di·vine
di·vin·i·ty
di·vis·i·bil·i·ty
di·vis·i·ble
di·vi·sion
di·vi·sive
di·vi·sor
di·vorce
di·vor·cée
div·ot
di·vulge
div·vy
diz·zi·ness
diz·zy
DNA fin·ger·
   print·ing
do·cent
doc·ile
dock·age
dock·et
doc·tor·ate
doc·tri·naire
doc·trin·al
doc·trine
doc·u·ment
doc·u·men·ta·ry
doc·u·men·ta·tion
dod·der·ing
dodg·er
do·do
does·n't
doff
dog·ger·el

dog·gy

dog·ma

dog·mat·ic

dog·ma·tism

dog·nap·per

do-good·er

Doh!/D'oh!*

doi·ly

dol·drums

dole·ful

dol·lar

dol·lop

dol·ly

dol·men

do·lor·ous

dol·phin

dolt

do·main name

do·mes·tic

   vi·o·lence

do·mes·ti·cate

do·mes·tic·i·ty

do·mi·cile

dom·i·nance

dom·i·nate

dom·i·na·tion

dom·i·neer·ing

do·min·ion

dom·i·no

do·nate

do·na·tion

don·key

don·nish

Don·ny·brook

don't

doo·dle

doom·say·er

do·pa·mine

dop·ey

dor·man·cy

dor·mant

dor·mer

dor·mi·to·ry

dor·sal

dos·age

do-si-do

dos·sier

dot·age

dot com

dot com·mer

dou·ble

dou·ble-bar·reled

dou·ble-breast·ed

dou·ble-click

dou·ble-cross (v)

dou·ble-date (v)

dou·ble en·ten·dre

dou·blet

doubt

doubt·ful

douche

dough+

dough·nut

dough·ty

dour

douse+

dove·tail

dow·a·ger

dowdy

dow·el

Dow Jones

   av·er·age

down·grade

down·hill

down-home (adj)

down·load

down-mar·ket (adj)

down·pour

down·right

down·size

Down's syn·drome

down·stage

down-the-line

down·time

down-to-earth

Down Un·der

dow·ry

dowse*+

dox·ol·o·gy

doy·en

dra·co·ni·an

draft

drafts·man

drag·net

drag·on

dra·goon

drag race

drag racing

drain·age

drake

dra·ma

dra·mat·ic

dra·mat·ics

dra·ma·tis

   per·so·nae

dra·ma·tist

dra·ma·ti·za·tion

dra·ma·tize

drap·ery

dras·tic

draught

drawl

dread·ful

dread·locks

dread·nought

dream team

dreamy

drea·ry

dredge

dreg

dress·er

dress·mak·er

dress·mak·ing

drib·ble

drib·let

dried-up (adj)

dri·er
dri·est
dril·ling
drill·mas·ter
drink·able
drip-dry
drip·less
drip·ping
drive-in (n)
driv·el
driv·en
drive·way
driv·ing
driz·zle
droll
droll·ery
drom·e·dary
drone
droopy
drop-out (n)
drop·per
drop·si·cal
drop·sy
dross
drought
drowse
drowsy
drudg·ery
drug·gist
dru·id
drum ma·chine
drunk·ard
drunk·en
druth·ers
du·al·ism
du·al·i·ty
du·al-pur·pose
du·bi·ous
du·cal
duc·at
duch·ess
duchy

duck·ling
duct
duc·tile
Duct Tape™
dud·geon
du·el
du·en·na
du·et
duf·fel bag
duf·fer
du jour
dul·cet
dul·ci·mer
dull·ard
dum·my
dun·geon
dun·nage
duo
duo·dec·i·mal
du·o·de·num
du·plex
du·pli·cate
du·pli·ca·tion
du·pli·ca·tor
du·plic·i·tous
du·plic·i·ty
du·ra·ble
du·ra·tion
du·ress
du·ti·ful
dwell·ing
dwin·dle
dyed-in-the-wool
dye·ing
dy·ing
dy·nam·ic
dy·na·mism
dy·na·mite
dy·nas·ty
dys·en·tery
dys·func·tion
dys·lex·ia

dys·pep·tic
dys·pha·gia
dys·pnea
dys·tro·phy

E

ea·ger
ea·ger·ly
ea·gle
ea·glet
ear·ache
ear·bud
ear·drum
ear·ful
earl+
ear·li·er
ear·li·est
ear·lobe
ear·ly
ear·mark
ear·muff
earn
ear·nest
earn·ings
ear·phone
ear·ring
ear·shot
ear·split·ting
earth·en
earth·en·ware
earth·ly
earth·quake
earth·shak·ing
earth·shat·ter·ing
earth·ward
earth·worm
earthy
ear·wax
ear·wig
ea·sel
ease·ment
eas·i·er

eas·i·ly
Eas·ter
east·er·ly
east·ern
east·ern·most
east·ward
easy·go·ing
eat·able
eat·ery
eat·ing
eau de co·logne
eaves
eaves·drop
ebb tide
Ebo·la vi·rus
Ebon·ics
eb·o·ny
ebul·lience
ebul·lient
ec·cen·tric
ec·cen·tric·i·ty
ec·cle·si·as·tic
ec·cle·si·ol·o·gy
ec·dys·i·ast
ech·e·lon
ech·i·na·cea
echo
echo·car·dio·gram
ech·oed
ech·oes
echo·ing
echo·la·lia
éclair
eclamp·sia
éclat
eclec·tic
eclec·ti·cism
eclipse
ec·logue
eco·fem·i·nism
E. co·li

ecol·o·gist
ecol·o·gy
e-com·merce
eco·nom·ics
econ·o·mist
econ·o·mize
econ·o·my
eco·ter·ror·ism
eco·tour·ism
ecru
ec·sta·sy
ec·stat·ic
ec·to·mor·phic
ec·to·plasm
ec·u·men·i·cal
ecu·me·nism
ec·ze·ma
ed·dies
ed·dy
edel·weiss
edge
edge·wise
edg·ing
edgy
edict
ed·i·fi·ca·tion
ed·i·fice
ed·i·fy
ed·it
edi·tion
ed·i·tor
ed·i·to·ri·al
ed·i·to·ri·al·ize
ed·u·ca·ble
ed·u·cate
ed·u·ca·tion
ed·u·ca·tor
educe
eel
ee·rie
ee·ri·ly

ee·ri·ness
ef·face
ef·fect[+]
ef·fec·tive
ef·fec·tu·al
ef·fec·tu·al·ly
ef·fem·i·na·cy
ef·fem·i·nate
ef·fer·ent
ef·fer·ves·cence
ef·fer·ves·cent
ef·fete
ef·fi·ca·cious
ef·fi·ca·cy
ef·fi·cien·cy
ef·fi·cient
ef·fi·gy
ef·flo·res·cence
ef·flu·ence
ef·flu·ent
ef·flu·vi·um
ef·fort
ef·fort·ful
ef·fron·tery
ef·ful·gence
ef·fuse
ef·fu·sion
ef·fu·sive
egal·i·tar·i·an
egal·i·tar·i·an·ism
egg·nog
egg·plant
egg roll
egg·shell
ego·cen·tric
ego·ism
ego·ist
ego·is·tic
ego·ma·ni·ac
ego·tism
ego·tist

ego·tis·tic
ego·tis·ti·cal
ego-trip (v)
egre·gious
egress
egret
ei·der·down
eigh·teen
eigh·teenth
eight·fold
eighth
eight·i·eth
eighty
Ein·stein's the·o·ry
ei·ther
ejac·u·late
ejac·u·la·tion
ejac·u·la·to·ry
eject
ejec·tor
eke
eked
EKG
ek·ing
elab·o·rate
elab·o·ra·tion
élan
elapse
elas·tic
elas·tic·i·ty
elas·ti·cized
elate
elat·ed
ela·tion
el·bow
el·der
el·der·ly
elect
elec·tion
elec·tion·eer
elec·tive
elec·tor

elec·tor·al
elec·tric
elec·tri·cian
elec·tric·i·ty
elec·tri·fied
elec·tri·fy
elec·tri·fy·ing
elec·tro·car·dio·
    gram
elec·tro·cute
elec·trode
elec·trol·y·sis
elec·tro·lyte
elec·tro·mag·net
elec·tron
elec·tron·ic
elec·tro-op·ti·cal
elec·tro·plate
elec·tro·shock
elec·tro·sta·tic
elec·tro·type
el·ee·mo·sy·nary
el·e·gance
el·e·gant
ele·gi·ac
ele·gi·a·cal
el·e·gy
el·e·ment
el·e·men·tal
el·e·men·ta·ry
el·e·phant
el·e·phan·ti·a·sis
el·e·phan·tine
el·e·vate
el·e·va·tion
el·e·va·tor
elev·en
elev·enth
elf·in
elf·ish
elic·it
elide

el·i·gi·ble
elim·i·nate
elim·i·na·tor
elim·i·na·to·ry
eli·sion
elite
elit·ism
elix·ir
elk
el·lipse
el·lip·sis
el·lip·tic
el·lip·ti·cal
El Niño
el·o·cu·tion
el·o·cu·tion·ist
elon·gate
elon·ga·tion
elope
el·o·quence
el·o·quent
else·where
elu·ci·date
elu·ci·da·tor
elude
elu·sive
elu·so·ry
elves
el·vish
ely·sian
ema·ci·at·ed
e-mail
em·a·nate
em·a·na·tion
eman·ci·pate
eman·ci·pa·tion
eman·ci·pa·tor
emas·cu·late
emas·cu·lat·ed
em·balm
em·balm·er
em·bank·ment

em·bar·go
em·bar·goes
em·bark
em·bar·ka·tion
em·bar·rass
em·bar·rass·ing·ly
em·bar·rass·ment
em·bas·sy
em·bat·tle
em·bed
em·bed·ded
em·bed·ding
em·bel·lish
em·bel·lish·ment
em·ber
em·bez·zle
em·bez·zle·ment
em·bez·zler
em·bit·ter
em·bla·zon
em·blem
em·blem·at·ic
em·bod·ied
em·bodi·ment
em·body
em·body·ing
em·bold·en
em·bo·lism
em·bo·lus
em·boss
em·bou·chure
em·brace
em·brace·able
em·brac·ing
em·bra·sure
em·broi·der
em·broi·dery
em·broil
em·bryo
em·bry·ol·o·gist
em·bry·ol·o·gy
em·bry·on·ic

em·cee
em·ceed
em·cee·ing
emend
emen·da·tion
em·er·ald
emerge
emer·gence
emer·gen·cy
emer·gent
emer·i·tus
em·ery
emet·ic
em·i·grant
em·i·grate
émi·gré
em·i·nence
em·i·nent
emir
emir·ate
em·is·sary
emis·sion
emit
Em·my
emol·lient
emol·u·ment
emote
emo·ti·con
emot·ing
emo·tion
emo·tion·al
emo·tion·less
emo·tive
em·pa·thet·ic
em·pa·thize
em·pa·thy
em·per·or
em·pha·sis
em·pha·size
em·phat·ic
em·phy·se·ma
em·pire

em·pir·ic
em·pir·i·cal
em·pir·i·cism
em·plane*
em·ploy
em·ploy·able
em·ploy·abil·i·ty
em·ploy·ee
em·ploy·ment
em·po·ri·um
em·pow·er
em·press
emp·ti·ness
emp·ty-nest
   syn·drome
em·py·re·an
EMT
em·u·late
em·u·la·tion
em·u·la·tor
emul·si·fi·er
emul·si·fy
emul·sion
en·able
en·act
en·act·ment
enam·el
enam·el·ware
en·am·or
en bloc
en·camp
en·camp·ment
en·cap·su·late
en·case·ment
en·ceinte
en·ceph·a·lit·ic
en·ceph·a·li·tis
en·chant
en·chant·ment
en·chant·ress
en·chi·la·da
en·ci·pher

en·cir·cle
en·clasp
en·clave
en·clit·ic
en·close
en·clo·sure
en·code
en·co·mi·um
en·com·pass
en·core
en·coun·ter
en·cour·age
en·croach·ment
en·cum·ber
en·cum·brance
en·cyc·li·cal
en·cy·clo·pe·dia
en·cy·clo·pe·dic
en·dan·ger
en·dear·ment
en·deav·or
en·dem·ic
en·dive
end·less
en·do·crine
en·do·cri·nol·o·gy
en·dog·a·my
en·dog·e·nous
en·do·me·tri·osis
en·do·mor·phic
en·dor·phin
en·dorse
en·dors·ee
en·dorse·ment
en·dors·er
en·dow
en·dow·ment
en·due
en·dur·able
en·dur·ance
en·dure
en·dur·ing

en·e·ma
en·e·my
en·er·get·ic
en·er·get·i·cal·ly
en·er·gize
en·er·giz·er
en·er·gy
en·er·vate[+]
en·er·va·tion
en·fant ter·ri·ble
en·fee·ble
en·fold
en·force
en·force·able
en·fran·chise
en·gage
en·gaged
en·gage·ment
en·gag·ing
en·gen·der
en·gine
en·gi·neer
en·gi·neer·ing
en·gorge
en·grave
en·grav·ing
en·grossed
en·gross·ing
en·gulf
en·hance
enig·ma
enig·mat·ic
en·join
en·joy
en·joy·ment
en·kin·dle
en·large
en·large·ment
en·light·en
en·light·en·ment
en·list
en·liv·en

en masse
en·mesh
en·mi·ty
en·no·ble
en·nui
enor·mi·ty
enor·mous
enough
en pas·sant
en·plane
en·rage
en·rap·ture
en·rich
en·robe
en·roll
en·roll·ment
en route
en·sconce
en·sem·ble
en·shrine
en·shroud
en·sign
en·slave
en·slave·ment
en·snare
en·sue
en·sure
en·tail
en·tan·gle
en·tan·gle·ment
en·tente
en·ter
en·ter·ic
en·ter·i·tis
en·ter·prise zone
en·ter·pris·ing
en·ter·tain
en·ter·tain·ing
en·ter·tain·ment
en·thrall
en·throne
en·thu·si·asm

en·thu·si·ast
en·thu·si·as·tic
en·tice
en·tice·ment
en·tire
en·tire·ty
en·ti·tle
en·ti·tle·ment
en·ti·ty
en·tomb
en·to·mol·o·gy
en·tou·rage
en·tr'acte
en·trails
en·train
en·trance
en·trant
en·trap
en·treat
en·treaty
en·tre·chat
en·trée
en·trench
en·tre·pre·neur
en·tre·pre·neur·
  ial
en·tro·py
en·trust
en·try
en·try·way
en·twine
enu·mer·ate
enu·mer·a·tor
enun·ci·ate
en·ure·sis
en·vel·op
en·ve·lope
en·vi·able
en·vi·ous
en·vi·ron·ment
en·vi·ron·men·
  tal·ly

en·vi·ron·men·
  tal·ism
en·vi·ron·men·
  tal·ist
en·vi·rons
en·vis·age
en·vi·sion
en·voi[+]
en·voy*[+]
en·vy
en·zyme
eon
ep·au·let
épée
ephed·rine
ephem·er·al
ep·ic
ep·i·cene
epi·cen·ter
ep·i·cure
ep·i·cu·re·an
ep·i·cu·re·an·ism
epi·cy·cle
ep·i·dem·ic
ep·i·de·mi·ol·o·gy
epi·der·mal
epi·der·mis
epi·glot·tis
ep·i·gram
ep·i·gram·mat·ic
ep·i·graph
ep·i·lep·sy
ep·i·lep·tic
ep·i·logue
epiph·a·ny
epi·phyte
epis·co·pa·cy
epis·co·pal
Epis·co·pa·lian
epi·si·ot·o·my
ep·i·sode
ep·i·sod·ic

epis·te·mol·o·gy
epis·tle
ep·i·taph
ep·i·the·li·um
ep·i·thet
epit·o·me
epit·o·mize
e plu·ri·bus unum
ep·och
ep·och·al
ep·ode
ep·onym
epon·y·mous
ep·oxy
EPROM
equa·ble
equa·bly
equal
equal·i·ty
equal·ize
equal·iz·er
equal·ly
equa·nim·i·ty
equate
equa·tion
equa·tor
equa·to·ri·al
eques·tri·an
equi·an·gu·lar
equi·dis·tant
equi·lat·er·al
equil·i·brate
equil·i·bra·tion
equi·lib·ri·um
equine
equi·nox
equip
eq·ui·page
equip·ping
equip·ment
equi·poise
eq·ui·ta·ble

eq·ui·ta·tion
eq·ui·ty
equiv·a·lence
equiv·a·len·cy
equiv·a·lent
equiv·o·cal
equiv·o·cate
erad·i·cate
erad·i·ca·tion
erase
eras·er
era·sure
erect
erec·tile
   dys·func·tion
erec·tion
erec·tor
er·got
er·mine
erode
erod·ing
erog·e·nous
ero·sion
erot·ic
erot·i·ca
erot·i·cism
er·rand
er·rant
er·ra·ta
er·rat·ic
er·ro·ne·ous
er·ror
erst·while
er·u·dite
er·u·di·tion
erupt+
erup·tion
erup·tive
ery·sip·e·las
es·ca·late
es·ca·la·tion
es·ca·la·tor

es·cap·able
es·ca·pade
es·cape
es·cap·ee
es·cap·ing
es·cap·ism
es·car·got
es·ca·role
es·carp·ment
es·cha·to·log·i·cal
es·cha·tol·o·gy
es·chew
es·cort
es·cri·toire
es·crow
es·cutch·eon
Es·ki·mo
ESL
esoph·a·gus
es·o·ter·ic
es·pa·drille
es·pal·ier
es·pe·cial·ly
es·pi·o·nage
es·pla·nade
es·pouse
espres·so
es·prit de corps
es·quire
es·say
es·say·ist
es·sence
es·sen·tial
es·sen·tial·ism
es·sen·tial·ly
es·tab·lish
es·tab·lish·ment
es·tate
es·teem
es·ti·ma·ble
es·ti·mate
es·ti·ma·tion

es·ti·ma·tor
es·top·pel
es·trange
es·tranged
es·tro·gen
es·tu·ary
éta·gère
et alia
et·cet·era
etch
etch·ing
eter·nal
eter·ni·ty
ether
ethe·re·al
ethe·re·al·ly
ether·ize
eth·ic
eth·i·cal
eth·i·cist
eth·nic cleans·ing
eth·nic·i·ty
eth·no·cen·tric
eth·nol·o·gy
ethos
eti·ol·o·gy
et·i·quette
étude
et·y·mo·log·i·cal
et·y·mol·o·gy
eu·ca·lyp·tus
Eu·cha·rist
eu·chre
Eu·clid·e·an
eu·gen·ic
eu·gen·i·cist
eu·gen·ics
eu·lo·gis·tic
eu·lo·gize
eu·lo·gy
eu·nuch
eu·phe·mism

eu·phe·mis·ti·cal·ly
eu·pho·ni·ous
eu·pho·ny
eu·pho·ria
eu·re·ka
Eu·ro
Eu·ro·pe·an
eu·ryth·mics
eu·sta·chian tube
eu·tha·na·sia
evac·u·ate
evac·u·a·tion
evac·u·ee
evade
eval·u·ate
ev·a·nesce
ev·a·nes·cence
ev·a·nes·cent
evan·gel·i·cal
evan·ge·lism
evan·ge·list
evan·ge·lize
evap·o·rate
evap·o·ra·tion
evap·o·ra·tor
eva·sion
eva·sive
even·hand·ed
eve·ning
event
event·ful
even·tu·al
even·tu·al·i·ty
even·tu·al·ly
ev·er·glade
ev·er·green
ev·er·last·ing
ev·er·more
ev·ery
ev·ery·body
ev·ery·day

ev·ery·man
ev·ery·one
ev·ery·place
ev·ery·thing
ev·ery·where
evict
ev·i·dence
ev·i·dent
ev·i·dent·ly
evil
evil·do·er
evil-mind·ed
evince
evis·cer·ate
evo·ca·tion
evoc·a·tive
evoke
evo·lu·tion
evolve
ew·er
ex·ac·er·bate
ex·act
ex·ac·ti·tude
ex·act·ly
ex·ag·ger·ate
ex·alt
ex·al·ta·tion
ex·am
ex·am·i·na·tion
ex·am·ine
ex·am·in·er
ex·am·ple
ex·as·per·ate
ex·as·per·a·tion
ex ca·the·dra
ex·ca·vate
ex·ca·va·tion
ex·ca·va·tor
ex·ceed
ex·cel
ex·cel·lence
ex·cel·len·cy

ex·cel·lent
ex·cel·si·or
ex·cept[+]
ex·cep·tion
ex·cep·tion·able
ex·cep·tion·al
ex·cerpt
ex·cess
ex·ces·sive
ex·ces·sive·ly
ex·change
ex·change·able
ex·che·quer
ex·cise
ex·ci·sion
ex·cit·able
ex·ci·ta·tion
ex·cite
ex·cite·ment
ex·cit·er
ex·claim
ex·cla·ma·tion
ex·clam·a·to·ry
ex·clude
ex·clu·sion
ex·clu·sive
ex·com·mu·ni·cate
ex·co·ri·ate
ex·cre·ment
ex·cres·cence
ex·cre·ta
ex·cre·tion
ex·cru·ci·at·ing
ex·cul·pate
ex·cul·pa·to·ry
ex·cur·sion
ex·cus·able
ex·cus·ably
ex·cuse
ex·cus·ing
ex·e·cra·ble
ex·e·crate

ex·e·cra·tion
ex·e·cute
ex·e·cu·tion
ex·ec·u·tive
ex·ec·u·tor
ex·ec·u·trix
ex·e·ge·sis
ex·e·gete
ex·em·plar
ex·em·pla·ry
ex·em·pli·fy
ex·empt
ex·emp·tion
ex·er·cise
ex·ert
ex·er·tion
ex·e·unt
ex·fo·liant
ex·hal·ant
ex·ha·la·tion
ex·hale
ex·haust
ex·haust·ible
ex·haus·tion
ex·haus·tive
ex·hib·it
ex·hi·bi·tion
ex·hi·bi·tion·ism
ex·hil·a·rate
ex·hil·a·ra·tion
ex·hort
ex·hor·ta·tion
ex·hor·ta·tive
ex·hor·ta·to·ry
ex·hume
ex·i·gence
ex·i·gen·cy
ex·i·gent
ex·ile
ex·ist
ex·is·tence
ex·is·tent

ex·is·ten·tial
ex·is·ten·tial·ism
ex·it
ex li·bris
ex·o·dus
ex of·fi·cio
ex·og·a·my
ex·on·er·ate
ex·or·bi·tant
ex·or·cise
ex·or·cism
ex·o·ter·ic
ex·ot·ic
ex·panse
ex·pand·able
ex·pan·sion
ex·pan·sive
ex·pa·ti·ate
ex·pa·tri·ate
ex·pec·tan·cy
ex·pec·tant
ex·pec·ta·tion
ex·pec·to·rant
ex·pec·to·rate
ex·pe·di·ence
ex·pe·di·en·cy
ex·pe·di·ent
ex·pe·dite
ex·pe·di·tion
ex·pe·di·tion·ary
ex·pe·di·tious
ex·pe·di·tious·ly
ex·pel
ex·pelled
ex·pend
ex·pend·able
ex·pen·di·ture
ex·pense
ex·pen·sive
ex·pe·ri·ence
ex·pe·ri·en·tial
ex·per·i·ment

ex·per·i·ment·er
ex·per·i·men·tal
ex·pert
ex·per·tise
ex·pi·ate
ex·pi·a·tion
ex·pi·ra·tion
ex·pire
ex·plain
ex·pla·na·tion
ex·plan·a·to·ry
ex·ple·tive
ex·pli·ca·ble
ex·pli·cate
ex·plic·it
ex·plode
ex·ploit
ex·ploi·ta·tion
ex·plo·ra·tion
ex·plor·ato·ry
ex·plore
ex·plo·sion
ex·plo·sive
ex·po·nent
ex·po·nen·tial
ex·port
ex·por·ta·tion
ex·pose
ex·po·sé
ex·po·si·tion
ex·pos·i·to·ry
ex post fac·to
ex·pos·tu·late
ex·post·tu·la·tion
ex·po·sure
ex·pound
ex-pres·i·dent
ex·press
ex·pres·sion
ex·pres·sion·less
ex·pres·sive
ex·pres·sive·ness

ex·press·ly
ex·pro·pri·ate
ex·pro·pri·a·tion
ex·pul·sion
ex·punge
ex·pur·gate
ex·qui·site
ex·tant
ex·tem·po·ra·ne·ous
ex·tem·po·rary
ex·tem·po·re
ex·tem·po·rize
ex·tend
ex·ten·sion
ex·ten·sive
ex·ten·sive·ly
ex·tent
ex·ten·u·ate
ex·ten·u·a·ting
ex·te·ri·or
ex·ter·mi·nate
ex·ter·mi·na·tor
ex·ter·nal
ex·tinct
ex·tinc·tion
ex·tin·guish
ex·tin·guish·er
ex·tir·pate
ex·tol
ex·tol·ling
ex·tort
ex·tor·tion
ex·tract
ex·trac·tion
ex·tra·cur·ric·u·lar
ex·tra·dit·able
ex·tra·dite
ex·tra·di·tion
ex·tra·mar·i·tal
ex·tra·mu·ral
ex·tra·ne·ous
ex·traor·di·nari·ly

ex·traor·di·nary
ex·trap·o·late
ex·tra·sen·so·ry
ex·trav·a·gance
ex·trav·a·gant
ex·trav·a·gan·za
ex·tra·vert*
ex·treme
ex·trem·ism
ex·trem·i·ty
ex·tri·cate
ex·trin·sic
ex·tro·ver·sion
ex·tro·vert
ex·trude
ex·tru·sion
ex·u·ber·ance
ex·u·ber·ant
ex·ude
ex·ult
ex·ul·tant
ex·ul·ta·tion
eye·brow
eyed
eye·ful
eye·lash
eye-open·er
eye·sight
eyes on·ly
eye·wash
eye·wit·ness
ey·rie
e-zine

F

fa·ble
fab·ric
fab·ri·cate
fab·u·lous
fa·cade
face·less·ness
face-off (n)

face-sav·ing
fac·et
fa·ce·tious
fa·cial
fa·cies
fac·ile
fa·cil·i·tate
fa·cil·i·ta·tion
fa·cil·i·ty
fac·ing
fac·sim·i·le
fac·tion
fac·tious
fac·ti·tious
fac·toid
fac·tor
fac·to·ri·al
fac·to·ry
fac·to·tum
fac·tu·al
fac·ul·ty
fa·er·ie+
fag·got
Fahr·en·heit
fail·ure
faint·heart·ed
fair·ground
fair·ly
fair-trade
fair·way
fair-weath·er
fairy+
fairy·land
fairy tale (n)
fairy-tale (adj)
fait ac·com·pli
faith·ful
faith·less
fa·kir
fal·con
fal·con·er
fal·con·ry

fal·la·cious

fal·la·cy

fal·li·bil·i·ty

fal·li·ble

fal·lo·pi·an tube

fal·low

fal·set·to

fals·ie

fal·si·fy

fal·ter

famed

fa·mil·ial

fa·mil·iar·i·ty

fa·mil·iar·ize

fam·i·ly leave

fam·ine

fam·ish

fa·mous

fa·nat·ic

fa·nat·i·cism

fan·cied

fan·ci·er

fan·ci·ful

fan·ci·ly

fan·ci·ness

fan·cy

fan·fare

fan·light

fan·ta·sia

fan·ta·size

fan·tasm*

fan·tas·tic

fan·ta·sy

fan·zine

FAQ

far·ad

far·away

farce

far·ci·cal

far·fetched

far·flung

fa·ri·na

farm·er

faro

far·ra·go

far·ri·er

far·row+

far·sight·ed

far·ther

far·thing

fas·cia

fas·ci·nate

fas·ci·na·tion

fas·cism

fas·cist

fash·ion

fash·ion·able

fash·ion·is·ta

fas·ten

fas·tid·i·ous

fast-twitch

fa·tal

fa·tal·ism

fa·tal·i·ty

fa·tal·ly

fat·ed

fate·ful

fa·ther

fa·ther-in-law

fa·ther·land

fath·om

fath·om·less

fa·tigue

fat·ten

fat·ty

fa·tu·i·ty

fat·u·ous

fau·cet

fault

faulty

faun

fau·na

fau·vism

faux pas

fa·vor

fa·vor·able

fa·vor·ite

fa·vor·it·ism

fawn·ing

fax mo·dem

faze+

fe·al·ty

fear·ful

fear·some

fea·si·ble

feast

feath·er

feath·er·bed

feath·er·weight

feath·ery

fea·ture

fe·brile

Feb·ru·ary

fe·cal oc·cult blood test

fe·ces

feck·less

fe·cund

fe·cun·di·ty

fed·er·al

fed·er·ate

fed·er·a·tion

fe·do·ra

fee·ble

feed·back (n)

feel·er

feel·ing

feign

feint

feisty

fe·lic·i·tate

fe·lic·i·ta·tion

fe·lic·i·tous

fe·lic·i·ty

fe·line

fell

fel·low·man
fel·low·ship
fel·on
fe·lo·ni·ous
fel·o·ny
fe·male
fem·i·nine
fem·i·nin·i·ty
fem·i·nism
femme fa·tale
fe·mo·ral
fe·mur
fence
fen·es·trat·ed
fen·es·tra·tion
feng shui
fen·nel
fe·ral
fer·ment
fer·men·ta·tion
fern
fe·ro·cious
fe·roc·i·ty
fer·ret
Fer·ris wheel
fer·rous
fer·ry[+]
fer·tile
fer·til·i·ty
fer·til·iza·tion
fer·til·ize
fer·ule
fer·vent
fer·vid
fer·vor
fes·ter
fes·ti·val
fes·tive
fes·tiv·i·ty
fes·toon
fe·tal al·co·hol
  syn·drome

fetch·ing
fete
fet·id
fe·tish
fet·lock
fet·ter
fet·tle
fet·tuc·ci·ne
fe·tus
feud
feu·dal
fe·ver·ish
fey
fi·an·cé[+]
fi·an·cée[+]
fi·as·co
fi·at
fi·ber
fi·ber·glass
fi·ber·op·tic
fi·bril·la·tion
fi·broid
fi·bro·my·al·gia
fi·brous
fib·u·la
fick·le
fic·tion
fic·ti·tious
fid·dling
fi·del·i·ty
fidg·et
fidg·ety
fi·du·cial
fi·du·cia·ry
fief
fief·dom
fiend
fiend·ish
fierce
fi·ery
fi·es·ta
fife

fifth
fif·ty
fif·ty-fif·ty
fight-or-flight
fig·ment
fig·u·ra·tive
fig·ure
fig·u·rine
fil·a·ment
fil·bert
filch
fi·let
fi·let mi·gnon
fil·ial
fil·i·bus·ter
fil·i·gree
fil·ing
Fil·i·pi·no
fil·let
fill·ing
fil·lip
fil·ly
film·dom
filmy
fil·ter
fil·ter·able
filth
filthy
fil·trate
fil·tra·tion
fi·na·gle
fi·nal
fi·nal·ly
fi·na·le
fi·nal·ist
fi·nal·i·ty
fi·nal·ize
fi·nance
fi·nan·cial
fi·nan·cier
fine·ly
fin·ery

fines herbes
fi·nesse
fin·est
fin·ger·ing
fin·ger·nail
fin·ger·print
fin·icky
fi·nis
fin·ish
fi·nite
fire·brand
fire·break
fir·ing
fir·ma·ment
first
first·ly
fis·cal
fish·able
fish-and-chips
fish·ery
fish-eye
fishy
fis·sion
fis·sion·able
fis·sure
fist·ful
fist·ic
fist·i·cuffs
fit·ful
fit·ting
fiv·er
fix·ate
fix·a·tion
fix·a·tive
fixed
fix·er
fix·i·ty
fix·ture
fizz
fiz·zle
fjord
flab·ber·gast

flab·by
flac·cid
fla·con
flag·el·late
flag·el·la·tion
flag·ging
flag·on
fla·grant
flail
flair[+]
flak
flaky
flam·bé
flam·beau
flam·boy·ance
flam·boy·ant
fla·men·co
flam·ing
fla·min·go
flam·ma·bil·i·ty
flam·ma·ble
flange
flank·er
flan·nel
flan·nel·ette
flap·jack
flap·per
flare[+]
flar·ing
flash·back
flash·er
flash·ing
flashy
flat·ten
flat·ter
flat·tery
flat·tish
flat·u·lence
flat·u·lent
flaunt
flau·tist
fla·vor

fla·vor·ful
flaw·less
flax·en
flax·seed
flay
flea
fleck
fledge
fledg·ling
fleece
fleecy
flesh·i·ness
flesh·ly
fleshy
fleur-de-lis
flex·i·bil·i·ty
flex·i·ble
flick
flick·er
fli·er
flighty
flim·flam
flim·sy
flinch
flint·lock
flinty
flip-flop
flip·pan·cy
flip·pant
flip·per
flip side
flir·ta·tious
flitch
flit·ter
float·er
floc·cu·lent
flock·ing
floe
floor·ing
floo·zy
flop·py
flop·py disk

flo·ra
flo·ral
flo·res·cence
flo·ret
flo·ri·cul·ture
flor·id
flo·rist
flo·ta·tion
flo·til·la
flot·sam
flounce
floun·der
flour·ish
flout
flow·chart
flow·er
flow·ery
flown
fluc·tu·ate
fluc·tu·a·tion
flue
flu·en·cy
flu·ent
fluffy
flu·id
flu·id·i·ty
fluke
flunk
fluo·resce
fluo·res·cence
fluo·res·cent
fluo·ri·date
fluo·ride
fluo·ri·nate
fluo·rine
fluo·ro·scope
flur·ry
flus·ter
flut·ing
flut·ist
flut·ter
flu·vi·al

flux
fly·by
fly-by-night
fly·er
fly·ing
fly·over
foamy
fo·cac·cia
fo·cal
fo·cal·ize
fo'·c'sle*
fo·cus group
fod·der
fog·gy
fo·gy
foi·ble
foie gras
foil
foist
fold·er
fol·de·rol
fo·liage
fo·li·ate
fo·li·a·tion
fo·lio
folk·lore
folksy
fol·li·cle
fol·low·er
fol·low·ing
fol·low-up
fol·ly
fo·ment
fon·dle
fond·ly
fon·due
food court
food pro·ces·sor
fool·ery
fool·har·dy
fool·ish
fool·ish·ness

fools·cap
foos·ball
foot·age
foot·ing
foot·lights
foot·note
foot·race
foot·wear
foot·work
fop·pery
fop·pish
for·age
for·ay
for·bear*+
for·bear·ance
for·bid
for·bid·ding
for·bode*
force·ful
for·ceps
forc·ible
fore-and-aft
fore·arm
fore·bear+
fore·bode
fore·bod·ing
fore·cast
fore·cast·ing
fore·cas·tle
fore·close
fore·clo·sure
fore·fa·ther
fore·fin·ger
fore·front
fore·go*+
fore·hand
fore·head
for·eign
fore·leg
fore·lock
fore·man
fore·mast

fore·most
fore·noon
fo·ren·sic
fore·or·dain
fore·play
fore·run·ner
fore·see
fore·see·able
fore·shad·ow
fore·shore
fore·short·en
fore·sight
fore·skin
for·est
fore·stall
for·est·er
for·est·ry
fore·taste
fore·tell
fore·thought
for·ev·er
for·ev·er·more
fore·warn
fore·wom·an
fore·word[+]
for·feit
for·fei·ture
for·fend
forge
forg·er
forg·ery
for·get
for·get·ful
for·get-me-not
for·get·ta·ble
for·give
for·give·ness
for·giv·ing
for·go[+]
for·gone
forked
for·lorn

for·mal
for·mal·ly
form·al·de·hyde
for·mal·ism
for·mal·i·ty
for·mal·ize
for·mat
for·ma·tion
for·ma·tive
formed
for·mer
for·mer·ly
form·fit·ting
For·mi·ca™
for·mi·da·ble
for·mu·la
for·mu·late
for·mu·la·tion
for·ni·cate
for·ni·ca·tion
for·sake
for·sooth
for·swear
for·sworn
for·syth·ia
forte
forth·com·ing
forth·right
for·ti·fi·ca·tion
for·ti·fi·er
for·ti·fy
for·tis·si·mo
for·ti·tude
fort·night
FORTRAN
for·tress
for·tu·itous
for·tu·ity
for·tu·nate
for·ty
for·ty-nin·er
fo·rum

for·ward[+]
fosse
fos·sil
fos·sil·ize
fos·ter
foul line
foul·ly
foul up (v)
foun·da·tion
foun·der ef·fect
found·ling
found·ry
foun·tain
foun·tain·head
four-flush (v)
four·fold
4-H'·er
four-poster
four·ra·gère
four·some
four·teen
fourth
fowl
foxy
foy·er
fra·cas
frac·tal
frac·tion
frac·tious
frac·ture
frag·ile
frag·ment
frag·men·tary
fra·grance
fra·grant
frail·ty
frame-up (n)
frame·work
fram·ing
franc
fran·chise
Fran·co·phile

Fran·co·phobe
fran·gi·ble
fran·gi·pane
Fran·ken·food
frank·furt·er
frank·in·cense
frank·ly
fran·tic
frap·pe
fra·ter·nal
fra·ter·ni·ty
frat·er·nize
frat·ri·cide
Frau
fraud
fraud·u·lence
fraud·u·lent
fraught
Fräu·lein
fray
fraz·zled
freak·ish
freak-out (n)
freaky
freck·le
free·bie
free·dom
free-fall (v)
free-for-all
free·hand·ed
free·heart·ed
free·hold
free·lance
free·ma·son·ry
free spir·it
free·style
free trade
free·ware
free·way
free·wheel·ing
freeze-dried
freez·er

freight
freight·age
freight·er
french fry
fre·net·ic
fren·zied
fren·zy
fre·quen·cy
fre·quent
fre·quent·ly-asked
  ques·tions
fres·co
fresh·en
fresh·et
fresh·man
fret
fret·ful
fret·saw
fret·work
Freud·ian
fri·a·ble
fri·ar+
fri·ary
fric·as·see
fric·tion
friend·ly
fri·er*
frieze
frig·ate
fright·en
fright·ful
frig·id
fri·gid·i·ty
fringe
frip·pery
Fris·bee™
frisky
frit·ter
fri·vol·i·ty
friv·o·lous
friz·zies
friz·zle

frol·ic
frol·ic·some
front·age
fron·tal
fron·tier
fron·tiers·man
fron·tis·piece
front-line
frost·bite
frost·ing
frosty
frost·i·ly
frothy
frow·sy
fro·zen
fruc·ti·fy
fruc·tose
fru·gal
fru·gal·i·ty
fruit·ful
fru·ition
fruit·less
fruity
frumpy
frus·trate
frus·trat·ed
frus·trat·ing
frus·tra·tion
fry·er+
fuch·sia
fudge
fu·el
fu·gi·tive
fu·gu
fugue
füh·rer
ful·crum
ful·fill
ful·gent
full-fledged
ful·mi·nate
ful·mi·nat·ing

ful·some
fum·ble
fu·mi·gate
func·tion
func·tion·al
func·tion·ary
fun·da·men·tal
fun·da·men·tal·ism
fun·da·men·tal·ist
fund-rais·er
fund-rais·ing
fu·ner·al
fu·ne·re·al
fun·gi·cide
fun·go
fun·gus
fu·nic·u·lar
fun·nel
fur·bish
fu·ri·ous
fur·long
fur·lough
fur·nace
fur·nish
fur·ni·ture
fu·ror
fur·ri·er
fur·row
fur·ry
fur·ther·ance
fur·ther·more
fur·ther·most
fur·thest
fur·tive
fu·ry
furze
fu·se·lage
fus·ible
fu·sil·ier
fu·sil·lade
fu·sion
fussy

fus·tian
fus·ty
fu·tile
fu·til·i·ty
fu·tur·ism
fu·tur·is·tic
fu·tu·ri·ty
fuzzy

G

gab
gab·ber
gab·by
gab·fest
ga·ble
ga·bled
gad·fly
gad·get
gad·get·ry
Gael·ic
gaff⁺
gaffe⁺
ga·ga
gage*⁺
gag·gle
gag·man
gai·ety
gai·ly
gain·ful
gain·say
gait
gait·ed
gai·ter
ga·la
ga·lac·tic
gal·an·tine
gal·a·vant
gal·axy
gal Fri·day
Gal·i·leo
gall
gal·lant

gal·lant·ry
gal·le·on
gal·lery
gal·ley
Gal·lic
gal·li·cism
gall·ing
gal·li·vant
gal·lon
gal·lop
gal·lows
gall·stone
Gal·lup poll
ga·loot
ga·lore
ga·losh·es
gal·van·ic
gal·va·nize
gam·bit
gam·ble⁺
gam·bol⁺
game·ly
games·man·ship
gam·ete
gam·ing
gam·ma ray
gam·mon
gam·ut
gamy
gan·der
gan·gling
gan·gli·on
gang·plank
gan·grene
gang·sta
gang·ster
gang·way
gan·try
gape
gap·er
ga·rage
garb

gar·bage
gar·ban·zo
gar·ble
gar·bled
gar·çon
gar·den
gar·de·nia
gar·gan·tuan
gar·gle
gar·goyle
gar·ish
gar·land
gar·lic
gar·licky
gar·ment
gar·ner
gar·net
gar·nish
gar·nish·ee
gar·nish·ment
gar·ni·ture
gar·ri·son
gar·rote
gar·ru·lous
gar·ter
gas·eous
gas·eous·ness
gas-guz·zler
gash
gas·ket
gas·o·line
gasp
gas·sy
gas·tric
gas·tri·tis
gas·tro-en·ter·i·tis
gas·tro-in·tes·ti·nal
gas·tro·nome
gas·tro·nom·ic
gas·tron·o·my
gate-crash·er
gate·keep·er

gate·way
gath·er
gath·er·er
gath·er·ing
gauche
gau·che·rie
gau·cho
gaud·i·ness
gaudy
gauge+
gauged
gaunt
gaunt·let
gauss
gauze
gav·el
gawk
gawky
gay·ety*
gay·ly*
ga·ze·bo
ga·zelle
gaz·et·teer
ga·zil·lion
gaz·pa·cho
gear
gear·ing
gear·shift
gecko
gee·gaw
geese
gee·zer
ge·fil·te fish
Ge·hen·na
Gei·ger coun·ter
gei·sha
gel·a·tin
ge·lat·i·nous
gel·cap
geld·ing
gel·id
gem·i·nate

Gem·i·ni
gem·ol·o·gist
gem·ol·o·gy
ge·müt·lich·keit
gen·darme
gen·der
gene
ge·ne·al·o·gist
ge·ne·al·o·gy
gen·era
gen·er·al
gen·er·a·lis·si·mo
gen·er·al·ist
gen·er·al·i·ty
gen·er·al·iza·tion
gen·er·al·ize
gen·er·al·ly
gen·er·ate
Gen·er·a·tion X
gen·er·a·tive
gen·er·a·tor
ge·ner·ic
gen·er·os·i·ty
gen·er·ous
gen·e·sis
gene splic·ing
ge·net·ic
ge·net·i·cal·ly
  en·gi·neered
ge·net·ics
ge·nial
ge·nial·i·ty
ge·nial·ly
ge·nie
gen·i·tal
gen·i·ta·lia
gen·i·tive
ge·nius
geno·cide
ge·nome
ge·no·type
genre

gen·teel
gen·tian
gen·tile
gen·til·i·ty
gen·tle
gen·tle·man
gen·tle·ness
gen·tle·wom·an
gen·try
gen·u·flect
gen·u·ine
ge·nus
Gen X
geo·cen·tric
geo·de·sic
ge·od·e·sy
ge·og·ra·pher
geo·graph·ic
ge·og·ra·phy
geo·log·ic
ge·ol·o·gy
geo·met·ric
ge·om·e·try
geo·pol·i·tics
geo·ther·mal
ge·ra·ni·um
ger·bil
ge·ri·at·ric
ger·i·a·tri·cian
ge·ri·at·rics
Ger·man
ger·mane
ger·mi·cid·al
ger·mi·cide
ger·mi·nal
ger·mi·nate
ger·on·tol·o·gist
ger·on·tol·o·gy
ger·ry·man·der
ger·und
ge·run·dive
ge·stalt

ge·sta·po
ges·ta·tion
ges·tic·u·late
ges·tic·u·la·tion
ges·ture
ge·sund·heit
get-to·geth·er
gew·gaw
gey·ser
ghast·ly
gher·kin
ghet·to
ghost
ghost·ly
ghost·writer
ghoul
gi·ant
gi·ant·ism
giar·dia
gib·ber
gib·ber·ish
gib·bet
gib·bon
gib·bous
gibe⁺
gib·lets
gid·dy
giga·bit
giga·byte
giga·hertz
gi·gan·tesque
gi·gan·tic
gi·gan·tism
gig·gle
gig·o·lo
gild·ing
gilt
gim·crack
gim·let
gim·mick
gim·mick·ry
gimp

gin·ger
gin·ger·ly
ging·ham
gin·gi·vi·tis
gink·go
gin·seng
gi·raffe
gird·er
gir·dle
girl·friend
girl·ish
girth
gist
giv·en
giz·mo
giz·zard
gla·cial
gla·cier
glad·den
glad·i·a·tor
glad·i·o·la
glad·i·o·lus
glam·or·ize
glam·or·ous
glance
glanc·ing
gland
glan·du·lar
glar·ing
glas·nost
glass ceil·ing
glassy
glau·co·ma
glaze
gla·zier
glaz·ing
gleam
glean
glee·ful
glib
glide
glid·er

glim·mer
glimpse
glint
glis·ten
glitch
glit·ter
gloam·ing
gloat
Glob·al Po·si·tion·
    ing Sys·tem
glob·al·ism
globe
glob·u·lar
glob·ule
gloom
gloomy
glo·ri·fy
glo·ri·ous
glo·ry
gloss
glos·sa·ry
glossy
glot·tal
glove
glow
glow·er
glox·in·ia
glu·cose
glue
glued
glu·ing
glum
glut
glu·ten
glu·te·us max·i·mus
glu·ti·nous
glut·ton
glut·ton·ous
glut·tony
glyc·er·in
gly·co·gen
gnarl

gnarled
gnarly
gnash
gnat
gnaw
gneiss
gnome
gnos·ti·cism
gnu
go·er
goad
goal·ie
goal·keep·er
goal line
go-around (n)
goat
goa·tee
gob·ble
gob·ble·dy·gook
go-be·tween
gob·let
go-cart
god·child
god·daugh·ter
god·dess
god·fa·ther
God-fear·ing
god·for·sak·en
god·head
god·less
god·ly
god·moth·er
god·par·ent
god·send
god·son
go-get·ter
gog·gle
go-go
go·ings-on
goi·ter
gold·brick
gold dig·ger

gold·en
golden age
gol·den hand·cuffs
gol·den old·ie
gol·den para·chute
gold·en·rod
gold·finch
gold·fish
gold·smith
go·lem
golf·er
Go·li·ath
gol·li·wog
go·nad
gon·do·la
gon·do·lier
gon·er
gon·or·rhea
gon·zo
goo·ber
good-bye
good-for-noth·ing
good-heart·ed
good-hu·mored
good-look·ing
good·ly
good-na·tured
good·will
goody-goody
goofy
goose·ber·ry
go·pher
gore
gorge
gor·geous
gor·gon
go·ril·la[+]
gor·man·dize
gorse
gory
gos·ling
gos·pel

gos·sa·mer
gos·sip
gos·sipy
Goth·ic
gouache
Gou·da
gouge
gou·lash
gourd
gour·mand
gour·met
gout
gov·ern
gov·ern·ess
gov·ern·ment
gov·ern·men·tal
gov·er·nor
gown
goy·im
grab·ber
grab·by
grace·ful
grace·less
gra·cious
grack·le
gra·da·tion
gra·di·ent
grad·u·al
grad·u·ate
grad·u·a·tion
graf·fi·ti
grail
grainy
gram·mar
gram·mat·i·cal
Gram·my
gram·o·phone
gra·na·ry
grand·dad·dy
grand·daugh·ter
grande dame
gran·deur

grand·fa·ther
gran·dil·o·quence
gran·dil·o·quent
gran·di·ose
grand·ma
grand mal
grand·moth·er
grand prix
grand-slam
grange
gran·ite
gran·ny
gra·no·la
grant·ee
grant-in-aid
gran·u·lar
gran·u·late
gran·u·la·tion
gran·ule
grape·vine
graph·eme
graph·ic
graph·i·cal user
   in·ter·face
graph·ics
graph·ite
gra·phol·o·gy
grap·ple
grasp·ing
grass·hop·per
grassy
grate·ful
grat·i·fi·ca·tion
grat·i·fy
grat·i·fy·ing
gra·tin
grat·ing
gra·tis
grat·i·tude
gra·tu·itous
gra·tu·ity
grave

grav·el
grav·el·ly
grav·er
Graves's dis·ease
grav·i·tate
grav·i·ta·tion
grav·i·ty
gra·vy
gray·ish
graz·ing
grease
greas·i·er
greasy
Great Dane
Gre·cian
greedy
green·er pas·tures
green·ery
green·ish
green·room
Green·wich time
greet·ing
gre·gar·i·ous
Gre·go·ri·an chant
grem·lin
gre·nade
gren·a·dier
gren·a·dine
Gresh·am's law
grey·hound
grid·dle
grid·lock
grief
griev·ance
grieve
griev·ous
grif·fin
grill*+
grille+
gri·mace
gri·mal·kin
grime

grimy

grinch

grind·er

grind·stone

grin·go

gripe

grippe

gris·ly[+]

grist

gris·tle

gris·tly[+]

grit·ty

griz·zled

griz·zly bear

groan·er

gro·cer

gro·cery

grog·gy

grom·met

groom

groove

groovy

grope

gross do·mes·tic
   prod·uct

gross·ly

gro·tesque

grot·to

grouchy

Ground·hog Day

grounds·keep·er

group·ing

grouse

grout

grov·el

growl·er

grown-up

growth

grub·by

grudge

grudg·ing

gru·el

gru·el·ing

grue·some

gruff

grum·ble

grumpy

grunge

Gru·yère

G-string

gua·ca·mo·le

gua·no

guar·an·tee[+]

guar·an·tor

guar·an·ty[+]

guard

guard·ed

guard·ian

gua·va

gu·ber·na·to·ri·al

guern·sey

guer·ril·la[+]

guess·ti·mate

guess·work

guf·faw

guid·ance

guid·ed mis·sile

guide·line

guild

guile

guile·less

guil·lo·tine

guilty

guin·ea

guin·ea hen

guise

gui·tar

gulch

Gulf War
   syn·drome

gul·let

gull·ible

gul·ly

gulp

gum·bo

gum·boil

gum·my

gump·tion

gung ho

gunk

gun·nery

gun·ny·sack

gun·wale

gup·py

gur·gle

gu·ru

gush·er

gushy

gus·set

gus·ta·to·ry

gus·to

gus·ty

gutsy

gut·ter

gut·ter·snipe

gut·tur·al

gut·tur·al·ly

gut-wrench·ing

guz·zle

gym·kha·na

gym·na·si·um

gym·nast

gym·nas·tic

gy·ne·col·o·gist

gy·ne·col·o·gy

gyp·sum

gyp·sy

gy·rate

gy·ra·tion

gyre

gy·ro·com·pass

gy·ro·scope

H

ha·ba·ne·ra

ha·be·as cor·pus

hab·er·dash·er
hab·er·dash·ery
hab·it
hab·it·able
hab·i·tat
hab·i·ta·tion
ha·bit·u·al
ha·bit·u·ate
ha·bi·tué
ha·ci·en·da
hack·ie
hack·les
hack·man
hack·ney
hack·neyed
hack·saw
hack·work
hack·y sack
had·dock
Ha·des
hag·gard
hag·gis
hag·gle
ha·gi·og·ra·phy
ha·gi·ol·o·gy
ha-ha
hai·ku
hail·stone
hail·storm
hair·breadth
hair·do
hair·dress·er
hair fol·li·cle
hair·less
hair·line
hair·piece
hair·pin
hair-rais·ing
hair·styl·ing
hair·styl·ist
hairy
hake

hal·cy·on
hale
half-baked
half-cocked
half-dol·lar
half-glas·ses
half·heart·ed
half-life
half-mast
half·pen·ny
half-pint
half-truth
half-wit
half-wit·ted
hal·i·but
hal·i·to·sis
hal·le·lu·jah
hall·mark
hal·low
hal·lowed
Hal·low·een
hal·lu·ci·nate
hal·lu·ci·na·tion
hal·lu·ci·na·to·ry
hal·lu·ci·no·gen
ha·lo
hal·ter
halt·ing
hal·vah
halve
halves
hal·yard
ham·burg·er
ham-fist·ed
ham-hand·ed
Ham·il·to·ni·an
ham·let
ham·mer
ham·mer-and=
    tongs
ham·mered
ham·mer·lock

ham·mi·er
ham·mock
ham·per
ham·ster
ham·string
hand·bag
hand·ball
hand·bill
hand·book
hand·clasp
hand·craft
hand·cuff
hand·ed·ness
hand-fed
hand·ful
hand·gun
hand·i·cap
hand·i·cap·per
hand·i·craft
hand·i·ly
hand·ker·chief
han·dle
han·dle·bars
han·dler
han·dling
hand·made
hand·maid·en
hand-me-down
hand-off
hand·out
hand·rail
hand·saw
hands·breadth
hands-down (adj)
hand·set
hand·shake
hands-off (adj)
hand·some+
hand·spike
hand·spring
hand·stand
hand-to-hand

hand-to-mouth
hand·wo·ven
hand·writ·ten
hand·writ·ing
hand·wrought
handy·man
han·gar⁺
hang·dog
hang·er⁺
hang·er-on
hang·ing
hang·man
hang·nail
hang·out
hang·over
hang·time
hang-up
han·ker
han·ker·ing
han·kie
han·ky-pan·ky
han·som⁺
han·ta·vi·rus
Ha·nuk·kah
hap
ha'·pen·ny
hap·haz·ard
hap·haz·ard·ly
hap·less
hap·pen
hap·pen·ing
hap·pen·stance
hap·pi·ly
hap·pi·ness
hap·py
hap·py camp·er
hap·py-go-lucky
hara-kiri
ha·rangue
ha·rangu·ing
ha·rass
har·bin·ger

har·bor
har·bor·age
hard-and-fast
hard·ball
hard-bit·ten
hard-boiled
hard·bound
hard-core (adj)
hard·cov·er
hard drive
hard-edge (adj)
hard·en
hard·en·ing
hard·fist·ed
hard·head·ed
hard·heart·ed
hard-hit·ting
har·di·ness
hard-line (adj)
hard·ly
hard·ness
hard-nosed
hard-of-hear·ing
hard-shell (adj)
hard·ship
hard·tack
hard·top
hard·ware
hard·wired
hard·work·ing
har·dy
hare·brained
Ha·re Krish·na
har·em
har·i·cot
ha·ri·jan
hari-kari
hark·en
har·le·quin
har·lot
har·lot·ry
harm·ful

harm·less
harm·less·ness
har·mon·ic
har·mon·i·ca
har·mon·ics
har·mo·ni·ous
har·mo·nize
har·ness
harp·ing
harp·ist
har·poon
harp·si·chord
har·py
har·ri·dan
har·ried
har·ri·er
har·row
har·ry
harsh
har·vest
har·vest·time
has-been
ha·sen·pfef·fer
hash·ish
hash mark
Ha·sid·ic
Ha·si·dim
hasn't
has·sle
has·sock
haste
has·ten
hast·i·ly
hasty
hat·band
hat·box
hatch
hatch·back
hat·check
hatch·ery
hatch·et
hatch·ing

hatch·way
hate crime
hate·ful
hatha yo·ga
hat·ing
ha·tred
hat·ter
haugh·ti·ness
haugh·ty
haul
haul·er
haunch
haunt
haute cou·ture
haute cui·sine
hau·teur
haut monde
ha·ven
have-not (n)
haven't
hav·er·sack
hav·ing
hav·oc
Ha·waii
Ha·wai·ian
hawk
hawk·er
hawk-eyed
haw·ser
haw·thorn
hay·cock
hay fe·ver
hay·fork
hay·loft
hay·mak·er
hay·rack
hay·rick
hay·ride
hay·stack
hay·wire
haz·ard
haz·ard·ous

haze
ha·zel
ha·zel·nut
haz·ing
hazy
head·ache
head·band
head·board
head·cheese
head·dress
head·ed
head·er
head·first
head·ing
head·lamp
head·land
head·less
head·light
head·line
head·lin·er
head·long
head·mas·ter
head·mis·tress
head-on
head·phone
head·piece
head·quar·ters
head·rest
head·room
head·set
head·stone
head·strong
head·wait·er
head·wa·ters
head·way
head wind
heady
heal·er
health
health·ful
health·i·er
health·i·ly

healthy
hear·ing
hear·ken
hear·say
hearse
heart·ache
heart at·tack
heart·break·ing
heart·bro·ken
heart·burn
heart·en
heart·felt
hearth
heart-healthy
hearth·stone
heart·i·ly
heart·land
heart·less
heart·rend·ing
heart·sick
heart·strings
heart·throb
heart-to-heart
heart·warm·ing
hearty
heat·er
heath
hea·then
heath·er
heat·stroke
heat wave
heave
heave-ho
heav·en·ly
heav·en-sent
heav·en·ward
heavi·ly
heavy-du·ty
heavy-hand·ed
heavy·weight
He·bra·ic
He·brew

heck·le

heck·ler

hect·are

hec·tic

hec·to·gram

hed·dle

hedge

hedge·hog

hedge·row

he·don·ist

he·do·nism

heed

heed·ful

heed·less

heel

heel·er

hefty

he·ge·mo·ny

he·gi·ra

heif·er

height

height·en

Heim·lich
   ma·neu·ver

hei·nous

heir

heir·ess

heir·loom

heist

he·li·a·cal

he·li·cal

he·li·cop·ter

he·lio·cen·tric

he·lio·graph

he·lio·trope

he·li·ot·ro·pism

he·li·pad

he·li·port

he·li·um

he·lix

he'll

hell-bent

Hel·len·ic

Hel·le·nism

Hel·le·nist

hel·le·nize

hell·fire

hell-for-leath·er

hel·lion

hell·ish

hel·lo

helm

hel·met

helms·man

hel·ot

help·er

help·ful

help·ing

help·less

help·mate

hel·ter-skel·ter

he·ma·tol·o·gist

he·ma·tol·o·gy

hemi·sphere

hem·line

hem·lock

he·mo·glo·bin

he·mo·phil·ia

he·mo·phil·i·ac

hem·or·rhage

hem·or·rhoids

he·mo·sta·sis

hence

hence·forth

hench·man

hen·na

hen·peck

hen·ry

hep·a·ti·tis

hep·ta·gon

her·ald

he·ral·dic

her·ald·ry

herb

her·ba·ceous

herb·age

herb·al

herb·al·ist

her·bar·i·um

her·bi·cide

her·biv·o·rous

Her·cu·le·an

herd·er

herds·man

here·abouts

here·af·ter

here and now

he·red·i·tary

he·red·i·ty

here·in

her·e·sy

her·e·tic

he·ret·i·cal

here·to·fore

here·up·on

here·with

her·i·tage

her·maph·ro·dite

her·me·neu·ti·cal

her·met·ic

her·met·i·cal·ly

her·mit

her·mit·age

her·nia

he·ro·ic

her·o·in[+]

her·o·ine[+]

her·o·ism

her·on

her·pes

her·pe·tol·o·gy

Herr

her·ring

her·ring·bone

her·ring gull

her·self

her·sto·ry
hertz
hes·i·tan·cy
hes·i·tant
hes·i·tate
hes·i·ta·tion
Hes·sian
het·ero·dox
het·ero·ge·ne·ity
het·ero·ge·neous
het·ero·sex·u·al
het·ero·sex·u·al·i·ty
heu·ris·tic
hew+
hexa·gon
hex·ag·o·nal
hex·am·e·ter
hey·day
hi·a·tus
hi·ba·chi
hi·ber·nate
Hi·ber·ni·an
hi·bis·cus
hic·cough*
hic·cup
hick·ey
hick·o·ry
hi·dal·go
hid·den
hide-and-seek
hide·away
hide·bound
hid·eous
hide·out
hie
hi·er·ar·chi·cal
hi·er·ar·chy
hi·er·at·ic
hi·ero·glyph
hi·ero·glyph·ic
hi·fi
high-and-mighty

high·ball
high·boy
high·brow
high chair
high-class
high·er-up
high·fa·lu·tin
high fi·del·i·ty
high fi·nance
high five
high-flown
high-fly·ing
high gear
high-grade
high-hand·ed
high·land
High·land fling
high-lev·el (adj)
high·light
high·ness
high-oc·tane
high-pitched
high-pow·ered
high-pres·sure
high-rise
high road
high-spir·it·ed
high-strung
high-ten·sion
high-test
high-toned
high·way·man
hi·jack
hike
hik·ing
hi·lar·i·ous
hi·lar·i·ty
hill·bil·ly
hill·ock
hill·side
hilly
Hi·ma·la·yan

him·self
hind
hin·der
Hin·di
hind·most
hind·quar·ter
hin·drance
hind·sight
Hin·du
hinge
hin·ter·land
hip-hop
hip·pie
Hip·po·crat·ic oath
hip·po·pot·a·mus
hire·ling
hir·ing
hir·sute
His·pan·ic
his·ta·mine
his·tol·o·gy
his·to·ri·an
his·tor·ic
his·tor·i·cal
his·to·ri·og·ra·phy
his·to·ry
his·tri·on·ic
hit-and-miss
hit-and-run
hitch
hitch·hike
hith·er
Hit·ler·ism
hit-or-miss
HIV
hive
hives
hoa·gie
hoard+
hoard·ing
hoar·frost
hoarse

hoars·en

hoary

hoax

hob·ble

hob·by

hob·by·horse

hob·gob·lin

hob·nail

hob·nob

ho·bo

Hob·son's choice

hock·ey

ho·cus-po·cus

hodge·podge

Hodg·kin's
   dis·ease

hoe·ing

ho·gan

hogs·head

hog-tie

hog·wash

hog wild

ho hum

hoi pol·loi

hoist

hoi·ty-toi·ty

hold·ing

hold·ing pat·tern

hold·out (n)

hold·over (n)

hold·up (n)

hol·ey[+]

hol·i·day

ho·li·er

ho·li·ness

ho·lis·tic

hol·lan·daise sauce

hol·ler

hol·low

hol·ly

hol·ly·hock

Hol·ly·wood

Ho·lo·caust

ho·lo·gram

ho·lo·graph

Hol·stein

hol·ster

ho·ly[+]

hom·age

hom·burg

home·body

home·bound

home·com·ing

home com·put·er

home eco·nom·ics

home·less

home·like

home·ly

home·made

home·mak·er

ho·meo·path·ic

ho·me·op·a·thy

ho·meo·sta·sis

home page

ho·mer

home school

home·spun

home·stead

home·stretch

home·work

hom·ey

ho·mi·cide

hom·ie*

hom·i·ly

hom·i·nid

hom·i·ny

ho·mo·ge·ne·ity

ho·mo·ge·neous

ho·mog·e·ni·za·tion

ho·mog·e·nize

ho·mog·e·nous

ho·mo·graph

ho·mol·o·gous

hom·onym

ho·mo·phobe

ho·mo·pho·bia

ho·mo·phone

Ho·mo sa·pi·ens

ho·mo·sex·u·al

ho·mo·sex·u·al·i·ty

hone

hon·est

hon·es·ty

hon·ey

hon·ey·comb

hon·ey·dew

hon·ey·moon

hon·ey·suck·le

hon·ky-tonk

hon·or·able

hon·o·rar·i·um

hon·or·ary

hooch

hood·lum

hoo·doo

hood·wink

hoof·er

hoof·print

hoo·kah

hooked

hook·er

hooky

hoo·li·gan

hoose·gow

Hoo·sier

hoo·te·nan·ny

hope·ful

hope·ful·ly

hope·less

Ho·pi

hop·ing

hop·per

hop·ping

hop·scotch

ho·ra

horde[+]

ho·ri·zon
hor·i·zon·tal
hor·mone
hor·net
horn·pipe
horny
horo·scope
hor·ren·dous
hor·ri·ble
hor·rid
hor·rif·ic
hor·ri·fy
hor·ror
hor·ror-struck
hors de com·bat
hors d'oeuvre
horse-and-bug·gy
horse·back
horse·fly
horse·man
horse·pow·er
horse race
horse·rad·ish
horse·wom·an
hor·ta·to·ry
hor·ti·cul·tur·al
hor·ti·cul·ture
ho·san·na
ho·siery
hos·pice
hos·pi·ta·ble
hos·pi·ta·bly
hos·pi·tal
hos·pi·tal·i·ty
hos·pi·tal·ize
hos·tage
hos·tel+
hos·tel·ry
host·ess
hos·tile+
hos·til·i·ty
hos·tler

hot·cake
hot·dog
ho·te·lier
hot flash·es
hot·foot
hot·head
hot·head·ed
hot·ly
hot·shot
hound
hour·glass
hour·ly
house·break
house·bro·ken
house·hold
house·hus·band
house·keep·er
house·keep·ing
house·wares
house·warm·ing
house·wife
house·work
hous·ing
hov·el
hov·er
how·ev·er
how·it·zer
howl
howl·ing
how·so·ev·er
hua·ra·che
hub·bub
hub·cap
hu·bris
huck·le·ber·ry
huck·ster
hud·dle
hue+
huge
Hu·gue·not
Hui·chol
hu·la

hul·la·ba·loo
hu·man
hu·man cho·ri·on·ic
  go·nad·o·tro·pin
hu·mane
hu·man im·mu·no·
  de·fi·cien·cy
  vi·rus
hu·man·ism
hu·man·i·tar·i·an
hu·man·i·tar·i·
  an·ism
hu·man·i·ty
hu·man·ize
hu·man·ly
hum·ble
hum·bug
hum·drum
hu·mer·us+
hu·mid
hu·mid·i·fi·er
hu·mid·i·fy
hu·mid·i·stat
hu·mid·i·ty
hu·mi·dor
hu·mil·i·ate
hu·mil·i·at·ing
hu·mil·i·ty
hum·ming·bird
hum·mock
hum·mus
hu·mor·esque
hu·mor·ist
hu·mor·less
hu·mor·ous+
hump·back
humped
hu·mus
hunch
hun·dred
hun·ger
hun·gry

hunt·er
hunt·ing
hunt·ress
hunts·man
hur·dle
hur·dy-gur·dy
hurl·ing
hur·rah
hur·ri·cane
hur·ried
hur·ry
hurt·ful
hur·tle
hus·band
hus·band·ry
hush-pup·py
husky
hus·sar
hus·sy
hus·tle
hutch
hy·a·cinth
hy·brid
hy·brid·ize
hy·dran·gea
hy·drant
hy·drate
hy·drau·lic
hy·drau·lics
hy·dro·chlo·ric
    acid
hy·dro·elec·tric
hy·dro·fluo·ro·
    car·bon
hy·dro·foil
hy·dro·gen
hy·dro·ge·nate
hy·drol·o·gy
hy·drom·e·ter
hy·dro·pho·bia
hy·dro·plane
hy·dro·pon·ics

hy·dro·stat·ics
hy·drox·ide
hy·e·na
hy·giene
hy·gien·ics
hy·men
hymn
hym·nal
hype
hy·per·ac·tive
hy·per·bar·ic
hy·per·bo·la
hy·per·bo·le
hy·per·bol·ic
hy·per·crit·i·cal
hy·per·ki·net·ic
hy·per·link
hy·per·son·ic
hy·per·space
hy·per·ten·sion
hy·per·text mark·up
    lan·guage
hy·per·text trans·fer
    pro·to·col
hy·per·thy·roid·ism
hy·phen
hy·phen·ate
hy·phen·at·ed
hyp·no·sis
hyp·not·ic
hyp·no·tism
hyp·no·tize
hy·po·chon·dria
hy·po·chon·dri·ac
hy·poc·ri·sy
hyp·o·crite
hyp·o·crit·i·cal
hy·po·der·mic
hy·po·gly·ce·mia
hy·pos·ta·sis
hy·po·ten·sion
hy·pot·e·nuse

hy·po·thal·a·mus
hy·poth·e·sis
hy·poth·e·size
hy·po·thet·i·cal
hy·po·thy·roid
hy·po·thy·roid·ism
hy·po·ton·ic
hys·sop
hys·ter·ec·to·my
hys·te·ria
hys·ter·i·cal
hys·ter·ics

I

iamb
Ibe·ri·an
ibex
ibis
ibu·pro·fen
ICBM
ice age
ice·berg
ice·bound
ice-cold
ice cream (n)
iced
ice-skate (v)
ich·thy·ol·o·gy
ici·cle
ic·ing
icon
icon·o·clast
icon·o·clas·tic
ico·nog·ra·pher
ico·nog·ra·phy
ic·tus
icy
ID card
idea
ide·al
ide·al·ism
ide·al·ist

ide·al·is·tic
ide·al·ize
ide·al·ly
ide·a·tion
iden·ti·cal
iden·ti·fi·ca·tion
iden·ti·fi·er
iden·ti·fy
iden·ti·ty theft
ideo·gram
ideo·log·i·cal
ide·ol·o·gy
id·i·o·cy
id·io·graph·ic
id·i·om
id·i·om·at·ic
id·i·o·syn·cra·sy
id·i·o·syn·crat·ic
id·i·ot
id·i·ot·ic
id·i·ot·proof
idle⁺
idol⁺
idol·a·ter
idol·a·trous
idol·a·try
idol·ize
idyll⁺
idyl·lic
ig·loo
ig·ne·ous
ig·nis fat·u·us
ig·nit·able
ig·nite
ig·ni·tion
ig·no·ble
ig·no·min·i·ous
ig·no·mi·ny
ig·no·ra·mus
ig·no·rance
ig·no·rant
ig·nore

igua·na
ike·ba·na
il·e·um⁺
ilex
Il·i·ad
il·i·um⁺
ilk
ill-ad·vised
ill-bred
il·le·gal
il·leg·i·ble
il·le·git·i·ma·cy
il·le·git·i·mate
ill-fat·ed
ill-fa·vored
ill-got·ten
ill-hu·mored
il·lib·er·al
il·lib·er·al·ly
il·lic·it
il·lit·er·a·cy
il·lit·er·ate
ill-man·nered
ill-na·tured
ill·ness
il·log·ic
il·log·i·cal
ill-sort·ed
ill-tem·pered
ill-treat
il·lu·mi·nate
il·lu·mi·na·tion
il·lu·mine
ill-us·age
ill-use
il·lu·sion
il·lu·sive
il·lu·so·ry
il·lus·trate
il·lus·tra·tion
il·lus·tri·ous
im·age

im·ag·ery
imag·in·able
imag·i·nary
imag·i·na·tion
imag·i·na·tive
imag·ine
im·ag·ing
im·ag·ism
Imam
im·bal·ance
im·be·cile
im·bibe
im·bri·cate
im·bro·glio
im·brue
im·bue
im·i·tate
im·i·ta·tion
im·i·ta·tive
im·mac·u·late
im·ma·nence⁺
im·ma·nent⁺
im·ma·te·ri·al
im·ma·ture
im·mea·sur·able
im·me·di·a·cy
im·me·di·ate
im·me·di·ate·ly
im·me·mo·ri·al
im·mense
im·men·si·ty
im·merge
im·merse
im·mers·ible
im·mer·sion
im·mi·grant
im·mi·grate
im·mi·nence⁺
im·mi·nent⁺
im·mo·bile
im·mo·bil·i·ty
im·mo·bi·lize

im·mod·er·ate
im·mod·est
im·mo·late
im·mor·al
im·mo·ral·i·ty
im·mor·tal
im·mor·tal·i·ty
im·mor·tal·ize
im·mov·able
im·mune
im·mu·ni·ty
im·mu·nize
im·mu·no·de·fi·
    cien·cy
im·mure
im·mu·ta·ble
im·pact
im·pac·tion
im·pair
im·pale
im·pal·pa·ble
im·pan·el
im·part
im·par·tial
im·pass·able+
im·passe
im·pas·si·ble*+
im·pas·sioned
im·pas·sive
im·pa·tience
im·pa·tient
im·peach
im·pec·ca·ble
im·pe·cu·nious
im·ped·ance
im·pede
im·ped·i·ment
im·pel
im·pend·ing
im·pen·e·tra·bil·
    i·ty
im·pen·e·tra·ble

im·pen·i·tent
im·per·a·tive
im·per·cep·ti·ble
im·per·fect
im·per·fec·tion
im·pe·ri·al
im·pe·ri·al·ism
im·per·il
im·pe·ri·ous
im·per·ish·able
im·per·ma·nence
im·per·me·able
im·per·mis·si·ble
im·per·son·al
im·per·son·ate
im·per·ti·nence
im·per·ti·nent
im·per·turb·able
im·per·turb·abil·i·ty
im·per·vi·ous
im·pe·ti·go
im·pet·u·os·i·ty
im·pet·u·ous
im·pe·tus
im·pi·ety
im·pinge
im·pi·ous
imp·ish
im·pla·ca·ble
im·plant
im·plau·si·ble
im·ple·ment
im·pli·cate
im·pli·ca·tion
im·plic·it
im·plore
im·plo·sion
im·ply
im·po·lite
im·pol·i·tic
im·pon·der·a·ble
im·port

im·por·tance
im·por·tant
im·por·ta·tion
im·por·tu·nate
im·por·tune
im·pose
im·pos·ing
im·po·si·tion
im·pos·si·bil·i·ty
im·pos·si·ble
im·pos·tor
im·pos·ture
im·po·tence
im·po·tent
im·pound
im·pov·er·ish
im·pov·er·ished
im·prac·ti·ca·ble
im·prac·ti·cal
im·pre·ca·tion
im·pre·cise
im·preg·na·ble
im·preg·nate
im·pre·sa·rio
im·press
im·pres·sion
im·pres·sion·able
im·pres·sion·ist
im·pres·sion·is·tic
im·pres·sive
im·pri·ma·tur
im·print
im·pris·on
im·prob·a·bil·i·ty
im·prob·a·ble
im·promp·tu
im·prop·er
im·pro·pri·ety
im·prove
im·prove·ment
im·prov·i·dent
im·pro·vi·sa·tion

im·pro·vise
im·pru·dence
im·pru·dent
im·pu·dence
im·pu·dent
im·pugn
im·pulse
im·pul·sive
im·pu·ni·ty
im·pu·ri·ty
im·pu·ta·tion
im·pute
in·abil·i·ty
in ab·sen·tia
in·ac·ces·si·ble
in·ac·cu·ra·cy
in·ac·tion
in·ac·ti·vate
in·ac·tive
in·ad·e·qua·cy
in·ad·e·quate
in·ad·mis·si·ble
in·ad·ver·tence
in·ad·ver·tent
in·ad·ver·tent·ly
in·ad·vis·able
in·alien·able
in·al·ter·able
in·amo·ra·ta
inane
in·an·i·mate
in·a·ni·tion
inan·i·ty
in·ap·pli·ca·ble
in·ap·po·site
in·ap·proach·able
in·ap·pro·pri·ate
in·apt
in·ap·ti·tude
in·ar·tic·u·late
in·as·much as
in·at·ten·tion

in·at·ten·tive
in·au·di·ble
in·au·gu·ral
in·au·gu·rate
in·au·gu·ra·tion
in·aus·pi·cious
in·au·then·tic
in·be·tween
in·bounds
in·bred
in·breed·ing
In·ca
in·cal·cu·la·ble
in·can·des·cence
in·can·des·cent
in·can·ta·tion
in·ca·pa·ble
in·ca·pac·i·tate
in·ca·pac·i·ty
in·car·cer·ate
in·car·na·dine
in·car·nate
in·car·na·tion
in·cau·tious
in·cen·di·ary
in·cense
in·cen·tive
in·cep·tion
in·ces·sant
in·cest
in·ces·tu·ous
in·cho·ate
inch·worm
in·ci·dence
in·ci·dent
in·ci·den·tal
in·ci·den·tal·ly
in·cin·er·ate
in·cin·er·a·tor
in·cip·i·ence
in·cip·i·ent
in·cise

in·ci·sion
in·ci·sive
in·ci·sor
in·cite
in·ci·vil·i·ty
in·clem·en·cy
in·clem·ent
in·cli·na·tion
in·cline
in·clin·ing
in·close
in·clude
in·clu·sion
in·clu·sive
in·cog·ni·to
in·co·her·ence
in·co·her·ent
in·com·bus·ti·ble
in·come
in·com·ing
in·com·men·su·
rate
in·com·mo·di·ous
in·com·mu·ni·ca·
ble
in·com·mu·ni·ca·do
in·com·pa·ra·ble
in·com·pat·i·bil·i·ty
in·com·pat·i·ble
in·com·pe·tence
in·com·pe·ten·cy
in·com·pe·tent
in·com·plete
in·com·pre·hen·
si·ble
in·com·pre·hen·
sion
in·con·ceiv·able
in·con·clu·sive
in·con·gru·ence
in·con·gru·i·ty
in·con·gru·ous

in·con·se·quen·tial
in·con·sid·er·able
in·con·sid·er·ate
in·con·sis·ten·cy
in·con·sis·tent
in·con·sol·able
in·con·spic·u·ous
in·con·stan·cy
in·con·stant
in·con·test·able
in·con·ti·nence
in·con·ti·nent
in·con·tro·vert·ible
in·con·ve·nience
in·con·ve·nient
in·con·vert·ible
in·con·vinc·ible
in·co·or·di·nate
in·co·or·di·na·tion
in·cor·po·rate
in·cor·po·rat·ed
in·cor·po·re·al
in·cor·rect
in·cor·ri·gi·ble
in·cor·rupt·ible
in·creas·ing·ly
in·cred·i·ble
in·cre·du·li·ty
in·cred·u·lous
in·cre·ment
in·cre·men·tal·ism
in·crim·i·nate
in·crus·ta·tion
in·cu·bate
in·cu·ba·tion
in·cu·ba·tor
in·cu·bus
in·cul·cate
in·cum·ben·cy
in·cum·bent
in·cur
in·cur·able

in·curred
in·cur·sion
in·debt·ed
in·debt·ed·ness
in·de·cen·cy
in·de·cent
in·de·ci·pher·able
in·de·ci·sion
in·de·ci·sive
in·de·co·rous
in·de·fat·i·ga·ble
in·de·fen·si·ble
in·de·fin·able
in·def·i·nite
in·del·i·ble
in·del·i·ca·cy
in·del·i·cate
in·dem·ni·fy
in·dem·ni·ty
in·dent
in·den·ta·tion
in·den·ture
in·de·pen·dence
in·de·pen·dent
in·depth
in·de·scrib·able
in·de·struc·ti·ble
in·de·ter·min·able
in·de·ter·mi·nate
in·dex
in·di·cate
in·di·ca·tion
in·dic·a·tive
in·di·ca·tor
in·dict
in·dict·able
in·dict·ment
in·dif·fer·ence
in·dif·fer·ent
in·di·gence
in·dig·e·nous
in·di·gent

in·di·gest·ible
in·di·ges·tion
in·dig·nant
in·dig·na·tion
in·dig·ni·ty
in·di·go
in·di·rect
in·di·rec·tion
in·dis·cern·ible
in·dis·creet
in·dis·cre·tion
in·dis·crim·i·nate
in·dis·pens·able
in·dis·pose
in·dis·po·si·tion
in·dis·put·able
in·dis·sol·u·ble
in·dis·tinct
in·dis·tin·guish·
    able
in·di·vid·u·al
    re·tire·ment
    ac·count
in·di·vid·u·al·ism
in·di·vid·u·al·i·ty
in·di·vid·u·al·ize
in·di·vid·u·ate
in·di·vid·u·a·tion
in·di·vis·i·ble
in·doc·tri·nate
in·do·lence
in·do·lent
in·dom·i·ta·ble
in·dorse*
in·du·bi·ta·ble
in·du·bi·ta·bly
in·duce
in·duce·ment
in·duct
in·duct·ee
in·duc·tion
in·duc·tive

in·dulge
in·dul·gence
in·dul·gent
in·dult
in·du·rate
in·dus·tri·al
in·dus·tri·al·ism
in·dus·tri·al·ist
in·dus·tri·al·ize
in·dus·tri·al=
   strength
in·dus·tri·ous
in·dus·try
in·dwell
in·dwell·ing
in·ebri·ate
in·ed·u·ca·ble
in·ef·fa·ble
in·ef·fec·tive
in·ef·fec·tu·al
in·ef·fi·ca·cious
in·ef·fi·ca·cy
in·ef·fi·cien·cy
in·ef·fi·cient
in·elas·tic
in·el·i·gi·ble
in·eluc·ta·ble
in·ept
in·equal·i·ty
in·eq·ui·ta·ble
in·eq·ui·ty
in·erad·i·ca·ble
in·ert
in·er·tia
in·es·cap·able
in·es·sen·tial
in·es·ti·ma·ble
in·ev·i·ta·bil·i·ty
in·ev·i·ta·ble
in·ev·i·ta·bly
in·ex·act
in·ex·cus·able

in·ex·haust·ible
in·ex·o·ra·ble
in·ex·pe·di·en·cy
in·ex·pe·di·ent
in·ex·pen·sive
in·ex·pe·ri·ence
in·ex·pert
in·ex·pi·a·ble
in·ex·pli·ca·ble
in·ex·press·ible
in·ex·tin·guish·able
in ex·tre·mis
in·ex·tri·ca·ble
in·fal·li·ble
in·fa·mous
in·fa·my
in·fan·cy
in·fan·ti·cide
in·fan·tile
in·fan·til·ism
in·fan·try
in·farct
in·fat·u·ate
in·fea·si·ble
in·fec·tion
in·fec·tious
in·fe·lic·i·tous
in·fe·lic·i·ty
in·fer
in·fer·ence
in·fe·ri·or
in·fer·nal
in·fer·no
in·fer·tile
in·fes·ta·tion
in·fi·del
in·fi·del·i·ty
in·fight·ing
in·fil·trate
in·fi·nite
in·fin·i·tes·i·mal
in·fin·i·tive

in·fin·i·tude
in·fin·i·ty
in·fir·ma·ry
in·fir·mi·ty
in fla·gran·te
   de·lic·to
in·flame
in·flam·ma·ble
in·flam·ma·tion
in·flam·ma·to·ry
   bow·el
   dis·ease
in·flat·able
in·flat·ed
in·fla·tion
in·fla·tion·ary
in·flect
in·flec·tion
in·flex·i·ble
in·flict
in·flu·ence
in·flu·en·tial
in·flu·en·za
in·flux
in·fo·mer·cial
in·form
in·for·mal
in·for·mant
in·for·ma·tion
   su·per high·way
in·for·ma·tive
in·form·er
in·frac·tion
in·fra dig
in·fra·red
in·fra·struc·ture
in·fre·quen·cy
in·fre·quent
in·fringe
in·fringe·ment
in·fu·ri·ate
in·fuse

in·fu·sion
in·ge·nious
in·ge·nue
in·ge·nu·ity
in·gen·u·ous
in·gest
in·glo·ri·ous
in·got
in·grained
in·grate
in·gra·ti·ate
in·gra·ti·at·ing
in·grat·i·tude
in·gre·di·ent
in·gress
in-group (n)
in·grown
in·hab·it
in·hab·it·ant
in·ha·la·tion
in·ha·la·tor
in·hal·er
in·har·mo·ni·ous
in·her·ent
in·her·it
in·her·i·tance
in·her·it·or
in·hib·it
in·hi·bi·tion
in·hib·i·tor
in·hos·pi·ta·ble
in-house
in·hu·man
in·hu·mane
in·hu·man·i·ty
in·im·i·cal
in·im·i·ta·ble
in·iq·ui·tous
in·iq·ui·ty
ini·tial
ini·tial·ize
ini·tiate

ini·ti·a·tion
ini·tia·tive
in·ject
in·jec·tion
in·ju·di·cious
in·junc·tion
in·jure
in·ju·ri·ous
in·ju·ry
in·jus·tice
ink-jet (adj)
in·kling
in·laid
in-law (n)
in·lay
in·let
in-line skate
in lo·co·pa·ren·tis
in·mate
in me·di·as res
in me·mo·ri·am
in-mi·gra·tion
in·most
in·nards
in·nate
in·ner
in·ner·vate+
in·ning
in·no·cence
in·no·cent
in·noc·u·ous
in·no·vate
in·no·va·tion
in·no·va·tive
in·nu·en·do
in·nu·mer·a·ble
in·oc·u·late
in·oc·u·la·tion
in·of·fen·sive
in·op·er·a·ble
in·op·er·a·tive
in·op·por·tune

in·or·di·nate
in·or·gan·ic
in·pa·tient
in per·so·nam
in·put
in·quest
in·qui·etude
in·quire
in·qui·ry
in·qui·si·tion
in·quis·i·tive
in·quis·i·tor
in rem
in·roads
in·sane
in·san·i·tary
in·san·i·ty
in·sa·tia·ble
in·scribe
in·scrip·tion
in·scru·ta·ble
in·sect
in·sec·ti·cide
in·sec·ti·vore
in·se·cure
in·sem·i·nate
in·sen·sate
in·sen·si·ble
in·sen·si·tive
in·sep·a·ra·ble
in·sert
in·ser·tion
in·ser·vice
in·set
in·sid·er
in·sid·i·ous
in·sight·ful
in·sig·nia
in·sig·nif·i·cance
in·sig·nif·i·cant
in·sin·cere
in·sin·u·ate

in·sin·u·at·ing
in·sin·u·a·tion
in·sip·id
in·si·pid·i·ty
in·sis·tence
in·sis·tent
in si·tu
in·so·bri·ety
in·so·far
in·so·lence
in·so·lent
in·sol·u·ble
in·solv·able
in·sol·ven·cy
in·sol·vent
in·som·nia
in·sou·ci·ance
in·sou·ci·ant
in·spect
in·spec·tion
in·spec·tor
in·spi·ra·tion
in·spire
in·spir·ing
in·sta·bil·i·ty
in·sta·ble
in·stall
in·stal·la·tion
in·stall·ment
in·stance
in·stant
in·stan·ta·neous
in·stead
in·sti·gate
in·still
in·stinct
in·stinc·tive
in·sti·tute
in·sti·tu·tion
in·sti·tu·tion·al·ism
in·sti·tu·tion·al·ize
in·struct

in·struc·tion
in·struc·tive
in·struc·tor
in·stru·ment
in·stru·men·tal·ist
in·stru·men·tal·i·ty
in·stru·men·ta·tion
in·sub·or·di·nate
in·sub·stan·tial
in·suf·fer·able
in·suf·fi·cien·cy
in·suf·fi·cient
in·su·lar
in·su·lar·i·ty
in·su·late
in·su·la·tion
in·su·la·tor
in·su·lin
in·sult
in·su·per·a·ble
in·sup·port·able
in·sur·able
in·sur·ance
in·sure
in·sur·gence
in·sur·gen·cy
in·sur·gent
in·sur·mount·able
in·sur·rec·tion
in·tact
in·ta·glio
in·tan·gi·ble
in·te·ger
in·te·gral
in·te·grate
in·te·gra·tion
in·teg·ri·ty
in·teg·u·ment
in·tel·lect
in·tel·lec·tu·al
in·tel·lec·tu·al·ize
in·tel·li·gence

in·tel·li·gent
in·tel·li·gent·sia
in·tel·li·gi·ble
in·tem·per·ance
in·tem·per·ate
in·tend·ed
in·tense
in·ten·si·fi·er
in·ten·si·fy
in·ten·si·ty
in·ten·tion
in·ter
in·ter·ac·tion
in·ter ali·a
in·ter·cede
in·ter·cel·lu·lar
in·ter·cept
in·ter·cep·tion
in·ter·cep·tor
in·ter·ces·sion
in·ter·change
in·ter·change·able
in·ter·col·le·giate
in·ter·com·mu·ni·
cate
in·ter·con·nect
in·ter·con·ti·nen·
tal
in·ter·cos·tal
in·ter·course
in·ter·cul·tur·al
in·ter·de·nom·i·na·
tion·al
in·ter·de·part·men·
tal
in·ter·de·pen·dence
in·ter·de·pen·dent
in·ter·dict
in·ter·dis·ci·plin·ary
in·ter·est
in·ter·est·ing
in·ter·face

in·ter·faith
in·ter·fere
in·ter·fer·ence
in·ter·fer·on
in·ter·im
in·te·ri·or
in·ter·ject
in·ter·jec·tion
in·ter·jec·tor
in·ter·lard
in·ter·li·brary
in·ter·lin·ear
in·ter·loc·u·to·ry
in·ter·lop·er
in·ter·lude
in·ter·me·di·ary
in·ter·me·di·ate
in·ter·ment
in·ter·mez·zo
in·ter·mi·na·ble
in·ter·min·gle
in·ter·mis·sion
in·ter·mit·tent
in·tern
in·ter·nal
in·ter·nal·ize
in·ter·na·tion·al
in·ter·ne·cine
In·ter·net
in·ter·nist
in·tern·ment
in·ter·nu·cle·ar
in·ter·of·fice
in·ter·pel·late
in·ter·pen·e·trate
in·ter·po·late
in·ter·pose
in·ter·po·si·tion
in·ter·pret
in·ter·pre·ta·tion
in·ter·pre·ta·tive
in·ter·pret·er

in·ter·ra·cial
in·ter·re·late
in·ter·re·li·gious
in·ter·ro·gate
in·ter·rog·a·tive
in·ter·ro·ga·tor
in·ter·rupt
in·ter·rupt·er
in·ter·scho·las·tic
in·ter·sect
in·ter·sec·tion
in·ter·ses·sion
in·ter·sperse
in·ter·stel·lar
in·ter·stic·es
in·ter·sti·tial
in·ter·twine
in·ter·val
in·ter·vene
in·ter·ven·tion·ism
in·ter·view
in·ter·view·ee
in·ter·weave
in·tes·tate
in·tes·ti·nal
in·tes·tine
in·ti·ma·cy
in·ti·mate
in·tim·i·date
in·tim·i·da·tion
in·tinc·tion
in·tol·er·a·ble
in·tol·er·ance
in·tol·er·ant
in·to·na·tion
in·tone
in to·to
in·tox·i·cate
in·tox·i·ca·tion
in·trac·ta·ble
in·tra·mu·ral
in·tra·net

in·tran·si·gence
in·tran·si·gent
in·tran·si·tive
in·tra·state
in·tra·uter·ine
in·tra·ve·nous
in·tra·zon·al
in·trep·id
in·tri·ca·cy
in·tri·cate
in·trigue
in·trigu·ing
in·trin·sic
in·trin·si·cal·ly
in·tro·duce
in·tro·duc·tion
in·tro·duc·to·ry
in·troit
in·tro·ject
in·tro·spect
in·tro·spec·tion
in·tro·spec·tive
in·tro·ver·sion
in·tro·vert
in·trude
in·tru·sion
in·tru·sive
in·tub·a·tion
in·tu·it
in·tu·i·tion
in·tu·i·tive
in·tu·mes·cence
In·u·it
in·un·date
in·ure
in utero
in·vade
in·val·id
in·val·i·date
in·valu·able
in·vari·able
in·vari·ant

in·va·sion
in·vec·tive
in·veigh
in·vei·gle
in·vent
in·ven·tion
in·ven·tive
in·ven·to·ry
in·verse
in·ver·sion
in·vert
in·ver·te·brate
in·vest
in·ves·ti·gate
in·ves·ti·ture
in·vest·ment
in·vet·er·ate
in·vi·a·ble
in·vid·i·ous
in·vig·o·rate
in·vin·ci·ble
in·vi·o·la·bil·i·ty
in·vi·o·la·ble
in·vi·o·late
in·vis·i·bil·i·ty
in·vis·i·ble
in·vi·ta·tion
in·vite
in·vit·ing
in vi·tro
in vi·vo
in·vo·ca·tion
in·voice
in·voke
in·vol·un·tary
in·vo·lute
in·vo·lu·tion
in·volve
in·volve·ment
in·vul·ner·a·ble
in·ward·ly
io·dine

ion·ize
ion·o·sphere
io·ta
ip·so fac·to
Irani
Ira·ni·an
Ira·qi
iras·ci·bil·i·ty
iras·ci·ble
irate
ire·nic
ir·i·des·cence
ir·i·des·cent
iris
irk·some
iron
iron·clad
iron·ic
iron·ic·al
iron·ing
iron out
iro·ny
Ir·o·quois
ir·ra·di·ate
ir·ra·di·a·tion
ir·rad·i·ca·ble
ir·ra·tio·nal
ir·re·claim·able
ir·rec·on·cil·able
ir·re·cov·er·able
ir·re·deem·able
ir·re·duc·ible
ir·re·form·able
ir·re·fut·able
ir·reg·u·lar
ir·reg·u·lar·i·ty
ir·rel·e·vance
ir·rel·e·van·cy
ir·rel·e·vant
ir·re·li·gious
ir·re·me·di·a·ble
ir·re·mov·able

ir·rep·a·ra·ble
ir·re·place·able
ir·re·press·ible
ir·re·proach·able
ir·re·sist·ible
ir·res·o·lute
ir·re·solv·able
ir·re·spec·tive of
ir·re·spon·si·bil·i·ty
ir·re·spon·si·ble
ir·re·spon·sive
ir·re·triev·able
ir·rev·er·ence
ir·rev·er·ent
ir·re·vers·ible
ir·rev·o·ca·ble
ir·ri·gate
ir·ri·ta·bil·i·ty
ir·ri·ta·ble
ir·ri·tant
ir·ri·tate
ir·ri·ta·tion
ir·rupt[+]
ISBN
isin·glass
Is·lam
is·land
isle[+]
isn't
iso·bar
iso·la·ble
iso·late
iso·la·tion
iso·la·tion·ism
iso·mer
iso·met·ric
iso·met·rics
isos·ce·les tri·an·gle
iso·therm
iso·tope
Is·ra·el
Is·rae·li

Is·ra·el·ite
is·su·ance
is·sue
isth·mus
Ital·ian
ital·ic
ital·i·cize
itch
item
item·i·za·tion
item·ize
it·er·ate
itin·er·ant
itin·er·ary
its
it's
it·self
I've
ivied
ivo·ry
ivy
Ivy League

J
jab·ber
jab·ber·wocky
jack·al
jack·a·napes
jack·ass
jack·daw
jack·et
jack·ham·mer
jack-in-the-box
jack-in-the-pul·pit
jack·knife
jack-of-all-trades
jack-o'-lan·tern
jack·pot
jack·rab·bit
Jack·so·ni·an
Jac·o·be·an
jac·quard

Ja·cuz·zi™
jad·ed
jag·ged
jag·uar
jai alai
jail·bait
jail·bird
jail·break
jail·er
Jain·ism
ja·la·pe·ño
ja·lopy
jam⁺
jamb⁺
jam·ba·laya
jam·bo·ree
jammed
jam·ming
jam ses·sion
Jane Doe
jan·gle
jan·gling
jan·i·tor
Jan·u·ary
Jap·a·nese
jape
jar·gon
jas·mine
jas·per
jaun·dice
jaun·diced
jaunt
jaun·ty
ja·va⁺
Java™⁺
jav·e·lin
jaw·break·er
jay
jay·bird
jay·gee
jay·vee
jay·walk

jazz
jazzy
jeal·ous
jeal·ou·sy
jeans
jeep
jeer
Je·ho·vah
je·june
jel·lied
jel·lies
jel·ly
jel·ly·fish
jen·net
jen·ny
jeop·ar·dize
jeop·ar·dy
jer·e·mi·ad
jerk·i·ly
jer·kin
jerky
jer·ry-built
jer·sey
jest
jest·er
Je·su·it
jet
je·té
jet lag
jet-pro·pelled
jet pro·pul·sion
jet·sam
jet stream
jet·ted
jet·ting
jet·ti·son
jet·ty
jew·el⁺
jew·el·er
jew·el·ry
jib
jibe*⁺

jig

jig·ger

jig·ging

jig·gle

jig·gly

jig·saw

jilt

jim crow

jim·my

jin·gle

jin·go·ism

jinx

jit·ney

jit·ter

jit·ter·bug

jit·tery

jiu·jit·su*

jive

job

job·ber

job·bery

jock·ey

jock·strap

jo·cose

joc·u·lar

jo·cund

jodh·purs

jog·ger

jog·gle

John Doe

John Han·cock

john·ny

john·ny·cake

John·ny-on-the=
    spot

joie de vi·vre

join·der

join·er

join·ery

join·ing

joint

join·ture

joist

jo·jo·ba

joke

jok·ing

jol·li·fi·ca·tion

jol·ly

Jol·ly Rog·er

jon·quil

josh

joss

jos·tle

jot

jot·ting

joule+

jounce

jour·nal

jour·nal·ism

jour·nal·ist

jour·nal·is·tic

jour·ney

jour·ney·man

joust

jo·vial

jowl

joy·ful

joy·ous

joy·ride

joy·stick

JPEG

ju·bi·lant

ju·bi·la·te Deo

ju·bi·la·tion

ju·bi·lee

Ju·da·ic

Ju·da·ica

Ju·da·ism

Ju·deo-Chris·tian

judge

judg·ment

ju·di·ca·ture

ju·di·cial

ju·di·cia·ry

ju·di·cious

ju·do

jug·ful

jug·ger·naut

jug·gle

jug·gler+

jug·u·lar+

juice

juic·er

juicy

ju·jit·su

ju·jube

juke·box

ju·lep

ju·li·enne

jum·ble

jum·bo

jump·er

jump·er's knee

jump-start

jump·suit

jumpy

junc·tion

junc·ture

Jung·ian

jun·gle

jun·gle gym

ju·nior

ju·nior col·lege

ju·nior high school

ju·nior miss

ju·nior var·si·ty

ju·ni·per

junk

jun·ket

junk·ie

junk mail

junk·yard

jun·ta

Ju·ras·sic

ju·rid·i·cal

ju·ris·dic·tion

ju·ris·pru·dence
ju·rist
ju·ror
ju·ry
ju·ry-rig
jus·sive
jus·tice
jus·ti·fi·able
jus·ti·fi·ca·tion
jus·ti·fy
jute
ju·ve·nile
ju·ve·nile de·lin·quen·cy
ju·ve·nil·ia
jux·ta·pose
jux·ta·po·si·tion

K
ka·bob
Ka·bu·ki
ka·chi·na
kad·dish
kaf·fee·klatsch
kaf·tan
ka·hu·na
kale
ka·lei·do·scope
ka·mi·ka·ze
kan·ga·roo
ka·pell·mei·ster
ka·pok
kap·pa
kar·a·bi·ner*
kar·a·o·ke
kar·at⁺
ka·ra·te
kar·ma
ka·ty·did
kay·ak
kayo
ka·zil·lion

ka·zoo
keel
keel·haul
keen
keen·ness
keep·ing
keep·sake
ke·fir
Ke·gel ex·er·cis·es
kelp
ken·do
ken·nel
ke·no
Ke·ogh plan
ker·a·to·sis
ker·chief
ker·nel
ker·o·sene
ke·ryg·ma
ketch
ketch·up
ket·tle
Kew·pie
key·board
key·board·ist
key·note
key·punch
key·stone
kha·ki
kib·ble
kib·butz
kib·butz·nik
ki·bitz
kick·back
kick·box·ing
kick·off
kid
kid·die
kid·ding
kid·nap
kid·ney
kid·skin

kiel·ba·sa
ki·lim
kill·er app
kill·er bee
kill·ing field
kill·joy
kiln
ki·lo
ki·lo·byte
ki·lo·cy·cle
ki·lo·gram
ki·lo·hertz
ki·lo·me·ter
ki·lo·watt
kilt
kil·ter
ki·mo·no
kin·der·gar·ten
kin·der·gart·ner
kind·heart·ed
kin·dle
kind·li·ness
kin·dling
kind·ly
kin·dred
kine
kin·e·scope
ki·ne·si·ol·o·gy
ki·ne·sis
ki·net·ic
ki·net·ics
kin·folk
king·dom
king·fish·er
King James Ver·sion
king·ly
king·mak·er
king·pin
King's En·glish
king·ship
king·side

king-size
kink
kinky
kins·folk
kin·ship
kins·man
kins·wom·an
ki·osk
kip·per
kirk
kirsch
kis·met
kitch·en
kitch·en·ette
kitch·en·ware
kite
kith
kit·ing
kitsch
kit·ten
kit·ten·ish
kit·ty
kit·ty-cor·ner
ki·va
ki·wi
Klee·nex™
klep·to·ma·nia
klep·to·ma·ni·ac
klutz
knack
knap·sack
knave⁺
knav·ery
knav·ish
knead⁺
knee
knee·cap
kneed⁺
knee-deep
kneel
knell
knick·er·bock·ers

knick·ers
knick·knack
knife
knight
knight·hood
knish
knit
knit·ting
knit·wear
knives
knob
knock
knock·down
knock-kneed
knock off (v)
knock·out (n)
knock·wurst
knoll
knot
knot·hole
knot·ty
knout
know
know-how
know·ing
know-it-all
knowl·edge
knowl·edge·able
known
knuck·le
knuck·le·ball
ko·ala
kohl·ra·bi
Ko·ran
ko·sher
kow·tow
kraal
kra·ken
krem·lin
Krish·na
ku·dos
Ku Klux Klan

kul·tur
kum·quat
kur·to·sis
Kwan·za
kwash·i·or·kor
ky·rie

L
la·bel
la·bi·a
la·bile
la·bor
lab·o·ra·to·ry
la·bo·ri·ous
lab·y·rinth
lab·y·rin·thine
lac·er·ate
lac·er·a·tion
lach·ry·mal
lach·ry·mose
lac·ing
lack·a·dai·si·cal
lack·ey
lack·lus·ter
la·con·ic
lac·quer
la·crosse
lac·tate
lac·tic
lac·tose
   in·tol·er·ance
lac·to-veg·e·tar·
   i·an
la·cu·na
lacy
lad·der
lad·die
lad·en
la-di-da
la·dies
la·dies' room
lad·ing

la·dle
la·dy·fin·ger
la·dy-in-wait·ing
la·dy·like
la·dy·ship
la·e·trile
la·ger+
lag·gard
lag·ging
la·goon
la·icism
la·icize
laid
lain
lair
lais·sez-faire
la·ity
lake·front
lake·shore
lake·side
la·ma+
La·maze
lam·baste
lam·bent
lamb·skin
la·mé
la·med
lame duck
la·ment
la·men·ta·ble
lam·en·ta·tion
la·ment·ed
lam·i·nate
lam·i·nat·ed
lam·i·na·tion
lamp·light
lam·poon
LAN
lance
lan·cet
land·fall
land·fill

land grant
land·la·dy
land·lord
land·lub·ber
land·mark
land-of·fice
    busi·ness
land·own·er
land·scape
land·slide
lands·man
lan·guage
lan·guid
lan·guish
lan·guor
lan·guor·ous
lank
lanky
lan·o·lin
lan·tern
lan·yard
lap·board
la·pel
lap·i·dar·i·an
lap·i·dary
lap·in
la·pis la·zu·li
lapse
lap·top
lar·ce·nous
lar·ce·ny
larch
lar·der
large·ly
large-scale
    (adj)
lar·gess
lar·go
lar·i·at
lar·va
lar·vi·cide
la·ryn·geal

lar·yn·gec·to·my
lar·yn·gi·tis
lar·yn·gol·o·gy
la·ryn·go·scope
lar·ynx
la·sa·gna
las·civ·i·ous
las·civ·i·ous·ly
la·ser print·er
lash·ings
LASIK™
lass·ie
las·si·tude
las·so
last-ditch
last·ing
latch
latch·key
late·com·er
late·ly
la·ten·cy
la·tent
la·ter
lat·er·al
lat·est
la·tex
lath
lathe
lath·ing
Lat·in·a
Lat·in·ism
lat·in·ize
Lat·in·o
lat·ish
lat·i·tude
lat·i·tu·di·nar·i·an
lat·ke
la·trine
lat·te
lat·ter
lat·ter·ly
lat·tice

lat·tice·work
laud
laud·able
lau·da·num
lau·da·to·ry
laugh
laugh·able
laugh·ing·stock
laugh·ter
launch
launch·er
launch·pad
laun·der
laun·der·ette
Laun·dro·mat
laun·dry
lau·re·ate
lau·rel
la·va
la·va·bo
la·va·lier
lav·a·to·ry
lave
lav·en·der
lav·ish
law·abid·ing
law·break·er
law·ful
law·ful·ly
law·giv·er
law·less
law·mak·er
lawn
law·suit
law·yer
lax
lax·a·tive
lax·ity
lax·ly
lay·er
lay·ette
lay·man

lay·off (n)
lay·out (n)
lay·over (n)
lay·per·son
lay-up (n)
lay·wom·an
la·zi·er
la·zi·ness
la·zy
la·zy Su·san
leach[+]
lead·en
lead·er
lead·er·ship
lead-in (n)
lead·ing
lead·less
lead·off (n)
lead pen·cil
leads·man
leaf·let
leafy
league
leak·age
leaky
lean·ing
lean-to
leap·frog
leap year
learn
learn·ing
lease
lease·hold
leash
least
leath·er
leath·er·neck
leath·ery
leave[+]
leav·en
leav·en·ing
leave-tak·ing

leav·ings
le·bens·raum
lech·er
lech·er·ous
lech·ery
lec·i·thin
lec·tern
lec·tion·ary
lec·tor
lec·ture
led
ledge
led·ger
leech[+]
leek
leer
leery
lee·ward
lee·way
left brain
left-click
left-hand·ed
left-hand·er
left·over
lefty
leg·a·cy
le·gal
le·gal·ese
le·gal·ism
le·gal·ist
le·gal·i·ty
le·gal·ize
leg·ate
leg·a·tee
le·ga·tion
le·ga·to
leg·end
leg·end·ary
leg·er·de·main
leg·ging
leg·gy
leg·hold trap

leg·horn
leg·i·ble
le·gion
le·gion·ary
le·gion·naire
Le·gion·naires'
   dis·ease
leg·is·late
leg·is·la·tion
leg·is·la·tive
leg·is·la·tor
leg·is·la·ture
le·git·i·ma·cy
le·git·i·mate
le·git·i·ma·tize
leg·man
leg-pull
le·gume
lei·sure
lei·sure·ly
leit·mo·tiv
lem·ming
lem·on law
lem·on·ade
le·mur
lend-lease
length
length·en
length·wise
le·nience
le·nien·cy
le·nient
len·til
le·o·nine
leop·ard
le·o·tard
lep·er
lep·i·dop·ter·ist
lep·re·chaun
lep·ro·sy
les·bi·an
les·bi·an·ism

lèse-maj·es·té
le·sion
les·see
less·en+
less·er+
les·son+
les·sor+
lest
le·thal
le·thar·gic
le·thar·gi·cal·ly
leth·ar·gy
le·the
let·ter bomb
let·tered
let·ter·head
let·ter·ing
let·ter-per·fect
let·tuce
leu·ke·mia
le·vee+
lev·el·er
lev·el-head·ed
le·ver·age
le·vi·a·than
lev·i·tate
lev·i·ta·tion
lev·i·ty
levy+
lewd
lex·i·cal
lex·i·cog·ra·pher
lex·i·cog·ra·phy
lex·i·con
Lha·sa ap·so
li·a·bil·i·ty
li·a·ble
li·ai·son
li·ar+
li·ba·tion
li·bel
li·bel·ous

lib·er·al
lib·er·al·ism
lib·er·al·i·ty
lib·er·al·ize
lib·er·ate
lib·er·a·tion
   the·ol·o·gy
lib·er·tar·i·an
lib·er·tine
lib·er·ty
li·bid·i·nal
li·bid·i·nous
li·bi·do
li·brar·i·an
li·brary
li·bret·tist
li·bret·to
li·cense
li·cens·ee
li·cen·tious
li·chee
li·chen+
lic·it
lick·ing
lic·o·rice
lid·less
lie
lied
lief+
liege
lie-in (n)
lien
lieu
lieu·ten·an·cy
lieu·ten·ant
life-and-death
life force
life-form
life-giv·ing
life·guard
life·less
life·like

life·line
life·long
life net
lif·er
life-sav·er
life-size
life span
life-style drug
life-sup·port (adj)
life·time
liftoff (n)
lig·a·ment
lig·a·ture
light·en
ligh·ter
light-fin·gered
light-foot·ed
light-head·ed
light·ing
light·ly
light·ning
light·weight
light-year
lig·ne·ous
lig·nite
lik·able
like·li·hood
like·ly
like-mind·ed
lik·en⁺
like·ness
like·wise
lik·ing
li·lac
lil·li·pu·tian
lilt·ing
lily-white
li·ma bean
lim·ber
lim·bic
lim·bo
Lim·burg·er

lime·ade
lime·light
lim·er·ick
lime·stone
lim·i·nal
lim·it·less
lim·i·ta·tion
lim·it·ed lia·bil·i·ty
   part·ner·ship
lim·it·ing
limn
lim·ou·sine
lim·pid
limp·ly
linch·pin
Lin·coln·ian
lin·den
lin·dy
lin·e·age
lin·e·a·ments
lin·e·ar
line·back·er
line judge
lin·en
lin·er
lines·man
line-up
lin·ger
lin·ge·rie
lin·go
ling·on·ber·ry
lin·gua fran·ca
lin·guist
lin·guis·tic
lin·i·ment
lin·ing
link·age
links⁺
link·up (n)
li·no·leum
Li·no·type™
lin·seed

lint
lin·tel
Lin·ux
li·on·heart·ed
li·on·ized
li·on's share
lip·id
Lip·iz·zan·er
li·po·gen·e·sis
li·po·suc·tion
lipped
lip-read
lip-read·ing
lip ser·vice
lip·stick
liq·ue·fac·tion
liq·ue·fy
li·queur
liq·uid
liq·ui·date
liq·ui·da·tion
li·quor
lisle
lisp
lis·some
lis·ten
list·ing
list·less
lit·a·ny
li·ter
lit·er·a·cy
lit·er·al
lit·er·ary
lit·er·ate
li·te·ra·ti
lit·er·a·ture
lithe
lithe·some
litho·graph
li·thog·ra·phy
lit·i·gant
lit·i·gate

lit·i·ga·tion
li·ti·gious
lit·mus
li·to·tes
lit·ter
lit·ter·bag
lit·ter·bug
lit·tle
lit·tle·neck
li·tur·gi·cal
lit·ur·gist
lit·ur·gy
liv·able
live-in (adj)
live·li·ness
live·long
live·ly
liv·en
liv·er
liv·er·ied
liv·er·wurst
liv·ery
live·stock
live wire
liv·id
liv·ing will
liz·ard
lla·ma[+]
load·ing
loaf
loam
loath
loathe
loath·ing
loath·some
lob·by
lob·by·er
lob·by·ist
lo·bot·o·my
lob·ster
lob·ster·man

lo·cal ar·ea
  net·work
lo·cale
lo·cal·ism
lo·cal·i·ty
lo·cal·ize
lo·cate
lo·ca·tion
loch
loci
lock·down
locked-in
lock·er
lock·jaw
lock·smith
lock·step
lo·co·mo·tion
lo·co·mo·tive
lo·cus
lo·cust
lo·cu·tion
lode
lode·star
lode·stone
lodge
lodg·er
lodg·ing
lofty
log·a·rithm
log·ger[+]
log·ger·heads
log·gia
log·ic
log·i·cal
log·i·cal·ly
lo·gi·cian
lo·gis·tics
log·jam
log on (v)
log·roll
lo·gy

loin
loi·ter
loi·ter·er
loll
lol·li·pop
lol·ly·gag
lone·li·ness
lone·ly
lon·er
lone·some
long-ago
lon·ga·nim·i·ty
long-dis·tance
long-drawn-out
lon·gev·i·ty
long·hand
long·ing
long·ish
lon·gi·tude
lon·gi·tu·di·nal
long johns
long-lived
long-play·ing
long-range (adj)
long·shore·man
long·sight·ed
long-stand·ing
long-suf·fer·ing
long-term
long-wind·ed
loo·fah
look-alike
look·er-on
look-in
loo·ny tunes
loop·hole
loose
loose-leaf
loos·en
loot[+]
lope

lop-eared
lop·sid·ed
lo·qua·cious
lo·quac·i·ty
lo·ran
lord·ly
lord·ship
lore
lor·gnette
lor·ry
lose-lose
los·er
los·ing
loss lead·er
lo·thar·io
lo·tion
lot·tery
lot·to
lo·tus
loud·mouth
loud·ness
loud·speak·er
lounge
louse
lousy
lout
lout·ish
lou·ver
lov·able
love·less
love·lorn
love·ly
lov·er
love·sick
lov·ing
lov·ing cup
low·boy
low·brow
low·er
low·er·case
low·er-class (adj)

low-grade (adj)
low-key (adj)
low-lev·el (adj)
low·ly
low-ly·ing
low-pro·file (adj)
low-tech
lox
loy·al
loy·al·ist
loy·al·ty
loz·enge
lu·au
lub·ber
lube
lu·bri·cant
lu·bri·cate
lu·bri·cious
lu·bric·i·ty
lu·cent
lu·cid
lu·cid·i·ty
Lu·ci·fer
Lu·cite™
lucky
lu·cra·tive
lu·cre
Lu·cul·lan
lu·di·crous
luff
luge
lug·gage
lug·ger
lu·gu·bri·ous
luke·warm
lull
lul·la·by
lum·ba·go
lum·bar[+]
lum·ber[+]
lum·ber·jack

lum·ber·yard
lu·men
lu·mi·nary
lu·mi·nes·cence
lu·mi·nes·cent
lu·mi·nos·i·ty
lu·mi·nous
lump·ec·to·my
lumpy
lu·na·cy
lu·nar
lu·na·tic
lun·cheon
lun·cheon·ette
lu·nette
lunge
lu·pine
lu·pus er·y·the·
    ma·to·sus
lurch
lure
lu·rid
lus·cious
lush
lus·ter
lust·ful
lus·trous
lusty
lute[+]
lu·te·nist
Lu·ther·an
lux·u·ri·ance
lux·u·ri·ant
lux·u·ri·ate
lux·u·ri·ous
lux·u·ry
ly·can·thro·py
ly·cée
ly·ce·um
lye
ly·ing

Lyme dis·ease
lymph
lynch
lynx[+]
lyre[+]
lyr·ic
lyr·i·cal
lyr·i·cism
lyr·i·cist
ly·sis

M
ma·ca·bre
mac·ad·am
mac·a·da·mia nut
ma·caque
mac·a·ro·ni
mac·a·roon
Mc·Car·thy·ism
mace
mac·er·ate
ma·chete
Ma·chi·a·vel·lian
mach·i·nate
mach·i·na·tions
ma·chine
ma·chine·like
ma·chine-read·able
ma·chin·ery
ma·chin·ist
ma·chis·mo
Mach number
ma·cho
mack·er·el
mack·i·naw
mack·in·tosh
mac·ra·mé
mac·ro (n)
mac·ro·bi·ot·ic
mac·ro·cosm
mac·ro·eco·nom·ics
ma·cron

mac·u·lar
de·gen·er·a·tion
mad
Mad·am[+]
Ma·dame[+]
mad·cap
mad cow dis·ease
mad·den
mad·den·ing
mad·der
mad·dest
ma·de·moi·selle
made-up (adj)
mad·house
mad·ly
mad·man
mad·ness
Ma·don·na
ma·dras
mad·ri·gal
mad·wom·an
mael·strom
mae·stro
Ma·fia
ma·fi·o·so
mag·a·zine
ma·gen·ta
mag·got
Ma·gi
mag·ic
mag·i·cal
ma·gi·cian
mag·is·te·ri·al
mag·is·te·ri·um
mag·is·trate
Mag·na Car·ta
mag·na cum lau·de
mag·na·nim·i·ty
mag·nan·i·mous
mag·nate
mag·ne·sia
mag·ne·sium

mag·net
mag·net·ic
res·o·nance
im·ag·ing
mag·net·ic flux
mag·ne·tism
mag·ne·tize
mag·ne·to
mag·ne·tom·e·ter
Mag·nif·i·cat
mag·ni·fi·ca·tion
mag·nif·i·cence
mag·nif·i·cent
mag·ni·fi·er
mag·ni·fy
mag·nil·o·quence
mag·nil·o·quent
mag·ni·tude
mag·no·lia
mag·num opus
mag·pie
ma·gus
ma·ha·ra·ja
ma·ha·ra·ni
ma·hat·ma
mah-jongg
ma·hog·a·ny
maid·en
maid·en·hood
maid·en name
maid-in-wait·ing
mail·bag
mail·box
mail·er
mail·man
maim
main·frame
main·land
main·line
main·ly
main·mast
main·sail

main·sheet
main·spring
main·stay
main·stream
main·tain
main·tain·able
main·te·nance
mai·son·ette
maî·tre d'
maî·tre d'hô·tel
maize⁺
ma·jes·tic
maj·es·ty
ma·jor·do·mo
ma·jor·ette
ma·jor·i·ty
ma·jus·cule
mak·able
make-be·lieve
make-do
mak·er
make·shift
make·up (n)
make-work
mak·ing
ma·ko
mal·adapt·ed
mal·ad·just·ed
mal·ad·just·ment
mal·adroit
mal·adroit·ly
mal·a·dy
mal·aise
mal·a·mute
mal·a·pert
mal·a·prop
mal·a·prop·ism
ma·lar·ia
mal·a·thi·on
mal·con·tent
mal de mer
mal·e·dict

mal·e·dic·tion
mal·e·fac·tion
mal·e·fac·tor
ma·lef·i·cence
ma·lef·i·cent
mal·e·mute*
ma·lev·o·lence
ma·lev·o·lent
mal·fea·sance
mal·for·ma·tion
mal·formed
mal·func·tion
mal·ice
ma·li·cious
ma·lign
ma·lig·nan·cy
ma·lig·nant
ma·lig·ni·ty
ma·li·hi·ni
ma·lin·ger
ma·lin·ger·er
mall⁺
mal·lard
mal·lea·ble
mal·let
mal·low
mal·nour·ished
mal·nu·tri·tion
mal·oc·clu·sion
mal·odor·ous
mal·prac·tice
malt
Mal·tese
Mal·thu·sian
mal·treat
mal·ver·sa·tion
ma·ma
mam·bo
mam·mal
mam·ma·ry
mam·mo·gram
mam·mog·ra·phy

mam·mon
mam·moth
man-about-town
man·a·cle
man·aged care
man·age·able
man·age·ment
man·ag·er
ma·ña·na
man·a·tee
man·da·la
man·da·mus
man·da·rin
man·date
man·da·to·ry
man·di·ble
man·do·lin
man·drake
mane
man-eat·er
ma·neu·ver
man·ful
man·ful·ly
man·ga·nate
man·ga·nese
mange
man·ger
man·gle
man·go
man·grove
mangy
man·han·dle
man·hat·tan
man·hole
man·hood
man-hour
ma·nia
ma·ni·ac
ma·ni·a·cal
man·ic
man·ic-de·pres·sive
ma·ni·cot·ti

man·i·cure
man·i·cur·ist
man·i·fest
man·i·fes·ta·tion
man·i·fes·to
man·i·fold
man·i·kin
ma·nila
ma·nip·u·late
ma·nip·u·la·tion
ma·nip·u·la·tor
man·kind
man·ly
man-made
man·na
manned
man·ne·quin
man·ner[+]
man·ner·ism
man·ner·ly
man·nish
man-of-war
man·or[+]
man·qué
man·sard
manse
man·sion
man·slaugh·ter
man·teau
man·tel[+]
man·tel·piece
man·til·la
man·tis·sa
man·tle[+]
man-to-man
Man·toux test
man·tra
man·u·al
man·u·fac·ture
man·u·fac·tur·er
man·u·mis·sion
ma·nure
man·u·script

many-sid·ed
Mao·ri
ma·ple
map·mak·er
map·ping
mar·a·schi·no
ma·ras·mus
mar·a·thon
ma·raud·er
mar·ble
mar·bled
mar·ble·ize
mar·ca·site
mar·cel
march
mar·che·sa
mar·chio·ness
Mar·di Gras
mare[+]
mare's nest
mar·ga·rine
mar·ga·ri·ta
mar·gin
mar·gin·al
mar·gi·na·lia
ma·ri·a·chi
mari·gold
mar·i·jua·na
ma·rim·ba
ma·ri·na
mar·i·nate
mar·i·ner
mar·i·o·nette
mar·i·tal
mar·i·time
mar·jo·ram
mar·ket·able
mar·ket·ing
mar·ket·place
marks·man
mar·lin
mar·ma·lade
mar·mo·re·al

mar·mo·set
mar·mot
ma·roon
mar·quee[+]
mar·quess
mar·que·try
mar·quis*[+]
mar·quise
marred
mar·riage
mar·ried
mar·row
mar·row·bone
mar·ry[+]
mar·shal[+]
marsh·mal·low
marshy
mar·su·pi·al
mart
mar·tial[+]
mar·tian
mar·tin
mar·ti·net
mar·tin·gale
mar·ti·ni
mar·tyr
mar·tyr·dom
mar·tyr·ol·o·gy
mar·vel
mar·vel·ous
Marx·ian
Marx·ism
Marx·ism=
    Le·nin·ism
mar·zi·pan
mas·cara
mas·cot
mas·cu·line
mash·er
mask[+]
mas·och·ism
mas·och·ist
ma·son

Ma·son-Dix·on line
Ma·son·ic
ma·son jar
ma·son·ry
masque[+]
mas·quer·ade
mass
mas·sa·cre
mas·sage
mas·seur
mas·seuse
mas·sive
mass-mar·ket (adj)
mass me·dia (n)
mast
mas·tec·to·my
mas·ter
mas·ter·ful
mas·ter·ly
mas·ter·mind
mas·ter·piece
mas·tery
mast·head
mas·ti·cate
mas·tiff
mas·to·don
mas·toid
mas·tur·bate
mat·a·dor
match
match·able
match·less
match·mak·er
mate
ma·te·ri·al
ma·te·ri·al·ism
ma·te·ri·al·ize
ma·té·ri·el
ma·ter·nal
ma·ter·ni·ty
math
math·e·mat·i·cal
math·e·ma·ti·cian

math·e·mat·ics
mat·i·nee
ma·tri·arch
ma·tri·ar·chy
ma·tri·ces
ma·tri·cide
ma·tric·u·late
mat·ri·mo·nial
mat·ri·mo·ny
ma·trix
ma·tron
ma·tron·ly
mat·ted
mat·ter
mat·ter-of-fact
mat·ting
mat·tress
mat·u·ra·tion
ma·ture
ma·tu·ri·ty
mat·zo
mat·zoh*
maud·lin
maul[+]
mau·so·le·um
mauve
ma·ven
mav·er·ick
maw
mawk·ish
max·im
maxi
max·i·mal
max·i·mize
max·i·mum
Ma·yan
may·be
May·day[+]
May Day[+]
may·fly
may·hap
may·hem
mayn't

may·on·naise
may·or[+]
may·or·al·ty
may·or·ess
maze[+]
ma·zur·ka
mea cul·pa
mead[+]
mead·ow
mead·ow·lark
mea·ger
meal
meal·time
mealy
mealy·bug
mean[+]
mean·ness
me·an·der
mean·ing
mean·ing·ful
mean·ing·less
meant
mean·while
mea·sles
mea·sly
mea·sur·ably
mea·sure·less
mea·sure·ment
mea·sur·ing
meat[+]
meat·ball
meaty
mec·ca
me·chan·ic
me·chan·i·cal
me·chan·ics
mech·a·nism
mech·a·nis·tic
mech·a·nize
med·al[+]
me·dal·lion
med·dle[+]
med·dle·some

me·dia event
me·di·al
me·di·an
me·di·ate
me·di·a·tion
me·di·a·tor
me·dic
Med·ic·aid
med·i·cal
Medi·care
med·i·cate
med·i·ca·tion
me·dic·i·nal
med·i·cine
me·di·e·val
me·di·e·val·ism
me·di·e·val·ist
me·di·o·cre
me·di·oc·ri·ty
med·i·tate
med·i·ta·tion
med·i·ta·tive
Med·i·ter·ra·nean
med·ley
meed[+]
meek
meer·schaum
meet and greet
meet·ing
mega·bucks
mega·byte
mega·cy·cle
mega·deal
mega·hertz
mega·lith
meg·a·lo·ma·nia
meg·a·lop·o·lis
mega·phone
mega·ton
mei·o·sis
mel·an·choly
mé·lange

mel·a·no·ma
mel·a·to·nin
mel·ba toast
meld
me·lee
me·lio·rism
mel·lif·lu·ent
mel·lif·lu·ous
mel·low
me·lod·ic
me·lo·di·ous
melo·dra·ma
melo·dra·mat·ic
mel·o·dy
mel·on
melt
mem·ber
mem·ber·ship
mem·brane
mem·bra·nous
me·men·to
mem·oir
mem·o·ra·bil·ia
mem·o·ra·ble
mem·o·ran·dum
me·mo·ri·al
me·mo·ri·al·ize
mem·o·rize
mem·o·ry
men·ace
mé·nage
me·nag·er·ie
mend
men·da·cious
men·dac·i·ty
Men·del's law
men·di·cant
me·nial
men·in·gi·tis
me·nis·cus
men·o·pause
me·no·rah

mensch
mens rea
men·stru·ate
men·stru·a·tion
mens·wear
men·tal
men·tal·i·ty
men·thol
men·tho·lat·ed
men·tion
men·tor
menu
me·ow
Meph·is·toph·e·les
mer·can·tile
mer·can·til·ism
Mer·ca·tor
 pro·jec·tion
mer·ce·nary
mer·cer·ized
mer·chan·dise
mer·chan·dis·ing
mer·chant
mer·ci·ful
mer·ci·ful·ly
mer·ci·less
mer·cu·ri·al
mer·cu·ric
Mer·cu·ro·chrome™
mer·cu·ry
mer·cy
mere
mer·e·tri·cious
merge
merg·er
me·rid·i·an
me·ringue
me·ri·no
mer·it
mer·i·toc·ra·cy
mer·i·to·ri·ous
Mer·lin

mer·maid
mer·man
mer·ri·ment
mer·ry[+]
mer·ry-go-round
mer·ry·mak·ing
me·sa
més·al·liance
mes·dames
mesh
mes·mer·ize
Me·so·lith·ic
me·so·mor·phic
Me·so·zo·ic
mes·quite
mess
mes·sage
mes·sen·ger
mes·si·ah
mes·si·an·ic
mes·sieurs
messy
mes·ti·zo
met·a·bol·ic
me·tab·o·lism
me·tab·o·lize
meta·car·pal
meta·cog·ni·tion
met·al[+]
me·tal·lic
met·al·lur·gi·cal
met·al·lur·gy
met·al·ware
meta·mor·pho·sis
met·a·phor
meta·phys·i·cal
meta·phys·ics
me·tas·ta·sis
me·tas·ta·size
me·tath·e·sis
meta·zo·an
mete[+]

me·te·or
me·te·or·ite
me·te·o·rol·o·gist
me·te·o·rol·o·gy
me·ter
meth·a·done
meth·ane
meth·od
me·thod·i·cal
Meth·od·ism
Meth·od·ist
meth·od·ol·o·gy
Me·thu·se·lah
me·tic·u·lous
mé·tier
me·ton·y·my
met·ric
met·ri·cal
met·ri·ca·tion
met·ro·nome
met·ro·nom·ic
me·trop·o·lis
met·ro·pol·i·tan
met·tle[+]
me·zu·zah
mez·za·nine
mez·zo-so·pra·no
mi·aow*
mi·as·ma
mic (n)[+]
mi·ca
mice
mi·crobe
mi·cro·brew·ery
mi·cro·cas·sette
mi·cro·com·put·er
mi·cro·con·trol·ler
mi·cro·cosm
mi·cro·eco·nom·ics
mi·cro·fiche
mi·cro·film
mi·cro·man·age

mi·crom·e·ter
Mi·cro·ne·sian
mi·cro·or·gan·ism
mi·cro·phone
mi·cro·pro·ces·sor
mi·cro·scope
mi·cro·scop·ic
mi·cro·tech·nol·o·gy
mi·cro·wave
mic·tu·rate
mid·air
mid-At·lan·tic
mid·day
mid·dle
mid·dle-aged
mid·dle-class
mid·dle-man
mid·dle-of-the=
    road
mid·dle school
mid·dle·weight
mid·dling
mid·dy
mid·field
midg·et
midi[+]
MIDI[+]
mid·land
mid·night
mid·point
mid·riff
mid·sec·tion
mid·ship·man
midst
mid·stream
mid·town
mid·way
mid·week
mid·wife
mien[+]
miff
might[+]

might·i·ly
mightn't
mighty
mi·graine
mi·grant
mi·grate
mi·gra·to·ry
mi·ka·do
mike (n, v)+
mil·dew
mile·age
mil·er
mile·stone
mi·lieu
mil·i·tan·cy
mil·i·tant
mil·i·ta·rism
mil·i·ta·rize
mil·i·tary
mil·i·tate
mi·li·tia
milk·man
milk·sop
milky
Milky Way
mil·len·ni·um
mill·er
mil·let
mil·li·gram
mil·li·li·ter
mil·li·me·ter
mil·li·ner
mil·li·nery
mill·ing
mil·lion
mil·lion·aire
mil·lion·air·ess
mill·pond
mill·stone
mill·stream
Milque·toast
mime

mim·eo·graph
mi·me·sis
mi·met·ic
mim·ic
mim·ic·ry
mi·mo·sa
min·a·ret
mi·na·to·ry
mince
minc·ing
mind
mind-blow·ing
mind·ful
mind·less
mind-set (n)
mine
min·er·al
min·er·al·o·gy
min·e·stro·ne
min·gle
mini
min·ia·ture
min·i·a·tur·ize
mini·bike
mini·bus
mini·car
mini·com·put·er
min·i·mal
min·i·mal·ly
mini-mart
min·i·mize
min·i·mum
min·ing
min·ion
min·is·cule
mini·se·ries
mini·skirt
min·is·ter+
min·is·te·ri·al
min·is·tra·tion
min·is·try
mink

min·now
mi·nor
mi·nor·i·ty
mi·nox·i·dil
min·ster+
min·strel
min·strel·sy
mint·age
mint ju·lep
min·u·et
mi·nus
mi·nus·cule
min·ute
mi·nute·ly
min·ute·man
min·ute steak
mi·nu·tia
mi·nu·tiae
minx
mir·a·cle
mi·rac·u·lous
mi·rage
Mi·ran·da rights
mire
mir·ror
mirth
mirth·ful·ness
mis·ad·ven·ture
mis·aligned
mis·al·li·ance
mis·an·thrope
mis·an·throp·ic
mis·ap·pli·ca·tion
mis·ap·ply
mis·ap·pre·hend
mis·ap·pre·hen·sion
mis·ap·pro·pri·ate
mis·be·got·ten
mis·be·have
mis·cal·cu·late
mis·car·riage
mis·car·ry

mis·cast
mis·ce·ge·na·tion
mis·cel·la·neous
mis·cel·la·ny
mis·chance
mis·chief
mis·chie·vous
mis·clas·si·fy
mis·con·ceive
mis·con·cep·tion
mis·con·duct
mis·con·struc·tion
mis·con·strue
mis·count
mis·cre·ant
mis·cue
mis·deal
mis·deed
mis·de·mean·or
mis·di·rect
mis·di·rec·tion
mise-en-scène
mi·ser
mis·er·a·ble
mi·ser·ly
mis·ery
mis·fea·sance
mis·file
mis·fire
mis·fit
mis·for·tune
mis·giv·ings
mis·gov·ern
mis·guide
mis·han·dle
mis·hap
mish·mash
mis·in·form
mis·in·ter·pret
mis·judge
mis·la·bel
mis·lay

mis·lead
mis·man·age
mis·match
mis·no·mer
mi·sog·a·mist
mi·sog·a·my
mi·sog·y·nist
mis·per·ceive
mis·place
mis·play
mis·print
mis·pri·sion
mis·pro·nounce
mis·pro·nun·ci·a·
  tion
mis·quote
mis·quo·ta·tion
mis·read
mis·re·mem·ber
mis·rep·re·sent
mis·rule
mis·sal[+]
mis·sent
mis·shap·en
mis·sile[+]
mis·sion
mis·sion·ary
mis·sive
mis·spell
mis·spend
mis·state
mis·step
mist
mis·tak·able
mis·take
mis·tak·en·ly
mis·ter
mis·tle·toe
mis·trans·late
mis·treat
mis·tress
mis·tri·al

mis·trust
misty
misty-eyed
mis·un·der·stand
mis·us·age
mis·use
mite[+]
mi·ter
mit·i·gate
mi·to·sis
mitt
mit·ten
mix·able
mixed
mixed-up (adj)
mix·er
mix·ture
mix-up (n)
miz·zen·mast
mne·mon·ic
moan[+]
moat[+]
mobbed
mo·bile phone
mo·bi·li·za·tion
mo·bi·lize
Mö·bi·us strip
mob·ster
moc·ca·sin
mo·cha
mock·ing·ly
mock·ery
mock-he·ro·ic
mock·u·men·ta·ry
mock-up
mod·al
mo·dal·i·ty
mode
mod·el
mod·em
mod·er·ate
mo·der·a·to

mod·er·a·tor
mod·ern
mod·ern·ism
mod·ern·iza·tion
mod·ern·ize
mod·est
mod·es·ty
mod·i·cum
mod·i·fi·able
mod·i·fi·ca·tion
mod·i·fi·er
mod·i·fy
mod·ish
mod·u·lar
mod·u·late
mod·u·la·tion
mod·ule
mo·dus ope·ran·di
mo·dus vi·ven·di
mo·gul
mo·hair
Mo·ham·med·an⁺
moi·e·ty
moil
moist·en
moist·en·er
mois·ture
mois·tur·ize
mo·jo
mo·lar
mo·las·ses
mold·able
mold·er
mold·ing
moldy
mole
mo·lec·u·lar
mol·e·cule
mole·skin
mo·lest
mo·les·ta·tion
mol·li·fy

mol·lusk
mol·ly·cod·dle
Mo·lo·tov cock·tail
molt
mol·ten
mo·ment
mo·men·tar·i·ly
mo·men·tary
mo·men·tous
mo·men·tum
mom·my
mom·my track
mon·arch
mo·nar·chi·cal
mon·ar·chism
mon·ar·chy
mon·as·te·ri·al
mon·as·tery
mo·nas·tic
mon·au·ral
mon·e·tary
mon·ey
mon·eyed
mon·ey·lend·er
mon·ger
mon·gol·ism
Mon·gol·oid
mon·grel
mon·i·ker
mo·nism
mon·i·tor
monk
mon·key
mon·key wrench
mono·chro·mat·ic
mon·o·cle
mon·oc·u·lar
mo·nog·a·my
mono·gram
mono·graph
mo·nog·y·ny
mono·lin·gual

mono·lith
mono·lith·ic
mono·logue
mono·ma·nia
mo·no·mi·al
mono·nu·cle·o·sis
mo·nop·o·lize
mo·nop·o·ly
mono·rail
mono·so·di·um
    glu·ta·mate
mono·syl·la·ble
mono·the·ism
mono·tone
mo·not·o·nous
mo·not·o·ny
mon·ox·ide
Mon·sieur
mon·si·gnor
mon·soon
mon·ster
mon·stros·i·ty
mon·strous
mon·tage
mon·te
Mon·tes·so·ri
month
mon·u·ment
mon·u·men·tal
mood
mood·i·ness
moody
moon·beam
moon·light
moon·lit
moon·shine
moon·stone
moor
moor·ing
moose⁺
moot
mope

mopped
mo·raine
mor·al
mo·rale
mor·al·ism
mor·al·is·tic
mo·ral·i·ty
mor·al·ize
mo·rass
mor·a·to·ri·um
mo·ray
mor·bid
mor·bid·i·ty
mor·dant
more·over
mo·res
mor·ga·nat·ic
morgue
mor·i·bund
Mor·mon
morn·ing breath
mo·ron
mo·ron·ic
mo·rose
mor·phine
Morse code
mor·sel
mor·tal
mor·tal·i·ty
mor·tal·ly
mor·tar
mor·tar·board
mort·gage
mort·gag·ee
mort·gag·or
mor·ti·cian
mor·ti·fi·ca·tion
mor·ti·fy
mor·tise
mort·main
mor·tu·ary
mo·sa·ic

Mos·lem*
mosque
mos·qui·to
mossy
most·ly
mote+
mo·tel
moth
moth-eat·en
moth·er
moth·er·board
moth·er-in-law
moth·er·ly
moth·er-of-pearl
mo·tif
mo·tile
mo·tion
mo·ti·vate
mo·ti·va·tion
mo·tive
mot juste
mot·ley
mo·tor
mo·tor·cade
mo·tor·cy·cle
mo·tor inn
mo·tor·ist
mot·tle
mot·tled
mot·to
mound
mount
mount·able
moun·tain
moun·tain·eer
moun·tain·ous
moun·tain·side
moun·te·bank
mourn
mourn·ful
mourn·ing
mouse

mous·er
mous·sa·ka
mousse+
mousy
mouth
mouth·ful
mouth·piece
mouth-to-mouth
mouthy
mov·able
mov·abil·i·ty
move·ment
mov·er
mov·ie
mov·ie·go·er
mow
mown+
mox·ie
moz·za·rel·la
MP3
mu·ci·lage
muck
muck·rake
mu·cus
mud·dle
mud·dy
mud·room
mud·sling·er
mues·li
muf·fin
muf·fle
muf·fler
mug·ger
mug·gy
mug·wump
Mu·ham·mad·an*+
mu·lat·to
mul·ber·ry
mulch
mule
mu·le·teer
mul·ish

mull
mul·let
mul·li·ga·taw·ny
mul·ti·col·ored
mul·ti·cul·tur·al
mul·ti·di·men·
  sion·al
mul·ti·di·rec·tion·al
mul·ti·dis·ci·plin·
  ary
mul·ti·fac·et·ed
mul·ti·far·i·ous
mul·ti·fold
mul·ti·form
mul·ti·lat·er·al
mul·ti·lay·ered
mul·ti·lev·el
mul·ti·lin·gual
mul·ti·mil·lion·aire
mul·ti·ple
mul·ti·ple
  scle·ro·sis
mul·ti·pli·ca·tion
mul·ti·plic·i·ty
mul·ti·pli·er
mul·ti·ply
mul·ti·pur·pose
mul·ti·ra·cial
mul·ti·sen·so·ry
mul·ti·tude
mul·ti·tu·di·nous
mum·ble
mum·bo jum·bo
mum·mer
mum·mi·fy
mum·my
mumps
munch
mun·dane
mu·nic·i·pal
mu·nic·i·pal·i·ty
mu·nif·i·cent

mu·ni·tion
mu·ral
mur·der
mur·der·er
mur·der·ous
murk·i·ness
murky
mur·mur
mus·ca·tel
mus·cle[+]
mus·cled
mus·co·vite
mus·cu·lar
mus·cu·lar
  dys·tro·phy
mus·cu·la·ture
muse
mu·se·um
mush
mush·room
mushy
mu·sic
mu·si·cal
mu·si·cale
mu·si·cal·i·ty
mu·si·cian
mu·si·cian·ship
mu·si·col·o·gy
musk
mus·kel·lunge
mus·ket
mus·ke·teer
mus·kie[+]
musk·mel·on
musk·rat
mus·ky[*][+]
Mus·lim
mus·lin
mus·sel[+]
mus·tache
mus·ta·chioed
mus·tang

mus·tard
mus·ter
mustn't
musty
mu·tant
mu·ta·tion
mu·ta·tis
  mu·tan·dis
mute
mut·ed
mu·ti·late
mu·ti·la·tion
mu·ti·la·tor
mu·ti·neer
mu·ti·nous
mu·ti·ny
mutt
mut·ter
mut·ton
mu·tu·al
mu·tu·al·i·ty
mu·tu·al·ize
muu·muu
muz·zle
my·col·o·gy
my·co·sis
My·lar™
my·nah
myo·car·di·al
  in·farc·tion
my·o·pia
my·o·pic
myr·i·ad
myrrh
myr·tle
my·self
mys·te·ri·ous
mys·tery
mys·tic
mys·ti·cal
mys·ti·cism
mys·ti·fi·ca·tion

mys·ti·fy
mys·tique
myth
myth·i·cal
myth·o·log·i·cal
my·thol·o·gize
my·thol·o·gy

N

na·bob
na·chos
na·dir
nag
nagged
nag·ging
na·if
nail
na·ive
na·ive·té
na·ked
name
name-call·ing
name·less
name·ly
name·sake
nan·ny
nano·sec·ond
nap
na·palm
nape
naph·tha
nap·kin
na·po·leon
napped
nap·ping
nar·cis·sism
nar·cis·sist
nar·cis·sus
nar·co·lep·sy
nar·co·sis
nar·cot·ic
nar·rate

nar·ra·tion
nar·ra·tive
nar·row
nary
na·sal
na·sal·ize
na·scent
na·so·gas·tric
nas·ti·ly
nas·ti·ness
nas·tur·tium
nas·ty
na·tal
na·ta·to·ri·um
na·tion
na·tion·al
na·tion·al·ism
na·tion·al·ist
na·tion·al·is·tic
na·tion·al·i·ty
na·tion·al·i·za·tion
na·tion·al·ize
na·tion-state
na·tion·wide
na·tive
na·tiv·ism
na·tiv·i·ty
nat·ty
nat·u·ral fam·i·ly
   plan·ning
nat·u·ral·ism
nat·u·ral·ist
nat·u·ral·ize
nat·u·ral·ly
nat·u·ral·ness
na·ture
na·tu·rop·a·thy
Nau·ga·hyde™
naught[+]
naugh·ty
nau·sea
nau·se·ate

nau·seous
nau·ti·cal
nau·ti·lus
na·val[+]
Na·va·jo
nave[+]
na·vel[+]
nav·i·ga·ble
nav·i·gate
nav·i·ga·tion
nav·i·ga·tor
na·vy
na·zi
Na·zi·ism*
Na·zism
Ne·an·der·thal
neap
Ne·a·pol·i·tan
near·by
near·ly
near·sight·ed
neat
neb·u·la
neb·u·lous
nec·es·sar·i·ly
nec·es·sary
ne·ces·si·tate
ne·ces·si·ty
neck·er·chief
neck·ing
neck·lace
neck·line
neck·tie
ne·crol·o·gy
nec·ro·man·cy
nec·rop·sy
nec·tar
nec·tar·ine
née[+]
need·ful
nee·dle
nee·dle·point

need·less
nee·dle·work
needn't
needy
ne'er-do-well
ne·far·i·ous
ne·gate
ne·ga·tion
neg·a·tive
neg·a·tiv·ism
ne·glect
ne·glect·ful
ne·glect·ful·ness
neg·li·gee
neg·li·gence
neg·li·gent
neg·li·gi·ble
ne·go·tia·ble
ne·go·ti·ate
ne·go·ti·a·tion
neigh+
neigh·bor
neigh·bor·hood
neigh·bor·li·ness
neigh·bor·ly
nei·ther
nel·son
ne·ma·tode
nem·e·sis
neo·clas·si·cal
Neo-Freud·ian
Neo-Im·pres·sion·ism
Neo·lith·ic
ne·ol·o·gism
ne·on
neo·na·tal
neo·phyte
neo·scho·las·ti·cism
neph·ew
ne·phrit·ic
ne·phri·tis

ne plus ul·tra
nep·o·tism
Nep·tune
nerve
nerve·less
nerve-rack·ing
ner·vous
nervy
nes·tle
nest·ling
neth·er
neth·er·world
net·i·quette
net·ted
net·ting
net·tle
net·work
neu·ral
neu·ral·gia
neur·as·the·nia
neu·ri·tis
neu·rol·o·gist
neu·rol·o·gy
neu·ro·mus·cu·lar
neu·ro·sis
neu·ro·sur·geon
neu·ro·sur·gery
neu·rot·ic
neu·ter
neu·tral
neu·tral·i·ty
neu·tral·i·za·tion
neu·tral·ize
neu·tron
nev·er·more
nev·er·the·less
New Age
new·bie
new·born
new·com·er
new·el
new·fan·gled

New·found·land
new·ly
new·ly·wed
news·agent
news·boy
news·break
news·cast·er
news·girl
news·let·ter
news·mag·a·zine
news·man
news·pa·per
news·wom·an
news·wor·thy
newsy
newt+
New Year's Day
New York min·ute
next-door (adj)
nex·us
Nez Perce
ni·a·cin
Ni·ag·a·ra
nib
nib·ble
nice·ly
nice·ty
niche
nick
nick·el
nick·el·ode·on
nick·nack*
nick·name
nic·o·tine
ni·dus
niece
nif·ty
nig·gard
nig·gard·ly
nig·gle
night·cap
night·clothes

night·club
night·gown
night·hawk
night·ie
night·in·gale
night·ly
night·mare
night·shirt
night·time
ni·hil·ism
nim·ble
nim·bus
NIMBY
nin·com·poop
nine·fold
nine·teen
nine·ti·eth
nine·ty
nin·ja
nin·ny
ninth
nip·ple
Nip·pon
nip·py
nir·va·na
Ni·sei
nit-pick·ing
ni·trate
ni·tric
ni·tro·gen
ni·tro·glyc·er·in
ni·trous
nit·ty-grit·ty
nit·wit
no-ac·count
No·bel·ist
No·bel prize
no·bil·i·ty
no·ble
no·blesse oblige
no-brain·er
noc·tur·nal

noc·turne
nod·ding
node
nod·ule
No·el
no-fault
nog·gin
no-go
no-hit
noise
noi·some
noisy
no-load
no·lo con·ten·de·re
no·mad
no·mad·ic
no-man's-land
nom de plume
no·men·cla·ture
nom·i·nal
nom·i·nal·ism
nom·i·nate
nom·i·na·tion
nom·i·na·tive
nom·i·nee
non·age
no·na·ge·nar·i·an
non·aligned
non·ca·lo·ric
nonce
non·cha·lance
non·cha·lant
non·com
non·com·ba·tant
non·com·mer·cial
non·com·mis·
    sioned of·fi·cer
non·com·mit·tal
non com·pos
    men·tis
non·con·cur·rence
non·con·form·ist

non·con·for·mi·ty
non·co·op·er·a·tion
non·co·op·er·a·tive
non·cus·to·di·al
non·dairy
non·de·duct·ible
non·de·script
non·de·struc·tive
non·di·rec·tive
non·en·ti·ty
none·such
none·the·less
non-Eu·clid·e·an
non·fic·tion
non·flam·ma·ble
non-Hodg·kin's
    lym·pho·ma
non·in·duc·tive
non·in·ter·ven·tion
non·in·volve·ment
non·judg·men·tal
non·match·ing
non·me·tal·lic
non·ob·jec·tive
no-non·sense
non·pa·reil
non·par·ti·san
non·per·son
non·plus
non·plussed
non·pro·duc·tive
non·prof·it
non·pro·lif·er·a·
    tion
non·read·er
non·re·fund·able
non·rep·re·sen·ta·
    tion·al
non·res·i·dent
non·re·sis·tance
non·re·turn·able
non·sec·tar·i·an

non·sense
non·sen·si·cal
non se·qui·tur
non·sig·nif·i·cant
non·skid
non·start·er
non·sup·port
non·ten·ured
non·ver·bal
non·vi·o·lence
non·vi·o·lent
non·white
noo·dle
noon·time
noose
Nor·dic
nor'·east·er*
nor·mal
nor·mal·cy
nor·mal·ize
nor·mal school
nor·ma·tive
normed
North Star
north·east·er
north·east·ern
North·east·ern·er
north·east·ward
north·er
north·er·ly
north·ern
north·ern·most
north·west
north·west·ern
North·west·ern·er
north·west·ward
nose·bleed
nose·gay
no-show
nos·ing
nos·tal·gia
nos·tril

nos·trum
nosy
no·ta be·ne
no·ta·bil·i·ty
no·ta·ble
no·ta·ri·za·tion
no·ta·rize
no·ta·ry pub·lic
no·tate
no·ta·tion
notch
note·book
not·ed
note·pa·per
note·wor·thy
noth·ing·ness
no·tice
no·tice·able
no·ti·fi·ca·tion
no·ti·fy
no·tion
no·to·ri·ety
no·to·ri·ous
no-trump
not·with·stand·ing
nou·gat
nour·ish
nour·ish·ment
nou·veau riche
nou·velle cui·sine
nov·el
nov·el·ist
nov·el·ty
no·ve·na
nov·ice
no·vi·tiate
no·vo·caine
now·a·days
no·where
nox·ious
noz·zle
nu·ance

nu·bile
nu·cle·ar
nu·cle·ate
nu·cle·on
nu·cle·us
nude
nudge
nud·ism
nu·di·ty
nu·ga·to·ry
nug·get
nui·sance
null hy·poth·e·sis
nul·li·fi·ca·tion
nul·li·fy
nul·li·ty
numb
num·ber·less
numb·skull*
nu·mer·al
nu·mer·a·tion
nu·mer·a·tor
nu·mer·i·cal
nu·mer·ol·o·gy
nu·mer·ous
nu·mi·nous
nu·mis·mat·ic
nu·mis·ma·tist
num·skull
nun·cio
nup·tial
nurse
nurs·ery
nurse's aide
nurs·ing
nur·ture
nut·crack·er
nut·meg
Nu·tra Sweet®
nu·tri·ent
nu·tri·ment
nu·tri·tion

nu·tri·tion·ist
nu·tri·tious
nu·tri·tive
nut·shell
nut·ty
nuz·zle
ny·lon
nymph
nym·phet

O

oaf
oaf·ish
oak-leaf clus·ter
oars·man
oa·sis
oath
oat·meal
ob·bli·ga·to
ob·du·ra·cy
ob·du·rate
obe·di·ence
obe·di·ent
obei·sance
obe·lisk
obese
obe·si·ty
obey
ob·fus·cate
Obie
obit
obi·ter dic·tum
obit·u·ary
ob·ject
ob·ject·ti·fy
ob·ject·ti·fi·ca·tion
ob·jec·tion
ob·jec·tion·able
ob·jec·tive
objec·tiv·ism
objet d'art
ob·jur·ga·tion

ob·late
ob·la·tion
ob·li·gate
ob·li·ga·tion
oblig·a·to·ry
oblige
oblig·ing
oblique
oblit·er·ate
obliv·i·on
obliv·i·ous
ob·long
ob·nox·ious
ob·nox·ious·ness
oboe
ob·scene
ob·scen·i·ty
ob·scu·ran·tism
ob·scure
ob·scu·ri·ty
ob·se·qui·ous
ob·se·quy
ob·serv·able
ob·ser·vance
ob·ser·vant
ob·ser·va·tion
ob·ser·va·to·ry
ob·serve
ob·serv·er
ob·sess
ob·ses·sion
ob·ses·sive
ob·sid·i·an
ob·so·les·cence
ob·so·les·cent
ob·so·lete
ob·sta·cle
ob·stet·ric
ob·ste·tri·cian
ob·stet·rics
ob·sti·na·cy
ob·sti·nate

ob·strep·er·ous
ob·struct
ob·struc·tion
ob·tain
ob·tru·sive
ob·tru·sive·ness
ob·tuse
ob·verse
ob·vi·ate
ob·vi·ous
Oc·cam's ra·zor
oc·ca·sion
oc·ca·sion·al
oc·ca·sion·al·ly
oc·ci·den·tal
oc·cip·i·tal
oc·clude
oc·clu·sion
oc·cult
oc·cult·ism
oc·cu·pan·cy
oc·cu·pant
oc·cu·pa·tion
oc·cu·pa·tion·al
oc·cu·py
oc·cu·py·ing
oc·cur
oc·cur·rence
oc·cur·ring
ocean
oce·an·ic
ocean·og·ra·phy
oce·lot
o'clock
oc·ta·gon
oc·tag·o·nal
oc·ta·he·dral
oc·ta·he·dron
oc·tane
oc·tave
oc·ta·vo
oc·tet

oc·to·ge·nar·i·an
oc·to·pod
oc·to·pus
oc·to·roon
oc·u·lar
oc·u·list
oda·lisque
odd·ball
odd·i·ty
odd·ly
odd·ment
odds
ode
odi·ous
odi·um
odom·e·ter
odon·tol·o·gy
odor·if·er·ous
odor·less
odor·ous
od·ys·sey
oe·di·pal
Oe·di·pus
    com·plex
oeu·vre
of·fal⁺
off·beat
off·col·or
of·fend
of·fense
of·fen·sive
of·fer·ing
of·fer·to·ry
off·hand
off·hand·ed·ness
of·fice
of·fi·cer
of·fi·cial
of·fi·ci·ate
of·fi·cious
off·ing
off·key

off·la·bel
off·lim·its
off·line
off-off-Broad·way
off·sea·son
off·set
off·shoot
off·shore
off·side
off·spring
off·stage
off-the-books
off-the-re·cord
of·ten·times
ogle
ogre
ohm
oiled
oil·er
oil·skin
oily
oint·ment
okra
old·en
old-fash·ioned
Old Glory
old guard
old·ie
old·ish
Old Nick
old·ster
old-time
ole·ag·i·nous
ole·an·der
oleo·mar·ga·rine
Olestra™
ol·fac·tion
ol·fac·to·ry
oli·garch
oli·gar·chy
ol·ive
olym·pi·ad

Olym·pi·an
Olym·pic Games
om·buds·man
om·buds·per·son
ome·ga
om·elet
omen
om·i·nous
omis·sion
omit
omit·ting
om·ni·bus
om·ni·di·rec·tion·al
om·nip·o·tence
om·nip·o·tent
om·ni·pres·ence
om·ni·pres·ent
om·ni·science
om·ni·scient
om·ni·um-
    gath·er·um
om·ni·vore
om·niv·o·rous
onan·is·tic
once-over
on·col·o·gy
on·com·ing
one-armed ban·dit
one bag·ger (n)
one-bag·ger (adj)
one-di·men·sion·al
one-hand·ed
one-horse
one-night stand
one-on-one
one-piece
oner·ous
one·self
one-shot
one-sid·ed
one-track (adj)
one-trick po·ny

one-up·man·ship
one-way
on·going
on·ion
on·ion·skin
on-line
on·look·er
on·ly
on·o·mato·poe·ia
on·rush
on·set
on·shore
on·side
on·site
on·slaught
on·stage
on-the-job
on·to
on·tog·e·ny
on·to·log·i·cal
on·tol·o·gy
onus
on·ward
on·yx
ooze
opac·i·ty
opal
opal·es·cent
opal·es·cence
opal·ine
opaque
op art
op-ed
open·ness
open-air
open-and-shut
open-cir·cuit
open-end
open·er
open-eyed
open·hand·ed
open-heart (adj)

open·ing
open-la·bel
open mike
open-mind·ed
open-mouthed
open ses·a·me
op·era
op·er·a·ble
op·éra bouffe
opé·ra comique
op·era·go·er
op·er·ant
op·er·ate
op·er·a·tion
op·er·a·tion·al
op·er·a·tive
op·er·a·tor
op·er·et·ta
oph·thal·mic
oph·thal·mol·o·gist
oph·thal·mol·o·gy
oph·thal·mo·scope
opi·ate
opine
opin·ion
opin·ion·at·ed
opi·um
opos·sum
op·po·nent
op·por·tune
op·por·tun·ism
op·por·tun·ist
op·por·tu·ni·ty
op·pos·able
op·pose
op·po·site
op·po·si·tion
op·press
op·pres·sion
op·pres·sive
op·pro·bri·ous
op·pro·bri·um

op·ta·tive
op·tic
op·ti·cal
op·ti·cian
op·tics
op·ti·mal
op·ti·mism
op·ti·mist
op·ti·mis·tic
op·ti·mize
op·ti·mum
op·tion
op·tion·al
op·tom·e·trist
op·tom·e·try
opt out
op·u·lence
op·u·lent
opus
or·a·cle
orac·u·lar
oral[+]
oral·ly
or·ange
or·ange·ade
orang·u·tan
orate
ora·tion
or·a·tor
or·a·to·rio
or·a·to·ry
orb
or·bit
or·bit·al
or·chard
or·ches·tra
or·ches·tral
or·ches·trate
or·ches·tra·tion
or·chid
or·dain
or·deal

or·der
or·der·ly
or·di·nal
or·di·nance[+]
or·di·nary
or·di·na·tion
ord·nance[+]
or·dure
ore
oreg·a·no
or·gan
or·gan·dy
or·gan·ic
or·gan·ism
or·gan·ist
or·ga·ni·za·tion
or·ga·nize
or·ga·niz·er
or·gan·o·phos·
     phate
or·gasm
or·gi·as·tic
or·gy
ori·ent
ori·en·tal
ori·en·ta·tion
ori·en·teer·ing
or·i·fice
ori·ga·mi
or·i·gin
orig·i·nal
orig·i·nal·i·ty
orig·i·nate
ori·ole
or·i·son
Or·lon™
or·na·ment
or·na·men·ta·tion
or·nate
or·nery
or·ni·thol·o·gist
or·ni·thol·o·gy

or·phan
or·phan·age
or·phic
orth·odon·tia
orth·odon·tics
orth·odon·tist
or·tho·dox
or·tho·doxy
or·thog·o·nal
or·thog·ra·phy
or·tho·pe·dic
or·tho·pe·dics
or·tho·pe·dist
or·thot·ics
Os·car®
os·cil·late
os·cil·la·tion
os·cil·la·tor
os·cil·lo·scope
os·cu·late
os·cu·la·tion
os·mo·sis
os·prey
os·si·fi·ca·tion
os·si·fy
os·ten·si·ble
os·ten·ta·tion
os·ten·ta·tious
os·te·o·ar·thri·tis
os·te·ol·o·gy
os·teo·path
os·te·op·a·thy
os·te·o·po·ro·sis
os·tler
os·tra·cism
os·tra·cize
os·trich
oth·er·wise
oth·er·world·ly
oti·ose
oto·lar·yn·gol·o·gy
ot·ter

ot·to·man
ought
Oui·ja™
ounce
our·selves
oust
oust·er
out·age
out-and-out
out·board
out·break
out·burst
out·cast
out·come
out·crop
out·cry
out·dat·ed
out·dis·tance
out·do
out·door
out·doors
out·doors·man
out·er·coat
out·field
out·fit
out·fit·ter
out·flank
out·fox
out·go
out·go·ing
out·group
out·grow
out·growth
out·guess
out·house
out·ing
out·land·ish
out·last
out·law
out·lay
out·let
out·line

out·live
out·look
out loud
out·ly·ing
out·ma·neu·ver
out·mi·gra·tion
out·mod·ed
out·num·ber
out-of-body
out-of-bounds
out-of-date
out-of-doors
out-of-pock·et
out-of-the-way
out·pa·tient
out·per·form
out·post
out·put
out·rage
out·ra·geous
ou·tré
out·reach
out·rig·ger
out·right
out·shine
out·side
out·sid·er
out·smart
out·source
out·sourc·ing
out·spent
out·spo·ken
out·stand·ing
out·stare
out·strip
out·ward
out·ward-bound
out·ward·ly
out·wit
out·worn
oval
ovar·i·an

ova·ry
ovate
ova·tion
ov·en
over·abun·dance
over·achiev·er
over·act
over·ac·tive
over·age
over·all
over·arch·ing
over·awe
over·bear
over·bear·ing
over·board
over·bur·den
over·cap·i·tal·ize
over·cast
over·cau·tious
over·charge
over·coat
over·come
over·com·pen·sa·tion
over·con·fi·dence
over·de·ter·mined
over·de·vel·op
over·di·ag·no·sis
over·do[+]
over·dose
over·draw
over·dress
over·drive
over·due[+]
over·em·pha·sis
over·es·ti·mate
over·ex·pose
over·fill
over·flow
over·hand
over·hang
over·haul

over·head
over·hear
over·in·dulge
over·kill
over·laid
over·land
over·lap
over·lay
over·load
over·lord
over·ly
over·much
over·night
over·pass
over·play
over·pop·u·la·tion
over·pow·er
over·price
over·pro·duce
over·qual·i·fied
over·rate
over·reach
over·re·act
over·rep·re·sent·ed
over·ride
over·ripe
over·rule
over·run
over·scale
over·seas
over·seer
over·sell
over·sen·si·tive
over·sexed
over·shoe
over·shot
over·sight
over·sim·pli·fy
over·size
over·sleep
over·sold
over·spend

over·state
over·stay
over·stock
over·sub·scribe
over·sup·ply
overt
over·take
over-the-count·er
over-the-top
over·time
over·ture
over·turn
over·view
over·ween·ing
over·weight
over·whelm
over·work
over·write
over·wrought
ovine
ovoid
ovo-lac·to
   veg·e·tar·ian
ovu·late
ovule
owe
owl·et
owl·ish
ox·blood
ox·ford
ox·i·da·tion
ox·ide
ox·i·dize
ox·tail
ox·tongue
ox·y·gen
ox·y·gen·ate
ox·y·mo·ron
oyez
oys·ter
oys·ter·man
ozone hole

P
PABA
pab·u·lum
pace
pace·mak·er
pac·er
pace·set·ter
pachy·derm
pa·cif·ic
pac·i·fi·ca·tion
pac·i·fi·er
pac·i·fism
pac·i·fist
pac·i·fy
pack·age
pack·ag·ing
pack·er
pack·et
pack·horse
pack·ing·house
pact
pad·ded
pad·ding
pad·dle
pad·dle·ball
pad·dle·board
pad·dock
pad·dy
pad·lock
pa·dre
pa·dro·ne
pae·an
pa·el·la
pa·gan
pa·gan·ism
page
pag·eant
pag·eant·ry
page boy
pag·i·nate
pag·i·na·tion
pag·ing

pa·go·da
paid
pail·ful
pain·kill·er
pain·less
pains·tak·ing
paint·ball
paint·brush
paint·er
paint·ing
pair
pais·ley
pa·ja·mas
pal·ace
pal·at·able
pal·a·tal
pal·a·tal·iza·tion
pal·a·tal·ize
pal·ate[+]
pa·la·tial
pa·la·ver
pa·laz·zo
pale
pale·face
pa·le·og·ra·phy
Pa·leo·lith·ic
pa·le·on·tol·o·gy
pal·ette[+]
pal·frey
pal·i·mo·ny
pal·in·drome
pal·ing
pal·i·sade
pall
pal·la·di·um
pall·bear·er
pal·let[+]
pal·lette[+]
pal·lia·tive
pal·lid
pal·lor
pal·ly

palm
pal·mate
palmed
pal·met·to
palm·ist·ry
palmy
pal·o·mi·no
pal·pa·ble
pal·pate
pal·pi·tant
pal·pi·tate
pal·sied
pal·sy
pal·try
pam·pas
pam·per
pam·phlet
pan·a·cea
pa·nache
pan·a·ma
Pan-Amer·i·can
pan·cake
pan·chro·mat·ic
pan·cre·as
pan·da
pan·dem·ic
pan·de·mo·ni·um
pan·der
pan·dit
pan·do·ra
Pan·do·ra's box
pane
pan·e·gy·ric
pan·el
pan·el·ing
pan·el·ist
pan·han·dle
Pan·hel·len·ic
pan·ic
pan·icked
pan·ick·ing
pan·i·cle

panned
pan·nier
pan·ning
pan·o·ply
pan·o·rama
pan·sy
pan·ta·loon
pan·the·ism
pan·the·on
pan·ther
pant·ies
pan·to·graph
pan·to·mime
pan·to·mim·ist
pan·try
pant·suit
pants suit*
panty hose
panty·waist
pan·zer
pa·pa·cy
pa·pal
pa·pa·raz·zi
pa·pa·ya
pa·per
pa·per·back
pa·per·er
pa·per·hang·er
pa·per-thin
pa·per·weight
pa·per·work
pa·pery
pa·pier-mâ·ché
pap·il·lo·ma
pa·pist
pa·poose
pa·pri·ka
Pap smear
pa·py·rus
par·a·ble
pa·rab·o·la
par·a·bol·ic

para·chute
para·chut·ist
pa·rade
par·a·digm
par·a·dig·mat·ic
par·a·dis·al
par·a·dise
par·a·dox
par·a·dox·i·cal
par·af·fin
par·a·gon
par·a·graph
par·a·keet
para·le·gal
par·al·lax
par·al·lel
par·al·lel·ism
par·al·lel·o·gram
pa·ral·o·gism
pa·ral·y·sis
par·a·lyt·ic
par·a·lyze
para·med·ic
para·med·i·cal
pa·ram·e·ter
para·mil·i·tary
par·a·mount
par·amour
para·noia
para·noi·ac
para·noid
par·a·pet
par·a·pher·na·lia
para·phrase
para·ple·gic
para·pro·fes·
   sion·al
para·psy·chol·o·gy
par·a·site
par·a·sit·ic
par·a·si·tol·o·gy
par·a·sol

para·sym·pa·thet·ic
para·thy·roid
   gland
para·troop·er
par·boil
par·cel
par·cel·ing
parched
Par·chee·si™
parch·ment
par·don
par·don·able
pare+
par·e·go·ric
par·ent
par·ent·age
pa·ren·the·sis
par·en·thet·i·cal
par·ent·hood
Pa·rent-Teach·er
   As·so·ci·a·tion
pa·re·ve
par ex·cel·lence
par·fait
pa·ri·ah
pa·ri·e·tal
pari-mu·tu·el
par·ing
par·ish
pa·rish·ion·er
par·i·ty
par·ka
Par·kin·son's
   dis·ease
Par·kin·son's law
park·way
par·lance
par·lay+
par·ley+
par·lia·ment
par·lia·men·tar·i·an
par·lia·men·ta·ry

par·lor
Par·me·san+
par·mi·gia·na+
pa·ro·chi·al
pa·ro·chi·al·ism
par·o·dist
par·o·dy
pa·role
pa·rol·ee
par·ox·ysm
par·quet
par·que·try
par·ra·keet
par·ri·cide
par·rot
par·ry
parse
pars·er
par·si·mo·ni·ous
par·si·mo·ny
pars·ley
pars·nip
par·son
par·son·age
par·take
part·ed
par·terre
par·the·no·gen·e·sis
par·tial
par·tial·i·ty
par·tial·ly
par·tic·i·pant
par·tic·i·pate
par·tic·i·pa·tion
par·tic·i·pa·to·ry
par·ti·cip·i·al
par·ti·ci·ple
par·ti·cle
par·ti-col·ored
par·tic·u·lar
par·tic·u·lar·i·ty
par·tic·u·lar·ize

par·tic·u·lar·ly
part·ing
par·ti·san
par·ti·tion
part·ner
part·ner·ship
par·tridge
part-time
par·tu·ri·tion
part·way
par·ty
par·ve·nu
pas de deux
pass·able
pas·sage
pas·sage·way
pas·sé
pas·sen·ger
pass·er·by
pas seul
pas·sim
pass·ing
pas·sion
pas·sion·ate
pas·sive re·straint
pas·sive smok·ing
pas·siv·ism
pass·key
Pass·over
pass·port
pass·word
pas·ta
paste
paste·board
pas·tel
pas·tern
pas·teur·iza·tion
pas·teur·ize
pas·tiche
pas·tille
pas·time
pas·tor

pas·to·ral
pas·tra·mi
past·ry
pas·tur·age
pas·ture
pas·ture·land
pas·tur·ing
pas·ty
patch·ou·li
patch
patchy
pate
pâ·té de foie gras
pa·tel·la
pat·en
pa·tent
pat·ent·able
pa·ter·nal
pa·ter·nal·ism
pa·ter·ni·ty
Pa·ter·nos·ter
pa·thet·ic
path·find·er
path·o·log·i·cal
pa·thol·o·gist
pa·thol·o·gy
pa·thos
path·way
pa·tience
pa·tient
pa·ti·na
pa·tio
pa·tois
pa·tri·arch
pa·tri·ar·chy
pa·tri·cian
pat·ri·cide
pat·ri·mo·ny
pa·tri·ot·ic
pa·tri·o·tism
pa·trol
pa·trol·man

pa·tron
pa·tron·age
pa·tron·ess
pa·tron·ize
pat·ro·nym·ic
pat·sy
pat·ter
pat·tern
pat·ty
pau·ci·ty
paunch
paunchy
pau·per
pause
paved
pave·ment
pa·vil·ion
pav·ing
Pav·lov·ian
pawn
pawn·bro·ker
pay·able
pay-as-you-go
pay down
pay·ee
pay·er
pay·load
pay·ment
pay·off
pay·ola
pay-per-view
pay·roll
peace ac·cord
peace·able
peace·ful
peace·keep·ing
peace·mak·er
peace·time
peach
peachy
pea·cock
pea·fowl

pea·hen
peaked
peal[+]
pea·nut
pear[+]
pearl[+]
pearly
peas·ant
peas·ant·ry
pease
peat
peb·ble
peb·bly
pe·can
pec·ca·dil·lo
pec·to·ral
pe·cu·liar
pe·cu·liar·i·ty
pe·cu·ni·ary
ped·a·gog·ic
ped·a·go·gy
ped·al[+]
ped·ant
pe·dan·tic
ped·ant·ry
ped·dle[+]
ped·dler
ped·er·ast
ped·es·tal
pe·des·tri·an
pe·des·tri·an·ism
pe·di·at·ric
pe·di·a·tri·cian
pe·di·at·rics
pe·dic·u·lo·sis
ped·i·cure
ped·i·gree
pe·dol·o·gy
pe·dom·e·ter
pe·do·phil·ia
peek·a·boo
peel

peep·er

Peep·ing Tom

peer

peer·age

peer·less

peeve

pee·vish

pee·wee

pegged

pei·gnoir

pe·jo·ra·tive

Pe·king·ese

pe·koe

pe·lag·ic

pelf

pel·i·can

pe·lisse

pel·la·gra

pel·let

pel·li·cle

pell-mell

pel·lu·cid

pelt

pel·vic
   in·flam·ma·to·ry
   dis·ease

pel·vis

pem·mi·can

pe·nal

pe·nal·i·za·tion

pe·nal·ize

pen·al·ty

pen·ance

pence

pen·chant

pen·cil

pen·cil·ing

pen·dant

pend·ing

pen·du·lous

pen·du·lum

pen·e·tra·ble

pen·e·tra·bil·i·ty

pen·e·trate

pen·e·trat·ing

pen·e·tra·tion

pen·guin

pen·i·cil·lin

pen·in·su·la

pe·nis

pen·i·tence

pen·i·tent

pen·i·ten·tial

pen·i·ten·tia·ry

pen·knife

pen·man·ship

pen·nant

pen·ni·less

pen·ny

pen·ny-pinch

pe·nol·o·gy

pen·sion

pen·sion·er

pen·sive

pen·ta·gon

pen·tam·e·ter

pen·tath·lon

pent·house

pe·nult

pen·ul·ti·mate

pen·um·bra

pe·nu·ri·ous

pen·u·ry

pe·on

pe·on·age

pe·o·ny

peo·ple

pep·per

pep·per·mint

pep·pery

pep·py

per·am·bu·late

per an·num

per·cale

per cap·i·ta

per·ceiv·able

per·ceive

per·cent

per·cent·age

per·cen·tile

per·cep·ti·ble

per·cep·tion

per·cep·tive

per·cep·tu·al

perch

per·chance

per·co·late

per·co·la·tor

per·cus·sion

per·cus·sive

per di·em

per·di·tion

per·e·gri·nate

pe·remp·to·ry

pe·ren·ni·al

per·e·stroi·ka

per·fect

per·fec·ta

per·fect·ibil·i·ty

per·fect·ible

per·fec·tion

per·fid·i·ous

per·fi·dy

per·fo·rate

per·fo·ra·tion

per·force

per·form

per·form·able

per·for·mance art

per·form·er

per·fume

per·fum·ery

per·func·to·ry

per·func·to·ri·ly

per·haps

peri·gee

per·il·ous
pe·rim·e·ter
pe·ri·od
pe·ri·od·ic
pe·ri·od·i·cal
peri·odon·tics
peri·odon·tist
peri·pa·tet·ic
pe·riph·er·al
pe·riph·ery
peri·phras·tic
peri·scope
per·ish·able
per·ish·ing
peri·stal·sis
peri·to·ni·tis
per·i·win·kle
per·jure
per·jur·er
per·ju·ry
perk
perky
perl⁺
Perl⁺
per·ma·frost
per·ma·nence
per·ma·nent
per·me·abil·i·ty
per·me·able
per·me·ate
per·mis·si·ble
per·mis·sion
per·mis·sive
per·mit
per·mu·ta·tion
per·ni·cious
per·ox·ide
per·pen·dic·u·lar
per·pe·trate
per·pet·u·al
per·pet·u·ate
per·pe·tu·ity

per·plex
per·plex·i·ty
per·qui·site
per se
per·se·cute
per·se·cu·tion
per·se·ver·ance
per·sev·er·a·tion
per·se·vere
per·sim·mon
per·sist
per·sis·tence
per·sis·tent
per·snick·e·ty
per·so·na
per·son·able
per·son·al
   com·put·er
per·son·al·i·ty
per·son·al·ize
per·son·al·ly
per·so·na non
   gra·ta
per·son·i·fi·ca·tion
per·son·i·fy
per·son·nel
per·spec·tive
per·spi·ca·cious
per·spi·cu·ity
per·spic·u·ous
per·spi·ra·tion
per·spire
per·suade
per·sua·sion
per·sua·sive
pert
per·tain
per·ti·na·cious
per·ti·nence
per·ti·nent
per·turb
per·tur·ba·tion

pe·rus·al
per·tus·sis
pe·ruse
per·vade
per·va·sive
per·va·sive·ness
per·verse
per·ver·sion
per·ver·si·ty
per·ver·sive
per·vert
pes·ky
pes·si·mism
pes·si·mis·tic
pest
pes·ter
pes·ti·cide
pes·ti·lence
pes·ti·lent
pes·ti·len·tial
pes·tle
pet·al
pe·tard
pe·ter
pe·tite
pe·tit four
pe·ti·tion
pet·it jury
pe·tit mal
pet·it point
pe·trel
pet·ri·fy
pet·rol
pe·tro·le·um
pe·trol·o·gy
pet·ti·coat
pet·ti·ness
pet·tish
pet·ty
pet·u·lance
pet·u·lant
pe·tu·nia

pew·ter
pey·o·te
pha·eton
pha·lanx
phal·lic
phan·tasm
phan·tas·ma·go·ria
phan·tasy
phan·tom
pha·raoh+
phar·i·sa·ical
phar·i·see
phar·ma·ceu·ti·cal
phar·ma·cist
phar·ma·col·o·gist
phar·ma·col·o·gy
phar·ma·cy
phar·ynx
phase+
pheas·ant
phe·nom·e·na
phe·nom·e·nal
phe·nom·e·nol·
    o·gy
phe·nom·e·non
phe·no·type
pher·o·mone
phi·al
Phi Be·ta Kap·pa
phi·lan·der
phil·an·throp·ic
phi·lan·thro·pist
phi·lan·thro·py
phi·lat·e·list
phi·lat·e·ly
phil·har·mon·ic
phi·lip·pic
phi·lis·tine
phil·o·den·dron
phi·log·y·ny
phi·lol·o·gist
phi·lol·o·gy

phi·los·o·pher
phil·o·soph·ic
phi·los·o·phize
phi·los·o·phy
phle·bi·tis
phle·bot·o·my
phlegm
phleg·mat·ic
phlox
pho·bia
phoe·be
phoe·nix
pho·nate
phone card
pho·neme
phone tag
pho·net·ic
pho·ne·ti·cian
pho·nics
pho·no·graph
pho·nol·o·gy
pho·ny-ba·lo·ney
phos·phate
phos·pho·res·cence
phos·pho·res·cent
phos·pho·rus
pho·to·copy
pho·to·di·ode
pho·to·elec·tric
pho·to·en·grav·ing
pho·to·ge·nic
pho·to·graph
pho·tog·ra·pher
pho·to·graph·ic
pho·tog·ra·phy
pho·to·gra·vure
pho·to·jour·nal·ism
pho·to·off·set
pho·to op
pho·to·stat
pho·to·syn·the·sis
phras·al

phrase
phra·se·ol·o·gy
phras·ing
phre·nol·o·gy
phthi·sis
phy·lac·tery
phy·log·e·ny
phy·lum
phys·ic
phys·i·cal
phys·i·cal·i·ty
phy·si·cian
phy·si·cian's
    as·sis·tant
phy·si·cian=
    as·sis·ted
    sui·cide
phys·i·cist
phys·ics
phys·i·og·no·my
phys·i·og·ra·phy
phys·i·o·log·i·cal
phys·i·ol·o·gy
phy·sique
pi·a·nis·si·mo
pi·a·nist
pi·a·no
pi·ano·forte
pi·az·za
pi·ca
pic·a·dor
pi·ca·resque
pic·a·yune
pic·ca·lil·li
pic·co·lo
pick·a·back*
pick·ax
picked
pick·er·el
pick·et
pick·le
pick·pock·et

picky
pic·nic
pic·nicked
pic·nick·ing
pic·to·graph
pic·to·ri·al
pic·to·ri·al·ly
pic·ture
pic·tur·esque
pid·dling
Pid·gin En·glish
pie·bald
piece
pièce de
 ré·sis·tance
piece·meal
piece·work
pied
pied·mont
Pied Pip·er
pier[+]
pierce
pierc·ing
pier glass
Pie·tà
pi·ety
pi·e·zom·e·ter
pif·fle
pi·geon
pi·geon-toed
pig·gish
pig·gy·back
pig·gy bank
pig·ment
pig·men·ta·tion
pig out
pig·pen
pig·skin
pig·sty
pig·tails
pike
pi·laf

pi·las·ter
pile
pi·le·at·ed
pile-up
pil·fer
pil·fer·age
pil·grim
pil·grim·age
pil·ing
pil·lage
pil·lar
pil·lo·ry
pil·low
pil·low·case
pi·lot
pil·sner
pi·men·to*[+]
pi·mien·to[+]
pim·per·nel
pim·ple
pin·afore
pi·ña·ta
pince-nez
pin·cer
pinch
pinch-hit
pin curl
pin·cush·ion
pine
pi·ne·al
pine·ap·ple
ping
Ping-Pong™
pin·head
pin·hole
pin·ion
pin·kie
pin·na·cle
pin·nate
pi·noch·le
pi·ñon
pi·not noir

pin·point
pin·to
pin-up
pi·o·neer
pi·ous
pipe
pipe·ful
pipe·line
pi·pette
pip·ing
pip·pin
pip-squeak
pi·quan·cy
pi·quant
pique
pi·ra·cy
pi·ra·nha
pir·ou·ette
pis·ca·to·ri·al
pis·ca·to·ry
pi·scine
pis·ta·chio
pis·tol
pis·ton
pitch
pitch-dark
pitch·er
pitch·man
pitch-out
pit·e·ous
pit·fall
pith
pithy
piti·able
piti·ful
piti·less
pi·ton
pit·tance
pit·ted
pit·ter-pat·ter
pi·tu·itary
pity

piv·ot
piv·ot·al
pix·el
pix·ie
piz·za
piz·zazz
piz·ze·ria
piz·zi·ca·to
pla·ca·ble
plac·ard
pla·cate
pla·ce·bo
place·ment
pla·cen·ta
plac·id
plack·et
pla·gia·rism
pla·gia·rist
pla·gia·rize
plague
plaice
plaid
plain·ness
plaint
plain·tiff
plain·tive
plain-va·nil·la
plait[+]
plane
plan·et
plan·e·tar·i·um
plan·e·tary
plan·gent
plank
plank·ton
plan·ning
plan·tain
plan·ta·tion
plaque
plas·ma
plas·ter
plas·tic

plas·tic·i·ty
plas·ti·cize
plat du jour
plate[+]
pla·teau
plate·let
plat·en
plat·form
plat·ing
plat·i·num rec·ord
plat·i·tude
pla·ton·ic
pla·toon
plat·ter
platy·pus
plau·dit
plau·di·to·ry
plau·si·bil·i·ty
plau·si·ble
play·back
play-by-play
play·ful
play·go·er
play-off (n)
play·pen
play·wright
pla·za
plea
plead
pleas·ant
pleas·ant·ry
please
pleas·ing
plea·sur·able
plea·sure
pleat
plebe
ple·be·ian
pleb·i·scite
pledge
ple·na·ry
plen·i·po·ten·tia·ry

plen·i·tude
plen·te·ous
plen·ti·ful
plen·ti·tude
plen·ty
ple·num
pleth·o·ra
pleu·ri·sy
Plex·i·glas™
pli·able
pli·an·cy
pli·ant
plié
pli·ers
plight
plod
plo·ver
plow
plow·share
ploy
pluck
plucky
plug and play
plugged
plug-in (n, adj)
plum·age
plumb
plumb·er
plume
plum·met
plump
plump·ness
plun·der
plunge
plu·per·fect
plu·ral·ism
plu·ral·is·tic
plu·ral·i·ty
plus fours
plush
plushy
plu·toc·ra·cy

plu·vi·al
ply·wood
pneu·mat·ic
pneu·mat·ics
pneu·mo·nia
poach
poach·er
pock·et
poc·ket-sized
pock·mark
po·di·a·trist
po·di·a·try
po·di·um
po·em
po·e·sy
po·et
po·et·as·ter
po·et·ic
po·et·i·cal
po·et lau·re·ate
po·et·ry
po·grom
poi·gnan·cy
poi·gnant
poin·set·tia
point-and-click
point-blank
poin·til·lism
point-of-service
pointy
poise
poi·son
poi·son·ous
poke
pok·er
poky
po·lar
po·lar·i·ty
po·lar·iza·tion
po·lar·ize
Po·lar·oid™
pole

pole·cat
po·lem·ic
po·len·ta
pole·star
pole vault
po·lice
pol·i·cy
po·lio
pol·ish
po·lit·bu·ro
po·lite
po·li·tesse
pol·i·tic
po·lit·i·cal
pol·i·ti·cian
po·lit·i·cize
po·lit·i·co
pol·i·tics
pol·i·ty
pol·ka
pol·ka dot
pol·lack
pol·len
pol·li·nate
pol·li·na·tion
pol·li·wog
poll·ster
pol·lut·ant
pol·lute
pol·lu·tion
po·lo
po·lo·naise
pol·ter·geist
pol·troon
poly·an·dry
poly·chrome
poly·es·ter
po·lyg·a·mist
po·lyg·a·mous
po·lyg·a·my
poly·glot
poly·gon

poly·graph
poly·he·dron
poly·mer
poly·mor·phous
poly·no·mi·al
pol·yps
poly·phon·ic
poly·syl·lab·ic
poly·tech·nic
poly·the·ism
poly·un·sat·u·rat·ed
poly·ure·thane
po·made
pome·gran·ate
Pom·er·a·nian
pom·mel
po·mol·o·gy
pomp
pom·pa·dour
pom·pa·no
pom-pom
pom·pos·i·ty
pomp·ous
pon·cho
pon·der
pon·der·a·ble
pon·der·ous
pon·tiff
pon·tif·i·cal
pon·tif·i·cate
pon·toon
po·ny
Pon·zi scheme
pooch
poo·dle
poor·house
poor·ly
pop art
pop·corn
pope
pop·ery

pop·in·jay
pop·ish
pop·lar
pop·lin
pop·py
pop·py·cock
pop·u·lace
pop·u·lar
pop·u·lar·i·ty
pop·u·lar·ize
pop·u·late
pop·u·la·tion
pop·u·list
pop·u·lous
por·ce·lain
porch
por·cine
por·cu·pine
pore
por·gy
pork·pie hat
por·nog·ra·pher
por·nog·ra·phy
po·ros·i·ty
po·rous
por·poise
por·ridge
por·rin·ger
por·ta·ble
por·tage
por·tal
por·tal-to-por·tal
port·cul·lis
por·tend
por·tent
por·ten·tous
por·ter
por·ter·house
port·fo·lio
por·ti·co
por·tiere
por·tion

port·ly
port·man·teau
por·trait
por·trait·ist
por·trai·ture
por·tray
por·tray·al
por·tu·laca
pos·er
po·seur
posh
pos·it
po·si·tion
pos·i·tive
pos·i·tron-emis·sion
  to·mog·ra·phy
pos·se
pos·sess
pos·ses·sion
pos·ses·sive
pos·si·bil·i·ty
pos·si·ble
pos·sum
post·age
post·al
post·bel·lum
post·card
post·con·sum·er
post·date
post·er
pos·te·ri·or
pos·ter·i·ty
pos·tern
post·fem·i·nist
post·grad·u·ate
post·haste
post hoc
post·hu·mous
post·man
post·mark
post me·ri·di·em
post·mod·ern

post·mor·tem
post·op·er·a·tive
post·pone
post·pran·di·al
post·script
Post·Script™
post·trau·mat·ic
  stress dis·or·der
pos·tu·lant
pos·tu·late
pos·tur·al
pos·ture
po·sy
po·ta·ble
po·tage
po·tas·si·um
po·ta·to
pot-au-feu
pot·bel·ly
pot·boil·er
po·ten·cy
po·tent
po·ten·tate
po·ten·tial
po·ten·ti·al·i·ty
po·tion
pot·latch
pot·luck
pot·pour·ri
pot·sherd
pot·shot
pot stick·er
pot·tage
pot·ted
pot·ter's field
pot·tery
pouch
poul·tice
poul·try
pounce
pound
pout

pov·er·ty
pov·er·ty-strick·en
pow·der
pow·dery
pow·er chord
pow·er·ful
pow·er·house
pow·er walk
pow·wow
prac·ti·ca·bil·i·ty
prac·ti·ca·ble
prac·ti·cal
prac·ti·cal·ly
prac·tice
prac·tic·ing
prac·ti·cum
prac·ti·tion·er
prag·mat·ic
prag·ma·tism
prag·ma·tist
prai·rie
praise
praise·wor·thy
pra·line
prance
pran·di·al
prank
prank·ish
prank·ster
prate
prat·tle
prat·tler
prawn
prax·is
prayer
prayer·ful
preach
preachy
pre·adapt·ed
pre·ad·o·les·cence
pre·am·ble
pre·ar·range

pre·as·signed
preb·end
preb·en·dary
pre·can·cer·ous
pre·car·i·ous
pre·cau·tion
pre·cede
pre·ce·dence
pre·ce·dent
pre·ced·ing
pre·cept
pre·cep·tor
pre·cinct
pre·cious
prec·i·pice
pre·cip·i·tate
pre·cip·i·ta·tion
pre·cip·i·tous
pré·cis
pre·cise
pre·ci·sion
pre·clude
pre·co·cious
pre·cog·ni·tion
pre·con·ceive
pre·con·cep·tion
pre·con·di·tion
pre·cur·sor
pre·da·tion
pred·a·tor
pred·a·to·ry
pre·de·cease
pre·de·ces·sor
pre·des·ti·na·tion
pre·de·ter·mi·na·
   tion
pre·de·ter·mine
pred·i·ca·ble
pre·dic·a·ment
pred·i·cate
pre·dict
pre·dic·tion

pre·di·lec·tion
pre·dis·pose
pre·dis·po·si·tion
pred·ni·sone
pre·dom·i·nant
pre·dom·i·nant·ly
pre·dom·i·nate
pre·em·i·nence
pre·em·i·nent
pre·empt
pre·emp·tive
preen
pre·ex·is·tence
pre·fab·ri·cate
pref·ace
pref·a·to·ry
pre·fect
pre·fec·ture
pre·fer
pref·er·a·ble
pref·er·ence
pref·er·en·tial
pre·fer·ment
pre·ferred
   pro·vid·er
   or·ga·ni·za·tion
pre·fer·ring
pre·fig·u·ra·tion
pre·fig·u·ra·tive
pre·fig·ure
pre·fix+
preg·nan·cy
preg·nant
pre·hen·sile
pre·his·tor·ic
pre·in·duc·tion
pre·judge
prej·u·dice
prej·u·di·cial
prel·a·cy
prel·ate
pre·lim·i·nary

pre·lude
pre·mar·i·tal
pre·ma·ture
pre·med
pre·med·i·tate
pre·med·i·ta·tion
pre·med·i·ta·tive
pre·men·stru·al
  syn·drome
pre·mier*+
pre·miere+
pre·mier·ship
prem·ise
pre·mi·um
pre·mix
pre·mo·ni·tion
pre·mon·i·to·ry
pre·na·tal
pre·nup·tial
  agree·ment
pre·oc·cu·pan·cy
pre·oc·cu·pa·tion
pre·oc·cu·pied
pre·or·dain
prep·a·ra·tion
pre·par·a·tive
pre·pa·ra·to·ry
pre·pare
pre·pared·ness
pre·pay
pre·pay·ment
pre·plan
pre·pon·der·ance
pre·pon·der·ant
prep·o·si·tion
pre·pos·sess·ing
pre·pos·ter·ous
pre·pran·di·al
pre·pub·li·ca·tion
pre·quel
pre·reg·is·ter
pre·reg·is·tra·tion

pre·req·ui·site
pre·rog·a·tive
pres·age
pres·by·ter
Pres·by·te·ri·an
pres·by·tery
pre·school
pre·science
pre·scribe
pre·scrip·tion
pre·scrip·tive
pres·ence
pres·ent
pre·sent·able
pre·sen·ta·tion
pre·sen·ti·ment
pres·ent·ly
pre·sent·ment
pres·er·va·tion·ist
pre·ser·va·tive
pre·serve
pre·set
pre·shrunk
pre·side
pres·i·den·cy
pres·i·dent
pre·sid·i·um
pre·soak
press
press·ing
press·run
pres·sure
pres·sure gauge
pres·sur·i·za·tion
pres·sur·ize
pres·ti·dig·i·ta·tion
pres·tige
pres·ti·gious
pres·to
pre·sum·ably
pre·sume
pre·sump·tion

pre·sump·tive
pre·sump·tu·ous
pre·sup·pose
pre·tend
pre·tense
pre·ten·sion
pre·ten·tious
pre·ter·nat·u·ral
pre·test
pre·text
pret·ti·fy
pret·ti·ness
pret·ty
pret·zel
pre·vail
prev·a·lence
prev·a·lent
pre·var·i·cate
pre·vent
pre·ven·ta·tive
pre·ven·tive
pre·view
pre·vi·ous
pre·vi·sion
pre·war
prey
price·less
prick·ly
pride·ful
prie-dieu
priest
priest·hood
prig
prig·gish
prim
pri·ma bal·ler·ina
pri·ma·cy
pri·ma don·na
pri·ma fa·cie
pri·mal
pri·mar·i·ly
pri·ma·ry care

pri·mate
prim·er
pri·me·val
prim·ing
prim·i·tive
prim·i·tiv·ism
pri·mo·gen·i·tor
pri·mo·gen·i·ture
pri·mor·di·al
primp
prim·rose
prince
prince·dom
prince·ly
prin·cess
prin·ci·pal[+]
prin·ci·pal·i·ty
prin·ci·ple[+]
print·able
print·ery
print·out
pri·or
pri·or·ess
pri·or·i·ty
pri·o·ry
prism
pris·mat·ic
pris·on
pris·on·er
pris·sy
pris·tine
pri·va·cy
pri·vate
pri·va·teer
pri·va·tion
priv·a·tive
priv·et
priv·i·lege
priv·i·ly
privy
prix fixe[+]
prize

prize·win·ning
pro·abor·tion
pro·ac·tive
prob·a·bil·i·ty
prob·a·ble
pro·bate
pro·ba·tion
pro·ba·tive
probe
pro·bi·ty
prob·lem
prob·lem·at·ic
pro bono
pro·bos·cis
pro·ce·dur·al
pro·ce·dure
pro·ceed
pro·cess
pro·ces·sion
pro·ces·sor
pro·choice
pro·claim
proc·la·ma·tion
pro·cliv·i·ty
pro·cras·ti·nate
pro·cre·ate
pro·crus·te·an
proc·tol·o·gy
proc·tor
proc·u·ra·tor
pro·cure
prod
prod·i·gal
pro·di·gious
prod·i·gy
pro·duce
prod·uct
pro·duc·tion
pro·duc·tive
pro·duc·tiv·i·ty
pro·em
prof·a·na·tion

pro·fane
pro·fan·i·ty
pro·fess
pro·fessed·ly
pro·fes·sion
pro·fes·sion·al
  cor·por·a·tion
pro·fes·sor
pro·fes·so·ri·al
prof·fer
pro·fi·cien·cy
pro·fi·cient
pro·file
pro·fil·ing
prof·it[+]
prof·it·able
prof·i·teer
prof·li·ga·cy
prof·li·gate
pro for·ma
pro·found
pro·fun·di·ty
pro·fuse
pro·fu·sion
pro·gen·i·tor
prog·e·ny
pro·ges·ter·one
prog·no·sis
prog·nos·ti·cate
prog·nos·ti·ca·tion
pro·gram
pro·gram·mer
pro·gram·ming
pro·gress (v)
prog·ress (n)
pro·gres·sion
pro·gres·sive
pro·gres·siv·ism
pro·hib·it
pro·hi·bi·tion
pro·hib·i·tive
pro·hib·i·to·ry

pro·ject (v)
proj·ect (n)
pro·jec·tile
pro·jec·tion
pro·jec·tion·ist
pro·jec·tor
pro·lapse
pro·le·tar·i·an
pro·le·tar·i·at
pro-life
pro·lif·er·ate
pro·lif·ic
pro·lix
pro·lix·i·ty
pro·logue
pro·long
pro·lon·gate
pro·lon·ga·tion
prom
prom·e·nade
prom·i·nence
prom·i·nent
pro·mis·cu·ity
pro·mis·cu·ous
prom·ise
prom·is·ing
prom·is·so·ry
prom·on·to·ry
pro·mot·er
pro·mo·tion
prompt
prompt·er
pro·mul·gate
pro·nate
prone
prong
pro·noun
pro·nounce
pro·nounce·ment
pro·nounc·ing
pro·nun·ci·a·tion
proof

proof·read·ing
prop
pro·pa·gan·da
pro·pa·gan·dize
prop·a·gate
prop·a·ga·tor
prop·a·ga·tion
pro·pane
pro·pel
pro·pel·lant
pro·pel·ler
pro·pen·si·ty
prop·er
prop·er·tied
prop·er·ty
proph·e·cy[+]
proph·e·sy*[+]
proph·et[+]
pro·phet·ic
pro·phy·lac·tic
pro·phy·lax·is
pro·pin·qui·ty
pro·pi·ti·ate
pro·pi·ti·a·tion
pro·pi·ti·a·to·ry
pro·pi·tious
pro·po·nent
pro·por·tion
pro·por·tion·al
pro·pos·al
pro·pose
prop·o·si·tion
pro·pound
pro·pri·e·tary
pro·pri·e·tor
pro·pri·e·ty
prop·ter hoc
pro·pul·sion
pro·pul·sive
pro·rate
pro·sa·ic
pro·sa·i·cal·ly

pro·sce·ni·um
pro·sciut·to
pro·scribe
pro·scrip·tion
prose
pros·e·cute
pros·e·cu·tion
pros·e·cu·tor
pros·e·ly·tize
pro·sit
pros·o·dy
pros·pect
pro·spec·tive
pro·spec·tus
pros·per
pros·per·ous
pros·tate
pros·the·sis
pros·ti·tute
pros·trate
pros·tra·tion
prosy
pro·tag·o·nist
pro·te·an
pro·tect
pro·tec·tion
pro·tec·tor
pro·tec·tor·ate
pro·té·gé[+]
pro·té·gée[+]
pro·tein
pro tem
pro tem·po·re
pro·test
Prot·es·tant
Prot·es·tant·ism
pro·tes·ta·tion
pro·test·er
pro·tes·tor
pro·to·col
pro·to·mar·tyr
pro·ton

pro·to·plasm
pro·to·type
pro·to·typ·i·cal
pro·to·zo·an
pro·tract
pro·trac·tion
pro·trac·tor
pro·trude
pro·tru·sion
pro·tu·ber·ance
proud·heart·ed
prov·able
prove
prov·e·nance
prov·en·der
prov·erb
pro·ver·bi·al
pro·vide
prov·i·dence
prov·i·dent
prov·i·den·tial
prov·ince
pro·vin·cial
pro·vi·sion
pro·vi·sion·al
pro·vi·so
pro·voc·a·teur
prov·o·ca·tion
pro·voc·a·tive
pro·voke
pro·vo·lo·ne
pro·vost
prow
prow·ess
prowl
prox·i·mal
prox·i·mate
prox·im·i·ty
proxy
prude
pru·dence
pru·dent

pru·den·tial
prud·ery
prud·ish
prune
pru·ri·ence
pru·ri·ent
psalm
psalm·o·dy
p's and q's
pseu·do·code
pseu·do·ephed·rine
pseu·do·nym
pseu·do·sci·ence
pso·ri·a·sis
psych
psy·che
psy·che·del·ic
psy·chi·at·ric
psy·chi·a·trist
psy·chi·a·try
psy·chic
psy·cho
psy·cho·anal·y·sis
psy·cho·an·a·lyt·ic
psy·cho·an·a·lyze
psy·cho·bab·ble
psy·cho·dra·ma
psy·cho·gen·ic
psy·cho·log·i·cal
psy·chol·o·gize
psy·chol·o·gy
psy·cho·met·rics
psy·cho·path
psy·cho·path·ic
psy·cho·pa·thol·o·gy
psy·cho·sis
psy·cho·so·mat·ic
psy·cho·ther·a·py
pto·maine
pu·ber·tal
pu·ber·ty
pu·bes·cence

pu·bes·cent
pu·bic
pub·lic
pub·lic-ad·dress
    sys·tem
pub·li·can
pub·li·ca·tion
pub·li·cist
pub·lic·i·ty
pub·li·cize
pub·lic·ly
pub·lish
puck
puck·ish
pud·ding
pud·dle
pu·den·dum
pudgy
pueb·lo
pu·er·ile
puff·ery
pu·gi·lism
pu·gi·list
pug·na·cious
pug·nac·i·ty
puis·sance
puis·sant
pul·chri·tude
pul·chri·tu·di·nous
Pu·lit·zer prize
pul·let
pul·ley
Pull·man
pull·over (n, adj)
pul·mo·nary
    ede·ma
pulp
pul·pit
pulpy
pul·sate
pul·sa·tion
pulse

pul·ver·ize

pu·ma

pum·ice

pum·mel

pump·er

pum·per·nick·el

pump·kin

punch

punch-drunk

punc·til·i·ous

punc·tu·al

punc·tu·ate

punc·tu·a·tion

punc·ture

pun·dit

pun·gen·cy

pun·gent

pun·ish

pun·ish·able

pu·ni·tive

pun·ster

punt

pu·ny

pu·pa

pu·pae

pu·pil

pup·pet

pup·pe·teer

pup·pet·ry

pup·py·ish

pur·chase

pur·chas·er

pur·dah

pu·ree

pure·ly

pur·ga·tion

pur·ga·tive

pur·ga·to·ri·al

pur·ga·to·ry

purge

pu·ri·fi·ca·tion

pu·ri·fi·er

pu·ri·fy

Pu·rim

pur·ist

pu·ri·tan

pu·ri·tan·i·cal

pu·ri·tan·ism

pu·ri·ty

purl⁺

pur·loin

pur·ple

pur·port

pur·pose

pur·pose·ful

pur·pose·ful·ly

pur·pose·ly

pur·po·sive

purr

purse

purs·er

pur·su·ant to

pur·sue

pur·suit

pu·ru·lent

pur·vey

pur·vey·ance

pur·vey·or

pur·view

pus

push

push·over (n)

pushy

pu·sil·lan·i·mous

pus·sy·cat

pus·tule

pu·ta·tive

put-down (n)

put-on (n)

pu·tre·fac·tion

pu·tre·fy

pu·tres·cence

pu·trid

putsch

putt

put·ter

put·ty

put-up (adj)

puz·zle

puz·zle·ment

pyg·my

py·ja·mas*

py·lon

py·or·rhea

pyr·a·mid scheme

pyre

py·ro·ma·nia

py·ro·ma·ni·ac

py·ro·tech·nics

Pyr·rhic vic·tory

Py·thag·o·re·an

py·thon

Q

quack

quack·ery

quad

quad·ran·gle

qua·dran·gu·lar

quad·rant

quad·ra·phon·ic

quad·rate

qua·drat·ic

qua·drat·ics

qua·dren·ni·al

quad·ri·ceps

quad·ri·lat·er·al

qua·drille

qua·dril·lion

quad·ri·ple·gic

qua·driv·i·um

qua·droon

quad·ru·ped

qua·dru·ple

qua·dru·plet

qua·dru·pli·cate

qua·dru·pling
quaff
quag·mire
qua·hog
quail
quaint
quake
quak·er
Quak·er·ism
qual·i·fi·able
qual·i·fi·ca·tion
qual·i·fied
qual·i·fi·er
qual·i·fy
qual·i·ta·tive
qual·i·ty
   as·sur·ance
qualms
quan·da·ry
quan·ti·fi·ca·tion
quan·ti·fi·er
quan·ti·fy
quan·ti·ta·tive
quan·ti·ty
quan·tize
quan·tum
quar·an·tin·able
quar·an·tine
quark
quar·rel
quar·rel·some
quar·ri·er
quar·ry
quar·ry·ing
quart
quar·ter
quar·ter·back
quar·ter·deck
quar·ter·fi·nal
quar·ter horse
quar·ter·ing
quar·ter·ly

quar·ter·mas·ter
quar·ter·staff
quar·ter·staves
quar·tet
quar·tile
quar·to
quartz
qua·sar
quash
qua·si
qua·si-ju·di·cial
qua·si-leg·is·la·
   tive
qua·si-pub·lic
Qua·ter·na·ry
qua·ter·ni·on
qua·train
qua·ver
quay
quay·side
quea·sy
queen
queen mo·ther
queen·side
queen-size
queer
quell
quench
que·ried
quer·u·lous
que·ry
quest
ques·tion
ques·tion·able
ques·tion·naire
queue
quib·ble
quiche Lor·raine
quick
quick·en
quick-freeze
quick·sil·ver

quick-wit·ted
quid
quid pro quo
qui·es·cence
qui·es·cent
qui·et
qui·et·ism
qui·etude
qui·etus
quill
quilt
quince
qui·nie·la
qui·nine
quin·quen·ni·al
quin·sy
quin·tes·sence
quin·tet
quin·tile
quin·tu·ple
quin·tu·plet
quip
quip·ster
quire
quirk
quis·ling
quit
quit·claim
quite
quits
quit·tance
quit·ter
quiv·er
quix·ot·ic
quix·ot·i·cal·ly
quiz
quiz·mas·ter
quiz·zi·cal
quoin
quoit
quon·dam
quo·rum

quo·ta
quot·able
quo·ta·tion
quote
quo·tid·i·an
quo·tient

R
rab·bet[+]
rab·bi
rab·bin·ate
rab·bin·ic
rab·bit[+]
rab·ble
rab·ble-rous·er
ra·bid
ra·bies
rac·coon
race
ra·ceme
rac·er
race·track
race·way
ra·cial
rac·ing
rac·ism
rack·et
rack·e·teer
rack rent (n)
ra·con·teur
racy
ra·dar
ra·di·al
ra·di·a·l
   ker·a·tot·o·my
ra·di·al·ly
ra·di·an
ra·di·ance
ra·di·an·cy
ra·di·ant
ra·di·ate
ra·di·a·tion

ra·di·a·tor
rad·i·cal[+]
rad·i·cal·ism
rad·i·cal·ize
rad·i·cand
rad·i·cle[+]
ra·dii
ra·dio
ra·dio·ac·tive
ra·dio·ac·tiv·i·ty
ra·dio as·tron·o·my
ra·dio broad·cast
ra·dio·car·bon
   dat·ing
ra·dio fre·quen·cy
ra·dio·graph
ra·dio·iso·tope
ra·di·ol·o·gist
ra·di·ol·o·gy
ra·di·ol·y·sis
ra·dio·phar·ma·
   ceu·ti·cal
ra·dio·tele·phone
ra·dio tele·scope
ra·dio·ther·a·py
rad·ish
ra·di·um
ra·di·us
ra·dix
raf·fia
raff·ish
raf·fle
raft
rag·a·muf·fin
rag·bag
rage
rag·ged
rag·gedy
rag·ing
rag·lan
ra·gout
rag·time

raid
raid·er
rail
rail·ing
rail·lery
rail·road
rail-split·ter
rail·way
rai·ment
rain[+]
rain·bow
rain·coat
rain gauge
rain·mak·er
rain·wear
rainy
raise[+]
rai·sin
rai·son d'être
raj
ra·ja
rake
rake-off
rak·ish
rak·ish·ness
ral·ly
RAM[+]
ram[+]
ram·ble
ram·bunc·tious
ram·e·kin
ra·mie
ram·i·fi·ca·tion
ramp
ram·page
ram·pan·cy
ram·pant
ram·part
ram·rod
ram·shack·le
ranch
ran·cho

ran·cid
ran·cor
ran·cor·ous
ran·dom
ran·dom-access
   mem·o·ry
ran·dom·iza·tion
ran·dom·ize
rang
range
rang·i·er
rang·ing
rangy
rank
rank·ing
ran·kle
ran·sack
ran·som
rant
ra·pa·cious
ra·pac·i·ty
rape
rap·id
rap·id eye
   move·ment
rap·id-fire
ra·pid·i·ty
ra·pi·er
rap·ine
rap·pel
rap·per
rap·port
rap·proche·ment
rap·scal·lion
rapt
rap·tor
rap·ture
rap·tur·ous·ly
ra·ra avis
rar·e·fac·tion
rar·e·fied
rar·e·fy

rare·ly
rar·ing
rar·i·ty
ras·cal
ras·cal·ly
rash
rasp
rasp·ber·ry
raspy
ras·ter
rat·able
ra·ta·tou·ille
ratch·et
rate
rath·er
raths·kel·ler
rat·i·fy
rat·ing
ra·tio
ra·ti·o·ci·nate
ra·ti·o·ci·na·tion
ra·tion
ra·tio·nal
ra·tio·nale
ra·tio·nal·ism
ra·tio·nal·i·ty
ra·tio·nal·i·za·tion
ra·tio·nal·ize
rat·tail
rat·tan
rat·ter
rat·tle
rat·tler
rat·tle·snake
rat·tle·trap
rat·tling
rat·ty
rau·cous
raun·chy
rav·age
rave
rav·el

ra·ven
rav·en·ous
ra·vine
rav·ing
rav·i·o·li
rav·ish·ing
raw·hide
rayed
Ray·naud's
   dis·ease
ray·on
raze[+]
ra·zor
ra·zor·back
razz
raz·zle-daz·zle
razz·ma·tazz
reach
reach·able
re·act
re·ac·tant
re·ac·tion
re·ac·tion·ary
re·ac·ti·vate
re·ac·tive
re·ac·tor
read·abil·i·ty
read·able
read·i·ly
read·ing
re·ad·just·ment
read-only
read·out (n)
ready
read·i·ness
ready-made
ready-to-wear
re·agent
re·al[+]
re·al·ism
re·al·i·ty
re·al·i·za·tion

re·al·ize
re·al·ly
realm
re·al·po·li·tik
re·al·ty
ream
ream·er
reap
re·ap·por·tion
rear
rear·guard (adj)
re·arm
re·ar·ma·ment
rear·view mir·ror
rear·ward
rea·son
rea·son·able
rea·son·ing
re·as·sur·ance
re·as·sure
re·bate
reb·be
reb·el
re·bel·lion
re·bel·lious
re·birth
re·born
re·bound
re·buff
re·buke
re·bus
re·but
re·but·tal
re·cal·ci·trance
re·cal·ci·trant
re·cal·cu·late
re·call
re·cant
re·cap
re·ca·pit·u·late
re·ca·pit·u·la·tion
re·cap·ture

re·cast
re·cede⁺
re·ceipt
re·ceiv·able
re·ceiv·ables
re·ceive
re·cent
re·cep·ta·cle
re·cep·tion
re·cep·tion·ist
re·cep·tive
re·cep·tor
re·cess
re·ces·sion
re·ces·sion·al
re·ces·sive
re·charge
re·cher·ché
re·cid·i·vism
re·cid·i·vist
rec·i·pe
re·cip·i·ent
re·cip·ro·cal
re·cip·ro·cate
re·cip·ro·ca·tion
rec·i·proc·i·ty
re·ci·sion
re·cit·al
rec·i·ta·tion
rec·i·ta·tive
re·cite
reck·less
reck·on
re·claim
rec·la·ma·tion
re·cline
re·clos·able
re·cluse
rec·og·ni·tion
re·cog·ni·zance
rec·og·nize
re·coil

rec·ol·lect
rec·ol·lec·tion
re·com·bi·nant
rec·om·mend
rec·om·men·da·tion
re·com·mit
rec·om·pense
re·com·pose
rec·on·cil·able
rec·on·cile
rec·on·cil·i·a·tion
re·con·dite
re·con·di·tion
re·con·firm
re·con·nais·sance
re·con·noi·ter
re·con·sid·er
re·con·sti·tute
re·con·struct
re·con·struc·tion
re·con·ver·sion
re·con·vert
re·con·vey
re·cord (v)
rec·ord (n)
re·cord·ing
re·count
re·coup
re·coup·able
re·course
re·cov·er
re·cov·ery
rec·re·ant
rec·re·ate
re·cre·a·tion
re·crim·i·nate
re·crim·i·na·tion
re·cruit
re·crys·tal·lize
rec·tal
rect·an·gle

rect·an·gu·lar
rec·ti·fi·able
rec·ti·fi·er
rec·ti·fy
rec·ti·lin·e·ar
rec·ti·tude
rec·tor
rec·to·ry
rec·tum
re·cum·ben·cy
re·cum·bent
re·cu·per·ate
re·cu·per·a·tive
re·cur
re·curred
re·cur·rent
re·cur·sive
re·cu·sant
re·cy·cla·ble
re·cy·cle
re·dac·tion
re·dac·tor
red-bait·ing
red·breast
red·den
red·dish
re·dec·o·rate
re·dec·o·ra·tion
re·deem
re·de·fine
re·demp·tion
re·demp·tive
re·demp·to·ry
re·de·ploy
re·de·sign
re·de·ter·mine
re·de·vel·op
red-eye
red·head
red-hot
re·di·rect
re·dis·trib·ute

red-let·ter
red-neck
re·do
red·o·lence
red·o·lent
re·dou·ble
re·doubt
re·doubt·able
re·dound
re·dox
red-pen·cil
re·dress
re·duce
re·duc·tio ad ab·
    sur·dum
re·duc·tion
re·duc·tion·ism
re·duc·tive
re·dun·dan·cy
re·dun·dant
re·du·pli·cate
re·du·pli·ca·tion
re·dux
re·echo
reed
re·edit
re·ed·u·cate
reedy
reef·er
reek[+]
reel[+]
re·elect
re·elec·tion
reel-to-reel
re·em·ploy
re·en·act
re·en·force
re·en·ter
re·en·try
reeve
re·fash·ion
re·fec·tion

re·fec·to·ry
re·fer
re·fer·able
ref·er·ee
ref·er·ence
ref·er·en·dum
ref·er·ent
ref·er·en·tial
re·fer·ral
re·fill
re·fi·nance
re·fine
re·fine·ment
re·fin·ery
re·fin·ish
re·flect
re·flec·tion
re·flec·tive
re·flec·tor
re·flex
re·flexed
re·flex·ive
re·flex·ol·o·gy
re·flux
re·for·est
re·for·es·ta·tion
re·forge
re·form
re·form·able
ref·or·ma·tion
re·for·ma·to·ry
re·form·er
re·fract
re·frac·tion
re·frac·tive
re·frac·tor
re·frac·to·ry
re·frain
re·fresh
re·fresh·ment
re·frig·er·ant
re·frig·er·ate

re·frig·er·a·tor
re·fu·el
ref·uge
ref·u·gee
re·ful·gence
re·fund
re·fur·bish
re·fus·al
re·fut·able
ref·u·ta·tion
re·fute
re·gain
re·gal
re·gale
re·ga·lia
re·gard
re·gard·less
re·gat·ta
re·gen·cy
re·gen·er·ate
re·gen·er·a·tion
re·gen·er·a·tive
re·gen·er·a·tor
re·gent
reg·gae
reg·i·cide
re·gime
reg·i·men
reg·i·ment
reg·i·men·tal
re·gion
re·gion·al
re·gion·al·ism
reg·is·ter
reg·is·trant
reg·is·trar
reg·is·tra·tion
reg·is·try
re·gress
re·gres·sion
re·gres·sive
re·gres·sor

re·gret·ta·ble
re·group
re·grow
reg·u·lar
reg·u·lar·i·ty
reg·u·lar·ize
reg·u·late
reg·u·la·to·ry
reg·u·la·tion
reg·u·la·tor
re·gur·gi·tate
re·gur·gi·ta·tion
re·ha·bil·i·tate
re·ha·bil·i·ta·tion
re·hash
re·hears·al
re·hearse
re·ifi·ca·tion
re·ify
reign[+]
re·im·burse
re·im·burse·ment
rein[+]
re·in·car·nate
rein·deer
re·in·fec·tion
re·in·force
re·in·force·ment
re·in·forc·er
reins
re·in·state
re·in·sur·ance
re·in·sure
re·in·te·grate
re·in·ter·pret
re·in·vent
re·is·sue
re·it·er·ate
re·ject
re·jec·tion
re·joic·ing
re·join·der

re·ju·ve·nate
re·kin·dle
re·lapse
re·late
re·la·tion
re·la·tion·ship
rel·a·tive
rel·a·tiv·ism
rel·a·tiv·is·tic
rel·a·tiv·i·ty
re·lax
re·lax·ant
re·lax·ation
re·laxed
re·lay
re·lease
rel·e·gate
rel·e·ga·tion
re·lent·less
rel·e·vance
rel·e·van·cy
rel·e·vant
re·li·abil·i·ty
re·li·able
re·li·ance
re·li·ant
rel·ic
rel·ict
re·lief
re·lieve
re·li·gion
re·li·gious
re·line
re·lin·quish
rel·i·quary
rel·ish
re·live
re·lo·cate
re·luc·tance
re·luc·tant
re·main
re·main·der

re·make
re·mand
re·mark+
re·mark·able
re·marque+
re·match
re·me·di·a·ble
re·me·di·al
re·me·di·a·tion
rem·e·dy
re·mem·ber
re·mem·brance
rem·i·nisce
rem·i·nis·cence
rem·i·nis·cent
re·mise
re·miss
re·mis·si·ble
re·mis·sion
re·mit
re·mit·tal
re·mit·tance
re·mit·tent
rem·nant
re·mod·el
re·mon·strance
re·mon·strate
rem·o·ra
re·morse
re·morse·ful
re·morse·less
re·mote
re·mount
re·mov·able
re·mov·al
re·move
REM sleep
re·mu·ner·ate
re·mu·ner·a·tion
re·mu·ner·a·tive
Re·nais·sance
re·nal

Re·na·scence*
rend
ren·der
ren·dez·vous
ren·di·tion
ren·e·gade
re·nege
re·ne·go·tia·ble
re·ne·go·ti·ate
re·new
re·new·able
re·new·al
re·nom·i·nate
re·nounce
ren·o·vate
re·nown
rent-a-car
rent·al
ren·tier
re·num·ber
re·nun·ci·a·tion
re·of·fer
re·open
re·or·ga·ni·za·tion
re·or·ga·nize
re·pair
rep·a·ra·ble
rep·a·ra·tion
rep·ar·tee
re·past
re·pa·tri·ate
re·peal
re·peal·er
re·peat
re·peat·er
re·pel
re·pel·lent
re·pent
re·pen·tance
re·pen·tant
re·per·cus·sion
rep·er·toire

rep·er·to·ry
rep·e·ti·tion
rep·e·ti·tious
re·pet·i·tive strain
  in·ju·ry
re·pine
re·place·able
re·place·ment
re·play
re·plen·ish
re·plete
rep·li·ca
rep·li·cate
rep·li·ca·tion
re·ply
re·port
re·port·ed·ly
re·port·er
re·pos·al
re·pose
re·po·si·tion
re·pos·i·to·ry
re·pos·sess
rep·re·hen·si·ble
rep·re·sent
rep·re·sen·ta·tion
rep·re·sen·ta·tive
re·press
re·pres·sion
re·pres·sor
re·prieve
rep·ri·mand
re·print
re·pri·sal
re·prise
re·pro
re·proach
re·proach·ful·ness
rep·ro·bate
re·pro·cess
re·pro·duce
re·pro·duc·tion

re·pro·duc·tive
re·pro·gram
re·proof
re·prove
rep·tile
rep·til·ian
re·pub·lic
re·pub·li·can
re·pub·li·ca·tion
re·pub·lish
re·pu·di·ate
re·pu·di·a·tion
re·pug·nance
re·pug·nant
re·pulse
re·pul·sion
rep·u·ta·ble
rep·u·ta·tion
re·pute
re·quest
re·qui·em
re·qui·es·cat
re·quire
re·quire·ment
req·ui·site
req·ui·si·tion
re·quite
re·run
re·sal·able
re·sale
re·scind
re·scis·sion
res·cue
res·cu·er
re·search
re·seed[+]
re·sem·blance
re·sem·ble
re·sent
re·sent·ment
res·er·va·tion
re·serve

re·serv·ist
res·er·voir
re·set
re·shape
re·shuf·fle
re·side
res·i·dence
res·i·den·cy
res·i·den·tial
re·sid·u·al
res·i·due
re·sign
re·signed
re·sign·ed·ly
res·ig·na·tion
re·sil·ien·cy
re·sil·ient
res·in
res·in·ate[+]
res·in·ous
re·sist
re·sis·tance
re·sist·er[+]
re·sist·ible
re·sis·tor[+]
re·sole
res·o·lu·tion
re·solve
res·o·nance
res·o·nant
res·o·nate[+]
res·o·na·tor
re·sorb
re·sorp·tion
re·sort
re·sound
re·source
re·source·ful
re·spect
re·spect·abil·i·ty
re·spect·ful
re·spect·ful·ly

re·spec·tive
re·spec·tive·ly
res·pi·ra·tion
res·pi·ra·tor
re·spi·ra·to·ry
re·spite
re·splen·dence
re·splen·dent
re·spond
re·spon·dent
re·spond·er
re·sponse
re·spon·si·bil·i·ty
re·spon·si·ble
re·spon·sive
re·spon·sive·ness
re·stage
re·start
re·state
res·tau·rant
res·tau·ra·teur
rest·ful
res·ti·tu·tion
res·tive
res·tive·ness
rest·less
re·stor·able
res·to·ra·tion
re·stor·ative
re·store
re·strain
re·strained
re·straint
re·strict
re·stric·tion
re·stric·tive
re·struc·ture
re·study
re·sult
re·sul·tant
re·sume
ré·su·mé

re·sump·tion
re·sup·ply
re·sur·gence
re·sur·gent
res·ur·rect
Res·ur·rec·tion
re·sus·ci·tate
re·sus·ci·ta·tor
re·tail
re·tain
re·tain·er
re·take
re·tal·i·ate
re·tard
re·tar·dant
re·tar·da·tion
re·tell
re·ten·tion
re·ten·tive
re·test
ret·i·cence
ret·i·cent
re·tic·u·lar
re·tic·u·late
ret·i·cule
ret·i·na
ret·i·nue
re·tire
re·tir·ee
re·tire·ment
re·tir·ing
re·tool
re·tort
re·touch
re·trace
re·tract
re·trac·tion
re·trac·tor
re·train
re·tread
re·treat
re·trench

re·trench·ment
re·tri·al
ret·ri·bu·tion
re·trib·u·tive
re·trib·u·to·ry
re·triev·al
re·trieve
re·triev·er
ret·ro
ret·ro·ac·tive
ret·ro·fit
ret·ro·flex
ret·ro·grade
ret·ro·gress
ret·ro·gres·sion
ret·ro·gres·sive
ret·ro·rock·et
ret·ro·spect
ret·ro·spec·tion
ret·ro·spec·tive
ret·ro·ver·sion
ret·ro·vi·rus
re·turn
re·turn·able
re·turn·ee
re·uni·fy
re·union
re·unite
re·up
re·us·able
re·use
re·val·i·date
re·val·u·ate
re·val·ue
re·vamp
re·veal
rev·eil·le
rev·el
rev·e·la·tion
re·ve·la·to·ry
rev·el·er
rev·el·ry

re·venge
rev·e·nue
re·ver·ber·ant
re·ver·ber·ate
re·ver·ber·a·tion
re·vere
rev·er·ence
rev·er·end
rev·er·ent
rev·er·en·tial
rev·er·ie
re·ver·sal
re·verse en·gi·neer
re·verse mort·gage
re·vers·ible
re·ver·sion
re·vert
re·view[+]
re·vile
re·vise
re·vi·sion
re·vis·it
re·vi·so·ry
re·vi·tal·ize
re·viv·al
re·viv·al·ist
re·vive
re·viv·i·fy
re·viv·i·fi·ca·tion
rev·o·ca·ble
re·vo·ca·tion
re·voke
re·volt
rev·o·lu·tion
rev·o·lu·tion·ary
rev·o·lu·tion·ize
re·volve
re·volv·er
re·vue[+]
re·vul·sion
re·ward
re·wind

re·word
re·work
re·write
Reye's syn·drome
re·zone
rhap·sod·ic
rhap·so·dize
rhap·so·dy
rheo·stat
rhet·o·ric
rhe·tor·i·cal
rhet·o·ri·cian
rheum
rheu·mat·ic
rheu·ma·tism
rheu·ma·toid
rheu·ma·tol·o·gy
rheumy
Rh fac·tor
rhine·stone
rhi·ni·tis
rhi·noc·er·os
rhi·zome
Rh-neg·a·tive
Rhodes schol·ar
rhom·boid
rhom·bus
Rh-pos·i·tive
rhu·barb
rhyme
rhym·er
rhyme·ster
rhythm
rhyth·mic
ri·a·ta
rib·ald
rib·ald·ry
rib·bing
rib·bon
ri·bo·fla·vin
rich·es
rich·ness

Rich·ter scale
rick·ets
rick·ety
rick·shaw
ric·o·chet
ri·cot·ta
rid·dance
rid·den
rid·dle
rid·dling
rid·er
ridge
rid·i·cule
ri·dic·u·lous
ri·ding
rife
riff
rif·fle
riff·raff
ri·fle
ri·fling
rift
rig·a·ma·role
rig·a·to·ni
rig·ger⁺
rig·ging
right brain
right-click
righ·teous
righ·teous·ness
right·ful
right-hand
right·ly
right-mind·ed
right-of-way
right-to-life
right-to-work law
rig·id
ri·gid·i·ty
rig·ma·role
rig·or⁺
rig·or mor·tis

rig·or·ous
rile⁺
rill
rimmed
ring-a-le·vio
ring-around-the=
  rosy
ring·er
ring·let
ring·mas·ter
ring·side
ring·toss
rink
rinky-dink
rinse
rins·ing
ri·ot
ri·ot·ous
rip cord
rip·en
rip-off (n)
ri·poste
rip·per
rip·ping
rip·ple
rip·rap
rip·saw
rip·snort·er
Rip van Win·kle
ris·er
ris·i·bil·i·ty
ris·i·ble
risky
ri·sor·gi·men·to
ri·sot·to
ris·qué
rite⁺
rite of pas·sage
rit·u·al
rit·u·al·ize
ritzy
ri·val

ri·val·ry
rive
riv·er·bank
riv·er·bed
riv·er·side
riv·et
riv·et·er
Ri·vi·era
riv·u·let
RNA
roach
road·bed
road·block
road·house
road·kill
road rage
road show
road·side
road·ster
road war·rior
road·way
roam
roan[+]
roast·er
robbed
rob·bery
robe
rob·in
ro·bot
ro·bot·ics
ro·bust
rock·a·bil·ly
rock and roll
rock-bottom
rock candy
rock·er
rock·et
rock·e·teer
rock·et·ry
rock garden
rock 'n' roll
rock-ribbed

rock wool
rocky
ro·co·co
ro·dent
ro·deo
roe
roe·buck
roent·gen ray
rog·er
rogue
rogu·ery
rogues' gal·lery
roil[+]
role[+]
role-play
roll[+]
roll·back
roll·er coast·er
roll·er skate
rol·lick
ro·ly-po·ly
ROM
ro·maine
ro·man à clef
ro·mance
ro·man·tic
ro·man·ti·cism
ro·man·ti·cize
Ro·meo
romp
ron·deau
rood
roof
roof·ing
roof·top
rook
rook·ery
rook·ie
room·ful
room·mate
roomy
roost·er

rope
ropy
Roque·fort
Ror·schach test
ro·sa·cea
ro·sa·ry
ro·sé
ro·se·ate
rose·bud
rose-col·ored
    glas·ses
rose·mary
Ro·set·ta stone
ro·sette
Rosh Ha·sha·nah
Ro·si·cru·cian
ros·in
ros·ter
ros·trum
rosy
Ro·tar·i·an
ro·ta·ry
ro·tate
ro·ta·tion
ro·ta·tor
rote[+]
ro·tis·ser·ie
ro·to·gra·vure
ro·tor
ro·to·till
rot·ten
ro·tund
ro·tun·da
ro·tun·di·ty
roué
rouge
rough[+]
rough·age
rough-and-ready
rough-and=
    tum·ble
rough·en

rough-hewn
rough·house
rough·ly
rough·neck
rough·rid·er
rough·shod
rou·lette
round
round·about
roun·de·lay
round·er
round-ro·bin
round-shoul·dered
round-up (n)
rouse
roust·about
rout+
route+
rout·er
rou·tine
roux+
ro·ver
row·an+
row·di·ness
row·dy
roy·al·ly
roy·al·ist
roy·al·ty
rub-a-dub
rub·ber
rub·ber·neck
rubber-stamp
rub·bery
rub·bing
rub·bish
rub·ble
ru·bel·la
Ru·bi·con
ru·bi·cund
ru·bric
ru·by
ruck·sack

ruck·us
rud·der
rud·dy
rude·ness
ru·di·ment
ru·di·men·ta·ry
rue+
rue·ful
ruff+
ruf·fi·an
ruf·fle
RU 486
rug·by
rug·ged
ru·in
ru·in·ation
ru·in·ous
rul·er
rul·ing
rum·ba
rum·ble
rum·bling
ru·mi·nant
ru·mi·nate
rum·mage
rum·my
ru·mor
rump
rum·ple
rum·pus
rum·run·ner
run·about
run·around
run·away
run·down
rune
rung
run in (v)
run·nel
run·ner
run·ner's high
run·ny

run·off
run-of-the-mill
run-on (adj)
runt
run-through
run·way
ru·pee
rup·ture
ru·ral
ruse
rush
rush·ee
rus·set
Rus·sian rou·lette
rust
rus·tic
rus·tle
rus·tler
rusty
ru·ta·ba·ga
ruth·less
rye whis·key

S

Sab·ba·tar·i·an
Sab·bath
sab·bat·i·cal
sa·ber
sa·ble
sa·bot
sab·o·tage
sab·o·teur
sac
sac·cha·rin+
sac·cha·rine+
sac·er·do·tal
sac fungus
sa·chem
sa·chet+
sack
sack·cloth
sack·ing

sa·cral
sac·ra·ment
sac·ra·men·tal
sa·cred
sac·ri·fice
sac·ri·fi·cial
sac·ri·lege
sac·ri·le·gious
sac·ris·tan
sac·ris·ty
sa·cro·il·i·ac
sac·ro·sanct
sa·crum
sad·den
sad·dle
sad·dler
sad·dlery
sa·dism
sa·dist
sa·dis·tic
sa·do·mas·och·ism
sad sack
sa·fa·ri
safe-con·duct
safe-de·pos·it
  box
safe·guard
safe·keep·ing
safe·ty
saf·flow·er
saf·fron
sa·ga
sa·ga·cious
sa·gac·i·ty
sage
sage·brush
sa·go
sa·gua·ro
sa·hib
sail·er⁺
sail·or⁺
saint

Saint El·mo's
  fire
saint·hood
saint·like
sake⁺
sa·ke⁺
sa·ki*
sa·laam
sal·abil·i·ty
sal·able
sa·la·cious
sal·ad
sal·a·man·der
sa·la·mi
sal am·mo·ni·ac
sal·a·ry
sale
sales check
sales·clerk
sales·man
sales·per·son
sales·wo·man
sa·lic·y·late
sa·lience
sa·lient
sa·line
sa·lin·i·ty
sa·li·va
sal·i·vary
sal·i·vate
sal·low
sal·ly
sal·ma·gun·di
salm·on
sal·mo·nel·la
sa·lon
sa·loon
sal·sa
salt
sal·ta·tion
sal·ta·to·ri·al
salt·cel·lar

salt·i·er
sal·tine
salt·pe·ter
salt·shak·er
salty
sa·lu·bri·ous
sal·u·tary
sal·u·ta·tion
sa·lu·ta·to·ri·an
sa·lute
sa·lut·ing
sal·vage
sal·vage·able
sal·va·tion
salve
sal·ver
sal·vif·ic
sal·vo
Sa·mar·i·tan
same
same·ness
sam·o·var
Sam·o·yed
sam·ple
sam·pler
sam·pling
sam·u·rai
san·a·to·ri·um⁺
sanc·ti·fi·ca·tion
sanc·ti·fy
sanc·ti·mo·ni·ous
sanc·tion
sanc·ti·ty
sanc·tu·ary
sanc·tum
  sanc·to·rum
san·dal
san·dal·wood
sand·bag
sand·bank
sand·bar
sand·blast

sand-cast
sand-er
sand-lot
sand-man
sand-paint-ing
sand-pa-per
sand-pip-er
sand-storm
sand-wich
sandy
sane
sang-froid
san-gria
san-gui-nary
san-guine
san-i-tar-i-an
san-i-tar-i-ly
san-i-tar-i-um*
san-i-tary
san-i-ta-tion
san-i-tize
san-i-to-ri-um+
san-i-ty
san-sei
san-se-vie-ria
San-skrit
sans ser-if
sap-head
sa-pi-ence
sa-pi-ent
sap-ling
sap-per
sap-phic
sap-phire
sap-pi-ness
sap-py
sap-suck-er
sa-ra-pe*
sar-casm
sar-cas-tic
sar-co-ma
sar-coph-a-gus

sar-dine
sar-don-ic
sa-ri
sa-rong
SARS
sar-sa-pa-ril-la
sar-to-ri-al
sa-shay+
sa-shi-mi
sas-sa-fras
sassy
Sa-tan
sa-tan-ic
sa-tan-ism
satch-el
sat-ed
sa-teen
sat-el-lite dish
sa-tia-ble
sa-ti-ate
sa-ti-ety
sat-in
sat-iny
sat-ire
sa-tir-ic
sa-tir-i-cal
sat-i-rist
sat-i-rize
sat-is-fac-tion
sat-is-fac-to-ri-ly
sat-is-fac-to-ry
sat-is-fi-able
sat-is-fy
sat-is-fy-ing-ly
sa-to-ri
sa-trap
sat-u-rate
sat-u-ra-tion
Sat-ur-day
sat-ur-nine
sa-tyr
sauce

sauce-pan
sau-cer
sauc-i-ness
saucy
sau-er-bra-ten
sau-er-kraut
sau-na
saun-ter
sau-sage
sau-té
sau-téed
sau-té-ing
sau-terne
sav-age
sav-age-ry
sa-van-na
sa-vant
sav-ior
sa-voir faire
sa-vor
sa-vory
Sa-voy-ard
sav-vy
saw
saw-dust
sawed
sawed-off
sawn
saw-yer
sax-o-phone
sax-o-phon-ist
say-ing
say-so
scab-bard
scab-by
sca-bies
sca-brous
scaf-fold
scaf-fold-ing
scal-able
sca-lar
scal-a-wag

scald
scald·ing
scale
sca·lene
scal·lion
scal·lop
scal·lo·pi·ni
scal·ly·wag*
scalp
scal·pel
scalp·er
scaly
scamp
scam·per
scam·pi
scan
scan·dal
scan·dal·ize
scan·dal·mon·ger
scan·dal·ous
Scan·di·na·vian
scanned
scan·ner
scan·sion
scant
scanty
scape
scape·goat
scap·u·la
scap·u·lar
scar
scar·ab
scarce·ly
scar·ci·ty
scare
scare·crow
scaredy-cat
scare·mon·ger
scarf
scar·i·fy
scar·la·ti·na
scar·let

scary
scat
scathe
scath·ing
scat·o·log·i·cal
sca·tol·o·gy
scat·ter
scat·ter·brained
scat·ter·gram
scat·ter·ing
scav·enge
scav·en·ger
sce·nar·io
scene
scen·ery
sce·nic
scent
scep·ter
scep·tered
scep·tic
scep·ti·cal
scep·ti·cism
sched·ule
Sche·her·a·zade
sche·ma
sche·mat·ic
sche·mat·i·cal·ly
scheme
schem·ing
scher·zo
Schick test
schip·per·ke
schism
schis·mat·ic
schiz·oid
schizo·phre·nia
schizo·phren·ic
schle·miel
schlock
schmaltz
schmooze
schnapps

schnau·zer
schnit·zel
schnook
schnoz
schol·ar
schol·ar·ship
scho·las·tic
scho·las·ti·cism
scho·lia
school
school·ing
school·mas·ter
school·mate
school·mis·tress
school·teach·er
schoo·ner
schtick
schuss
schwa
sci·at·ic
sci·at·i·ca
sci·ence
sci·en·tif·ic
sci·en·tif·i·cal·ly
sci·en·tism
sci·en·tist
scim·i·tar
scin·til·la
scin·til·late
sci·o·lism
sci·on
sci·re fa·cias
scis·sors
sclaff
scle·ro·sis
scle·rot·ic
scoff
scoff·law
scold
sco·li·o·sis
scol·lop*
sconce

scone
scoop
scoot
scoot·er
scope
scorch
score
score·board
score·card
score·keep·er
scorn
scorn·ful
scorn·ful·ly
scor·pi·on
Scot
scotch
Scotch
scot-free
Scot·land Yard
Scots·man
Scot·tish
scoun·drel
scour
scourge
scourg·ing
scour·ing
scout
scout·mas·ter
scow
scowl
scrab·ble
scrag
scrag·gly
scrag·gy
scram
scram·ble
scram·bling
scrap
scrap·book
scrape
scraped
scrap·er

scrap·ple
scrap·py
scratch
scratchy
scrawl
scraw·ni·ness
scraw·ny
scream
scream·ing·ly
scree
screech
screed
screen sav·er
screw
screw·ball
screw driv·er
screwy
scrib·ble
scrib·bler
scribe
scrim
scrim·mage
scrimp
scrim·shaw
scrip
script
scrip·tur·al
scrip·ture
script·writ·er
scriv·en·er
scrod
scrof·u·la
scrof·u·lous
scroll
scrooge
scro·tum
scrounge
scrub
scrub·ber
scrub·by
scruff
scruffy

scrump·tious
scrunch
scrunch·ie
scru·ple
scru·pu·los·i·ty
scru·pu·lous
scru·ti·nize
scru·ti·ny
scu·ba
scud
scud·ding
scuff
scuf·fle
scuf·fling
scull+
scul·lery
scul·lion
sculpt
sculp·tor
sculp·tur·al
sculp·ture
sculp·tur·esque
scum
scum·my
scup·per
scup·per·nong
scurf
scur·ri·lous
scur·ry
scur·vy
scut·tle
scut·tle·butt
scythe
sea bass
Sea·bee
sea·borne
sea·coast
sea·far·er
sea·far·ing
sea·food
sea·go·ing
sea gull

seal
seal·ant
seal·er
seal point
seal·skin
Sea·ly·ham ter·ri·er
seam
sea·man
sea·man·ship
seam·less
seam·stress
seamy
sé·ance
sea·plane
sea·port
sear*+
search
search·ing·ly
search·light
search war·rant
sea·scape
sea·shell
sea·shore
sea·sick·ness
sea·side
sea·son
sea·son·able
sea·son·al af·fec·tive
   dis·or·der
sea·son·al·ly
sea·son·ing
seat
sea·ward
sea·way
sea·wor·thy
se·ba·ceous
se·cant
se·cede
se·ces·sion
se·ces·sion·ist
se·clude
se·clu·sion

sec·ond·ari·ly
sec·ond·ary
sec·ond-best
sec·ond-class
sec·ond-guess
sec·ond·hand smoke
sec·ond mort·gage
sec·ond-rate
sec·ond-string
se·cre·cy
sec·re·tar·i·al
sec·re·tar·i·at
sec·re·tary
sec·re·tary=
   gen·er·al
se·crete
se·cre·tion
se·cre·tive
se·cret·ly
sect
sec·tar·i·an
sec·tar·i·an·ism
sec·tion·al
sec·tion·al·ism
sec·tor
sec·u·lar
sec·u·lar·ism
sec·u·lar·ize
se·cure
se·cure·ly
se·cu·ri·ty
se·dan
se·date
se·da·tion
sed·a·tive
sed·en·tary
Se·der
sedge
sed·i·ment
sed·i·men·ta·ry
sed·i·men·ta·tion
se·di·tion

se·di·tious
se·duce
se·duce·ment
se·duc·tion
se·duc·tive
se·duc·tive·ness
se·duc·tress
sed·u·lous
seed+
seed·i·er
seed·ling
seedy
see·ing
See·ing Eye™
seek
seem·ing
seem·ly
seep
seep·age
seer+
seer·suck·er
see·saw
seethe
seeth·ing
seg·ment
seg·men·tal
seg·men·ta·tion
seg·ment·ed
seg·re·gate
seg·re·ga·tion
seg·re·ga·tion·ist
se·gue
seine
seis·mic
seis·mo·graph
seis·mol·o·gy
seize
seiz·ing
sei·zure
sel·dom
se·lect
se·lect·ee

se·lec·tion
se·lec·tive
se·lec·tiv·i·ty
se·lect·man
self-abase·ment
self-ab·sorbed
self-ab·sorp·tion
self·ac·ti·vat·ed
self-ac·tiv·i·ty
self-ad·dressed
self-ad·just·ing
self-ad·vance·ment
self-anal·y·sis
self-as·sured
self-cen·tered
self-clos·ing
self-com·pla·cent
self-com·posed
self-con·cept
self-con·cern
self-con·fi·dence
self-con·scious
self-con·tained
self-con·trol
self-crit·i·cal
self-de·cep·tion
self-de·feat·ing
self-de·fense
self-de·ni·al
self-de·struc·tion
self-de·ter·mi·na·
    tion
self-dis·ci·pline
self-dis·cov·ery
self-ed·u·cat·ed
self-ef·fac·ing
self-em·ploy·ment
self-es·teem
self-ev·i·dent
self-ex·am·i·na·tion
self-ex·plan·a·to·ry
self-ex·pres·sion

self-ful·fill·ing
self-gov·ern·ing
self-grat·i·fi·ca·tion
self-help
self-hyp·no·sis
self-im·age
self-im·por·tance
self-imposed
self-im·prove·ment
self-in·duced
self-in·flict·ed
self-ini·ti·at·ed
self-in·sur·er
self-in·ter·est
self·ish
self-jus·ti·fi·ca·tion
self·less
self-mas·tery
self-op·er·at·ing
self-per·cep·tion
self-per·pet·u·at·ing
self-pity
self-por·trait
self-pos·sessed
self-pos·ses·sion
self-pres·er·va·tion
self-pro·claimed
self-pro·pelled
self-pub·lish
self-pun·ish·ment
self-ques·tion·ing
self-re·al·iza·tion
self-re·crim·i·na·
    tion
self-re·flec·tion
self-re·gard
self-reg·u·lat·ing
self-re·li·ance
self-re·proach
self-re·spect
self-re·straint
self-righ·teous

self-sa·cri·fic·ing
self·same
self-seek·ing
self-ser·vice
self-serv·ing
self-start·er
self-stim·u·la·tion
self-suf·fi·cien·cy
self-suf·fi·cient
self-sup·port
self-sus·tain·ing
self-taught
self-treat·ment
self-wind·ing
sell·er+
sell-off
sell·out
selt·zer
sel·vage
se·man·tic
se·man·ti·cist
sema·phore
sem·blance
se·men
se·mes·ter
semi·an·nu·al
semi·au·to·mat·ic
semi·au·ton·o·mous
semi·cir·cle
semi·civ·i·lized
semi·co·lon
semi·con·duc·tor
semi·con·scious
semi·dark·ness
semi·de·tached
semi·fi·nal
semi·for·mal
semi·gloss
semi·in·de·pen·dent
semi·lit·er·ate
semi·month·ly
sem·i·nal

sem·i·nar
sem·i·nar·i·an
sem·i·nary
se·mi·ot·ic
semi·pal·mat·ed
semi·per·ma·nent
semi·per·me·able
semi·pre·cious
semi·pri·vate
semi·pro
semi·pro·fes·sion·al
semi·re·tired
semi·skilled
Se·mit·ic
semi·tone
semi·trop·i·cal
semi·week·ly
sem·o·li·na
sen·ate+
sen·a·tor
sen·a·to·ri·al
send-off (n)
se·nes·cence
sen·e·schal
se·nile
se·nil·i·ty
se·nior
se·nior·i·ty
sen·nit+
Se·ñor
Se·ño·ra
Se·ño·ri·ta
sen·sate
sen·sa·tion
sen·sa·tion·al·ism
sense
sen·sei
sense·less
sen·si·bil·i·ty
sen·si·ble
sen·si·tive
sen·si·tiv·i·ty

sen·si·tize
sen·sor+
sen·so·ry
sen·su·al
sen·su·al·ly
sen·su·ous
sen·su·ous·ness
sen·tence
sen·ten·tious
sen·tience
sen·tient
sen·ti·ment
sen·ti·men·tal·i·ty
sen·ti·nel
sen·try
se·pal
sep·a·ra·ble
sep·a·rate
sep·a·ra·tion
sep·a·rat·ist
sep·a·ra·tor
se·pia
sep·tet
sep·tic
sep·tu·a·ge·nar·i·an
sep·tum
sep·ul·cher
se·pul·chral
se·qua·cious
se·quel
se·quence
se·quen·tial
se·ques·ter
se·ques·tra·tion
se·quin
se·qui·tur
se·quoia
se·ra·glio
se·ra·pe
ser·aph
sere+
ser·e·nade

ser·en·dip·i·tous
ser·en·dip·i·ty
se·rene
se·ren·i·ty
serf+
serge+
ser·geant
se·ri·al kill·er
se·ri·al·i·za·tion
se·ries
ser·if
seri·graph
se·rio·com·ic
se·ri·ous
se·ri·ous·ness
ser·mon
ser·mon·ize
se·rol·o·gy
se·ro·to·nin
ser·pent
ser·pen·tine
ser·rate
ser·rat·ed
ser·ra·tion
se·rum
ser·vant
serv·er
ser·vice
ser·vice·able
ser·vice·man
ser·vice·wom·an
ser·vic·ing
ser·vi·ette
ser·vile
ser·vile·ly
ser·vil·i·ty
ser·vi·tude
ser·vo·mo·tor
ses·a·me
ses·qui·cen·te·na·ry
ses·qui·cen·ten·
    ni·al

ses·qui·pe·da·lian
ses·sion
ses·tet
se·ta
se·ta·ceous
set-aside
set·back (n)
set-in (adj, n)
set·screw
set·tee
set·ter
set·ting
set·tle
set·tle·ment
set·tler
set-to
set·up
sev·en·fold
sev·en·teen
sev·enth
sev·en·ty
sev·er·able
sev·er·al
sev·er·ance
se·vere·ly
se·ver·i·ty
sew·age
sew·er
sew·er·age
sew·ing
sex·a·ge·nar·i·an
sex·ism
sex·less
sex-linked
sex·ol·o·gy
sex·tant
sex·tet
sex·ton
sex·tu·ple
sex·tu·plet
sex·u·al
  as·sault

sex·u·al
  ha·rass·ment
sex·u·al·i·ty
sex·u·al·ly trans·
  mit·ted dis·ease
sexy
sfer·ics
sfor·zan·do
Shab·bat
shab·bi·ness
shab·by
Sha·bu·oth
shack
shack·le
shad
shade
shad·i·er
shad·i·ness
shad·ing
shad·ow
shad·owy
shady
shaft
shag
shag·gi·er
shag·gy
shah
shake[+]
shak·er
Shak·er
Shake·spear·ean
shake-up (n)
shak·i·ly
shak·i·ness
shaky
shale
shal·lot
shal·low
sha·lom
sha·lom alei·chem
shalt
sham

sha·man
sha·man·ic
sha·man·ism
sham·bles
shame·faced
shame·ful
sham·poo
sham·rock
shang·hai
Shan·gri-la
shank
shan·ty
shape
shape·less
shape·ly
shape-up (n)
shard
share
share·crop·per
share·hold·er
share-ware
shark
shark·skin
shar-pei
sharp·en
sharp·er
sharp·shoot·er
sharp-wit·ted
shat·ter
shat·ter·proof
shave
shav·ing
shav·er
Sha·vi·an
shawl
shay
sheaf
shear[+]
sheath
sheathe
sheath·ing
she'd

shed·der
sheep
sheep·fold
sheep·herd·er
sheep·ish
sheep·skin
sheer⁺
sheet
sheet·ing
sheet·rock
sheik*
sheikh⁺
sheikh·dom
shek·el
shelf
she'll
shel·lac
shel·lacked
shell·fish
shell-shocked
shel·ter
shel·tie
shelve
shelv·ing
she·nan·i·gans
shep·herd
shep·herd·ess
shep·herd's pie
Sher·a·ton
sher·bet
sher·iff
sher·lock
sher·ry
she's
shi·at·su
shib·bo·leth
shied
shield
shift
shift·less
shifty
Shih Tzu

shii·ta·ke
Shi·ite
shik·sa
shill
shil·le·lagh
shil·ling
shim
shim·mer
shim·mery
shim·my
shin
shin·dig
shine
shin·gle
shin·gles
shin·ing
shin·ny
shin splints
Shin·to
shiny
ship·board
ship·ment
ship·pa·ble
ship·per
ship·ping
ship·shape
ship·wreck
ship·wright
ship·yard
shire
shirk
shirr
shirt
shirt-sleeve
shirt·tail
shish ke·bab
shiv·a·ree
shiv·er
shoal
shoat
shock
shod

shod·di·ness
shod·dy
shoe
shoe·horn
shoe·lace
shoe·mak·er
shoe·string
sho·far⁺
sho·gun
shone
shoo
shoo·fly
shoo-in (n)
shook-up (adj)
shoot⁺
shop·a·hol·ic
shop·keep·er
shop·lift
shop·per
shop·talk
shop·worn
shore
shore·line
shore·ward
shoring
shorn
short
short·age
short·cake
short-change
short-cir·cuit
short·com·ing
short·en
short·en·ing
short·hand
short·list
short-lived
shortly
short shrift
short·sight·ed
short-tem·pered
short-term

short·wave
short-wind·ed
shot·gun
should
shoulder
shouldn't
shout
shove
shov·el
shov·el·er
shov·el·ful
show biz
show·case
show·down
show·er
show·i·er
show·man
show-off (n)
show·piece
show·stop·per
showy
shrank
shrap·nel
shred
shrew
shrewd
shrew·ish
shriek
shrift
shrike
shrill
shrimp
shrine
shrink
shrink·age
shrive
shriv·en
shriv·el
shroud
shrub·bery
shrug
shrunk

shtick
shuck
shud·der
shuf·fle
shuf·fle·board
shun
shunt
shush
shut
shut-eye
shut-in (n, adj)
shut·ter
shut·ter·bug
shut·tle
    di·plo·ma·cy
shut·tle·cock
shy
shy·ing
shy·lock
shy·ster
Si·a·mese
sib·i·lant
sib·ling
sib·yl·line
sick build·ing
    syn·drome
sick·en
sick·en·ing
sick·le
sick·le-cell ane·mia
sick·li·ness
sick·ly
sick·ness
side
side arm
side·burns
side·kick
side·light
side·line
si·de·re·al
side·slip
side·step

side·swipe
side·track
side·ways
side·wind·er
sid·ing
si·dle
si·dling
siege
si·er·ra
si·es·ta
sieve
sift
sigh
sight⁺
sight·less
sight-read
sight-see·ing
sig·ma
sign⁺
sign·age
sig·nal
sig·nal·man
sig·na·to·ry
sig·na·ture
signed
sig·net
sig·ni·fi·able
sig·nif·i·cance
sig·nif·i·cant
sig·ni·fi·ca·tion
sig·ni·fy
Si·gnor
Si·gno·ra
Si·gno·re
Si·gno·ri·na
sign·post
Sikh
si·lage
si·lence
si·lent
sil·hou·ette
sil·i·cate

sil·i·con
silk
silk·en
silk·i·er
silk screen
silk-stock·ing
silky
sill
sil·ly
si·lo
silt
sil·ver
sil·ver·fish
sil·ver·smith
sil·ver·ware
sil·very
sim·i·an
sim·i·lar
sim·i·lar·i·ty
sim·i·le
si·mil·i·tude
sim·mer
si·mo·nize
si·mo·ny
sim·pa·ti·co
sim·per·ing
sim·ple
sim·ple·ton
sim·plex
sim·plic·i·ty
sim·pli·fi·ca·tion
sim·pli·fy
sim·plis·tic
sim·plis·ti·cal·ly
sim·ply
sim·u·la·crum
sim·u·late
sim·u·la·tion
si·mul·cast
si·mul·ta·neous
since
sin·cere

sin·cere·ly
sin·cer·i·ty
sine⁺
si·ne·cure
si·ne die
si·ne qua non
sin·ew
sin·ewy
sin·ful
sing-along
singe
singe·ing
sin·gle
sin·gle-hand·ed
sin·gle-lens
   re·flex
sin·gle·ness
sin·glet
sin·gle·ton
sin·gle-track
sin·gly
sing·song
sin·gu·lar
sin·gu·lar·i·ty
sin·is·ter
sink·er
sink·hole
sin·less
sin·ner
si·nol·o·gy
sin·u·os·i·ty
sin·u·ous
si·nus
si·nus·i·tis
Sioux
si·phon
sire
si·ren
sir·loin
si·roc·co
si·sal
sis·sy

sis·ter
sis·ter·hood
sis·ter-in-law
sis·ter·ly
Sis·y·phus
si·tar
sit-down (n, adj)
site⁺
sit-in (n)
sit·ter
sit·ting
sit·u·ate
sit·u·at·ed
sit·u·a·tion
sit-up (n)
six-pack
six·pence
six-shoot·er
six·teen
sixth
six·ty
siz·able
size
siz·ing
siz·zle
siz·zler
skate
skeet
skein
skel·e·tal
skel·e·ton
skep·ti·cal
skep·ti·cism
skep·tics
sketch
skew
skew·er
skew·ness
ski
skid
skid·der
skid·dy

skid row
skied
skiff
ski·ing
skill
skil·let
skill·ful
skim
skim·mer
skim·ming
skimp
skimp·i·ly
skimpy
skin-deep
skin·flint
skin·head
skinned
skin·ny
skip
skip·per
skirl
skir·mish
skirt
skit
skit·ter
skit·tish
skit·tles
skoal
skul·dug·gery
skulk
skull[+]
skull·cap
skunk
sky·cap
sky·div·ing
sky-high
sky·jack·er
sky·lark
sky·light
sky·line
sky·rock·et
sky·scrap·er

sky·ward
sky·writ·ing
slab
slack
slack·en
slack·er
slag
slain
slake
slak·ing
sla·lom
slam
slam-bang
slam dunk
slam·ming
slan·der
slan·der·ous·ly
slang
slang·i·ness
slangy
slant
slant·wise
slap·dash
slap·hap·py
slap·stick
slash
slash·ing
slat
slate
slat·tern
slaty
slaugh·ter
slaugh·ter·ous
slave
sla·ver
slav·ery
Slav·ic
slav·ish
slay[+]
slea·zy
sled·ding
sledge

sledge·ham·mer
sleek
sleep
sleep ap·nea
sleep·er
sleep-in (adj)
sleep·i·ness
sleep·walk·er
sleepy
sleepy·head
sleet
sleeve
sleigh[+]
sleight
slen·der·ize
sleuth
slew*[+]
slice
slice-of-life
slick
slide
slid·ing
slight
slim
slime
slim·i·ness
slim·ming
slimy
sling
sling·shot
slink
slinky
slip·cov·er
slip·knot
slip·page
slip·per
slip·pery
slip·shod
slip·stream
slith·er
slith·ery
sliv·er

slob
slob·ber
slob·bered
sloe-eyed
slog
slo·gan
slo·gan·eer
sloop
slop
slope
slop·pi·ness
slop·py
slosh
slot
sloth
sloth·ful
slouch
slouchy
slough+
slo·ven·li·ness
slov·en·ly
slowly
slow-twitch
slub
sludge
slue*+
slug
slug·fest
slug·gard
slug·ger
slug·gish
sluice
sluice·way
slum
slum·ber
slum·lord
slum·my
slump
slur
slurp
slurred
slur·ring

slur·ry
slush
slushy
slut
smack
smack·er
small
small-fry
small-mind·ed
small·pox
small-scale
small-time
smarmy
smart
smart al·eck
smart·en
smarty-pants
smash
smash·ing
smash·up
smat·ter·ing
smear
smeared
smell
smelly
smelt
smelt·er
smid·gen
smile
smil·ey face
smirk
smite
smith
smith·er·eens
smithy
smock
smog
smog·gy
smok·able
smoke and
    mir·rors
smoky

smol·der
smooch
smooth
smooth·ie*+
smooth-tongued
smoothy+
smor·gas·bord
smote
smoth·er
smudge
smug
smug·gle
smug·gler
smug·ly
smut
snack
snaf·fle
sna·fu
snag
snail mail
snake
snaky
snap
snap·drag·on
snap·per
snap·pish
snap·py
snap·shot
snare
snarl
snatch
snaz·zy
sneak
sneak·er
sneaky
sneer
sneeze
sneezy
snick·er
snide
sniff
snif·fle

snif·fling

snif·ter

snig·ger

snip

snipe

snip·ing

snip·pet

snip·py

snitch

sniv·el

sniv·el·ing

snob

snob·bery

snob·bish

snood

snook·er

snoop

snoop·er

snoopy

snooty

snooze

snore

snor·kel

snort

snot·ty

snout

snow

snow·ball

snow·bank

snow·bird

snow·board

snow·bound

snow·drift

snow·fall

snow·flake

snow·mo·bile

snow·plow

snow·shoe

snowy

snub

snub-nosed

snuff

snuff·er

snuf·fle

snug

snug·gle

snug·gling

soak

so-and-so

soap

soap·box

soap opera

soapy

soar

soar·ing

sob

so·ber

so·ber·ly

so·bri·ety

so·bri·quet

so-called

soc·cer mom

so·cia·bil·i·ty

so·cia·ble

so·cial

so·cial·ism

so·cial·ist

so·cial·ite

so·cial·ize

so·cial·ly

so·ci·e·tal

so·ci·ety

so·cio·eco·nom·ic

so·cio·log·i·cal

so·ci·ol·o·gy

so·ci·om·e·try

so·cio·path

sock

sock·et

So·crat·ic

sod

so·da

so·da·list

so·dal·i·ty

sod·den

so·di·um

sod·omy

so·fa

soft

soft·ball

soft-cov·er

soft·en

soft·heart·ed

soft-ped·al

soft-shell (adj)

soft-shoe

soft-soap (v)

soft-spo·ken

soft·ware

softy

sog·gi·ness

sog·gy

soi·gnée

soil·age

soi·ree

so·journ

so·lace

so·lar

so·lar·i·um

solar plexus

sol·der

sol·der·ing iron

sol·dier

sole

so·le·cism

sol·emn

so·lem·ni·fy

so·lem·ni·ty

sol·em·nize

so·le·noid

so·lic·it

so·lic·i·ta·tion

so·lic·i·tor

so·lic·i·tous

so·lic·i·tude

sol·id

sol·i·dar·i·ty
so·lid·i·fi·ca·tion
so·lid·i·fy
so·lid·i·ty
sol·id-state
sol·i·dus
so·lil·o·quist
so·lil·o·quize
so·lil·o·quy
sol·ip·sism
sol·i·taire
sol·i·tary
sol·i·tude
so·lo
so·lo·ist
so·lon
so long
sol·stice
sol·u·bil·i·ty
sol·u·ble
so·lu·tion
solv·able
solve
sol·ven·cy
sol·vent
so·mat·ic
so·ma·tol·o·gy
som·ber
som·bre·ro
some
som·er·sault
som·er·set*
some·thing
some·time
some·times
some·where
som·me·lier
som·nam·bu·lant
som·nam·bu·lism
som·nam·bu·list
som·no·lence
som·no·lent

so·nant
so·nar
so·na·ta
song·fest
song·ster
son·ic
son·ic boom
son-in-law
son·net
son·ny
so·nor·i·ty
so·no·rous
soon·er
soot⁺
soothe
sooth·say·er
sooth·say·ing
soot·i·ness
sooty
soph·ism
soph·ist
so·phis·ti·cate
so·phis·ti·cat·ed
so·phis·ti·ca·tion
soph·ist·ry
soph·o·more
soph·o·mor·ic
so·po·rif·ic
sop·ping
sop·py
so·pra·no
sor·bet
sor·cer·er
sor·cer·ess
sor·cery
sor·did
sore·head
sore·ly
sor·ghum
so·ror·i·ty
sor·rel
sor·row

sor·row·ful
sor·ry
sor·tie
SOS
so-so
sot·to vo·ce
sou·brette
sou·bri·quet
souf·flé
sought
soul·ful
sound
sound-bite
sound·less
sound·stage
soup
soup·çon
soup du jour
soupy
source code
sou·sa·phone
souse
sou·tane
south
South·east·ern·er
south·er·ly
south·ern
South·ern·er
south·land
south·paw
sou·ve·nir
sou·vla·ki
sou'·west·er
sov·er·eign
sov·er·eign·ty
So·vi·et
sow·bel·ly
soy·bean
spa
space ca·det
space·craft
space lab

spac·ing
spa·cious
spack·le
spade
spa·ghet·ti strap
spam
span
spa·na·ko·pi·ta
span·dex
span·gle
span·iel
spank
span·ner
spar
spare
spare·ribs
spar·ing
spark
spar·kle
spar·kler
spar·row
sparse·ness
spar·si·ty
Spar·tan
spasm
spas·mod·ic
spas·tic
spat
spate
spa·tial
spa·tial·ly
spat·ter
spat·u·la
spav·in
spawn
speak·easy
speak·er
spear
spear·gun
spear·head
spear·mint
spe·cial

spe·cial·ist
spe·ci·al·i·ty
spe·cial·i·za·tion
spe·cial·ize
spe·cial·ly
spe·cial-needs
spe·cial·ty
spe·cies
spe·cif·ic
spec·i·fi·ca·tion
spec·i·fic·i·ty
spec·i·fy
spec·i·men
spe·cious
speck
speck·le
spec·ta·cle
spec·tac·u·lar
spec·ta·tor
spec·ter
spec·tral
spec·trom·e·ter
spec·tro·scope
spec·trum
spec·u·late
spec·u·la·tion
spec·u·la·tive
spec·u·la·tor
spec·u·lum
speech
speech·less
speed
speed·ball
speed bump
speed·om·e·ter
speed-read·ing
speed·way
speedy
spe·le·ol·o·gist
spe·le·ol·o·gy
spell·bind
spell·bound

spell-check
spell·er
spe·lunk·er
spe·lunk·ing
spend·able
spend·thrift
spent
sperm
sper·ma·ce·ti
spew
sphag·num
sphere
spher·i·cal
spher·oid
sphe·roi·dal
sphinx-like
spice
spic·i·ness
spick-and-span
spicy
spi·der
spi·dery
spiel
spig·ot
spike
spiky
spill·age
spill·way
spi·na bi·fi·da
spin·ach
spi·nal
spin·dle
spin·dly
spin doc·tor
spin·drift
spine
spine·less
spin·et
spin·na·ker
spin·ner
spin·ning
spin-off (n)

spin·ster
spiny
spi·ral
spire
spi·rea
spir·it
spir·it·ed
spir·it·ism
spir·it·less
spir·i·tu·al
spir·i·tu·al·ism
spir·i·tu·al·i·ty
spi·ro·chete
spite
spit·ed
spite·ful
spit·fire
spit·tle
spit·toon
splash
splat·ter
splay·foot·ed
spleen
splen·did
splen·did·ly
splen·dif·er·ous
splen·dor
sple·net·ic
splice
splint
splin·ter
split
split-level
split·ting
splotch
splurge
splut·ter
spoil
spoil·age
spoil·er
spoil·sport
spoke

spokes·per·son
spo·li·a·tion
spon·dee
spon·dy·li·tis
sponge
spongy
spon·sor
spon·ta·ne·i·ty
spon·ta·ne·ous
spoof
spooky
spool
spool·ing
spoon
spoo·ner·ism
spoon-feed
spoon·ful
spoor⁺
spo·rad·ic
spore⁺
spor·ran
sport
sport·ive
sports·cast
sports·man·ship
sport-util·i·ty
    ve·hi·cle
sporty
spot-check
spot·less
spot·light
spot·ted
spot·ter
spot·ty
spou·sal
spouse
spout
sprain
sprat
sprawl
spray
spread

spread-ea·gle
spread·er
spread·sheet
spree
sprig
spright·li·ness
spright·ly
spring
spring·board
spring·er
spring·time
springy
sprin·kle
sprin·kling
sprint
sprite
spritz·er
sprock·et
sprout
spruce
spry
spud
spume
spu·mo·ni
spunk
spunk·i·ly
spunky
spur
spu·ri·ous
spurn
spurred
spurt
sput·nik
sput·ter
spu·tum
spy·glass
squab
squab·ble
squad
squad·ron
squal·id
squall

squa·lor
squa·mous
squan·der
square
squar·ish
squash
squat
squat·ter
squaw
squawk
squeak
squeaky
squeal
squea·mish
squee·gee
squeeze
squelch
squib
squid
squig·gle
squint
squire
squirm
squir·rel
squirt
squishy
stab
sta·bil·i·ty
sta·bi·lize
sta·bi·liz·er
sta·ble
sta·bling
stac·ca·to
stack
stack·able
sta·dia
sta·di·um
staff[+]
stag
stage
stage·craft
stage·struck

stag·ger
stag·ing
stag·nant
stag·nate
stag·na·tion
stagy
staid
stain
stain·er
stain·less
stair·case
stair·way
stair·well
stake
stake·out (n)
sta·lac·tite
sta·lag
sta·lag·mite
stale
stale·mate
Sta·lin·ism
stalk
stall
stal·lion
stal·wart
sta·men
sta·mi·na (pl of
    stamen)[+]
stam·i·na[+]
stam·mer
stamp
stam·pede
stamp·er
stance
stanch*[+]
stan·chion
stand
stan·dard
stan·dard-bear·er
stan·dard·bred
stan·dard
    de·vi·a·tion

stan·dard·ize
stand·by
stand-in (n)
stand·ing
stand·off (n)
stand·off·ish
stand·pat
stand·point
stand·still
stand-up (n)
stan·za
staph·y·lo·coc·cus
sta·ple
sta·pler
star·board
starch
star-cham·ber
starchy
star-crossed
star·dom
stare
star·gaz·ing
stark
star·let
star·ling
star·ry
star-span·gled
start
star·tle
star·tling
star·va·tion
starve
stash
sta·sis
state
state·craft
stat·ed
state·hood
state·less
state·ly
state·ment
state·side

states·man
states' rights
stat·ic
sta·tion
sta·tion·ary[+]
sta·tio·ner
sta·tio·nery[+]
stat·ism
sta·tis·tic
sta·tis·ti·cal
stat·is·ti·cian
sta·tis·tics
stat·u·ary
stat·ue
stat·u·esque
stat·u·ette
stat·ure
sta·tus
sta·tus quo
stat·ute
stat·u·to·ry
staunch[+]
stave[+]
stay·sail
STD
stead
stead·fast
stead·ing
steady
steak[+]
steal[+]
stealth
stealth·i·ly
stealthy
steam
steam·er
steam·roll·er
steam·ship
steamy
steed
steel[+]
steely

steel·yard
steep
stee·ple
stee·ple·chase
stee·ple·jack
steer
steer·age
stein
stel·lar
stem cell
stem·less
stemmed
stem·ware
stem-wind·er
stench
sten·cil
ste·nog·ra·pher
ste·nog·ra·phy
steno·type
sten·to·ri·an
step aer·o·bics
step·broth·er
step·child
step·child·ren
step·daugh·ter
step·fa·ther
step·lad·der
step·moth·er
step·par·ent·ing
steppe
step·ping-stone
step·sis·ter
step·son
step stool
ste·reo
ste·reo·phon·ic
ste·reo·typed
ster·ile
ster·il·i·za·tion
ster·il·ize
ster·ling
stern

ster·num
ste·roid
stet
stetho·scope
Stet·son™
stet·ted
stet·ting
ste·ve·dore
stew
stew·ard
stew·ard·ship
stick
stick-in-the-mud
stick·ler
stick·pin
stick·up (n)
sticky
stiff
stiff·en
stiff-necked
stiff·ness
sti·fle
stig·ma
stig·mat·ic
stig·ma·tism
stig·ma·tize
stile[+]
sti·let·to
still·birth
still·born
still life
stil·ly
stilt·ed
Stil·ton
stim·u·lant
stim·u·late
stim·u·lus
sting
stin·gi·ness
sting·less
stin·gy
stink

stint
sti·pend
stip·ple
stip·u·late
stip·u·la·tion
stir
stirk
stir·ring
stir·rup
stitch
stitch·ery
stoat
stock
stock·ade
stock·bro·ker
stock·hold·er
Stock·holm
  syn·drome
stock·ing
stock-in-trade
stock·keep·er
stock·man
stock mar·ket
stock·pile
stock·pot
stock·room
stock split
stock-still
stock·tak·ing
stocky
stock·yard
stodgy
sto·ic
sto·i·cal
sto·i·cism
stoke
stole
sto·len
stol·id
stol·len
stom·ach
stom·ach·ache

stomp
stone
Stone Age
stone-broke
stoned
stone·ma·son
stone·wall
stone·ware
stony
stood
stooge
stoop[+]
stop-and-go
stop·cock
stop·gap
stop·light
stop·over (n)
stop·per
stop·ping
stop·watch
stor·age
store
store·front
store·house
store·keep·er
store·room
sto·ried
stork
storm
storm·i·ly
stormy
sto·ry
sto·ry·book
sto·ry·tell·er
stoup[+]
stout
stout·heart·ed
stove
stow
stow·age
stow·away
stra·bis·mus

strad·dle
Strad·i·var·i·us
strafe
strag·gle
strag·gly
straight[+]
straight·away
straight·edge
straight·en
straight·for·ward
straight-line (adj)
strain
strait[+]
strait·jack·et
strait·laced
strand
strange
stran·gle
stran·gle·hold
stran·gu·la·tion
strap·hang·er
strap·less
strapped
strap·ping
strat·a·gem
stra·te·gic
strat·e·gy
strat·i·fi·ca·tion
strat·i·fy
strato·sphere
strato·spher·ic
stra·tum
straw
straw·ber·ry
stray
streak
streak·ing
streaky
stream
stream·er
stream·line
street

street·walk·er
street·wise
strength
strength·en
stren·u·ous
strep·to·coc·cus
strep·to·my·cin
stress
stressed-out
stress·ful
stress test
stretch
stretch-out (n)
strew
stri·at·ed
stri·a·tion
strick·en
strict
strict·ly
stric·ture
stride
stri·dence
stri·den·cy
stri·dent
strife
strike
strike·bound
strike·break·er
strike·out
strik·er
strik·ing
string
strin·gen·cy
strin·gent
string·ing
string the·o·ry
strip
striped
strip mall
strip·per
strip·tease
strive

strobe
stro·bo·scope
strode
stroke
stroll·er
strong·hold
strong-mind·ed
stron·ti·um
stro·phe
stro·phic
strove
struck
struc·tur·al
struc·ture
stru·del
strug·gle
strum·ming
strung
strut
strych·nine
stub·ble
stub·born
stub·born·ness
stub·by
stuc·co
stud
stud·ding sail
stu·dent
stud·ied
stu·dio
stu·di·ous
study
study·ing
stuff·ing
stuffy
stul·ti·fi·ca·tion
stul·ti·fy
stum·ble
stump
stumpy
stung
stunk

stun·ner
stun·ning
stunt
stu·pe·fac·tion
stu·pe·fy
stu·pen·dous
stu·pid
stu·pid·i·ty
stu·pid·ly
stu·por
stur·dy
stur·geon
stut·ter
sty·gian
style[+]
styl·ish
sty·lis·tic
styl·ize
sty·lus
sty·mie
styp·tic
Sty·ro·foam™
suave·ness
sua·vi·ty
sub·arc·tic
sub·con·scious
sub·con·ti·nent
sub·con·tract
sub·cul·ture
sub·cu·ta·ne·ous
sub·dea·con
sub·di·vide
sub·due
sub·dued
sub·freez·ing
sub·group
sub·head
sub·head·ing
sub·hu·man
sub·ject
sub·jec·tive
sub·jec·tiv·ism

sub·join
sub·ju·gate
sub·ju·ga·tion
sub·junc·tive
sub·lease
sub·let
sub·lev·el
sub·li·mate
sub·lime
sub·lim·i·nal
sub·lux·a·tion
sub·ma·chine gun
sub·ma·rine
sub·merge
sub·merse
sub·mers·ible
sub·mis·sion
sub·mis·sive
sub·mit
sub·nor·mal
sub·or·di·nate
sub·orn
sub·plot
sub·poe·na
sub·ro·ga·tion
sub·Sa·ha·ran
sub·scribe
sub·script
sub·scrip·tion
sub·sec·tion
sub·se·quent
sub·ser·vi·ence
sub·ser·vi·ent
sub·side
sub·sid·iary
sub·si·di·za·tion
sub·si·dize
sub·si·dy
sub·sist
sub·sis·tence
sub·soil
sub·space

sub·spe·cies
sub·stance
sub·stan·dard
sub·stan·tial
sub·stan·ti·ate
sub·stan·tive
sub·sta·tion
sub·sti·tute
sub·sti·tu·tion
sub·stra·tum
sub·struc·ture
sub·sume
sub·teen
sub·tend
sub·ter·fuge
sub·ter·ra·nean
sub·ti·tle
sub·tle
sub·tle·ty
sub·top·ic
sub·to·tal
sub·tract
sub·trac·tion
sub·trop·i·cal
sub·urb
sub·ur·bia
sub·ven·tion
sub·ver·sion
sub·ver·sive
sub·vert
sub·vo·cal·i·za·tion
sub·way
suc·ceed
suc·cès d'es·time
suc·cess
suc·cess·ful
suc·ces·sion
suc·ces·sive
suc·ces·sor
suc·cinct
suc·cor
suc·co·tash

suc·cu·lence
suc·cu·lent
suc·cumb
suck·le
suck·ling
su·crose
suc·tion
sud·den in·fant
    death syn·drome
suds
sudsy
sue
suede
su·et
suf·fer
suf·fer·ing
suf·fice
suf·fi·cien·cy
suf·fi·cient
suf·fix
suf·fo·cate
suf·fo·ca·tion
suf·frage
suf·frag·ette
suf·frag·ist
suf·fuse
sug·ar
sug·ar·coat
sug·ary
sug·gest
sug·gest·ible
sug·ges·tion
sug·ges·tive
sui·cid·al
sui·cide
sui ge·ner·is
sui ju·ris
suit·able
suite[+]
suit·ing
suit·or
su·ki·ya·ki

Suk·koth
sul·fa drug
sul·fur
sul·fu·ric
sul·fu·rous
sulky
sul·len
sul·ly
sul·tan
sul·tan·ate
sul·try
su·mac
sum·ma cum
 lau·de
sum·ma·ri·za·tion
sum·ma·rize
sum·ma·ry
sum·ma·tion
sum·ma·tive
sum·mer·sault*
sum·mer·time
sum·mit
sum·mon
sum·mons
sum·mum bo·num
su·mo
sump
sump·tu·ary
sump·tu·ous
sun·baked
sun·bathe
sun·beam
sun·block
sun·bon·net
sun·burst
sun·dae
sun·der
sun·di·al
sun·down
sun·dries
sun·dry
sunk·en

sun·less
sun·light
sun·lit
sun·ny
sun·ny-side up
sun·screen
sun·set
sun·shine
sun·spot
sun·stroke
sun·tan
su·per
su·per·abun·dant
su·per·an·nu·at·ed
su·perb
su·per·car·go
su·per·cil·ious
su·per·col·lid·er
su·per·ego
su·per·er·o·ga·to·ry
su·per·fi·cial
su·per·fi·ci·al·i·ty
su·per·flu·ity
su·per·flu·ous
su·per·hea·vy·
 weight
su·per·high·way
su·per·hu·man
su·per·im·pose
su·per·in·ten·
 den·cy
su·per·in·ten·dent
su·pe·ri·or
su·pe·ri·or·i·ty
su·pe·ri·or·ly
su·per·la·tive
su·per·man
su·per·mar·ket
su·per·nal
su·per·nat·u·ral
su·per·nu·mer·ary
su·per·or·di·nate

su·per·pow·er
su·per·sede
su·per·son·ic
su·per·sti·tion
su·per·sti·tious
su·per·struc·ture
su·per·vise
su·per·vi·sion
su·per·vi·sor
su·per·wom·an
su·pine
sup·per
sup·plant
sup·ple
sup·ple·ment
sup·ple·men·tal
sup·ple·men·ta·ry
sup·pli·ant
sup·pli·cant
sup·pli·cate
sup·pli·ca·tion
sup·ply-side
sup·port
sup·port·able
sup·port·er
sup·port·ive
sup·pose
sup·posed
sup·po·si·tion
sup·pos·i·to·ry
sup·press
sup·press·ible
sup·pres·sion
sup·pres·sor
sup·pu·rate
sup·pu·ra·tion
su·pra·na·tion·al
su·prem·a·cist
su·prem·a·cy
su·preme
sur·cease
sur·charge

sur·cin·gle

surd

sure·foot·ed

sure·ly

sure·ty

surf[+]

sur·face

sur·face-to-air mis·sile

surf·board

surf cast·ing

sur·feit

surf·ing

surge[+]

sur·geon

sur·gery

sur·gi·cal

sur·ly

sur·mise

sur·mount

sur·name

sur·pass

sur·plice

sur·plus

sur·prise

sur·re·al

sur·re·al·ism

sur·re·al·is·tic

sur·ren·der

sur·rep·ti·tious

sur·rey

sur·ro·gate moth·er

sur·round

sur·round·ings

sur·tax

sur·tout

sur·veil·lance

sur·vey

sur·vey·or

sur·viv·able

sur·viv·al

sur·vive

sur·viv·or

sur·vi·vor·ship

sus·cep·ti·bil·i·ty

sus·cep·ti·ble

su·shi

sus·pect

sus·pend

sus·pend·er

sus·pense

sus·pen·sion

sus·pi·cion

sus·pi·cious

sus·tain

sus·tain·able

sus·te·nance

su·sur·ra·tion

sut·ler

sut·ra

sut·tee

su·ture

svelte

swab·ber

swad·dle

swag

swag·ger

Swa·hi·li

swain

swale

swal·low

swa·mi

swamp

swamp·i·ness

swampy

swan dive

swank

swap

sward

swarm

swar·thy

swash·buck·ling

swas·ti·ka

swat

swatch

swath

swathe

swat·ter

sway

sway·back

swear

sweat

sweat·pants

sweat·shirt

sweat·shop

sweaty

sweep

sweep-sec·ond hand

sweep·stakes

sweet[+]

sweet·en

sweet·en·ing

sweet·heart

sweet·meat

swell

swell·ing

swel·ter

swept-back

swerve

swift

swift·ly

swift·ness

swig

swill

swim

swim·ming·ly

swim·suit

swin·dle

swind·ler

swine

swine·herd

swing

swing·er

swin·ish

swipe

swirl
swish
Swiss chard
switch
switch·back
switch·blade
switch·board
switch-hit·ter
swiv·el
swiv·el-hipped
swiz·zle
swol·len
swoon
swoop
sword
swords·man
swore
sworn
syb·a·rite
syc·a·more
sy·co·phant
sy·co·phan·tic
syl·lab·ic
syl·lab·i·cate
syl·lab·i·ca·tion
syl·lab·i·fi·ca·tion
syl·lab·i·fy
syl·la·ble
syl·la·bus
syl·lo·gism
syl·lo·gize
sylph
syl·van
sym·bi·o·sis
sym·bi·o·tic
sym·bol⁺
sym·bol·ic
sym·bol·ism
sym·bol·ize
sym·met·ri·cal
sym·me·try
sym·pa·thet·ic

sym·pa·thize
sym·pa·thy
sym·phon·ic
sym·pho·nist
sym·pho·ny
sym·po·sium
symp·tom
symp·tom·at·ic
symp·tom·atol·
   o·gy
syn·a·gogue
syn·apse
syn·ap·sis
syn·chro·nic·i·ty
syn·chro·nize
syn·chron·ous
syn·co·pate
syn·co·pa·tion
syn·co·pe
syn·cre·tism
syn·di·cal·ism
syn·di·cate
syn·drome
syn·ec·do·che
syn·er·get·ic
syn·er·gism
syn·er·gy
syn·od
syn·o·nym
syn·on·y·mous
syn·op·sis
syn·op·size
syn·op·tic
syn·tax
synth
syn·the·sis
syn·the·size
syn·thet·ic
syph·i·lis
sy·ringe
syr·up
sys·tem

sys·tem·at·ic
sys·tem·a·tize
sys·tem·ic
sys·to·le
sys·to·lic
syz·y·gy

T
Ta·bas·co™
tabbed
tab·bing
tab·bou·leh
tab·by
tab·er·na·cle
ta·bla
tab·la·ture
ta·ble
tab·leau
ta·ble-cloth
ta·ble d'hôte
ta·ble-hop
ta·ble·spoon·ful
tab·let
ta·bling
tab·loid
ta·boo
tab·u·lar
ta·bu·la ra·sa
tab·u·late
tab·u·la·tor
ta·cet
ta·chom·e·ter
tachy·car·dia
tac·it
tac·i·turn
tac·i·tur·ni·ty
tack·board
tack·i·ness
tack·le
tack·ling
tacky
tact

tact·ful
tac·tic
tac·ti·cal
tac·ti·cian
tac·tics
tac·tile
tact·less
tad·pole
Tae Kwon Do
taf·fe·ta
taff·rail
taf·fy
tag sale
ta·hi·ni
Ta·hi·tian
Tai Chi
tail
tail·back
tail·er+
tail·gate
tail·light
tai·lor+
tail·or·ing
tai·lor-made
tail·spin
taint·ed
take·down (n)
take-home pay
take-no-pris·on·ers
take·off (n)
take·over (n)
tak·ing
talc
tal·cum pow·der
tale·bear·er
tal·ent
tales·man
tal·is·man
talk·ative
talk·ie
talk·ing-to (n)
talk ra·dio

talk ther·a·py
talky
tall·boy
tal·lith
tal·low
tal·ly
tal·ly·ho
tal·ly·man
Tal·mud
tal·on
ta·ma·le
ta·ma·ri
tam·bour
tam·bou·rine
tame
tam-o'-shanter
ta·mox·i·fen
tamp
tam·per
tam·pon
tan·a·ger
tan·bark
tan·dem
tan·doori
tang
tan·ge·lo
tan·gent
tan·gen·tial
tan·ger·ine
tan·gi·ble
tan·gle
tan·go
tangy
tan·kard
tank·er
tan·ner
tan·nery
tan·nic
tan·ning
tan·ta·lize
tan·ta·mount
tan·tric

tan·trum
Tao·ism
Tao·ist
tap-dance
tape deck
tape mea·sure
ta·per+
tape re·cord·er
tap·es·try
tape·worm
tap·i·o·ca
ta·pir+
tap·pet
tap·room
tap·root
taps
tar·a·did·dle
ta·ran·tu·la
tar·di·ly
tar·dy
tare
tar·get
tar·iff
tar·mac
tar·nish
ta·ro+
tar·ot+
tar·pau·lin
tar·pon
tar·ra·gon
tar·ry
tar·sus
tart
tar·tan
tar·tar
task
task·mas·ter
task·mis·tress
tas·sel
taste
taste·ful
taste·less

tast·er
tasty
ta·ta·mi
tat·ter
tat·tered
tat·ting
tat·tle
tat·tler
tat·too
taught[+]
taunt
taut[+]
taut·en
tau·to·log·i·cal
tau·tol·o·gy
tav·ern
taw·dry
taw·ny
tax·able
tax·a·tion
tax-ex·empt
taxi
taxi·cab
taxi·der·my
tax·ied
taxi·ing
taxi·me·ter
tax·on·o·my
tax·pay·er
T-bone
T cell
teach
teach·able
teach·er
teach·ers col·lege
teach-in
tea·cup
teak
tea·ket·tle
teak·wood
teal
team[+]

team·mate
team·ster
team·work
tear·ful
tear·ing
tear·jerk·er
teary
tease
tea·spoon·ful
teat
tech·ni·cal
tech·ni·cal·i·ty
tech·ni·cian
tech·nique
tech·no·bab·ble
tech·noc·ra·cy
tech·no·crat
tech·no·crat·ic
tech·no·log·i·cal
tech·nol·o·gy
tech·no·pho·bia
tec·ton·ics
Te De·um
te·dious
te·di·um
tee
teem[+]
teen·age
teen·ag·er
teen·sy
teen·sy-ween·sy
tee·ny-wee·ny
tee shirt
tee·ter
tee·ter·tot·ter
teeth
teethe
teeth·ing
tee·to·tal
tee·to·tal·er
Tef·lon™
tele·cast

tele·com·mu·ni·
  ca·tion
tele·com·mute
tele·con·fer·enc·
  ing
tele·ge·nic
tele·gram
tele·graph
te·leg·ra·phy
tele·mar·ket·ing
tele·me·try
te·le·o·log·i·cal
te·le·ol·o·gy
te·lep·a·thy
tele·phone
tele·phon·ic
tele·pho·to
tele·print·er
Tele·Promp·Ter™
tele·scope
tele·scop·ic
tele·thon
tele·type
tele·type·writ·er
tele·typ·ist
tel·evan·ge·list
tele·vise
tele·vi·sion
tel·ex
tell·er
tell·tale
tel·lu·ric
tem·blor
te·mer·i·ty
tem·per
tem·pera
tem·per·a·ment
tem·per·a·men·tal
tem·per·ance
tem·per·ate
tem·per·a·ture
tem·pered

tem·pes·tu·ous
tem·plate
tem·ple
tem·po
tem·po·ral
tem·po·ral·i·ty
tem·po·rar·i·ly
tem·po·rary
tem·po·rize
tem·po·ro·
   man·dib·u·lar
tempt
temp·ta·tion
tempt·er
tempt·ing
tem·pu·ra
ten·a·ble
te·na·cious
te·nac·i·ty
ten·an·cy
ten·ant
ten·ant farm·er
ten·den·cy
ten·den·tious
ten·der·foot
ten·der·heart·ed
ten·der·ize
ten·der·loin
ten·der-mind·ed
ten·don
ten·dril
ten·e·ment
te·net
ten·nis
ten·on
ten·or
ten·pin
tense
ten·sile
ten·sion
ten·sor
ten-speed

ten·ta·cle
ten·ta·tive
ten·ter·hooks
tenth-rate
ten·u·ous
ten·ure-track
te·pee
tep·id
te·qui·la
ter·cen·te·na·ry
ter·i·ya·ki
term
ter·mi·nal
ter·mi·nate
ter·mi·na·tion
ter·mi·nol·o·gy
ter·mi·nus
ter·mite
tern[+]
terp·si·cho·re·an
ter·race
ter·ra-cot·ta
ter·ra fir·ma
ter·rain
ter·ra in·cog·ni·ta
ter·ra·pin
ter·rar·i·um
ter·raz·zo
ter·res·tri·al
ter·ri·ble
ter·ri·er
ter·rif·ic
ter·ri·fy
ter·ri·to·ri·al
ter·ri·to·ri·al·i·ty
ter·ri·to·ry
ter·ror
ter·ror·ism
ter·ror·ize
ter·ry
terse
Ter·tia·ry

tes·sel·late
tes·sel·lat·ed
tes·ta·ment
tes·tate
tes·ta·tor
test-drive
tes·ter
test-fly
tes·ti·cle
tes·ti·fy
tes·ti·mo·ni·al
tes·ti·mo·ny
test·ing
tes·tos·ter·one
tes·ty
tet·a·nus
tetchy
tête-à-tête
teth·er
teth·er·ball
tet·ra·chlo·ride
tet·ra·he·dral
tet·ra·he·dron
te·tral·o·gy
te·tram·e·ter
te·traz·zi·ni
Teu·ton·ic
text·book
tex·tile
tex·tu·al
tex·ture
T for·ma·tion
T-group
thane
thank·ful
thank·less
thanks·giv·ing
thatch
thau·ma·tur·gist
thau·ma·tur·gy
thaw
the·ater

the·ater·go·er
the·atre
the·at·ri·cal
the·at·ri·cal·ly
theft
their
the·ism
the·ist
the·mat·ic
theme
them·selves
thence
thence·forth
theo·cen·tric
the·oc·ra·cy
theo·crat·ic
theo·lo·gian
theo·log·i·cal
the·ol·o·gize
the·ol·o·gy
the·o·rem
the·o·ret·i·cal
the·o·re·ti·cian
the·o·rist
the·o·rize
the·o·ry
the·os·o·phist
the·os·o·phy
ther·a·peu·tic touch
ther·a·pist
ther·a·py
there·abouts
there·af·ter
there·by
there·fore
there·in
there·in·af·ter
there·of
there·upon
ther·mal
ther·mo·dy·nam·
    ics

ther·mom·e·ter
ther·mo·nu·cle·ar
ther·mos
ther·mo·stat
the·sau·rus
the·sis
thes·pi·an
thew
they'd
they'll
they're
they've
thi·amine
thick
thick·en
thick·et
thick·ness
thick·set
thick-skinned
thief
thiev·ery
thigh
thigh·bone
thim·ble
thim·ble·rig
thine
think
think·able
think·ing
thin·ly
thin·ner
thin·ness
thin·nish
thin-skinned
third
third-class
third-rate
third world
thirst
thirst·i·ly
thirst·i·ness
thirsty

thir·teen
thir·ty·some·thing
this·tle
thith·er
thole
thong
tho·rac·ic
tho·rax
thorn
thorny
thor·ough
thor·ough·bred
thor·ough·fare
thor·ough·go·ing
though
thought
thought·ful
thought·less
thought·less·ness
thou·sand
thrall
thrash
thrash·er
thread
thread·bare
threat
threat·en
three-di·men·
    sion·al
three·fold
three-peat
three-piece
three-point line
three-quar·ter
three·some
thren·o·dy
thresh·er
thresh·old
threw
thrice
thrift·i·er
thrift·less

thrifty
thrill
thril·ler
thrips
thrive
throat
throat·i·ness
throaty
throb
throes
throm·bo·sis
throm·bus
throne
throng
throt·tle
throt·tle·hold
through
through·out
throw
throw·away (n)
throw·back (n)
throw-in (n)
thrush
thrust
thrust stage
thumb
thumb·nail
thumb·tack
thun·der
thun·der·bolt
thun·der·clap
thun·der·head
thun·der·ous
thun·der·show·er
thun·der·storm
Thurs·day
thus
thwart
thyme
thy·mus
thy·roid
thy·self

ti·ara
Ti·bet·an
tib·ia
tic
tick·er
tick·et
tick·ing
tick·le
tick·ler
tick·lish
tick-tack-toe*
tic-tac-toe
tid·al
tid·bit
tid·dle·dy·
   winks
tide
tide·wa·ter
ti·di·ness
tid·ings
ti·dy
tie-dyed
tie-in (n)
tiered
tie-rod
tie tack
tie-up
ti·ger
tight
tight·en
tight·fist·ed
tight-lipped
tight·rope
tights
tight·wad
ti·gress
ti·ki
tile
til·ing
till
till·age
till·er

til·ler·man
tim·ber*+
tim·bered
tim·ber·land
tim·ber·line
tim·bre+
tim·brel
time-con·sum·ing
time·keep·er
time·less
time·ly
time-out (n)
tim·er
time-sav·er
time·shar·ing
time·ta·ble
tim·id
ti·mid·i·ty
tim·ing
tim·o·rous
tim·o·thy
tim·pa·ni
tim·pa·nist
tinc·ture
tin·der
tin·foil
tinge
tin·gle
tin·horn
tin·ker
tin·kle
tin·ni·tus
tin·ny
Tin Pan Al·ley
Tin·sel·town
tin·tin·nab·u·la·tion
ti·ny
ti·ni·ness
tip-in (n)
tip-off (n)
tip·pet
tip·ple

tip·si·ly

tip·ster

tip·sy

tip·toe

tip-top

ti·rade

tire·less

tire·some

ti·sane

tis·sue

ti·tan·ic

tit for tat

tithe

tith·ing

ti·tian

tit·il·late

tit·il·lat·ing

ti·tle

ti·tle·hold·er

ti·tlist

tit·mouse

tit·ter

tit·u·lar

toad

toad·stool

toady

to-and-fro

toast

toast·mas·ter

toast·mis·tress

toasty

to·bac·co

to·bac·co·nist

to·bog·gan

toc·ca·ta

toc·sin[+]

to·day

tod·dle

tod·dler

tod·dy

to-do

toed

toe·hold

toe-in

toe·nail

tof·fee

to·fu

to·ga

to·geth·er

tog·gle

toil

toi·let

toi·let·ry

toi·lette

toil·some

to·ken

to·ken·ism

tole

tol·er·a·ble

tol·er·ance

tol·er·ant

tol·er·ate

tol·er·a·tion

toll·booth

toll·gate

tom·a·hawk

to·ma·to

tomb

tom·boy

tomb·stone

tom·cat

tome

tom·fool·ery

tom·my·rot

to·mog·ra·phy

to·mor·row

tom-tom

ton·al

to·nal·i·ty

tone-deaf

tone·less

tongs

tongue

tongued

tongu·ing

tongue-in-cheek

tongue-lash

tongue-tie

tongue twist·er

ton·ic

to·night

ton·nage

ton·neau

ton·sil

ton·sil·lec·to·my

ton·sil·li·tis

ton·so·ri·al

ton·sure

tony

To·ny Award

tool[+]

tool·mak·ing

tooth

tooth·ache

toothed

tooth·less

tooth·paste

tooth·pick

tooth·some

toothy

to·paz

top·coat

top-down

top-dress·ing

top-heavy

to·pi·ary

top·i·cal

top·less

top-lev·el

top-notch

to·po·graph·i·cal

to·pog·ra·phy

to·pol·o·gy

top·o·nym

top·per

top·ping

top·ple
top·pling
top·sail
top·side
top·sy-tur·vy
toque
torch·bear·er
to·re·a·dor
tor·ment
tor·men·tor
tor·na·do
tor·pe·do
tor·pid
tor·por
torque
tor·rent
tor·ren·tial
tor·rid
tor·sion
tor·so
tort[+]
torte[+]
tor·tel·li·ni
tor·ti·lla
tor·toise
tor·to·ni
tor·tu·ous
tor·ture
tor·tur·ous
toss-up (n)
to·tal
to·tal·i·tar·i·an
to·tal·i·tar·i·an·ism
to·tal·i·ty
to·tal·ly
tote
to·tem
to·tem·ism
totem pole
tot·ter
tot·tery
touch

touch·able
touch·down
tou·ché
touch-me-not
touch·stone
touch-type
touch-up
touchy
tough
tough·en
tough-mind·ed
tou·pee
tour
tour de force
Tou·rette's
   syn·drome
tour·ism
tour·ist
tour·na·ment
tour·ne·dos
tour·ney
tour·ni·quet
tou·sle
tout
to·ward
tow·el
tow·el·ing
tow·er
tow·head
town
towns·folk
town·ship
tow·path
tow·rope
tox·e·mia
tox·ic shock
   syn·drome
tox·ic·i·ty
tox·i·col·o·gist
tox·i·col·o·gy
tox·in[+]
tox·o·plas·mo·sis

trace
trac·er
trac·ery
tra·chea
tra·cho·ma
trac·ing
track
track·er
track·ing
tract
trac·ta·ble
trac·tion
trac·tor
trade·mark
trade-off (n)
trades·per·son
trade union
trade wind
tra·di·tion
tra·di·tion·al·ism
tra·duce
traf·fic
traf·ficked
traf·fick·ing
tra·ge·di·an
tra·ge·di·enne
trag·e·dy
trag·ic
tragi·com·e·dy
trail
trail·blaz·er
trail·er
train
train·bear·er
train·ee
traipse
trait[+]
trai·tor
trai·tor·ous
tra·jec·to·ry
tram·car
tram·line

tram·mel
tra·mon·tane
tramp
tram·ple
tram·po·line
tram·way
trance
tran·quil
tran·quil·iz·er
tran·quil·li·ty
trans·act
trans·ac·tion
trans·at·lan·tic
tran·scend
tran·scen·dence
tran·scen·dent
tran·scen·den·tal
tran·scen·den·tal·ism
trans·con·ti·nen·tal
tran·scribe
tran·script
tran·scrip·tion
tran·sect
tran·sept
trans·fer
trans·fer·al
trans·fer·ence
trans·fer·ring
trans·fig·u·ra·tion
trans·fix
trans·form
trans·for·ma·tion
trans·form·er
trans·fuse
trans·fu·sion
trans·gress
trans·gres·sion
tran·sience
tran·sient
tran·sis·tor
tran·sit

tran·si·tion
tran·si·tive
tran·si·to·ry
trans·late
trans·la·tion
trans·lit·er·ate
trans·lo·cate
trans·lu·cent
trans·mis·sion
trans·mit
trans·mit·tance
trans·mit·ter
trans·mog·ri·fy
trans·mu·ta·tion
trans·mute
trans·oce·an·ic
tran·som
trans·pa·cif·ic
trans·par·en·cy
trans·par·ent
tran·spire
trans·plant
trans·port
trans·port·able
trans·por·ta·tion
trans·port·er
trans·pose
trans·po·si·tion
trans·sex·u·al
trans·ship
trans·sub·stan·ti·ate
tran·sub·stan·ti·a·tion
trans·val·ue
trans·verse
trans·ves·tite
trap·door
tra·peze
trap·e·zoid
trap·e·zoid·al
trap·ping
trap·shoot·er

tra·pun·to
trash
trashy
trat·to·ria
trau·ma
trau·ma·tic
trau·ma·tize
tra·vail
trav·el
trav·eled
trav·el·er
trav·el·ogue
tra·verse
trav·es·ty
tra·vois
trawl·er
tray[+]
treach·er·ous
treach·ery
trea·cle
tread
trea·dle
tread·mill
trea·son
trea·son·able
trea·son·ous
trea·sure
trea·sur·er
trea·sury
treat
treat·able
trea·tise
treat·ment
trea·ty
tre·ble
tree hug·ger
tree·less
tre·foil
trek
trekked
trek·king
trel·lis

trel·lised
trem·ble
tre·men·dous
trem·o·lo
trem·or
trem·u·lous
trench
tren·chant
tren·cher·man
trend
trendy
trep·i·da·tion
tres·pass
tress
tres·tle
T. rex
trey[+]
tri·ad
tri·age
tri·al
tri·an·gle
tri·an·gu·lar
tri·an·gu·late
tri·an·gu·la·tion
tri·ath·lete
tri·bal
trib·al·ism
tribe
trib·u·la·tion
tri·bu·nal
tri·bune
trib·u·tary
trib·ute
tri·ceps
trich·i·no·sis
trick
trick·ery
trick·le
trick·ster
tricky
tri·col·or
tri·cor·nered

tri·cot
tri·cy·cle
tri·dent
trid·u·um
tried
tri·en·ni·al
tries
tri·fle
tri·fling
trig·ger
trig·ger-hap·py
tri·glyc·er·ides
trig·o·no·met·ric
trig·o·nom·e·try
tril·lion
tril·li·um
tril·o·gy
trim
tri·mes·ter
trim·mer
trim·ming
trim·ness
trin·ket
tri·no·mi·al
trio
tri·o·let
tri·par·tite
tripe
trip-ham·mer
triph·thong
tri·ple-team
tri·plex
trip·li·cate
tri·pod
trip·per
trip·ping·ly
trip·tych
trite
trite·ness
tri·umph
tri·um·phant
tri·um·vi·rate

tri·une
triv·et
triv·ia
triv·i·al
triv·i·al·ize
triv·i·um
tri·week·ly
tro·chee
trod
trog·lo·dyte
troll
trol·ley
trol·lop
trom·bone
trom·bon·ist
trompe l'oeil
troop[+]
trope
tro·phy
trop·ic
trop·i·cal
tro·po·sphere
trot
trot·ter
trou·ba·dour
trou·ble
trou·ble·mak·er
trou·ble·shoot·er
trou·ble·some
trough
trounce
troupe
trou·sers
trous·seau
trout
trow·el
tru·an·cy
tru·ant
tru·ant·ry
truce
truck·er
tru·cu·lence

tru·cu·lent
trudge
true
true-blue
true-false test
truf·fle
tru·ism
tru·ly
trump
trum·pery
trum·pet
trum·pet·er
trun·cate
trun·cheon
trun·dle
trunk
truss
trust
trust·bust·er
trust·ee
trust·wor·thy
trusty
truth·ful
try·ing
try·out
tryst
tset·se
T-shirt
T square
tsu·na·mi
tu·ba
tub·by
tube
tu·ber
tu·ber·cu·lar
tu·ber·cu·lo·sis
tu·ber·ous
tub·ing
tu·bu·lar
tuck
tuck·er
'tude

Tues·day
tuft
tug-of-war
tu·i·tion
tu·lip
tulle⁺
tum·ble
tum·bling
tu·mes·cence
tu·mid
tum·my
tu·mor
tu·mor·ous
tu·mult
tu·mul·tu·ous
tun
tu·na
tun·dra
tune·ful
tun·er
tune-up (n)
tung·sten
tu·nic
tun·nel
tur·ban
tur·bid
tur·bine
tur·bo·jet
tur·bo·prop
tur·bot
tur·bu·lence
tur·bu·lent
tu·reen
turf
tur·gid
tur·key
tur·mer·ic
tur·moil
turn⁺
turn·coat
tur·nip
turn·key

turn·over (n)
turn·pike
turn·stile
turn·ta·ble
tur·pen·tine
tur·pi·tude
tur·quoise
tur·ret
tur·tle
tur·tle·back
tur·tle·neck
tusk
tus·sle
tus·sock
tu·te·lage
tu·tor
tu·to·ri·al
tut·ti-frut·ti
tu·tu
tux·e·do
twain
twang
tweak
tweed
tweedy
tween·er
tweet·er
twee·zers
twelfth
twelve
twice
twi·light
twill
twin bed
twine
twinge
twin·kle
twin-size
twirl
twist
twist·er
twitch

twit·ter
twixt
two-by-four
two-faced
two·fer
two·fold
two-piece
two·some
ty·coon
tyke
tym·pa·num
type A
type·face
type·set·ter
type·writ·er
ty·phoid
ty·phoon
ty·phus
typ·i·cal
typ·i·fy
typ·ist
ty·po
ty·pog·ra·pher
ty·pog·ra·phi·cal
ty·pog·ra·phy
ty·ran·ni·cal
ty·ran·ni·cide
tyr·an·nize
tyr·an·nous
tyr·an·ny
ty·rant
ty·ro
tzar

U
über·cool
ubiq·ui·tous
ubiq·ui·ty
ud·der
UFO
ug·li·ness
ug·ly

Ukrai·ni·an
uku·le·le
ul·cer
ul·cer·ate
ul·cer·ation
ul·cer·ous
ul·na
ul·ster
ul·te·ri·or
ul·ti·mate
ul·ti·ma·tum
ul·tra
ul·tra·con·ser·va·
   tive
ul·tra·high
   fre·quen·cy
ul·tra·lib·er·al
ul·tra·light
ul·tra·mil·i·tant
ul·tra·mod·ern
ul·tra·na·tion·al·ist
ul·tra·son·ic
ul·tra·sound
ul·tra·vi·o·let
ul·tra vi·res
ul·u·late
um·ber
um·bil·i·cal
um·bi·li·cus
um·bra
um·brage
um·brel·la
um·laut
um·pire
un·abat·ed
un·able
un·abridged
un·ac·cept·able
un·ac·com·mo·
   dat·ed
un·ac·com·pa·nied
un·ac·count·able

un·ac·count·ed
un·ac·cus·tomed
un·adorned
un·adul·ter·at·ed
un·af·fect·ed
un·alien·able
un·aligned
un·al·loyed
un·al·ter·able
un·am·big·u·ous
un·Amer·i·can
una·nim·i·ty
unan·i·mous
un·an·swer·able
un·an·tic·i·pat·ed
un·ap·peal·ing
un·ap·peas·able
un·ap·pe·tiz·ing
un·ap·proach·able
un·ar·gu·able
un·armed
un·ar·tic·u·lat·ed
un·ashamed
un·asked
un·as·sail·able
un·as·ser·tive
un·as·sist·ed
un·as·suage·able
un·as·sum·ing
un·at·tached
un·at·trac·tive
un·avail·able
un·avail·ing
un·avoid·able
un·aware
un·awares
un·bal·anced
un·barred
un·bear·able
un·beat·able
un·beat·en
un·be·com·ing

un·be·knownst
un·be·lief
un·be·liev·able
un·be·liev·er
un·be·liev·ing
un·bend
un·bend·ing
un·bi·ased
un·bid·den
un·bind
un·blessed
un·blink·ing
un·block
un·blush·ing
un·born
un·bo·som
un·bound
un·bri·dled
un·bro·ken
un·buck·le
un·budg·ing
un·bur·dened
un·bur·ied
un·but·toned
un·called-for
un·can·ny
un·ceas·ing
un·ceas·ing·ly
un·cer·e·mo·ni·ous
un·cer·tain
un·cer·tain·ty
un·chal·lenge·able
un·change·able
un·chang·ing
un·char·ac·ter·is·tic
un·char·i·ta·ble
un·chart·ed
un·chiv·al·rous
un·chris·tian
un·cir·cum·cised
un·civ·i·lized
un·clasp

un·clas·si·fied
un·cle
un·clean
un·clench
Uncle Tom·ism
un·climb·able
un·clothed
un·cloud·ed
un·clut·ter
un·coiled
un·com·fort·able
un·com·mer·cial
un·com·mit·ted
un·com·mon
un·com·mu·ni·ca·ble
un·com·mu·ni·ca·tive
un·com·plain·ing
un·com·pli·cat·ed
un·com·pli·men·ta·ry
un·com·pre·hend·ing
un·com·pro·mis·ing
un·con·cerned
un·con·di·tion·al
un·con·for·mi·ty
un·con·ge·nial
un·con·quer·able
un·con·scio·na·ble
un·con·scious
un·con·sid·ered
un·con·sti·tu·tion·al
un·con·trol·la·ble
un·con·ven·tion·al
un·con·vinc·ing
un·cork
un·cor·rupt
un·cou·ple
un·couth
un·cov·er

un·cov·ered
un·crit·i·cal
un·crush·able
unc·tion
unc·tu·ous
un·curl
un·daunt·ed
un·de·bat·able
un·de·fend·ed
un·dem·o·crat·ic
un·de·mon·stra·tive
un·de·ni·able
un·der
un·der·achiev·er
un·der·age
un·der·arm
un·der·bid
un·der·body
un·der·brush
un·der·bud·get·ed
un·der·cap·i·tal·ized
un·der·class·man
un·der·clothes
un·der·cloth·ing
un·der·coat
un·der·cov·er
un·der·cur·rent
un·der·cut
un·der·de·vel·oped
un·der·dog
un·der·ed·u·cat·ed
un·der·em·pha·sis
un·der·em·ployed
un·der·es·ti·mate
un·der·ex·pose
un·der·foot
un·der·gird
un·der·go
un·der·grad·u·ate
un·der·ground

un·der·growth
un·der·hand·ed
un·der·in·sured
un·der·laid
un·der·lie
un·der·line
un·der·ling
un·der·ly·ing
un·der·manned
un·der·mine
un·der·neath
un·der·nour·ished
un·der·paid
un·der·pass
un·der·pin
un·der·play
un·der·priv·i·leged
un·der·pro·duc·tion
un·der·rate
un·der·rep·re·sen·ta·tion
un·der·rep·re·sent·ed
un·der·score
un·der·sea
un·der·sell
un·der·shirt
un·der·side
un·der·signed
un·der·sized
un·der·staffed
un·der·stand
un·der·state
un·der·stood
un·der·study
un·der·take
un·der·tak·er
und·er-the=coun·ter
un·der·tone
un·der·tow
un·der·used
un·der·uti·lize

un·der·val·ue
un·der·wa·ter
un·der·way
un·der·wear
un·der·weight
un·der·world
un·der·write
un·der·writ·er
un·de·sir·able
un·de·vi·at·ing
un·dip·lo·mat·ic
un·dis·guised
un·do+
un·do·ing
un·doubt·ed·ly
un·dra·mat·ic
un·dreamed
un·dress
un·due+
un·du·late
un·du·la·tion
un·du·ly
un·dy·ing
un·earned
un·earth
un·earth·ly
un·ease
un·eas·i·ly
un·easy
un·eco·nom·i·cal
un·emo·tion·al
un·em·ploy·able
un·em·ployed
un·end·ing
un·en·dur·able
un·en·thu·si·as·tic
un·equal
un·equiv·o·ca·bly
un·equiv·o·cal
un·err·ing·ly
un·es·sen·tial
un·even

un·even·ness
un·event·ful
un·ex·cep·tion·able
un·ex·cep·tion·al
un·ex·pect·ed
un·ex·ploit·ed
un·ex·pres·sive
un·fad·ing
un·fail·ing
un·fair
un·faith·ful
un·fal·ter·ing
un·fa·mil·iar
un·fash·ion·able
un·fas·ten
un·fath·om·able
un·fa·vor·able
un·feel·ing
un·feigned
un·fet·tered
un·fin·ished
un·fit
un·fit·ting
un·flag·ging
un·flap·pa·ble
un·flat·ter·ing
un·fledged
un·flinch·ing
un·fo·cused
un·fold
un·for·get·ta·ble
un·for·giv·ing
un·formed
un·for·tu·nate
un·found·ed
un·fre·quent·ed
un·friend·ly
un·fruit·ful
un·furl
un·gain·ly
un·glue
un·glued

un·god·ly
un·gov·ern·able
un·gra·cious
un·gram·mat·i·cal
un·grate·ful
un·guard·ed
un·guent
un·hal·lowed
un·hand
un·hap·pi·ly
un·hap·py
un·healthy
un·heard-of
un·help·ful
un·hes·i·tat·ing
un·hinge
un·ho·ly
un·hook
un·hos·pit·able
un·hur·ried
uni·cam·er·al
uni·cel·lu·lar
uni·corn
uni·cy·cle
uni·di·rec·tion·al
uni·fi·ca·tion
uni·form
uni·for·mi·ty
uni·fy
uni·lat·er·al
uni·lin·ear
un·imag·in·able
un·im·pas·sioned
un·im·peach·able
un·im·proved
un·in·for·ma·tive
un·in·hib·it·ed
un·in·stall
un·in·tel·li·gent
un·in·tel·li·gi·ble
un·in·ten·tion·al
un·in·ter·rupt·ed

union·ism
union·i·za·tion
union·ize
unique
uni·sex
uni·son
Uni·tar·i·an
uni·tary
unite
uni·ty
Uni·ver·sal
    Pro·duct Code
uni·ver·sal
    re·source
    lo·cat·or
uni·ver·sal se·ri·al
    bus
uni·ver·sal·i·ty
uni·verse
uni·ver·si·ty
univ·o·cal
UNIX®
un·just
un·kempt
un·kind
un·know·able
un·know·ing
un·known
un·lace
un·latch
un·law·ful
un·lead·ed
un·leash
un·let·tered
un·like
un·like·li·hood
un·like·ly
un·lim·it·ed
un·list·ed
un·load
un·lock
un·loose

un·made
un·man·ly
un·man·nered
un·man·ner·ly
un·mask
un·men·tion·able
un·mer·ci·ful
un·mer·ci·ful·ly
un·mind·ful
un·mis·tak·able
un·mit·i·gat·ed
un·nat·u·ral
un·nec·es·sar·i·ly
un·nec·es·sary
un·nerve
un·num·bered
un·ob·tru·sive
un·oc·cu·pied
un·of·fi·cial
un·or·ga·nized
un·or·tho·dox
un·pack
un·paid
un·pal·at·able
un·par·al·leled
un·pin
un·pleas·ant
un·plugged
un·plumbed
un·pop·u·lar
un·prec·e·dent·ed
un·pre·dict·able
un·prej·u·diced
un·pre·ten·tious
un·prin·ci·pled
un·print·able
un·pro·fes·sion·al
un·prof·it·able
un·prom·is·ing
un·qual·i·fied
un·ques·tion·able
un·rav·el

un·re·al·is·tic
un·re·al·i·ty
un·rea·son·able
un·rea·son·ing
un·re·gen·er·ate
un·re·lent·ing
un·re·mit·ting
un·re·served
un·re·spon·sive
un·re·strained
un·ripe
un·ri·valed
un·ruf·fled
un·ruly
un·san·i·tary
un·sat·u·rat·ed
un·sa·vory
un·say
un·scathed
un·schooled
un·sci·en·tif·ic
un·scram·ble
un·screw
un·scru·pu·lous
un·sea·son·able
un·seat
un·seem·ly
un·seg·re·gat·ed
un·self·ish
un·set·tle
un·shack·le
un·sheathe
un·shod
un·sight·ly
un·skilled
un·snarl
un·so·cia·ble
un·so·cial
un·so·phis·ti·cat·ed
un·sought
un·sound
un·spar·ing

un·speak·able
un·sports·man·like
un·spot·ted
un·sta·ble
un·stat·ed
un·steady
un·stop·pa·ble
un·stressed
un·struc·tured
un·stud·ied
un·sub·stan·tial
un·suc·cess·ful
un·suit·able
un·sul·lied
un·sung
un·swerv·ing
un·tan·gle
un·tapped
un·taught
un·ten·a·ble
un·ten·ured
un·think·able
un·think·ing
un·thought
un·ti·dy
un·tie
un·til
un·time·ly
un·ti·tled
un·to
un·told
un·touch·able
un·to·ward
un·tried
un·trod·den
un·trou·bled
un·true
un·truth·ful
un·tu·tored
un·twist
un·used
un·usu·al

un·ut·ter·able
un·var·nished
un·veil
un·voiced
un·war·rant·able
un·wary
un·washed
un·wa·ver·ing
un·wea·ried
un·whole·some
un·wieldy
un·will·ing
un·wind
un·wise
un·wit·ting
un·world·ly
un·worn
un·wor·thy
un·wrap
un·writ·ten
un·yield·ing
un·zip
up-and-coming
up-and-down
up·beat
up·braid
up·bring·ing
up·com·ing
up·date
up·draft
up·end
up·field
up·grade
up·heav·al
up·hill
up·hold
up·hol·ster
up·hol·stery
up·keep
up·land
up·lift
up·link

up·mar·ket
up·per-class
up·per crust
up·per-cut
up·per hand
up·per·most
up·pi·ty
up·right
up·ris·ing
up·roar·i·ous
up·root
up·scale
up·set
up·shot
up·side down
up·stage
up·stairs
up·stand·ing
up·start
up·sweep
up·tight
up-to-date
up-to-the-min·ute
up·town
up·ward
up·wind
ura·ni·um
ur·ban leg·end
ur·bane
ur·ban·ism
ur·ban·i·ty
ur·ban·i·za·tion
ur·chin
ure·mia
ure·ter
ure·thra
urge
ur·gen·cy
ur·gent
uri·nal
uri·nal·y·sis
uri·nary

uri·nate
urine
URL+
urol·o·gist
ur·sine
us·age
use·ful
use·less·ness
us·er-friend·ly
ush·er
ush·er·ette
us·ing
usu·al
usu·al·ly
usu·al·ness
usu·rer
usu·ri·ous
usurp
usur·pa·tion
usu·ry
uten·sil
uter·us
util·i·tar·i·an
util·i·tar·i·an·ism
util·i·ty
uti·lize
ut·most
uto·pia
uto·pi·an
uto·pi·an·ism
ut·ter
ut·ter·ance
uvu·la
ux·o·ri·ous

V
va·can·cy
va·cant
va·cate
va·ca·tion
va·ca·tion·er
vac·ci·nate

vac·ci·na·tion
vac·cine
vac·il·late
vac·il·la·tion
va·cu·ity
vac·u·ous
vac·u·um
va·de me·cum
vag·a·bond
va·ga·ry
va·gi·na
vag·i·nal
va·gran·cy
va·grant
vague
vague·ness
vagu·er
vagu·est
va·gus nerve
vain+
vain·glo·ri·ous
vain·glo·ry
vain·ness
va·lance+
vale
vale·dic·tion
vale·dic·to·ri·an
vale·dic·to·ry
va·lence+
val·en·tine
va·let
val·e·tu·di·nar·i·an
val·iant
val·id
val·i·date
val·i·da·tion
va·lid·i·ty
val·ley
val·or
val·or·ous
valu·able
val·u·ate

val·u·a·tion
val·ue
va·lu·ta
valve
val·vu·lar
va·moose
vam·pire
van·dal
van·dal·ism
van·dal·ize
Van·dyke
vane+
van·guard
va·nil·la
van·ish
van·i·ty
van·quish
van·tage
va·pid
va·pid·i·ty
va·por
va·por·iza·tion
va·por·iz·er
va·por·ous
vari·able rate
  mort·gage
vari·ance
vari·ant
vari·a·tion
vari·col·ored
var·i·cose
var·ied
var·ie·gat·ed
var·ie·ga·tion
va·ri·ety
var·io·cou·pler
var·i·ous
var·let
var·mint
var·nish
var·si·ty
vary

vary·ing
vas·cu·lar
vase
va·sec·to·my
Vas·e·line
vas·sal
vas·sal·age
vast
Vat·i·can
vaude·ville
vault
vault·ing
vaunt
VBAC
V-chip
VCR
veal
vec·tor
veep
veer
veg·an
veg·e·ta·ble
veg·e·tal
veg·e·tar·i·an
veg·e·tar·i·an·ism
veg·e·tate
veg·e·ta·tion
veg·e·ta·tive
veg·gie bur·ger
ve·he·mence
ve·he·ment
ve·hi·cle
veil·ing
vein+
ve·lar
Vel·cro™
veld
vel·lum
ve·loc·i·pede
ve·loc·i·rap·tor
ve·loc·i·ty
ve·lour

ve·lum
vel·vet
vel·ve·teen
vel·vety
ve·na ca·va
ve·nal
vend·er
ven·det·ta
ven·dor
ve·neer
ven·er·a·ble
ven·er·ate
ven·er·a·tion
ve·ne·re·al
ve·ne·tian blind
ven·geance
venge·ful
ve·nial
ve·ni·punc·ture
ven·i·son
ven·om·ous
ve·nous
vent
ven·ti·late
ven·ti·la·tion
ven·ti·la·tor
ven·tral
ven·tri·cle
ven·tril·o·quism
ven·tril·o·quist
ven·ture
ven·tur·er
ven·ture·some
ven·tur·ous
ven·ue
ve·ra·cious
ve·rac·i·ty
ve·ran·da
ver·bal
ver·bal·ism
ver·bal·ize
ver·ba·tim

ver·biage
ver·bose
ver·bos·i·ty
ver·bo·ten
ver·dant
ver·dict
ver·di·gris
ver·dure
verge
ve·rid·i·cal
ver·i·fi·able
ver·i·fi·ca·tion
ver·i·fy
ver·i·ly
veri·si·mil·i·tude
ver·i·ta·ble
ver·i·ty
ver·mi·cel·li
ver·mic·u·lite
ver·mil·ion
ver·min
ver·min·ous
ver·mouth
ver·nac·u·lar
ver·nal
ver·ni·er
ver·sa·tile
ver·sa·til·i·ty
verse
ver·si·cle
ver·si·fi·ca·tion
ver·si·fi·er
ver·si·fy
ver·sion
vers li·bre
ver·sus
ver·te·bra
ver·te·brae
ver·te·brate
ver·tex
ver·ti·cal
ver·tig·i·nous

ver·ti·go
verve
very low den·si·ty
    li·po·pro·tein
ves·pers
ves·sel
vest·ee
ves·ti·bule
ves·tige
vest·ing
vest·ment
ves·try
vet·er·an
vet·er·i·nar·i·an
vet·er·i·nary
ve·to
vexed
vex·ing
vex·a·tion
vex·a·tious
vi·a·ble
via·duct
vi·ands
vi·at·i·cum
vibes
vi·brant
vi·bra·phone
vi·brate
vi·bra·tion
vi·bra·tor
vic·ar·age
vi·car·i·ous
vice-pres·i·den·cy
vice-pres·i·dent
vice·re·gal
vice·roy
vice ver·sa
vi·chys·soise
vi·cin·i·ty
vi·cious
vi·cis·si·tude
vic·tim

vic·tim·ize
vic·tor
Vic·to·ri·an
vic·to·ri·ous
vic·to·ry
vict·uals
vict·ual·ler
vi·cu·ña
vi·de·li·cet
vid·eo
vid·eo·cas·sette
vid·e·og·ra·phy
vid·eo·tape
vie
vied
vi·er
Viet·cong
Viet·minh
Viet·nam·ese
view·er
view·find·er
view·ing
view·point
vig·il
vig·i·lance
vig·i·lant
vig·i·lan·te
vi·gnette
vig·or
vig·or·ous
vile[+]
vil·i·fi·ca·tion
vil·i·fy
vil·la
vil·lage
vil·lain
vil·lain·ous
vil·lainy
vin·ai·grette
vin·cu·lum
vin·di·cate
vin·di·ca·tion

vin·dic·tive
vine
vin·e·gar
vin·ery
vine·yard
vi·nous
vin·tage
vint·ner
vi·nyl
vi·ol[+]
vi·o·la
vi·o·late
vi·o·la·tion
vi·o·lence
vi·o·lent
vi·o·let
vi·o·lin
vi·o·lon·cel·lo
vi·per
vi·ra·go
vi·ral
vi·res·cence
vir·gin
vir·gin·al
vir·gin·i·ty
vir·gule
vi·rid·i·ty
vir·ile
vi·ril·i·ty
vir·tu·al·ly
vir·tu·al re·al·i·ty
vir·tue
vir·tue·less
vir·tu·os·i·ty
vir·tu·o·so
vir·tu·ous
vir·u·lence
vir·u·lent
vi·rus
vi·sa
vi·saed
vis·age

vis·à·vis
vis·cera
vis·cer·al
vis·cos·i·ty
vis·count
vis·cous[+]
viscus[+]
vise
vis·i·bil·i·ty
vis·i·ble
vi·sion
vi·sion·ary
vis·it
vis·i·tant
vis·i·ta·tion
vis·i·tor
vi·sor
vis·ta
vi·su·al
vi·su·al·i·za·tion
vi·su·al·ize
vi·ta
vi·tal
vi·tal·i·ty
vi·tals
vi·ta·min
vi·ti·ate
vit·i·cul·ture
vit·re·ous
vit·ri·fy
vit·ri·ol·ic
vi·tu·per·ate
vi·tu·per·a·tion
vi·va
vi·va·cious
vi·vac·i·ty
vi·va vo·ce
viv·id
viv·i·fy
vi·vip·a·rous
vivi·sect
vivi·sec·tion

vix·en
vo·ca·ble
vo·cab·u·lary
vo·cal
vo·cal·ic
vo·cal·ist
vo·cal·ize
vo·ca·tion
vo·ca·tion·al
voc·a·tive
vo·cif·er·ous
vod·ka
vogue
vogu·ish
voice mail
voice·less
voice-over
void·able
voile
voir dire
vol·a·tile
vol·a·til·i·ty
vol·ca·nic
vol·ca·no
vol·ca·nol·o·gist
vole
vo·li·tion
vol·ley
vol·ley·ball
volt·age
vol·ta·ic
volt·me·ter
volte-face
vol·u·ble
vol·ume
vo·lu·mi·nous
vol·un·ta·rism[+]
vol·un·tary
vol·un·tar·i·ly
vol·un·teer
vol·un·teer·ism*[+]
vo·lup·tu·ous

vom·it
voo·doo
voo·doo·ism
vo·ra·cious
vo·rac·i·ty
vor·la·ge
vor·tex
vor·tic·i·ty
vo·ta·ry
vot·er
vo·tive
vouch
vouch·er
vouch·safe
vow·el
vox po·pu·li
voy·age
voy·eur
voy·eur·ism
vul·ca·ni·za·tion
vul·ca·nize
vul·gar
vul·gar·i·ty
vul·gate
vul·ner·a·ble
vul·pine
vul·ture
vul·va
vying

W
wacki·ness
wacky
wad·ding
wad·dle
wa·di
wa·fer
waf·fle
waft
wage
wa·ger
wag·gery

wag·gish
wag·gle
Wag·ne·ri·an
wag·on
wa·gon-lit
wa·hi·ne
waif
wail[+]
wain·scot·ing
waist[+]
waist·band
waist·coat
waist·line
wait·er
wait·per·son
wait·ress
wait·staff
waive
waiv·er[+]
wake
wake·ful
wake·ful·ness
wak·en
wake-up call
wale[+]
walk·about
walk·a·thon
walk·er
walk·ie·talk·ie
walk-in (n, adj)
walk-up (n, adj)
wal·la·by
wall·board
wal·let
wall·eyed
wall·flow·er
wal·lop
wal·low·ing
wal·nut
wal·rus
waltz
wam·pum

wan
wand
wan·der
wan·der·ing
wan·der·lust
wane
wan·gle
wan·ly
wan·na·be
wan·ton
wan·ton·ness
war·ble
war·bler
war·bling
war·den
ward·er
ward·robe
ward·room
ware·house
war·fare
war·horse
war·i·er
war·like
war·lock
war·lord
warm-blood·ed
warmed-over
warm·heart·ed
war·mon·ger
warmth
warm-up (n)
warn·ing
warp
warp and woof
war·path
war·plane
war·rant
war·rant·able
war·ran·tee[+]
war·ran·tor
war·ran·ty
war·ren

war·ring
war·rior
war·ship[+]
wart
war·time
wary[+]
wash·able
wash·bowl
wash·cloth
washed-out
wash·er
wash·ing
wash·out
wash·stand
wasn't
wasp
WASP
wasp·ish
was·sail
wast·age
waste[+]
waste·bas·ket
waste·ful
waste·land
waste·pa·per
waste·wa·ter
wast·ing
wast·rel
watch
watch·dog
watch·er
watch·ful
watch·mak·ing
watch·man
watch·word
wa·ter
wa·ter clos·et
wa·ter·col·or
wa·ter·cool·er
wa·ter·course
wa·ter·cress
wa·ter·fall

wa·ter·fowl
wa·ter·front
wa·ter·ing place
wa·ter·line
wa·ter·log
wa·ter·logged
wa·ter·loo
wa·ter·mark
wa·ter·mel·on
wa·ter me·ter
wa·ter park
wa·ter·pow·er
wa·ter·proof
wa·ter-re·pel·lent
wa·ter-re·sis·tant
wa·ter·shed
wa·ter-ski·er
wa·ter snake
wa·ter sup·ply
wa·ter ta·ble
wa·ter wings
wa·tery
watt·age
wat·tle
wave·length
wa·ver[+]
wav·i·ness
wavy
wax
waxed paper
wax·en
wax·works
waxy
way·bill
way·far·er
way·lay
way-out
way·side
way·ward
weak·en
weak·fish
weak·heart·ed

weak-kneed
weak·ling
weak-mind·ed
weak·ness
weal[+]
wealth
wealth·i·er
wealthy
wean
weap·on
weap·on·ry
wear·able
wea·ri·ly
wea·ri·ness
wear·ing
wea·ri·some
wea·ry
wea·sel
weath·er[+]
weath·er-beat·en
weath·er bu·reau
weath·er·cock
weath·ered
weath·er·man
weath·er map
weath·er·worn
weave
weav·er
web·bing
web·cam
web·cast
web·cast·ing
web·foot
web·mas·ter
web press
web·zine
wed·ding
we·deln
wedge
Wedg·wood
wed·lock
Wed·nes·day

weed·er
weed·less
weedy
week·day
week·end war·rior
week·end·er
week·ly
week·night
weep·ing
weepy
wee·vil
weigh-in (n)
weight
weight·ed
weight·less
weight lift·er
weighty
Wei·ma·ra·ner
wei·ner
weir
weird
weird·ness
weirdo
welch
wel·come
wel·com·ing
weld·er
wel·fare
wel·far·ism
well-ad·vised
well-ap·point·ed
well-be·ing
well-be·loved
well-born
well-bred
well-de·fined
well-dis·posed
well-done
well-fixed
well-groomed
well-han·dled
well-heeled

Wel·ling·tons
well-in·ten·tioned
well-knit
well-mean·ing
well-off
well-read
well-round·ed
well-spo·ken
well·spring
well-tak·en
well-timed
well-to-do
well-wish·er
well-worn
welsh
Welsh corgi
Welsh rab·bit
Welsh rare·bit
welt
wel·ter
wel·ter·weight
wench
wend
weren't
were·wolf
wes·kit*
west·er·ly
west·ern
west·ern·i·za·tion
west·ern·ize
West In·dies
west·ing
West Nile vi·rus
west·ward
wet·back
wet-blan·ket
wet·lands
wet-nurse
wet suit
we've
whack
whal·er

whal·ing
wham·my
wharf
wharf·age
wharf·mas·ter
what·ev·er
what·not
what·so·ev·er
wheat
wheat·en
wheat germ
whee·dle
wheel[+]
wheel·bar·row
wheel·base
wheel·chair
wheeled
wheel·er-deal·er
wheels·man
wheeze
wheezy
whelk
whelp
whence
when·ev·er
where·abouts
where·as
where·at
where·by
where·fore
where·in
where·of
where·on
where·to
where·up·on
wher·ev·er
where·with·al
wher·ry[+]
whet
wheth·er[+]
whet·stone
whey

whey-faced

which·ev·er

whiff

whif·fle

while

whilst

whim

whim·per

whim·si·cal

whim·sy

whine

whin·ny

whip·cord

whip·lash

whip·per·snap·per

whip·pet

whip·ping

whip·poor·will

whip·saw

whir

whirl

whirl·i·gig

whirl·pool

whirl·wind

whish

whisk

whisk broom

whis·ker

whis·key

whis·per

whis·per·ing

whis·pery

whist

whis·tle blow·er

whis·tler

whis·tling

whit

white·cap

white-col·lar (adj)

white el·e·phant

white-head·ed

white hole

white-hot

whit·en

white·ness

whit·en·ing

white noise

white pages

white-tie

white·wall

white·wash

whith·er[+]

whit·ing

whit·ish

whit·tle

whit·tling

whiz

whoa

who·dun·it

who·ev·er[+]

whole

whole·heart·ed·ly

whole-hog

whole lan·guage

whole·sal·er

whole·sal·ing

whole·some

whol·ly[+]

whom·ev·er[+]

whom·so·ev·er[+]

whoop

whoop-ee

whoop·ing cough

whoops

whoosh

whop·per

whop·ping

whore

whore·house

whorl[+]

whose

who·so·ev·er[+]

who's who

wick·ed

wick·er

wick·er·work

wick·et

wick·i·up

wide-an·gle

wide ar·ea
net·work

wide-eyed

wide·ly

wide receiver

wide·spread

wid·get

wid·ow

wid·ow·er

wid·ow·hood

widow's walk

width

wield

wie·ner

Wie·ner schnit·zel

wie·nie

wife·ly

wig·gle room

wig·wam

wil·co

wild·cat

wil·der·ness

wild-eyed

wild·fowl

wild·life

wild oat

Wild West

wiles

will·ful

wil·lies

wil·li·waw

will-o'-the-wisp

wil·low

wil·low·ware

wil·lowy

wil·ly-nil·ly

wilt

wily

wim·ple

wimpy

wince

winch

wind·age

wind·bag

wind·blown

wind·borne

wind·break·er

wind·chill

wind·fall

wind·ing

wind·jam·mer

wind·lass

wind·mill

win·dow

win·dow dress·ing

win·dow·pane

win·dow-shop

wind·pipe

wind·row

wind·shield

wind sock

wind·storm

wind·swept

wind-up (n)

wind·ward

windy

wine·glass

win·ery

wing·back

wing-foot·ed

wing·man

wing·span

wing·spread

win·ner

win·ning

win·now

wino

win·some

win·ter

win·ter·green

win·ter·ize

win·ter·kill (n)[+]

win·ter·kill (v)[+]

win·ter·time

win·try

win-win

wip·er

wire·less

wire-pull·er

wire·tap

wir·ing

wiry

wis·dom

wise·acre

wise·crack

wise guy

wish·bone

wish·ful

wish list

wish-wash

wishy-washy

wisp

wispy

wist·ful

witch

witch·craft

witch·ery

witch ha·zel

witch-hunt

with·al

with·draw

with·draw·al

with·drawn

with·er[+]

with·er·ing

with·ers

with·hold

with·in

with-it

with·out

with·stand

wit·less

wit·ness

wit·ti·cism

wit·ti·ness

wit·ty

wiz·ard

wiz·ard·ry

wiz·en

wiz·ened

wob·ble

wob·bly

woe·be·gone

woe·ful

wok

woke

woken

wolf·hound

wolf·ish

wol·ver·ine

wom·an

wom·an·hood

wom·an·ize

wom·an·kind

wom·an·ly

womb

wom·en

wom·en's stud·ies

won·der

won·der·ful

won·der·ment

won·drous

wont

won·ton

wood-carv·er

wood-chop·per

wood·chuck

wood·craft

wood·cut

wood·cut·ting

wood·ed

wood·en

wood·en·ware

wood·land
wood·lot
wood·man
wood·pile
wood pulp
wood·shed
woods·man
woodsy
wood·wind
wood·work
wood·work·ing
woody
woof
woof·er
wool·en
wool·gath·er·ing
wool·ly
woo·zy
word·age
word·ing
word·less
word-of-mouth
word pro·ces·sing
word pro·ces·sor
wordy
work·able
work·a·day
work-around
work·bas·ket
work·bench
work·book
work·box
work·er
work·ing
work·ing-class
working·man
work·man·like
work·man·ship
work·out
work·ta·ble
work-up (n)
work·week

world·ly
world·ly·wise
world pre·miere
world series
world·wide
World Wide Web
worm-eat·en
worm gear
worm's-eye
   view
wormy
worn-out
wor·ri·some
wor·ry
wor·ry·wart
worse
wors·en
wor·ship+
wor·ship·ful
worst+
wor·sted
wor·thi·er
worth·less
worth·while
wor·thy
would
would-be (adj)
wouldn't
wound
wrack
wraith
wran·gle
wran·gler
wrap·per
wrap·ping
wrap up
wrath
wrath·ful
wreak+
wreath+
wreathe+
wreck·age

wreck·er
wreck·er's ball
wrench
wrest
wres·tle
wres·tling
wretch
wretch·ed
wrig·gle
wring·er
wrin·kle
wrist·band
wrist·lock
wrist·watch
writ
write+
write-in (n)
write-off (n)
writ·er
write-up (n)
writhe
writ·ing
writ·ten
wrong·do·er
wrong·do·ing
wrong·er
wrong·est
wrong·ful
wrong·head·ed
wrought
wrung
wry
wry·neck
wun·der·kind
wurst+
www
WYSIWYG

X

x-ax·is
X chro·mo·some
x-co·or·di·nate

xe·nia
xe·non
xe·no·phile
xe·no·phobe
xe·no·pho·bia
xe·rog·ra·phy
xe·ro·phyte
Xe·rox™
X-rat·ed
X-ray
xy·log·ra·phy
xy·lo·phone

Y
Y2K
yacht
yacht·ing
yachts·man
ya·hoo
Yah·weh
yack·ing
yak
yam
yam·mer
yang
Yan·kee
Yan·kee-Doo·dle (n)
yap·ping
yard·age
yard·arm
yard·bird
yard goods
yard line
yard·stick
yar·mul·ke
yaw
yawl
yawn
y-ax·is
Y chro·mo·some
y-co·or·di·nate

year·book
year-end
year·ling
year·long
year·ly
yearn
yearn·ing
yeast
yeasty
yel·low·ish
yelp
yen
yen·ta
yeo·man
ye·shi·va
yes-man
yes·ter·day
yes·ter·year
yew
yield·ing
yip·pee
yo·del
yo·del·er
yo·ga
yo·gi
yo·gurt
yoke*+
yo·kel
yolk+
yon·der
yoo-hoo
yore+
you'll+
young·er
young·ster
your+
you're+
your·self
your·selves
youth·ful
you've
yowl

yo-yo
yule+
Yule log
yule·tide
yum·my
yup·pie
yurt

Z
za·ba·glio·ne
za·ny
zap
zapped
zap·ping
z-ax·is
zeal
zeal·ot
zeal·ot·ry
zeal·ous
ze·bra
zeit·geist
ze·nith
zeph·yr
zep·pe·lin
ze·ro-based
ze·ro tol·er·ance
zest
zesty
zig·zag
zig·zagged
zig·zag·ging
zilch
zil·lion
zinc
zin·fan·del
zin·nia
Zi·on·ism
zip
zip-code
zipped
zip·per
zip·ping

zip·py

zir·con

zith·er

zo·di·ac

zom·bie

zon·al

zonked

zoo·log·i·cal

zo·ol·o·gy

zoom

zuc·chi·ni

zwie·back

zy·de·co

zy·gote

zy·mur·gy

Homophones: Words Commonly Confused and Misspelled

INTRODUCTION

Homographs and Homophones

Homographs (literally "written the same") are words that have the same spelling but differ in either meaning or pronunciation. The first kind of homograph is sometimes called a *homonym* (literally, "having the same name"), and examples include *cricket* (the game) and *cricket* (the insect). The second kind would include the word *schedule,* which has a US English pronunciation beginning \sked\ but a Canadian and British pronunciation that begins \shed\. There is no problem telling which spelling to use, since there is only one, and no spelling issue arises because the words are homographs.

Homophones (literally "same sound") are words that are spelled differently but sound the same. Merriam-Webster's allows that words with the same sound but different points of stress, such as *insight* and *incite*, are homophones, so such words are found among those on the list. Homophones cause the most confusion in writing because having them in your oral vocabulary does not mean that you will be able to identify which of the written versions has the meaning you are trying to convey. In addition, because there are many dialects of English in which words are pronounced differently, it is actually true that different people have different homophones! This means that in order to serve the greatest number of readers, a broad range of pronunciations has been considered for this list, but this also suggests that some words that are listed as homophones may prove not to be homophones for you. Merriam-Webster's distinguishes between pronunciations phonetically spelled /är/ and /ȯr/, although many speakers of US English do not. Because such words are stored with different pronunciation information in the dictionary database, the task of locating such words and verifying that they are, in fact, homophones for someone, would prove too difficult, so it has not been attempted.

Words with Variant Spellings

Homophones are clearly different words with different meanings: for example, *chauffeur* and *shofar* (only in English), or *dhow*, *Tao,* and *Dow*, or *bare* and *bear.* Careful examination shows that some words that look like they may be homophones are simply the same word with two or more variant spellings, like *bur* and *burr*, *cookie* and *cooky,* and *coolabah* and *coolibah* (the tree in the song "Waltzing Matilda"). These words are included on the list with slash marks between them, but only if they are homophones for another word. (The first word is the main entry. There are some oddities: I have followed Merriam-Webster's if the word appears there and in the rare case that it does not, a reliable source that lists the word.) The whole range of British and US English spelling variants falls into this category, and the following kinds of differences, which are manifestations of that, are not included in the homophone list.

US		British	
Spelling	**Example**	**Spelling**	**Example**
e	encyclopedia	*ae*	encyclopaedia
e	fetus	*oe*	foetus
er	meter	*re*	metre
f	draft	*ugh*	draught
ize	apologize	*ise*	apologise
single *l*	traveler	double *l*	traveller
o	color	*ou*	colour
se	defense	*ce*	defence
drop *e* before *-ment*	judgment	keep *e* before *-ment*	judgement

Sometimes it can be difficult to determine if two words are variant spellings or homophones because their history is unclear, or dictionaries are at odds, or they may possibly both be homophones AND also have variant spellings. In this category are *bogey, bogy,* and *bogie*; *amok* and *amuck*; *gallipot* and *galipot*; and *analog* and *analogue*. Examples that are too unclear have been omitted from the list.

Homographs and Words with Multiple Meanings

Homographs are distinguished in the dictionary by having separate entries. But there are also words that have only one entry with multiple meanings. Another level of difficulty can arise when one or more words in a set of homophones is a word with multiple meanings—then you have to connect each meaning to the correct spelling. Even more complicated is the case when homographs are also homophonic. For example, the homographs:

air—(n) odorless gasses we breathe *and*
air—(v) to broadcast

also have the homophones:

are—(n) 1/100th of a hectare
Ayr—(n) Scottish seaport
e'er—(adv) contraction of *ever*
ere—(conj) before
err—(v) to make a mistake
heir—(n) person who will inherit

About the List

What follows is a list of homophones—one of the
longest lists anywhere. Because of the list's length, only
ONE of any multiple meanings is usually given. For the
same reason, homophone groups are listed only once—
by the word that comes first in alphabetical order. So the
group above is listed by *air*, not by any of the other
words. Thus the list is organized partly alphabetically,
but also partly by sound. If you do not find a word
where you expect it, this may be because it has a homophone that falls earlier in the alphabet—use the Sound
Chart on page 51 to check for alternate spellings, or scan
the list to find it. A word or *orthography* (sequence of
letters) that has two different pronunciations, both of
them homophonic, will be listed twice. Thus, you will
find *bade* with *bad* and *bade* also grouped with *bayed*.

Note that the pronunciation that places a word in a
homophone group is not necessarily its only pronunciation, nor is it necessarily the first pronunciation for
that word in the dictionary. It is always the first pronunciation unless marked otherwise.

Also because of length, proper names of people are
included only if a group has two members without it (so

the homophones *an, Ann/Anne* are not included because
only one word in the groups is not a proper name—
which, in this particular case, has variant spellings).
Proper nouns that name geographical locations and
proper adjectives formed from them are treated differently: they are included if they are homophones of only
one other word (so *let, Lett* will be found listed).

Although, as stated in the introduction, *Merriam-
Webster's Collegiate Dictionary, Eleventh Edition* is
THE source for this book, on occasion other sources
have been consulted for enlightenment on sticky points.

Each homophone is identified, using the following
abbreviations:

abbr—abbreviation
adj—adjective
adv—adverb
art—article
conj—conjunction
interj—interjection
n—noun
part—participle
prep—preposition
pres—present
pron—pronoun
pt—past tense
v—verb

As in The Word List, centered dots show word divisions for hyphenating at the end of a line of print or
type. Words that are not broken into syllables should
not be hypenated (see page 41 if you wish to further
develop your understanding of hyphenation rules).
Hyphens that are part of the word are shown as
hyphens and as double hyphens (=) if the word breaks
at the hyphen.

THE HOMOPHONE LIST

a—(art) indefinite article (rhymes with *say*)
ay/aye—(adv) always
eh—(interj) request for confirmation or repetition

ac·cept—(v) to receive willingly
ex·cept—(v) to leave out

ac·ci·dence—(n) part of grammar dealing with inflections
ac·ci·dents—(n) unplanned events

ad—(n) short for advertisement
add—(v) total up

adds—(v) totals up
ads—(n) short for advertisements
adze—(n) cutting tool

adieu—(n) farewell
ado—(n) time-wasting bother

ae·rie/aery—(n) mountaintop nest (rhymes with *dairy*)
aery—(adj) ethereal
ai·ry—(adj) open to circulation of air

ae·rie/aery—(n) mountaintop nest (2nd pronunciation; rhymes with *dearie*)
ee·rie/ee·ry—(adj) weird
Erie—(n) a Native American/American Indian people

aero—(adj) of aircraft
ar·row—(n) slender, pointed shaft

af·fect—(v) to change
ef·fect—(n) result

aid—(v) to assist
aide—(n) helper

aides—(n) helpers
aids—(v) assists
AIDS—(n) acquired immune deficiency syndrome

ail—(v) be sick
ale—(n) beer

air—(n) odorless gasses we breathe
Aire—(n) river in northern England
are—(n) 1/100th of a hectare
Ayr—(n) Scottish seaport
e'er—(adv) contraction of *ever*
ere—(prep) before
err—(v) to make a mistake
eyre—(n) court circuit in medieval England
heir—(n) person who will inherit

aisle—(n) walkway
I'll—(pron + v) contraction of *I will*
isle—(n) island

ait—(n) little island
ate—(v—pt of *eat*) consumed food
eight—(n) number 8

all—(adv) everything
auld—(adj) old
awl—(n) tool for piercing

al·lot—(v) to assign a share
a lot—(adv) large amount

al·lowed—(v) permitted
aloud—(adv) with the speaking voice

all ready—(adv) completely prepared
al·ready—(adv) before a specified time

al·tar—(n) place where sacrifice is offered
al·ter—(v) to change

all to·geth·er—(adv) as one
al·to·geth·er—(adv) in all

amn't—(v + adv) chiefly Scottish and Irish contraction of *am not*
ant—(n) insect
aunt—(n) sister of a parent

an—(indefinite art) one (rhymes with *bun)*
and—(conj) in addition

in—(adv) within a particular place
'n—(conj) abbr for *than*
'n'—(conj) abbr for *and* as in *fish 'n' chips*

an·a·log—(adj) timepiece with hour and minute hands
an·a·logue—(adj) something analogous

an·te—(n) poker stakes
an·ti—(prep) against
aunt·ie/aunty—(n) sister of a parent

any one—(phrase) any single
any·one—(pron) any person at all

arc—(n) portion of a circle
ark—(n) a ship

as·cent—(n) an upward climb
as·sent—(v) to agree

as·sis·tance—(n) act of helping
as·sis·tants—(n) helpers

at·ten·dance—(n) number of people present
at·ten·dents—(n) people who serve others

au·ger—(n) a drill
au·gur—(n) person who foretells

aught—(adv) anything
ought—(v) should

au·ral—(adj) related to the hearing
oral—(adj) related to the mouth

au·tar·chy—(n) absolute sovereignty
au·tar·ky—(n) condition of national self-sufficiency

away—(adv) distant
aweigh—(adj) raised just clear of the bottom

awed—(adj) in a state of wonder
odd—(adj) unusual

aw·ful—(adj) very bad
of·fal—(n) waste

ax·el—(n) figure-skating jump
ax·il—(n) angle between a leaf and the point at which it arises
ax·le—(n) shaft on which wheels revolve

ay—(interj) expression of regret (rhymes with *sigh*)
aye—(adv) sea goer's "yes"
eye—(n) organ of sight
I—(pron) oneself

baa—(n) bleat of a sheep
bah—(interj) exclamation of disdain

baal—(n) Canaanite or Phoenician deity
bail—(v) to remove water from a boat
bale—(v) to bundle hay into a bale

bach—(v) to live alone as a bachelor (rhymes with *catch*)
batch—(n) a group

bad—(adj) disobedient (rhymes with *mad*)
bade—(v—pt of *bid*) issued an order

bade—(v—pt of *bid*) issued an order (2nd pronunciation; rhymes with *made*)
bayed—(v—pt of *bay*) barked

bailed—(v—pt of *bail*) removed water from a boat
baled—(v—pt of *bale*) gathered hay into bales

bail·ee—(n) person to whom property is bailed
bai·ley—(n) outer wall of a castle
bai·lie—(n) municipal officer in Scotland

bail·er—(n) person who bails water
bail·or—(n) person who entrusts goods to a bailee
bal·er—(n) person who bales hay

bail·ing—(pres part of *bail*) removing water from a boat
bal·ing—(pres part of *bale*) creating hay bales

bait—(v) to lure
bate—(v) to lessen

bait·ed—(v—pt of *bait*) lured
bat·ed—(v—pt of *bate*) lessened

bait·ing—(pres part of *bait*) luring
bat·ing—(pres part of *bate*) lessening

baize—(n) green felt
bays—(v) barks
beys—(n) Turkish officials

bald—(adj) hairless
balled—(v—pt of *ball*) rolled into a ball
bawled—(v—pt of *bawl*) cried loudly

ball—(n) spherical body used in games and sports
bawl—(v) to cry loudly

balm—(n) healing ointment
bomb—(n) explosive device

ba·lo·ney/bo·lo·ney—(n) nonsense
bo·lo·gna/ba·lo·ney—(n) smoked sausage

band—(n) a group
banned—(adj) forbidden

bang—(n) loud noise
bhang—(n) hemp

ban·zai—(n) Japanese war cry
bon·sai—(n) dwarfed potted plant

bard—(n) poet
bard/barde—(n) piece of armor for a horse
barred—(adj) enclosed by poles

bare—(adj) naked
bear—(v) to carry

bar·ing—uncovering
bear·ing—(pres part of *bear*) carrying

bark—(n) outer sheath of a tree
bark/barque—(n) square-rigged sailing ship

ba·ron—(n) minor royalty
bar·ren—(adj) not reproducing

Bar·ry—(n) masculine name
ber·ry—(n) type of pulpy fruit
bury—(v) to deposit in the earth
Bury—(n) town in northwestern England

bas·al—(adj) forming the foundation
ba·sil—(n) type of herb

base—(n) foundation
bass—(n) deep-voiced male singer
beth—(n) 2nd letter of the Hebrew alphabet

based—(part) supported
baste—(v) to coat with liquid during cooking

bas·es—(n) foundations
ba·sis—(n) principal component
bass·es—(n) deep-voiced male singers

bas·i·net—(n) light steel helmet
bas·si·net—(n) baby's basket-shaped bed

bask—(v) to enjoy a pleasant warmth
basque—(n) tight-fitting bodice
Basque—(n) inhabitant of the Pyrenees

bat—(n) flying nocturnal mammal
batt—(n) flat pad

baud—(n) unit of data transmission (rhymes with *clawed*)
bawd—(n) one who keeps a brothel

baud—(n) unit of data transmission (2nd pronunciation; rhymes with *cod*)
bod—(n) body

baud—(n) unit of data transmission (British pronunciation; rhymes with *code*)
bode—(v—pt of *bide*) stayed
bowed—(v—pt of *bow*) bent

bay—(v) to bark
bey—(n) Turkish official

be—(v) exist
Bea—(n) feminine name, nickname for *Beatrice*
bee—(n) insect that feeds on pollen and nectar and stores honey

beach—(n) seashore
beech—(n) hardwood tree

bean—(n) type of legume (rhymes with *keen*)
been—(v—pt part of *be*) existed (chiefly British pronunciation)

beat—(v) to hit repeatedly
beet—(n) edible purplish-red root

beau—(n) male friend
bow—(n) a simple curve or bend

beaut—(n) slang for a beauty
bute—(n) abbr for *phenylbutazone*—an analgesic
Bute—(n) Scottish island
butte—(n) steep, isolated hill
Butte—(n) city in Montana

been—(v) (pt part of *be*) existed (rhymes with *kin*)
bin—(n) a storage box

been—(v) (pt part of *be*) existed (2nd pronunciation; rhymes with *Ken*)
ben—(prep) Scottish for within
Ben—(n) masculine name, nickname for *Benjamin*

beer—(n) brewed drink
bier—(n) stand for a coffin
birr—(n) 100 cents in Ethiopia

bel—(n) ten decibels
bell—(n) hollow, metallic, reverberating device
belle—(n) beautiful woman
Belle—(n) feminine name

Bern—(n) capital of Switzerland
burn—(v) to undergo combustion

berth—(n) shipboard accommodations
birth—(n) emergence of a baby from the body of its mother

be·sot—(v) to muddle, especially with drink
be·sought—(v—pt of *beseech*) begged

bet·ter—(adj) superior
bet·tor/bet·ter—(n) one who bets

bi—(adj) bisexual
buy—(v) to purchase
by—(prep) near
bye—(n) slot in a tournament through which a participant advances
without competing

bight—(n) bay
bite—(n) morsel of food
byte—(n) unit of computer information

billed—(adj) having a bill
build—(v) to construct

bit—(v—pt of *bite*) seized with the teeth
bitt—(n) post on ship deck for securing lines

blew—(v—pt of *blow*) sent forth a current of air
blue—(adj) color of the sky

bloc—(n) alliance
block—(n) cube

blond—(adj) yellow-haired male
blonde—(adj) yellow-haired female

boar—(n) wild pig (rhymes with *more*)
Boer—(n) South African of Dutch descent
bore—(v—pt of *bear*) carried

board—(n) a plank
bored—(adj) not interested

board·er—(n) person provided with meals and lodging
bord·er—(n) perimeter

Boer—(n) South African of Dutch descent (rhymes with *moor*)
boor—(n) rude, insensitive person
bourg—(n) town neighboring a castle

bo·gey/bo·gie/bo·gy—(n) specter
bo·gie/bo·gey—(n) low, strong cart

bold—(adj) brave
bowled—(v—pt of *bowl)* knocked over

bold·er—(adj) more courageous
boul·der/bowl·der—(n) large rock

bole—(n) a trunk
boll—(n) plant pod
bowl—(n) to roll a ball at pins

boos—(n) shouts of disapproval
booze—(n) liquor

boo·tee/boo·tie—(n) baby's sock
boo·ty/boo·tie—(n) plunder

born—(adj) brought forth by birth
borne—(v—pt part of *bear*) carried
bourn/bourne—(n) small stream

bor·ough—(n) municipal corporation in some states
burgh—(n) incorporated town in Scotland
bur·ro—(n) donkey
bur·row—(v) to dig into the ground

bough—(n) tree branch
bow—(n) front of a ship; respectful bend

bouil·lon—(n) broth
bul·lion—(n) gold or silver bar

boy—(n) male child
buoy—(n) navigational aid

bra—(n) abbr for *brassiere*
braw—(adj) well-dressed

braes—(n) chiefly Scottish for hillsides
braise—(v) to cook slowly in a closed pot with fat and a little
    moisture
brays—(n) loud, harsh cries
braze—(v) to solder

braid—(n) three strands woven together
brayed—(v—pt of *bray*) uttered a loud, harsh cry

brake—(n) device for stopping motion
break—(v) to split apart

breach—(v) to commit an infraction
breech—(n) hind part of the body

breach·es—(v) violates
breech·es—(n) short pants

bread—(n) baked and leavened food made from flour
bred—(v—pt of *breed*) propagated

breast—(n) a mammary gland
Brest—(n) a port in northwestern France

brede—(n) archaic: embroidery
breed—(v) propagate
Brighid—(n) variant of the feminine name *Brigit*

brewed—(adj) fermented
brood—(n) family

brews—(v) ferments
bruise—(n) contusion

brid·al—(adj) relating to a bride
bri·dle—(n) horse's headgear

Brit·ain—(n) the United Kingdom
Brit·on—(n) native of Great Britain

broach—(v) to open for the first time
brooch—(n) ornament fastened at or near the neck

broom—(n) tool for sweeping
brougham—(n) horse-drawn carriage
brume—(n) mist

brows—(n) foreheads
browse—(v) to graze

bruit—(n) noise
brut—(adj) very dry (of champagne)
brute—(adj) of or relating to beasts

bru·net—(n) male with dark hair and complexion
bru·nette—(n) female with dark hair and complexion

bundt—(n) type of cake pan
bunt—(v) to tap a baseball with a bat without swinging

bur·ger—(n) abbr for *hamburger*
bur·gher—(n) merchant

bur·ley—(n) type of tobacco
bur·ly—(n) husky

bus—(n) motor vehicle, usually for mass transit
buss—(v) to kiss

bussed—(v—pt of *buss*) kissed
bust—(v) to smash

but—(conj) excepting
butt—(v) to hit with the head or horns

buy·er—(n) person who buys
byre—(n) cow barn

cache—(n) hidden storage
cash—(n) legal tender

cached—(v—pt of *cache*) hidden away
cashed—(v—pt of *cash*) converted to legal tender

cad·die/cad·dy—(n) golfer's assistant
cad·dy—(n) small chest to hold tea

cal·en·dar—(n) register of days
cal·en·der—(v) to press between plates

call—(v) to summon
caul—(n) amniotic membrane

cal·ler—(n) person who calls
cho·ler—(n) irascibility
col·lar—(v) to arrest

cal·lous—(adj) hard-hearted
cal·lus—(v) to form thick, protective skin

can·non—(n) large gun
can·non/can·on—(n) projecting part of a bell by which it's hung
can·on—(n) accepted principle

cant—(n) private language of the underworld
can't—(v + adv) contraction of *cannot*

can·vas/can·vass—(n) cloth
can·vass/can·vas—(v) to solicit

cap·i·tal—(n) city that is the seat of government
cap·i·tol—(n) building that is the legislative meeting place

car—(n) automobile (dialect pronunciation; rhymes with *more*)
cor/kor—(n) ancient Hebrew/Phoenician unit of measure
core—(n) inner part
corps—(n) body

car·at—(n) unit of weight for precious stones, equal to 200 milligrams
car·et—(n) proofreader's insertion mark
car·rot—(n) edible orange root
kar·at/car·at—(n) unit of fineness of gold

car·ies—(n) dental cavities
car·ries—(v) transports

car·ol—(n) Christmas song
Car·ol/Car·ole—(n) feminine name; sometimes nickname for *Caroline*
car·rel—(n) study enclosure
Kar·ol—(n) masculine name

car·pal—(n) all of the bones at the wrist
car·pel—(n) structural part of a flower

cask—(n) barrel
casque—(n) helmet

cast—(v) to throw
caste—(n) Hindu social class

cast·er—(n) person who casts
cast·or—(n) beaver hat
Cast·or—(n) star in Gemini

cause—(n) reason for action
'cause—(conj) abbr for *because*
caws—(n) sounds made by crows

cay—(n) low island or reef (rhymes with *me*)
chi—(n) 22nd letter of the Greek alphabet
chi/ch'i/ki/qi—(n) animating energy
key—(n) device that opens locks
quay—(n) landing place

cay—(n) low island or reef (2nd pronunciation; rhymes with *may*)
kay—(n) the letter *k*
Kay—(n) feminine name
Kay—(n) knight of the Round Table, Arthur's adopted brother
quay/quai—(n) landing place

ce·dar—(n) evergreen tree
seed·er—(n) person who broadcasts seeds

cede—(v) to yield
seed—(v) to plant

ced·ing—(v—pres part of *cede*) yielding
seed·ing—(v—pres part of *seed*) planting

cee—(n) the letter *c*
sea—(n) great body of salt water
see—(v) to perceive with the eye
See—(n) cathedral town
si—(n) 7th tone of the diatonic scale in solmization in Italian

cees—(n) multiple occurrences of the letter *c*
seas—(n) great bodies of salt water
sees—(n) perceives with the eyes
Sees—(n) cathedral towns
seise—(v) to put in possession of something
seize—(v) to take possession of

ceil—(v) to furnish with a ceiling
seal—(v) to close an envelope
SEAL—(n) SEa, Air, Land team (Navy SEAL)
seel—(v) to sew closed the eyes of a hawk

ceil·ing—(n) top of the room
seal·ing—(pres part of *seal*) closing an envelope
seel·ing—(pres part of *seel*) sewing closed the eyes of a hawk

cel/cell—(n) abbr for *celluloid*; material on which to draw to make cartoons
cell—(n) small room
sell—(v) to exchange for money

cel·lar—(n) small room under a house
sell·er—(n) person who sells

cen·ser—(n) vessel for burning incense
cen·sor—(v) to examine for objectionable material
sen·sor—(n) device that detects

cen·sus—(n) numbering
sen·ses—(n) faculties

cent—(n) 1/100th of a dollar
scent—(n) aroma
sent—(v—pt of *send*) dispatched

cents—(n) hundredths of a dollar
scents—(n) aromas
sense—(v) to be aware of

cere—(n) area at the base of a bird's bill
sear—(v) to scorch
seer—(n) prophet
sere/sear—(adj) withered

ce·re·al—(n) food made of grain(s)
se·ri·al—(n) numbers in sequence

Ce·res—(n) Roman Goddess of agriculture
se·ries—(n) sequence of things

ces·sion—(n) yielding to another
ses·sion—(n) meeting

cham·pagne—(n) French sparkling wine
cham·paign—(n) expanse of level open country

chance—(n) luck
chants—(n) rhythmic utterances

chan·tey/chan·ty/shan·ty—(n) sailor's song
shan·ty—(n) crudely built dwelling

chard—(n) spinach-like vegetable
charred—(v—pt of *char*) burnt

chased—(v—pt of *chase*) quickly followed
chaste—(adj) pure

chauf·feur—(n) person employed as a driver
sho·far—(n) rams-horn trumpet (2nd pronunciation)

check—(v) to slow or stop
Czech—(n) native or inhabitant of the Czech Republic

chews—(v) masticates
choose—(v) to select

chic—(adj) stylish (rhymes with *seek*)
sheikh/sheik—(n) Arab chief

Chi·le—(n) South American country
chili/chile/chil·li—(n) hot pepper
chilly—(adj) uncomfortably cool

choir—(n) group of singers
quire—(n) one-twentieth of a ream of paper

cho·ral—(adj) made to be sung by a choir
cor·al—(n) marine polyp's skeleton

cho·rale—(n) choir
cor·ral—(n) pen for livestock

chord—(n) three or more musical tones rendered simultaneously
cord—(n) very light rope
cored—(v—pt of *core*) removed the central part of

chough—(n) crow-like bird (rhymes with *puff*)
chuff—(v) to produce noisy exhaust

chute—(n) slide
shoot—(n) immature stem or branch

chow—(n) food
ciao—(interj) Italian expression for greeting or parting

cist—(n) stone-lined neolithic burial chamber (soft *c*: \s\)
cyst—(n) closed sac

cist—(n) stone-lined neolithic burial chamber (hard *c*: \k\)
kist—(n) Scottish or South African for a cupboard for first aid supplies

cite—(v) to refer to
sight—(n) vision
site—(n) location

cit·ed—(v—pt of *cite*) referenced
sight·ed—(adj) having sight
sit·ed—(adj) located

cites—(v) refers to
sights—(n) things to be seen
sites—(n) locations

clack—(n) chattering sound
claque—(n) group hired to applaud; sycophants

Claus—(n) Santa
clause—(n) group of words with a subject and predicate
claws—(n) animal's sharp, curved nails

cleek—(n) chiefly Scottish for large hook to hang pot over fire
    (rhymes with *seek*)
clique—(n) exclusive group

clew—(n) ball of yarn
clue—(n) hint

click—(n) slight, sharp noise (rhymes with *trick*)
clique—(n) exclusive group (2nd pronunciation)

climb—(v) to ascend
clime—(n) climate

close—(v) to shut
clothes—(n) garments (alternate pronunciation)
cloze—(adj) style of fill-in test to check reading comprehension

coal—(n) ember
cole—(n) group of plants including cabbage and kale
kohl—(n) eye shadow

coaled—(v—pt of *coal*) supplied with coal
cold—(adj) opposite of hot

coarse—(adj) rough
cors/kors—(n) ancient Hebrew/Phoenician units of measure
corse—(n) corpse
course—(n) path for travel

coat—(n) jacket
cote—(n) shed or coop for small animals
Côte—(n) coast
quote—(v) to speak someone else's words, giving credit (alternate pronunciation)

coax—(v) to persuade
Cokes®—(n) soft drinks

cocks—(n) male birds
cox—(n) abbr for *coxswain*

cocks·comb—(n) flowering plant
cock's comb—(n) comb of a cock
cox·comb—(n) fop

cod·dling—(v—pres part of *coddle*) treating with care
cod·ling—(n) young cod

cof·fer—(n) chest
cough·er—(n) person who coughs

coin—(n) metal money
quoin—(n) keystone

co·la—(n) soft drink flavored with kola extracts
ko·la—(n) seed of a kola tree

col·lard—(n) kale
col·lared—(v—pt of *collar*) grabbed or apprehended

Co·lum·bia—(n) the United States
Co·lom·bia—(n) South American country

col·o·nel—(n) military officer
ker·nel—(n) seed

com·pla·cence—(n) self-satisfaction
com·plai·sance—(n) willingness to please

com·pla·cent—(adj) self-satisfied
com·plai·sant—(adj) willing to please

com·ple·ment—(n) something that completes
com·plim·ent—(n) praise

com·ple·men·ta·ry—(adj) serving to complete
com·pli·men·ta·ry—(adj) expressing a compliment

conch—(n) marine mollusk (rhymes with *honk*)
conk—(v) to hit on the head

con·fec·tion·ary—(n) sweets
con·fec·tion·ery—(n) the confectioner's art

con·fi·dant—(n) one who is trusted with secrets
con·fi·dante—(n) especially a confidant who is a woman

coo—(n) low, soft cry of a pigeon or dove (rhymes with *Sue*)
coup—(n) sudden, successful stroke

coo·lie—(n) unskilled laborer from the Far East; not acceptable
cool·ly/cooly—(adv) in a nonchalant manner
cou·lee—(n) stream of water or lava

cope—(v) to put up with difficulties (rhymes with *soap*)
coup—(n) chiefly Scottish for an upset

copped—(v—pt of *cop*) swiped
Copt—(n) person descended from ancient Egyptians

cops—(n) police officers
copse—(n) stand of trees

cork—(n) bottle stopper
Cork—(n) city and county in Ireland

co·sign—(v) to sign jointly
co·sine—(n) trigonometric function

coun·cil—(n) advisory group
coun·sel—(n) advice

coun·cil·lor/coun·cil·or—(n) member of a council
coun·sel·or/coun·sel·lor—(n) lawyer

cous·in—(n) child of one's aunt or uncle
coz·en—(v) to deceive

cow·ard—(n) person who shows disgraceful fear
cow·ered—(v—pt of *cower*) to crouch away from something

craft—(n) occupation requiring artistic skill
kraft—(n) strong paper made from wood pulp

crape—(n) band of fabric worn in mourning
crepe/crêpe—(n) small, thin pancake

cra·ter—(n) depression around the mouth of a volcano
kra·ter/cra·ter—(n) vessel from classical antiquity

creak—(v) to squeak (rhymes with *sleek*)
creek—(n) small stream

cream—(n) milk containing 18–40% butterfat
crème/creme—(n) cream or similar preparation used in cooking

crease—(n) ridge made by folding
kris—(n) Malay or Indonesian dagger

crewed—(adj) served by a crew
crude—(adj) coarse

crew·el—(n) embroidery done with crewel yarn
cru·el—(adj) merciless

crews—(v) acts as a crew member
cruise—(v) to travel by sea without purpose

crick—(n) muscle spasm (rhymes with *stick*)
creek—(n) small stream (2nd pronunciation)

cru·di·tés—(n) raw vegetables served as hors d'oeuvres
cru·di·ties—(n) the quality of being rude

cue—(v) to prompt for stage business
Kew—(n) home of the famous English gardens
queue—(n) waiting line

curd—(v) to curdle
Kurd—(n) one of the pastoral people from Turkey and neighboring areas

cur·rant—(n) small seedless raisin
cur·rent—(n) flow of electric charge

curs·er—(n) one who swears
cur·sor—(n) visual cue in a video display

cyg·net—(n) young swan
sig·net—(n) seal used in place of a signature

cym·bal—(n) brass plate used to create a musical sound
sym·bol—(n) representation

dam—(v) to create a barrier that prevents the flow of water
damn—(v) to curse

dammed—(v—pt of *dam*) prevented from flowing
damned—(v—pt of *damn*) cursed

Dane—(n) native of Denmark
deign—(v) to condescend reluctantly

days—(n) periods of light
daze—(v) to stun

dear—(adj) precious
deer—(n) mammal with brown fur and antlers

deb·u·tant—(n) person making a debut
deb·u·tante—(n) woman making her entrance into society

dense—(adj) marked by crowding
dents—(n) depressions made by blows

de·pendence/de·pen·dance—(n) state of being dependent
de·pen·dents/de·pen·dants—(n) those who rely on others

de·scent—(n) lineage
dis·sent—(n) difference of opinion

de·vis·er—(n) inventor
di·vi·sor—(n) number by which dividend is divided

dew—(n) morning condensation on cool surfaces
do—(v) to carry out
doux—(adj) used of champagne: very sweet
due—(adj) owed as a debt

dhow—(n) Arab boat
dow—(adj) chiefly Scottish for capable
Dow—(n) abbr for Dow Jones average
Tao—(n) guiding principle of all reality

Di—(n) nickname for feminine name *Diane*
die—(v) to expire
dye—(v) to give a new color to

died—(v—pt of *die*) expired
dyed—(v—pt of *dye*) gave new color to

dies—(v) expires
dyes—(v) gives new color to

dine—(v) to take dinner
dyne—(n) unit of force

dire—(adj) creating desperation
dyer—(n) person who dyes

dis·creet—(adj) discerning
dis·crete—(adj) separate

dis·cussed—(v—pt of *discuss*) talked about
dis·gust—(n) aversion

djinn/jinn—(n) genie—a spirit in human form who serves its master
gin—(n) alcoholic beverage made from juniper berries

do—(n) first tone of diatonic scale in solmization (rhymes with
   mow)
doe—(n) female deer
Doe—(n) pseudonym for someone whose true name is unknown:
   John if a man, Jane if a woman
Doh!—(interj) exclamation of annoyance
D'oh!—(interj) vocalization representing the script direction
   "Annoyed Grunt" by Homer Simpson of *The Simpsons*™
dough—(n) uncooked mixture of flour and liquid

doc—(n) abbr for *doctor*
dock—(n) wooden pier where boats are kept

does—(n) multiple female deer
doughs—(n) several uncooked bread mixtures
doze—(v) to nap

done—(adj) completed
dun—(adj) drab and dull

dos/do's—(n) opposite of *dont's*
dues—(n) membership payments

dost—(v) archaic present 2nd person singular of *do*
dust—(n) fine particles of matter

dour—(adj) stern (2nd pronunciation)
dower—(n) dowry

douse/dowse—(v) to throw liquid on
dowse—(v) to use a divining rod

doy·en—(n) senior member
doy·enne—(n) woman who is a doyen

droop—(v) to sink gradually
drupe—(n) one-seeded fruit

du·al—(adj) having two parts
du·el—(n) conflict between two antagonists

earl—(n) British nobleman
URL—(n) Internet address

earn—(v) to receive in return for work
erne—(n) sea eagle
urn—(n) ornamental vase

eau—(n) French for *water*: appears in compounds
O—(n) a blood type
oh/O—(interj) used to express emotion, etc.
owe—(v) to be under obligation to repay

eave—(n) lower border of a roof
eve—(n) abbr for *evening*
Eve—(n) first woman, wife of Adam; a feminine name

en·voi/en·voy—(n) concluding remarks to poem, essay, or book
en·voy—(n) representative from one government to another

erup·tion—(n) the breaking out of a rash
ir·rup·tion—(v) a violent rushing in

eu·nuchs—(n) those who lack virility or power
UNIX®—(n) a computer operating system

ev·ery·one—(pron) everybody
ev·ery one—(phrase) each individual example

ewe—(n) mature female sheep
U—(adj) characteristic of the upper class
yew—(adj) evergreen tree
you—(pron) the 2nd person singular or plural

ewes—(n) more than one female sheep
yews—(n) evergreen trees

eye·let—(n) small hole for laces
is·let—(n) little island

eyer—(n) person who eyes something
ire—(n) intense anger

facts—(n) information that is objectively real
FAQs—(n) frequently asked questions
fax—(n) image transmission machine; abbr for *facsimile*

fa·er·ie/fa·ery—(n) fairies' abode
fa·ery—(adj) having to do with the fairies' abode
fairy—(n) imaginary, minute, magical person
fer·ry—(n) abbr for *ferryboat*

fain—(adj) willing
fane—(n) temple or church
feign—(v) to give a false appearance
foehn/föhn—(n) warm, dry wind that blows down a mountainside

faille—(n) shiny, woven fabric
file—(n) tool for smoothing
phial—(n) vial

faint—(adj) lacking courage and spirit
feint—(n) something feigned

fair—(adj) pleasing to eye or mind
fare—(n) price charged for transport

fak·er—(n) one who deceives
fa·kir—(n) Dervish

far·row—(n) a litter of pigs
pha·raoh—(n) Egyptian king

fat—(adj) plump
phat—(adj) excellent

fate—(n) destiny
fete/fête—(n) festival

faun—(n) mythological half-man, half-goat
fawn—(n) young deer

faux—(adj) imitation
foe—(n) adversary

fay—(n) fairy or elf
Fay/Faye—(n) feminine name
fey—(adj) otherworldly

fays—(n) fairies or elves
faze—(v) to disconcert
feeze—(n) dialect for state of alarm
phase—(n) stage in a sequence

fazed—(adj) stunned
phased—(adj) done in sequential stages

feat—(n) notable deed
feet—(n) plural of *foot*

fer·rate—(n) salt containing iron and oxygen
fer·ret—(n) domesticated polecat

fe·ral—(adj) brutal
fer·rule—(n) strengthening metal cap
fer·ule—(n) school discipline

fet·ed/fêted—(v—pt of *fete/fête*) celebrated
fet·id—(adj) stinking

few—(pron) not many
phew—(interj) expression of relief or disgust

fi·an·cé—(n) man engaged to be married
fi·an·cée—(n) woman engaged to be married

fie—(interj) expression of disgust or disapproval
phi—(n) 21st letter of the Greek alphabet

fills—(v) completes
fils—(n) 1/1000th of dinar, dirham, and rial in various countries

fil·ter—(n) porous material to separate substances
phil·ter—(n) potion credited with magical power

fin—(n) flipper-like appendage
Finn—(n) native of Finland
Fyn—(n) Danish island in the Baltic Sea

find—(v) to locate
fined—(v—pt of *fine*) imposed a sum as punishment

fin·ish—(v) to terminate
Finn·ish—(adj) of Finland

fir—(n) evergreen tree
fur—(n) animal pelt

firs—(n) evergreen trees
furs—(n) animal pelts
furze—(n) gorse

fish·er—(n) person who fishes
fis·sure—(n) crack

fizz—(v) effervesce
phiz—(n) face; shortened and altered form for *physiognomy*

flair—(n) instinctive ability
flare—(n) signal light

flea—(n) blood-sucking insect
flee—(v) to run away

fleche—(n) spire
flesh—(n) part of an animal eaten as food

flecks—(n) specks
flex—(v) to bend

flew—(v—pt of *fly*) was airborne
flu—(n) any of several viruses; abbr for *influenza*
flue—(n) chimney pipe

Flo—(n) a feminine name; nickname for *Florence*
floe—(n) floating ice sheet
flow—(v) to move in a stream

floc—(n) woolly mass; abbr for *floccule*
flock—(n) group of birds or sheep

flocs—(n) woolly masses; abbr for *floccules*
flocks—(n) groups of birds or sheep
phlox—(n) flowering plant

floes—(n) floating ice sheets
flows—(v) glides along; moves in a stream

flour—(n) finely milled wheat
flow·er—(n) plant cultivated for its blossoms

foaled—(v—pt of *foal*) gave birth to a foal
fold—(n) enclosure for sheep

for—(prep) as being or constituting
fore—(interj) golfer's warning cry
four—(n) number 4

for·bear—(v) to hold back
fore·bear/for·bear—(n) ancestor

fore·go—(v) to precede
for·go/fore·go—(v) to do without (something)

fore·word—(n) prefatory comments
for·ward—(adv) toward what is ahead

fort—(n) permanent army post
forte—(n) person's strong point

forth—(adv) forward
fourth—(n) musical interval from tonic to subdominant

foul—(adj) loathsome
fowl—(n) bird

franc—(n) former monetary units of France, etc.
frank—(adj) candid
Frank—(n) masculine name; nickname for *Francis*

frays—(n) protracted fights
phrase—(n) word group with a single grammatical function

freak—(n) markedly unusual or abnormal
phreak—(n) person who gains illegal access to phone service

frees—(v) causes to be free
freeze—(v) to turn to ice
frieze—(n) sculptured band around a building, etc.

fri·ar—(n) member of a mendicant order; brother; monk
fry·er/fri·er—(n) something used for frying, as a small chicken

Gael—(n) Celtic inhabitant of Ireland, Scotland, or the Isle of Man
Gail—(n) feminine name
gale—(n) wind from 32–63 mph

gaff—(n) butcher's hook
gaffe—(n) noticeable mistake

gage—(n) token of defiance
gauge/gage—(n) instrument for measuring

gait—(n) rate of movement
gate—(n) opening in a wall or fence

gait·ed—(adj) any breed of horse that does not usually trot
gat·ed—(adj) having a gate

gall—(n) bile
Gaul—(n) ancient country of western Europe

gal·ley—(n) long, low ship
gal·ly—(v) chiefly dialect meaning to frighten or terrify

gal·lop—(n) horse's fastest gait
Gal·lup—(n) a company that does survey research through polling
ga·lop—(n) lively dance

gam·ble—(v) to play a game for money
gam·bol—(v) to frolic

gang—(n) group of persons working together
gangue—(n) worthless rock containing valuable minerals

gays—(n) homosexuals
gaze—(n) a languid look

gel—(v) to set
jell—(v) to come to the consistency of jelly

gene—(n) sequence of nucleotides in DNA or RNA
jean—(n) durable cotton cloth
Jean/Jeanne—(n) feminine name; sometimes nickname for *Jeanine*
   or *Jeanette*

genes—(n) sequences of nucleotides in DNA or RNA
jeans—(n) pants made of blue denim; abbr for *blue jeans*

gest/geste—(n) tale of adventures
geste/gest—(n) (obsolete) deportment
jessed—(adj) of a hawk: fitted with a strap for attaching a leash
jest—(n) quip

ghat—(n) steps from an Indian riverbank into the water
got—(v—pt of *get*) received possession of

gibe/jibe—(v) to tease
jibe/gybe—(v) to shift forcibly from one side to the other
jibe—(v) to agree

gild—(v)—to coat with gold
gilled—(adj) having gills
guild—(n) craft society

gilt—(adj) covered with gold
guilt—(n) feelings of culpability

glair/glaire—(n) sizing liquid made from egg white
glare—(n) bright light

glass—(n) tumbler (2nd pronunciation; rhymes with *boss*)
gloss—(n) shine

gloom—(n) partial or total darkness
glume—(n) grass bract

glows—(v) shines with intense heat
gloze—(v) to mask the true nature of

glu·ten·ous—(adj) having the quality of gluten
glu·ti·nous—(adj) having the quality of glue

gnawed—(v—pt of *gnaw*) chewed
nod—(n) quick downward motion of the head

gneiss—(n) metamorphic rock
nice—(adj) pleasing

gnu—(n) wildebeest
knew—(v—pt of *know*) perceived
new—(adj) recent
nu—(n) 13th letter of the Greek alphabet

gnus—(n) wildebeests
news—(n) reports of recent events

go·fer/go·pher—(n) lackey
go·pher—(n) burrowing rodent

gored—(v—pt of *gore*) pierced with something pointed
gourd—(n) fruit of a family of vines

go·ril·la—(n) large anthropoid ape
guer·ril·la/gue·ril·la—(n) person who carries out irregular warfare

grade—(n) a standard of food quality
grayed/greyed—(v—pt of *gray/grey*) turned gray/grey

graft—(v) to attach a scion to a stock
graphed—(v—pt of *graph*) plotted on a graph

grate—(v) to grind noisily
great—(adj) eminent

grays/greys—(n) neutral colors between black and white
graze—(v) to crop and eat in a field

grease—(n) thick lubricant
Greece—(n) country in southern Europe

greave—(n) shin armor
grieve—(v) to feel sorrow

greaves—(n) several pieces of shin armor
grieves—(v) feels sorrow

grill—(v) to broil on a grill
grille/grill—(n) grating forming a barrier

grip—(v) to seize
grippe—(n) virus accompanied with fever

gris·ly—(adj) inspiring horror (rhymes with *drizzly*)
gris·tly—(adj) being or consisting of gristle (3rd pronunciation; rhymes with *drizzly*)
griz·zly—(adj) grizzled

groan—(n) a deep moan
grown—(adj) mature

guar·an·tee—(n) assurance for the fulfillment of a condition
guar·an·ty—(n) something given as security

guessed—(v—pt of *guess*) formed an opinion from little evidence
guest—(n) person receiving hospitality

guide—(n) one who leads another
guyed—(v—pt of *guy*) reinforced with a guyline

guise—(n) costume
guys—(n) people

gun·nel—(n) small, eel-shaped marine fish; butterfish
gun·wale/gun·nel—(n) upper edge of a ship's side

hae—(v) chiefly Scottish variant of *have* (rhymes with *day*)
hay—(n) grass prepared for fodder
he—(n) 5th letter of the Hebrew alphabet
hey—(interj) exclamation of surprise or interrogation

hail—(n) precipitation that falls as small balls of ice and snow
hale—(adj) sound

hair—(n) the characteristic coat of a mammal
hare—(n) swift, long-eared mammal in the same family as the rabbit
Herr—(n) German equivalent of *Mister*

hairy—(adj) covered with hair
Har·ry—(n) masculine name
har·ry—(v) to torment by constant attack

hall—(n) large room for assembly
haul—(v) to tranport in a vehicle

halve—(v) to divide into two equal parts
have—(v) to hold as a possession

halves—(n) several portions that are 50% of the whole
haves—(n) those with material wealth

hand·made—(adj) made by hand
hand·maid—(n) something whose function is to serve

hand·some—(adj) having a pleasing appearance
han·som—(n) two-wheeled covered carriage

han·gar—(n) housing for aircraft
hang·er—(n) device by which something is hung

hart—(n) male red deer
heart—(n) the blood pump in vertebrates

hays—(n) grasses prepared for fodder
haze—(n) water, dust, or vapor obscuring the transparency of the air

heal—(v) to restore to health
heel—(n) back of the human foot
he'll—(pron + v) contraction of *he will* or *he shall*

hear—(v) to perceive with the ear
here—(adv) in or at this place

heard—(v—pt of *hear*) perceived with the ear
herd—(n) similar animals kept together and under control

he'd—(pron + v) contraction of *he had* or *he would*
heed—(v) to pay attention

height—(n) the highest part
hight—(adj) named

her·o·in—(n) addictive narcotic
her·o·ine—(n) woman admired and emulated

hew—(v) to fell with an ax (rhymes with *mew*)
hue—(n) color gradation
Hugh—(n) masculine name
whew—(interj) exclamation of amazement, relief, etc.
   (3rd pronunciation)

hi—(interj) greeting; informal for *hello*
hie—(v) to hasten
high—(adj) extending upward to a large degree

hied—(v—pt of *hie*) hastened
hide—(n) skin of an animal

higher—(adj) extending upward to a larger degree
hire—(v) to give employment to

him—(pron) objective case of *he*
hymn—(n) song of praise to God

ho—(interj) exclamation used to attract attention
hoe—(n) implement for tilling or raking
howe—(n) Scottish for *hollow* or *valley*
whoa—(verbal imperative) command to cease movement (2nd
   pronunciation)

hoar—(adj) hoary
whore—(n) woman who engages in sexual acts for money

hoard—(n) hidden supply
horde—(n) teeming crowd
whored—(v) sold oneself for money

hoarse—(adj) grating
horse—(n) stallion

hoes—(n) garden implements
hose—(n) flexible tubes for conveying liquid

hold—(v) to have possession of
holed—(adj) full of holes

hole—(n) opening through something
whole—(adj) free of wound or hurt

hol·ey—(adj) having holes
ho·ly—(adj) divine
whol·ly—(adv) completely

holm—(n) British for small island
home—(n) person's place of residence

hos·tel—(n) inn
hos·tile—(adj) relating to an enemy

hour—(n) sixty minutes
our—(adj) of or relating to ourselves

hours—(n) sets of sixty minutes
ours—(pron) belonging to us

Huai—(n) river in East China (2nd pronunciation; pronounced
   beginning with \hw\; rhymes with *my*)
why—(adv) for what reason (pronounced with initial *h*)

Hue—(n) city in central Vietnam (2nd pronunciation; pronounced
   with \w\; rhymes with *May*)
way—(n) thoroughfare for travel
Wei—(n) river in central China
weigh—(v) to ascertain the heaviness of
whey—(n) watery part of milk separated from curd in cheesemaking

hu·mer·us—(n) funny bone
hu·mor·ous—(adj) funny

Huy—(n) commune in eastern Belgium (pronounced beginning
   with *w*; rhymes with *me*)
we—(pron) I and the rest of the group that includes me
wee—(adj) very small
whee—(interj) exclamation of delight (2nd pronunciation)

idle—(adj) inactive
idol—(n) object of worship
idyll/idyl—(n) narrative poem

ileum—(n) last division of small intestines
ilium—(n) largest of pelvic bones
Ilium—(n) Troy

im·ma·nent—(adj) inherent
im·mi·nent—(adj) ready to take place

im·pass·able/ im·pas·si·ble—(adj) incapable of being passed
im·pas·si·ble—(adj) incapable of experiencing pain

in—(adv) within a particular place (rhymes with *bin*)
inn—(n) travelers' lodging
isn't—(v + adv) dialect: contraction of *is not*

Inc.—(adj) abbr for *Incorporated*
ink—(n) colored liquid for writing

in·ci·dence—(n) rate of occurrence
in·ci·dents—(n) occurrences

in·cip·i·ent—(adj) beginning to come into being
in·sip·i·ent—(adj) lacking wisdom

in·cite—(v) to move to action
in·sight—(n) act of seeing intuitively

in·dict—(v) to charge with an offense
in·dite—(v) to make up or compose

in·dis·creet—(adj) imprudent
in·dis·crete—(adj) not separated

in·no·cence—(adj) freedom from guilt
in·no·cents—(n) those who are free from guilt

in·tense—(adj) existing in an extreme degree
in·tents—(n) purposes

in·tern/in·terne—(n) advanced student in a professional field
in turn—(adv phrase) one at a time

in·ter·pel·late—(v) to question about an official action
in·ter·po·late—(v) to alter or corrupt by insertions

its—(pron) belonging to it
it's—(pron + v) contraction of *it is*

jam—(v) to block
jamb—(n) side post of a doorway

jew·el—(n) gem
joule—(n) unit of energy

jinks—(n) pranks
jinx—(v) to bring bad luck

jug·gler—(n) one skilled in keeping several objects in the air
jug·u·lar—(adj) of or relating to the jugular vein

knap—(n) chiefly dialect for crest of a hill (silent *k*)
nap—(n) short sleep
nape—(n) back of the neck (2nd pronunciation)
nappe—(n) large mass of rock

knave—(n) deceitful fellow
nave—(n) main part of a church interior

knead—(v) to work and press with the hands, as bread dough
kneed—(adj) possessing knees
need—(n) to require

knick·ers—(n) loose, short pants
nick·ers—(v) whinnies

knight—(n) mounted man-at-arms
night—(n) time from dusk to dawn

knit—(v) to link firmly
nit—(n) egg of a louse or other parasite

knits—(v) links firmly together
nits—(n) eggs of a louse or other parasite

knob—(n) rounded protuberance
nob—(n) head of a person or animal

knock—(v) to strike with a sharp blow
nock—(n) notch in an arrow

knot—(v) to entangle
naught/nought—(pron) nothing
not—(adv) negates a group of words
NOT—(n) logical operator to produce the inverse of the input

knout—(n) whip for flogging (alternate pronunciation; rhymes with *boot*)
newt—(n) small salamander

knout—(n) whip for flogging (rhymes with *out*)
nowt—(pron) dialect version of *nought*

know—(v) to perceive directly
no—(adv) not so
Noh—(n) classic Japanese dance-drama

knows—(v) perceives directly
noes/nos—(n) act or instance of refusing
nose—(n) olfactory organ

laa·ger—(n) South African camp
la·ger—(n) beer
log·ger—(n) person who logs

lac—(n) substance used in shellac (rhymes with *sack*)
Lac—(n) French for *lake* in place names
lack—(v) to be in need
lakh—(n) from Hindi/Urdu: a great number

lacks—(v) is in need of
lax—(adj) slack

lade—(v) to load
laid—(v—pt of *lay*) set down

lain—(v—pt part of *lie*) to have reclined
lane—(n) narrow roadway

lam—(n) sudden flight from the law
lamb—(n) young sheep
lame—(n) thin plate, especially of metal (2nd pronunciation)

la·ma—(n) Lamaist monk
lla·ma—(n) long-necked South American ruminant

lap—(n) one turn around a race track
Lapp—(n) language of the nomadic northern Scandanavian people

laps—(n) turns around a race track
lapse—(n) slight error

lase—(v) to emit coherent light
lays—(v) sets down
laze—(v) to idle
leis—(n) flower wreaths

la·ser—(n) beam of coherent electromagnetic radiation
la·zar—(n) person afflicted with a repulsive disease

lay—(v) to set down (rhymes with *bay*)
lay—(v—pt of *lie*) reclined
lea/ley—(n) grassland (2nd pronunciation)
Leh—(n) town in eastern Kashmir, India
lei—(n) flower wreath

lea/ley—(n) grassland (rhymes with *bee*)
lee—(n) protecting shelter

leach—(v) to dissolve out by percolation
leech—(n) blood-sucking worm

lead—(n) soft metallic element (rhymes with *red*)
led—(v—pt of *lead*) guided

leaf—(n) foliage
lief—(adv) gladly (2nd pronunciation)

leak—(v) to escape through an opening
leek—(n) herb related to onion

lean—(v) to incline
lien—(n) security interest created by a mortgage

leaned—(v—pt of *lean*) inclined (chiefly British pronunciation; rhymes with *bent*)
leant—(v—pt of *lean*) chiefly British: inclined
lent—(v—pt of *lend*) gave for temporary use
Lent—(n) forty weekdays from Ash Wednesday to Holy Saturday

leas—(n) grasslands
lees—(n) sediment of a liquor

leased—(v—pt of *lease*) contracted to rent property
least—(adj) lowest in importance; superlative of *little*

leave—(v) to bequeath
lief—(adv) gladly

less·en—(v) to decrease
les·son—(v) to instruct

less·er—(adj) lower in importance; comparative of *little*
les·sor—(n) person who conveys property by lease

let—(v) to give opportunity to
Lett—(n) native or inhabitant of Latvia

lev·ee—(n) pier on a river
levy—(v) to impose (a tax)

li·ar—(n) person who tells lies
li·er—(n) person who reclines
lyre—(n) stringed instrument of the harp family

li·chen—(n) symbiotic alga and fungus growth
lik·en—(v) to compare

lick·er·ish—(adj) greedy
lic·o·rice—(n) type of candy

lie—(v) to recline
lye—(n) a solid caustic

lieu—(n) French for instead: chiefly in phrase *in lieu*
loo—(n) chiefly British for toilet
Lou—(n) masculine or feminine nickname for *Louis, Louisa, Lucy*

light·en·ing—(v—pres part of *lighten*) making light or clear
light·ning—(n) discharge of atmospheric electricity

limb—(n) primary tree branch
limn—(v) to delineate

limbs—(n) branches
limns—(v) delineates

lime—(n) green citrus fruit
Lyme—(n) acute inflammatory disease transmitted by ticks; short for *Lyme disease*

links—(n) rings of chain
links—(n) golf course
lynx—(n) species of wildcat

linn (n) chiefly Scottish for waterfall
Lynn (n) city in Massachusetts, northeast of Boston
Lynn (n) feminine name

lit·er·al—(adj) taking words in their nonfigurative sense
lit·to·ral—(adj) relating to a shore

lo—(interj) exclamation to call attention or express wonder
low—(adj) not loud
low/lowe—(n) chiefly Scottish for flame

load—(n) what is carried
Lod—(n) city in Israel
lode—(n) ore deposit
lowed—(v—pt of *low*) mooed

loan—(n) money lent at interest
lone—(adj) solitary

lakh—(n) from Hindi/Urdu: a great number (rhymes with *sock*)
loch—(n) Scottish for lake
lock—(n) security device operated by key or combination
lough—(n) Irish for lake

lochs—(n) Scottish for lakes
locks—(n) security devices operated by key or combination
lox—(n) cured salmon
loughs—(n) Irish for lakes

loon—(n) water fowl
lown—(n) dialect for calm (2nd pronunciation)
lune—(n) crescent shape

loop—(n) curve formed by a line crossing itself
Loup—(n) river in Nebraska
loupe—(n) jeweler's or watchmaker's magnifier

loos—(n) chiefly British for toilets
lose—(v) to miss from among one's possessions

loot—(n) spoils
lute—(n) stringed instrument with a pear-shaped body

lum·bar—(adj) between the thoracic vertebrae and sacrum
lum·ber—(n) timber

Mach—(n) high speed expressed by a Mach number
moc—(n) short for *moccasin*
mock—(v) to deride

made—(v—pt of *make*) fashioned
maid—(n) unmarried girl or woman

mail—(n) material sent through the postal system
male—(n) man or boy

main—(adj) principle
Maine—(n) New England state
mane—(n) long, heavy hair growing about some animals' heads

maize—(n) Indian corn
Mays—(n) spring months
maze—(n) something confusingly elaborate

mall—(n) urban shopping area
maul—(n) hammer for driving wedges
moll—(n) gangster's girlfriend (2nd pronunciation)

man·ner—(n) kind
man·or—(n) house on an estate

man·tel—(n) shelf above a fireplace
man·tle—(n) cloak

marc—(n) coarse brandy
mark—(v) to indicate by a symbol
Mark—(n) masculine name
marque—(n) brand of a product

mare—(n) female horse
mayor—(n) chief executive of a city, town, or borough

mar·quee—(n) sign over a theater entrance
mar·quis—(n) rank of nobleman in Europe or Japan

mar·ry—(v) to join in marriage
Mary—(n) mother of Jesus; feminine name
mer·ry—(adj) full of high spirits

mar·shal/mar·shall—(n) officer in charge of prisoners
mar·tial—(adj) relating to military life

mask—(v) to disguise oneself
masque/mask—(n) masquerade

massed—(adj) collected into a mass
mast—(n) pole on a ship's deck supporting yard, booms, and rigging

may·be—(adv) perhaps
may be—(verb phrase) is possible

me—(pron) objective case of *I*
mi—(n) 3rd tone of diatonic scale in solmization

mead—(n) fermented beverage of water, honey, malt, and yeast
Mede—(n) inhabitant of ancient Media in Persia
meed—(n) fitting return

mean—(v) to intend
mesne—(adj) intermediate (law term)
mien—(n) manner

meat—(n) animal flesh used as food
meet—(v) to join
mete—(v) to give out by measure

Meaux—(n) commune of northern France
mho—(n) unit of conductance reciprocal of an ohm
mot—(n) from French: pithy or witty saying
mots—(n) from French: pithy or witty sayings
mow—(v) to cut (lawn)

med·al—(n) piece of metal awarded for excellence
med·dle—(v) to interfere

med·dler—(n) person who interferes
med·lar—(n) small deciduous tree

met·al—(n) element that conducts heat and electricity well
met·tle—(n) strength of spirit

mewl—(n) to whimper
mule—(n) hybrid of a mare and a male donkey

mews—(n) stables
muse—(n) nine sister goddesses in Greek mythology

mic—(n) short for *microphone*
mike—(n/v) microphone; to supply with a microphone (shortened and altered from *microphone*)
Mike—(n) masculine name, nickname for *Michael*

might—(v—pt of *may*) had the ability
mite—(n) small arachnid

mil—(n) unit equal to 1/1000 inch
mill—(n) machine for grinding grain
mille—(n) thousand

mince—(v) chop finely
mints—(n) confections flavored with mint

mind—(n) that in a person which thinks, reasons, feels, perceives, and wills
mined—(v—pt of *mine*) dug for ore or metal

min·er—(n) person who digs for ore or metal
mi·nor—(n) person who has not yet attained majority

minks—(n) pelts of the mink worn as wraps
minx—(n) pert girl

mis·sal—(n) book containing all that is said or sung at Mass
mis·sile—(n) an object projected to strike at a distance

missed—(v—pt of *miss*) failed to hit
mist—(n) water in the atmosphere in the form of particles

Miss·es—(n) title for unmarried women
Mrs.—(n) title for married woman

moan—(n) prolonged sound of grief or pain
Mon—(n) the dominant native people of Pegu division, Myanmar
mown—(v—pt part of *mow*) having been cut

moat—(n) deep trench around the rampart of a castle
mote—(n) a speck

mode—(n) style
mowed—(v—pt of *mow*) cut

moire—(n) watered mohair (2nd pronunciation; rhymes with *core*)
Moore—(n) city in Oklahoma
mor—(n) forest humus
more—(adj) comparative of *many*

moo—(v) to make the vocalization of a cow
moue—(n) pout
mu—(n) 12th letter of the Greek alphabet

mood—(n) feeling
mooed—(v—pt of *moo*) made the vocalization of a cow

moor—(n) boggy area
Mur—(n) European river

moose—(n) ruminant mammal in the deer family
mousse—(n) molded, chilled dessert

morn—(n) morning
mourn—(n) to feel grief or sorrow

morn·ing—(n) time from sunrise to noon
mourn·ing—(n) the act of sorrowing

mus·cle—(n) body tissue that contracts to produce motion
mus·sel—(n) marine bivalve mollusk

mussed—(v—pt of *muss*) disarranged
must—(v) to be commanded

mus·tard—(n) condiment made with powder from mustard seeds
mus·tered—(v—pt of *muster*) caused to gather

nan·ny/nan·nie—(n) woman who acts as child's caregiver
nan·ny—(n) short for *nanny goat* (female adult goat)
Nan·ny—(n) feminine name; nickname for *Ann* or *Anne*

na·val—(adj) of or relating to a navy
na·vel—(n) depression at the middle of the abdomen

nay—(adv) no
né—(adj) indicates original legal name of a man
née/nee—(adj) indicates original legal name of a woman
neigh—(n) horse's prolonged cry

nays—(n) noes
neighs—(n) horse's prolonged cries

neap—(n) the tide occurring at the 1st and 3rd quarters of the moon
neep—(n) chiefly Scottish for turnip

nib·ble—(n) very small quantity
nyb·ble/nib·ble—(n) half a byte

nicks—(v) makes a notch in
nix—(n) nothing

Nice—(n) port in southeastern France
niece—(n) daughter of one's brother or sister

nigh—(adv) near in place or time
nye—(n) brood or flock of pheasant

none—(pron) not any; not one
nun—(n) woman in a religious order

note—(n) symbol used to denote pitch and duration of music
nowt—(pron) dialect version of *nought*

oar—(n) long pole for propelling and steering a boat
o'er—(adv) contraction of *over*
or—(conj) expressing an alternative
OR—(n) logical operator that requires one of two inputs
ore—(n) mineral containing valuable constituent

Od/Odd—(interj) used as mild oath
odd—(adj) differing from the usual

ode—(n) lyric poem
owed—(v—pt of *owe*) was under obligation to repay

ohs—(interj) exclamations of emotion
owes—(v) is under obligation to repay

one—(n) number 1
when—(adv) at what time (3rd pronunciation)
won—(v—pt of *win*) earned

oohs—(interj) exclamations of amazement, joy, or surprise
ooze—(n) soft deposit of slime on the bottom of a body of water
Ouse—(n) name of several rivers in England

or·di·nance—(n) authoritative decree
ord·nance—(n) military supplies

over·do—(v) to do in excess
over·due—(adj) unpaid when due

paced—(v—pt of *pace*) measured by footsteps
paste—(n) preparation used as an adhesive

packed—(v—pt of *pack*) made into a compact bundle
pact—(n) international treaty

packs—(v) makes into a compact bundle
pax—(n) peace

pail—(n) bucket
pale—(adj) pallid

pain—(n) physical suffering
pane—(n) framed sheet of glass

pair—(n) two corresponding things
pare—(v) trim off outside part
pear—(n) juicy fruit with green to brown skin
père—(n) father, used after a name to distinguish father and son

pal·ate—(n) the roof of the mouth
pal·ette—(n) tablet that painter mixes paint on
pal·let—(n) small, hard bed
pal·lette—(n) plate at the armpit of a suit of armor

pall—(n) dwindle
Paul—(n) masculine name
pawl—(n) sliding bolt on a machine

par—(n) equality
parr—(n) young salmon feeding in fresh water

par·ish—(n) local church community
per·ish—(v) to become destroyed or ruined

par·lay—(v) to transform into something of greater value
par·ley—(v) to discuss terms with an enemy

pass·able—(adj) capable of being passed
pas·si·ble—(adj) capable of feeling or suffering

passed—(v—pt of *pass*) went beyond
past—(n) time gone by

pat·en—(n) plate used to carry the Eucharist
pat·ten—(n) shoe that elevates the wearer

pa·tience—(n) fact of being patient
pa·tients—(n) people awaiting medical care

pause—(n) temporary stop
paws—(n) quadruped feet

pea—(n) green edible seed of a legume
pee—(v) to urinate

peace—(n) state of tranquility
piece—(n) part of a whole

peak—(n) top of a hill
peek—(n) furtive look
pique—(n) transient feeling of hurt vanity

peaked—(v—pt of *peak*) reached the top
peeked—(v—pt of *peek*) looked furtively
piqued—(v—pt of *picque*) caused transient feelings of hurt vanity

peal—(n) loud ringing of bells
peel—(v) to strip off the outer wrapper

pealed—(v—pt of *peal*) rang bells loudly
peeled—(v—pt of *peel*) stripped off the outer wrapper

pearl—(v) lustrous gem formed in a mollusk
perl—(n) the implementation of Perl
Perl—(n) a computer language
purl—(n) a knitting stitch

pecks—(n) sets of 8 quarts
pecs—(n) pectoral muscles

ped·al—(n) lever pressed by the foot
ped·dle—(v) to travel with wares for sale

peer—(n) equal
pier—(n) structure forming a harbor
Pierre—(n) capital of South Dakota

pen·cel/pen·cil—(n) small pennon used in Medieval and
    Renaissance times
pen·cil—(n) writing implement

pen·dant/pen·dent—(n) something suspended
pen·dent/pen·dant—(adj) supported from above

per—(adv) for each
purr—(n) low vibratory sound typical of a cat

pi—(n) ratio of the circumference of a circle to its diameter
pi/pie—(n) spilled type
pie—(n) filling baked in pastry

pi·ca—(n) 12-point type
pi·ka—(n) mammal also called a rock rabbit (2nd pronunciation)

picks—(v) chooses
pyx—(n) container for transporting the Eucharist to the sick

pic·nic—(n) outing with food eaten in the open
pyk·nic—(adj) physiological type also called endomorphic

pid·gin—(n) rudimentary language for communicating without shared primary language
pi·geon—(n) bird of the rock dove family

pieced—(adj) joined into a whole
piste—(n) downhill ski trail

pin·cer—(n) instrument for gripping things (2nd pronunciation; rhymes with *clincher*)
pinch·er—(n) person who pinches
pin·scher—(n) breed of working dog

pis·til—(n) female part of a flower
pis·tol—(n) handgun

place—(n) physical location
plaice—(n) large European flounder

plain—(adj) lacking ornament
plane—(adj) lying on a geometric plane

plait—(n) braid (rhymes with *rate*)
plate—(n) dish on which food is served

plait—(n) braid (2nd pronunciation; rhymes with *rat*)
plat—(v) to braid
Platte—(n) name of several rivers in the Plains states

pla·nar—(adj) two-dimensional
plan·er—(n) person who planes

pleas—(n) appeals
please—(v) to give pleasure

pleu·ral—(adj) having to do with the membrane around the lungs
plu·ral—(adj) containing more than one

plum—(n) purple fruit with an oblong seed
plumb—(n) lead weight attached to a line to measure depth

po·lar—(adj) relating to the geographic poles
pol·er—(n) person who uses a pole (e.g., in a boat)
poll·er—(n) person who canvasses a group

pole—(n) long, slender length of wood
Pole—(n) native of Poland
poll—(n) canvassing of persons selected at random

poled—(v—pt of *pole*) used a pole to propel a boat
polled—(v—pt of *poll*) canvassed a group

po·ne—(n) dealer's opponent in two-handed cards; otherwise, player to dealer's right (rhymes with *phony*)
po·ny—(n) small horse

poof—(interj) to express disdain or immediacy
pouf/pouffe—(n) ottoman

poor—(adj) lacking material possessions
pore—(v) to study attentively
pour—(v) to dispense from a container

praise—(v) to commend
prase—(n) a quartz (chalcedony) of yellowish green
prays—(v) converses with God
preys—(v) raids for booty

pray—(v) to converse with God
prey—(v) to raid for booty

pre·ce·dence—(n) priority of importance
prec·e·dents—(n) acts that justify subsequent action

pre·mier—(n) first in time
pre·miere/pre·mière/pre·mier—(v) to give the first performance

pres·ence—(n) the condition of being present
pres·ents—(n) gifts

pride—(n) self-respect
pried—(v—pt of *pry*) opened with difficulty

pries—(v) opens with difficulty
prize—(n) something vied for in competition

prince—(n) son of the sovereign
prints—(n) reproductions of a work of art

prin·ci·pal—(n) head of school
prin·ci·ple—(n) fundamental law

prof·it—(n) gain
proph·et—(n) one who utters divinely inspired revelations

pros—(n) experts; short for *professionals*
pros—(n) arguments in the affirmative
prose—(n) literary medium often counterposed to poetry

pro·té·gé—(n) person who is mentored by a person of experience
pro·té·gée—(n) girl or woman who is a protégé

psi—(n) 23rd letter of the Greek alphabet
sigh—(n) deep, audible breath

pu·pal—(adj) having to do with a stage of a metamorphic insect
pu·pil—(n) student

quad—(n) quadrangle
quod—(n) British slang for prison

quarts—(n) several quarters of a gallon
quartz—(n) mineral with crystalline form

quean—(n) disreputable woman
queen—(n) female monarch

quince—(n) small, round fruit resembling a yellow apple
quints—(n) short for *quintuplets*

rab·bet—(n) a groove cut in a surface
rab·bit—(n) small, long-eared mammal

rack—(n) framework on which articles are placed
wrack—(n) ruin

rain—(n) precipitation in the form of water droplets
reign—(n) sovereignty
rein—(n) strap fastened to the bit to control an animal

raise—(v) to help to rise
rase—(v) archaic: to erase
rays—(n) beams of radiant energy
raze—(v) to demolish
reis—(n) plural of *real*, former monetary unit of Portugal

ram—(n) male sheep
RAM—(n) random-access memory on a computer

rap—(n) a sharp knock
wrap—(v) to envelop

rapped—(v—pt of *rap*) knocked sharply
rapt—(adj) transported with emotion
wrapped—(v—pt of *wrap*) enveloped

ray—(n) beam of radiant energy
re—(n) 2nd tone of the diatonic scale in solmization
Re—(n) Egyptian sun god

read—(v) to make meaning from written words (rhymes with *bead*)
rede—(v) archaic: advise
reed—(n) tall grass that grows in wetlands

read—(v—pt of *read*) made meaning from printed or written words (rhymes with *bed*)
red—(n) a primary color
redd—(n) spawning ground for various fish

read·ing—(pres part of *read*) making meaning from printed or written words
reed·ing—(n) small convex molding

reads—(v) receives meaning from printed or written words
reeds—(n) tall grasses that grow in wetlands

real—(adj) not artificial, fraudulent, or illusory
reel—(n) windlass on a fishing rod to hold the line

reave—(v) to plunder
reeve—(v) to pass a rope through
reive—(v) Scottish for *to raid*

re·cede—(v) to cede back to a former possessor
re·seed—(v) to sow seed on again

reck—(v) to worry
wreak—(v) to cause (2nd pronunciation)
wreck—(v) to ruin

recks—(v) worries
rex—(n) animal with genetic lack of guard hairs
Rex—(n) masculine name
wrecks—(v) ruins

reek—(v) to give off an offensive odor
wreak—(v) to cause

res·i·dence—(n) place where one lives
res·i·dents—(n) persons who reside in a place

res·in·ate—(v) to flavor with resin
res·o·nate—(v) to exhibit resonance

re·sist·er—(n) person who resists
re·sis·tor—(n) device that has electrical resistance

re·sist·ers—(n) people who resist
re·sis·tors—(n) devices that have electrical resistance

rest—(n) repose
wrest—(v) to gain with difficulty

retch—(v) to vomit
wretch—(n) miserable person

review—(n) a retrospective view
revue—(n) theatrical production of skits and songs

rheum—(n) watery discharge from mucous membranes
room—(n) partitioned space inside a building

rheumy—(adj) having a watery discharge from the mucous
   membranes
room·ie—(n) short for *roommate*
roomy—(adj) having ample room

rho—(n) 17th letter of the Greek alphabet
roe—(n) fish eggs
row—(v) to propel a boat with oars

Rhône—(n) river flowing out of the Alps (rhymes with *own*)
roan—(adj) having the base hair color lightened by a mixture of
   white (alternative pronunciation)

rhumb—(n) course on a single bearing
rum—(n) alcoholic beverage distilled from a cane product

rhyme/rime—(n) verse with corresponding sounds at the ends of
   lines
rime—(n) frost

Rheydt—(n) city in Germany (rhymes with *sight*)
right—(adj) correct
rite—(n) ceremonial action
wright—(n) a maker
write—(v) to set down in writing

rig·ger—(n) person who rigs
rig·or—(n) strict exactness

rile—(v) to upset (rhymes with *bile*)
roil—(v) to make agitated and angry (this pronunciation specific to this meaning)

ring—(n) circlet worn around the finger
wring—(v) to twist in order to dry

rise—(v) to ascend
ryes—(n) grasses grown for grain

road—(n) travel lane for vehicles
rode—(v—pt of *ride*) traveled on the back of an animal
rowed—(v—pt of *row*) propelled a boat with oars

roam—(v) to wander
Rom—(n) Gypsy
Rome—(n) name of several US cities and the Italian capital

roan—(adj) having the base hair color lightened by a mixture of white (rhymes with *Owen*)
row·an—(n) either of two types of mountain ash tree

roc—(n) legendary bird of great size and strength
rock—(n) large mass of stone

roes—(n) fish eggs
rose—(n) prickly shrubs with showy flowers
Rose—(n) feminine name
rows—(v) propels a boat with oars

roil—(v) to make turbid (rhymes with *boil*)
roy·al—(adj) suitable for royalty

role/rôle—(n) part played by an actor or actress
roll—(n) sound produced by rapid drum strokes

roll·over—(n) accident in which a motor vehicle overturns
roll over—(v) to defer payment

roo—(n) nickname for a kangaroo
roux—(n) cooked mixture of flour and fat used to thicken soup, etc.
rue—(v) to feel remorse

rood—(n) a cross
rude—(adj) simple
rued—(v—pt of *rue*) felt remorse

room·er—(n) occupant of a rented room in another's house
ru·mor/ru·mour—(n) statement with no known authority for its
authenticity

root—(n) underground part of a plant (rhymes with *boot*)
rout—(n) to low loudly (2nd pronunciation)
route—(n) highway

rote—(n) the use of memory (rhymes with *boat*)
rout—(v) to low loudly (pronunciation specific to this meaning)
wrote—(v—pt of *write*) set down in writing

rough—(adj) coarse
ruff—(n) large, round, pleated collar
ruff/ruffe—(n) small European perch

rout—(v) to drive out or dispel (rhymes with *bout*)
route—(n) highway (2nd pronunciation)

run·down—(n) summary
run-down—(adj) worn out
run down—(v) to collide with and knock down

rung—(v) sounded resonantly
wrung—(v—pt of *wring*) twisted in order to dry

rye—(n) grass grown for grain
wry—(adj) cleverly and ironically humorous

sac·cha·rin—(n) calorie-free sweetener
sac·cha·rine—(adj) sickly sweet

sa·chet—(n) a small bag containing potpourri
sa·shay—(v) to make a chassé

sacks—(n) rectangularly shaped bags
sax—(n) short for *saxophone*

sail—(v) to travel on water in a ship
sale—(n) the act of selling

sail·er—(n) ship or boat having specific capabilities
sail·or—(n) person who sails

sain—(v) British dialect meaning to cross oneself
sane—(adj) mentally sound
seine—(n) fishing net with sinkers on one end and floats on the
other

sav·er—(n) person who saves
sa·vor/sa·vour—(v) to taste with pleasure

sawer—(n) person who saws
soar—(v) to fly aloft
sore—(adj) inflamed

say·yid—(n) Islamic chief or leader (3rd pronunciation; rhymes with *tide*)
side—(v) to agree with
sighed—(v—pt of *sigh*) breathed deeply and audibly

scene—(n) one of the subdivisions of a play
seen—(v—pt of *saw*) perceived with the eye
sin—(n) 21st letter of the Hebrew alphabet

scot—(n) money assessed or paid
Scot—(n) native or inhabitant of Scotland
Scott—(n) masculine name
skat—(n) three-handed card game

scotch—(v) to put an end to
Scotch—(adj) Scottish

scull—(n) racing shell propelled with oars by one or two persons
skull—(n) skeleton of the head

seam—(n) line of stitching to join two pieces of cloth
seem—(v) to appear to the understanding
seme—(n) a linguistic sign

sea·man—(n) sailor
se·men—(n) male discharge containing spermatozoa

seams—(n) lines of stitching to join two pieces of cloth
seems—(v) appears to the understanding

seek—(v) to go in search of (rhymes with *peek*)
sic—(adv) intentionally so written (pronunciation: specific to this meaning only)
Sikh—(n) an adherent of Sikhism

sen·ate—(n) an assembly that usually has a legislative function
sen·net—(n) signal call on a trumpet
sen·nit—(n) braided cord or fabric

Seoul—(n) capital of South Korea
sol—(n) 5th tone of the diatonic scale in solmization
sole—(adj) functioning independently
soul—(n) person's immortal spirit

serf—(n) feudal servant
surf—(n) breaking waves

serge—(n) durable twilled fabric
surge—(v) to move in waves

sew—(v) to fasten with stitches
so—(adv) in the manner indicated
so—(n) 5th tone in the diatonic scale in solmization
sow—(v) to plant seed by scattering

sew·er—(n) person who stitches (rhymes with *knower*)
sow·er—(n) person who plants seed

sew·er—(n) waste drain (rhymes with *newer)*
su·er—(n) person who sues

shake—(v) to move something briskly to mix it
sheikh/sheik—(n) Arab chief (2nd pronunciation)

shear—(v) to cut off the hair from something
sheer—(v) to swerve

shears—(n) scissors
sheers—(v) swerves

sheave—(n) pulley
shiv—(n) knife

she'll—(pron + v) contraction of *she will* or *she shall* (2nd pronunciation; rhymes with *wheel*)
shiel—(n) chiefly Scottish for mountain hut used for shelter by shepherds

she'll—(pron + v) contraction of *she will* or *she shall* (rhymes with *will*)
shill—(v) to act as a spokesperson

shoe—(n) covering for the human foot
shoo—(interj) exclamation to drive away unwanted animal

shoes—(n) coverings for human feet
shoos—(interj) exclamations to drive away unwanted animal

shone—(v—pt of *shine*) emitted rays of light (rhymes with *Joan*)
shoon—(n) chiefly dialect plural of *shoe* (2nd pronunciation)
shown—(v—pt part of *show*) had caused to be seen

shone—(v—pt of *shine*) emitted rays of light (Canadian and British pronunciation; rhymes with *John*)
Shan—(n) member of people living in Myanmar and southern China

sic—(v) to set upon (rhymes with *pick)*
sick—(adj) ailing

sics—(v) sets upon
six—(n) number 6

sighs—(n) deep, audible breaths
size—(n) magnitude

sign—(n) signal
sine—(n) trigonometric function
syne—(conj/prep) Scottish for since

sink—(v) to submerge
sync/synch—(v) to synchronize

Sioux—(n) member of a group of Native Americans/American Indians
sou—(n) French coin worth five centimes
sue—(v) to seek justice by legal action
Sue—(n) feminine name, nickname for *Susan* or *Suzanne*
xu—(n) former South Vietnamese coin

sky—(n) the upper atmosphere
Skye—(n) Scottish island

slay—(v) to murder
sleigh—(n) horse-drawn vehicle for use on snow or ice

sleight—(n) dexterity
slight—(adj) having a slim build

slew—(v—pt of *slay*) murdered (rhymes with *do*)
slough/slew/slue—(n) swamp
slue—(n) position after turning on fixed axis

sloe—(n) fruit of the blackthorn
slow—(adj) without speed

smooth·ie—(n) creamy beverage of fruit and liquid
smooth·y/smooth·ie—(n) smooth-tongued person

soared—(v—pt of *soar*) flew aloft
sword—(n) weapon with a long blade

sold—(v—pt of *sell*) disposed of for profit
soled—(v—pt of *sole*) furnished with a sole
souled—(adj) possessing a soul

some—(adj) unspecified amount
Somme—(n) river in France (2nd pronunciation)
sum—(n) result of adding numbers

son—(n) male offspring
Sun—(n) star around which Earth orbits

Son·ny—(n) young boy, usually form of address
sunny—(adj) filled with sunshine

soot—(n) black byproduct of burning that adheres to inside of
   chimney (3rd pronunciation; rhymes with *hoot*)
suit—(n) set of garments
suite—(n) matching set of furniture (pronunciation specific to this
   meaning only)

sough—(v) to make a moaning sound (rhymes with *cow*)
sow—(n) adult female pig

spade—(n) digging implement
spayed—(v—pt of *spay*) removed the ovaries and uterus of a
   female animal

specks—(n) small spots
specs—(n) short for *spectacles*

spoor—(n) traces left by an animal (2nd pronunciation)
spore—(n) unicellular reproductive body

stade—(n) ancient Greek unit of length, 607–738 feet
staid—(adj) reserved
stayed—(v—pt of *stay*) remained

staff—(n) a supporting rod
staph—(n) short for *staphylococcus*

stair—(n) series of steps between levels of a building
stare—(v) to look fixedly

stake—(n) pointed wooden pole
steak—(n) cut of meat or fish

stat·ion·ary—(adj) immobile
sta·tio·nery—(n) materials for writing

steal—(v) to take unlawfully
steel—(n) commercial iron containing carbon
stele—(n) central vascular portion of the axis of a vascular plant

step—(n) single stride
steppe—(n) vast, treeless tract in southeastern Europe or Asia

sticks—(n) dry shoots or twigs broken off a bush or tree
Styx—(n) principal river of underworld in Greek mythology

stile—(n) steps for passing over a fence or wall
style—(n) idiosyncratic manner of expression

stoop—(v) to bend the body forward
stoup—(n) basin for holy water at church entrance
stupe—(n) dolt; short for *stupid*

sto·ry/sto·rey—(n) set of rooms between floors in a building
sto·ry—(n) fictional narrative, shorter than a novel

stow—(v) to store
Stowe—(n) town in Vermont

straight—(adj) free of bends or irregularities
strait—(adj) constricted

suc·cor/suc·cour—(n) relief
suck·er—(n) person who is easily deceived

suède/suede—(n) leather with napped surface
swayed—(v—pt of *sway*) swung slowly side to side

suite—(n) instrumental composition in several movements (rhymes
   with *feet*)
sweet—(adj) much loved

sum·ma·ry—(n) précis
sum·mery—(adj) fit for summer

sun·dae—(n) ice cream served with toppings
Sun·day—(n) first day of the week

swat—(v) to strike with a sharp blow
SWAT—(n) Special Weapons And Tactics police or military unit
Swat—(n) river in Pakistan
swot—(v) British for study hard

tach—(n) short for *tachometer*
tack—(n) small pointed nail

tacked—(v—pt of *tack*) attached with a small pointed nail
tact—(n) perceptive ability to deal in social situations

tacks—(n) small pointed nails
tax—(n) charge of money imposed for public purposes

tael—(n) any of several Chinese units of value or eastern Asian
    weights (rhymes with *mail*)
tail—(v) to follow for surveillance
taille—(n) tax formerly levied by a French king
tale—(n) imaginative narrative of an event

Tai—(n) group of languages including Thai and Shan
Thai—(n) native or inhabitant from Thailand
tie—(n) contest that ends in a draw

tail·er—(n) person who follows another for the purpose of surveillance
tai·lor—(n) person who makes or alters outer garments

ta·per—(n) slender candle
ta·pir—(n) herbivorous mammals of tropical America and
    Southeast Asia

tare—(n) allowance for the weight of a container (rhymes with *dare*)
tear—(n) damage from being torn

ta·ro—(n) Asian plant with edible starchy corms and cormels
tar·ot—(n) set of 78 cards used for fortune telling

taught—(v—pt and pt part of *teach*) conducted instruction in some-
    thing
taut—(adj) drawn tight

tea—(n) aromatic beverage from steeping leaves of the tea plant in
    boiling water
tee—(n) peg on which a golf ball is placed
ti—(n) 7th tone of the diatonic scale in solmization

team—(n) a group that works or plays together
teem—(v) to be present in large quantity

team·ing—(pres part of *team*) joining into a coordinated pair
teem·ing—(pres part of *teem*) being present in large quantities

tear—(n) drop of fluid from the eye (rhymes with *deer*)
tier—(n) row of articles, such as seats in a stadium
Tyr—(n) god of war in Norse mythology

teas—(n) aromatic beverages from steeping leaves of the tea plant
in boiling water
tease—(v) to pester
tees—(n) pegs for golf balls

tech·nic—(n) engineering (2nd pronunciation)
tech·nique—(n) body of technical methods

ten·ner—(n) ten-dollar bill
ten·or/ten·our—(n) usually male voice part next to lowest in 4-part
harmony

tense—(adj) rigid
tents—(n) collapsible shelters

terce/tierce—(n) 3rd of the canonical hours
terse—(adj) brief

tern—(n) marine bird related to the gull
terne—(n) alloy of lead and tin
turn—(n) pivoting movement

thane—(n) Scottish feudal lord
thegn—(n) free retainer of an Anglo-Saxon lord

the—(art) usual pronunciation before vowels and before names and
titles (rhymes with *me*)
thee—(pron) objective case of *thou*

their—(adj) of or relating to them (2nd pronunciation)
there—(adv) in or at that place
they're—(pron + v) second pronunciation: contraction of *they are*

threw—(v—pt of *throw*) propelled through the air by hand
thro—(prep) archaic: through
through—(prep) indicates movement into one side and out at the
other

throes—(n) pangs of pain
throws—(v) propels through the air by hand

throne—(n) chair of state of the sovereign
thrown—(pt part of *threw*) was propelled through the air by hand

Thun—(n) commune in central Switzerland (rhymes with *moon*)
toon—(n) tree of the mahogany family
toon—(n) famous character from a cartoon; short for *cartoon*
tune—(n) melody

thyme—(n) Eurasian mints with pungent aromatic leaves used in cooking
time—(n) duration of events

tic—(n) local and habitual spasmodic behavior
tick—(n) blood-sucking arachnid

ticks—(n) light rhythmic taps
tics—(n) local, habitual spasms

tide—(n) alternate rising and falling of the water of the ocean
tied—(v—pt of *tie*) fastened with a tie

tight·en—(v) to make tighter
ti·tan—(n) family of giants in Greek mythology

til—(n) sesame
till/'til/til—(prep or conj) short for *until*
till—(v) to cultivate

tim·ber—(n) wood for building
tim·bre/tim·ber—(n) the identifying quality(ies) of a particular voice or instrument (2nd pronunciation)

tire—(v) to fatigue
tire/tyre—(n) rubber cushion that fits around the wheel of a vehicle
tier/tyer—(n) person who ties
Tyre—(n) chief city of ancient Phoenicia

to—(adv) at hand
too—(adv) also
two—(adj) being 2 in number

toad—(n) amphibian related to frog, but more terrestrial
toed—(adj) having toes
towed—(v—pt of *tow*) drew behind

toc·sin—(n) warning signal
tox·in—(n) a poison

toc·sins—(n) warning signals
tox·ins—(n) poisons

toe—(n) fore end of a foot or hoof
tow—(v) to draw behind

told—(v—pt and pt part of *tell*) related in detail
tolled—(v—pt of *toll*) rang a bell

tole—(n) painted metalware
toll—(n) tax paid for some liberty or privilege

ton—(n) various weights, for example, 2000 lbs
tonne—(n) metric ton
tun—(n) a large cask

tongue—(n) mouth muscle of most vertebrates
tung—(n) short name for Chinese tree of the spurge family and its oil

tool—(n) handheld device to aid in a task
tulle—(n) stiffened netting used for veils and ballet costumes

tor—(n) high, craggy hill
tore—(v—pt of *tear*) damaged by tearing
torr—(n) unit of pressure equal to 1/760 of an atmosphere

tort—(n) wrongful act other than breach of contract
torte—(n) rich cake made with many eggs and often grated nuts or breadcrumbs

tough—(adj) not easily chewed
tuff—(n) rock composed of volcanic detritus

tracked—(v—pt of *track*) followed the traces of
tract—(n) defined area of land

trait—(n) distinguishing quality (British pronunciation only; rhymes with *day*)
tray—(n) flat, open receptacle for transporting, serving, exhibiting, etc.
trey—(n) card numbered 3

troop—(n) collection of people or flock of animals
troupe—(n) a company of theatrical performers

troop·er—(n) state police officer
troup·er—(n) person who persists uncomplainingly through hardship

troop·ers—(n) state police officers
troup·ers—(n) people who persist uncomplainingly through hardship

troy—(adj) expressed in troy weight
Troy—(n) several cities in the US or the ancient city of Ilium in the Dardanelles

trussed—(adj) bound tightly
trust—(n) reliance

un·do—(v) to open by releasing a fastening
un·due—(adj) excessive

un·real—(adj) lacking in reality
un·reel—(v) to unwind from a reel

un·want·ed—(adj) not wanted
un·wont·ed—(adj) rare

vail—(v) to lower as a sign of respect
Vail—(n) city in Colorado
vale—(n) valley
veil—(n) length of veiling or netting worn over the head or face

vain—(adj) worthless
vane—(n) device for showing wind direction
vein—(n) blood vessel

va·lance—(n) short drapery used as a heading to cover curtain tops
va·lence—(n) degree of combining power of an element
Va·lence—(n) commune in southeastern France

vary—(v) to diversify
very—(adv) to a high degree

vers·es—(n) poetry
ver·sus—(prep) against (2nd pronunciation)

vi·al—(n) small closed vessel for liquids
vile—(adj) foul
vi·ol—(n) bowed stringed instrument

vice—(n) moral corruption
vise—(n) tools with two jaws for holding work

vis·cous—(adj) characterized by viscosity
vis·cus—(n) internal organ of the body (plural is *viscera*)

WACs—(n) members of the Women's Army Corps
wax—(n) substance secreted by bees
whacks—(n) resounding blows

wade—(v) to step through a medium that resists more than air
weighed—(v—pt of *weigh*) ascertained heaviness

wail—(v) to lament
wale—(n) fabric ridges
whale—(n) cetacean: large marine mammal

wain—(n) large, heavy farm vehicle
wane—(v) to decrease in size or extent
Wayne—(n) masculine name

waist—(n) narrowed part of the human body between thorax and hips
waste—(v) to use extravagantly

wait—(v) to stop in expectation of
weight—(n) amount something weighs

waive—(v) to relinquish voluntarily
wave—(v) to motion with the hands in salute

waiv·er—(n) the act of voluntarily relinquishing
wa·ver—(v) to vacillate irresolutely

wales—(n) fabric ridges
Wales—(n) principality of southwestern Great Britain
whales—(n) cetaceans: large marine mammals

want—(n) thing desired
wont—(n) habitual way of doing

war—(n) armed hostilities between states or nations
wore—(v—pt of *wear*) had on as apparel

ware—(n) article of merchandise (rhymes with *pear*)
wear—(n) article of clothing
weir—(n) dam in a stream or river to raise the water level
where—(n) place

warn—(v) to give notice beforehand
worn—(v—pt part of *wear*) had on

war·ran·tee—(n) person to whom warranty is made
war·ran·ty—(n) guarantee of integrity

war·ship—(n) naval vessel
wor·ship—(n) reverence offered a divine being

wary—(adj) marked by caution
wher·ry—(n) light boat

watt—(n) unit of power equal to 1 joule/second
what—(adj) whatever (3rd pronunciation)
wot—(v) archaic: 1st and 3rd person singular: know

weak—(adj) lacking strength
week—(n) 7-day cycle used to measure time

weal—(n) healthy state
we'll—(pron + v) contraction for *we will* or *we shall*
wheal—(n) welt (2nd pronunciation)
wheel—(n) circular frame that can turn on an axle

weald—(n) heavily wooded spot
Weald—(n) region in southeastern England
wheeled—(adj) equipped with wheels
wield—(v) to handle effectively

wean—(v) to accustom a young child to stop nursing
ween—(v) archaic: to believe
wheen—(n) British for a considerable amount

weath·er—(n) state of the atmosphere
weth·er—(n) a castrated ram
wheth·er—(conj) to express alternative possibilities

weave—(v) to make cloth on a loom
we've—(pron + v) contraction of *we have*

we'd—(pron + v) contraction of *we had, we could,* or *we should*
weed—(n) plant not valued where it is growing

wee·ny—(adj) tiny
wie·nie—(n) frankfurter (short for *wienerwurst*)

weir—(n) dam in a stream or river to raise the water level (rhymes with *pier*)
we're—(pron + v) contraction of *we are*

welled—(v—pt of *well*) flowed forth
weld—(v) to unite metal by heating

wen—(n) cyst
wen—(n) Old English and Middle English runic letter
when—(adv) at what time

were—(v—pt of *be*) existed (rhymes with *purr*)
we're—(pron + v) contraction of *we are* (2nd pronunciation)
where—(adv) 2nd pronunciation: at what place
whir/whirr—(n) continuous vibratory sound made by rapid motion

wert—(v—pt of *be*) archaic
wort—(n) herbaceous plant, usually used as second part of a
   compound

wet—(adj) soaked with liquid
whet—(v) to sharpen (2nd pronunciation)

which—(adj) whichever (2nd pronunciation)
witch—(n) woman credited with evil supernatural powers

whig—(n) supporter of American revolution (2nd pronunciation)
wig—(n) hairpiece

while—(conj) during the time that
wile—(n) trick or strategem

whiled—(v—pt of *while*) passed the time
wild—(adj) living in a state of nature

whin—(n) gorse (2nd pronunciation)
win—(v) to earn
wynn/wyn—(n) Old English or Middle English runic letter (also
   wen with different pronunciation)

whine—(v) to utter a distressed cry (2nd pronunciation)
wine—(n) alcoholic fermented grape juice

whined—(v—pt of *whine*) uttered distressed cries
wind—(v) to tighten the spring of
wined—(v—pt of *wine*) drank a deal of wine

whirl—(v) to move speedily in a circle
whorl—(n) something that whirls or spirals

whirled—(v—pt of *whirl*) moved speedily in a circle
whorled—(adj) having or arranged in whorls
world—(n) Earth

whirred—(v—pt of *whir* and *whirr*) made a continuous vibratory
  sound by rapid motion
word—(n) written character representing a spoken speech sound

whist—(v) British dialect meaning to be silent
wist—(v) archaic: to know

whit—(n) smallest particle (2nd pronunciation)
wit—(n) reasoning power

white—(adj) the color of new snow
wight—(n) living being
wite—(v) chiefly Scottish for *blame*

whith·er—(adv) to what place? (2nd pronunciation)
with·er—(v) to shrivel up

whoa—(n) command to draft animal to stand still
woe—(n) sorrow

who's—(pron + v) contraction of *who is*
whose—(adj) of or relating to whom

why—(adv) for what reason (pronounced beginning with \hw\)
wye—(adj) the letter *y*
Wye—(n) river in East Wales and West England

wood—(n) dense growth of trees
would—(v) auxiliary used to express wish, desire, etc.
  (4th pronunciation)
wud—(adj) chiefly Scottish for *insane*

worst—(adj/adv) superlative of *bad* or *ill*
wurst—(n) sausage

yak/yack—(n) tireless chatter
yak—(n) long-haired central Asian ox
yak—(n) slang: joke

yauld—(adj) chiefly Scottish for *vigorous* (rhymes with *brawl*)
yawl—(n) ship's small boat
you-all/y'all—(pron) chiefly Southern to address two or more
  people

yogh—(n) Middle English letter ʒ
yoke—(n) wooden frame to join two draft animals to work together
yolk/yoke—(n) yellow center of an egg

yokes—(v) puts animals into a yoke
yolks—(n) yellow centers of eggs

yore—(n) time past (rhymes with *more*)
your—(adj) of or relating to you (3rd pronunciation)
you're—(pron + v) contraction of *you are* (3rd pronunciation)

you'll—(pron + v) contraction of *you will* or *you shall*
yule—(n) Christmas

your—(adj) of or relating to you (rhymes with *were*)
you're—(pron + v) contraction of *you are*

your—(adj) of or relating to you (2nd pronunciation; rhymes with *pure*)
you're—(pron + v) contraction of *you are* (2nd pronunciation)